Prophecy and Reason

Prophecy and Reason

THE DUTCH COLLEGIANTS
IN THE EARLY ENLIGHTENMENT

Andrew C. Fix

PRINCETON UNIVERSITY PRESS

PRINCETON, NEW JERSEY

Library of Congress Cataloging-in-Publication Data

Fix, Andrew C. (Andrew Cooper), 1955–
Prophecy and reason : the Dutch Collegiants in the early
Enlightenment / Andrew C. Fix.
p.   cm.
Revision of the author's thesis (Ph.D.)—Indiana University at
Bloomington, 1984.
Includes bibliographical references (p.   ) and index.
1. Collegiants—Netherlands—History. 2. Enlightenment—
Netherlands. 3. Netherlands—Intellectual life. 4. History
(Theology)—History of doctrines—17th century. 5. History—
Philosophy—History—17th century. 6. Netherlands—Church
history—17th century. 7. Prophecy (Christianity)—History of
doctrines—17th century. 8. Rationalism—History—
17th century. I. Title.
BX6195.15.F58   1991   284′.9—dc20   90–8784

ISBN 0-691-03141-X (cloth : acid-free paper)

This book has been composed in Linotron Sabon

Princeton University Press books are printed on acid-free paper,
and meet the guidelines for permanence and durability of the
Committee on Production Guidelines for Book Longevity of the
Council on Library Resources

Printed in the United States of America by Princeton University Press,
Princeton, New Jersey

1   3   5   7   9   10   8   6   4   2

For Lou Carol

Beproef dan alles
en behoud het goede
—1 Thess. 5:21

CONTENTS

LIST OF ILLUSTRATIONS

PREFACE

NEARLY TEN years ago I discovered the Dutch Collegiants almost by accident while I was working on a graduate seminar paper on Spinoza. As I found out more about this group of remarkable people my interest grew, and the research paper grew into a doctoral dissertation and then eventually into the present book. As my interest in the group grew so did my admiration for those noble spirits and for the fascinating culture and society in which they lived. I became convinced that the world of seventeenth-century Holland, with its rich diversity of intellectual, religious, and political groups, had a great deal in common with the pluralistic societies of modern Western Europe. I likewise became convinced that the rational and tolerant worldview that the Collegiants adopted could be a valuable guide for modern people in times of increasing complexity and tension. The study of history is certainly for naught if it bears no fruit for the lives of those who pursue it.

No scholarly work can be successfully completed without the assistance of many individuals and institutions. I am privileged to acknowledge the financial support of the Fulbright Foundation, whose fellowship made possible a year of research in the Netherlands, and of the Woodrow Wilson National Fellowship Foundation, whose Charlotte W. Newcombe Fellowship supported the writing of the first version of this manuscript. I would also like to acknowledge the support of the National Endowment for the Humanities, whose summer research stipend made possible an additional summer of source work in Europe, as well as the Newberry Library Renaissance Center in Chicago; the Centre Interuniversitaire d'Etudes Européenes in Montreal; Indiana University in Bloomington, Indiana, and Lafayette College in Easton, Pennsylvania.

No less tangible was the assistance provided by many expert historians and librarians on both sides of the Atlantic who interested themselves in my project. I am especially indebted to Professor Gerald Strauss of Indiana University, whose careful reading of my manuscript enabled me to present my ideas with greater precision, and to Dr. S.B.J. Zilverberg of the University of Amsterdam, who provided many helpful comments and much bibliographic direction. I would also like to thank Professor R. S. Westfall of Indiana University; Professor William Shetter of Indiana University; Professor Robin Barnes of Davidson College; Professors James Riley and Paul Spade of Indiana University; Dr. Clasina G. Manusov of Krommenie, the Netherlands; Mr. Wiep van Bunge of Erasmus University of Rotterdam; and my colleague Dr. Ellen S. Hurwitz for their kind assistance in reading various versions of this manuscript. Equally invaluable was the generous assistance of Dr. S. L. Verheus, curator of church history collections in the library of the University of Amsterdam, whose patience and advice enabled me to make full use of the magnificent collection of seventeenth-century materials held by his department. Mr. G. A. de Zeeuw of the Photographic Department of the University of Amsterdam library allowed me the use of his efficient facilities. I would also like to thank Mr. Jeff Beneke for an excellent job of editing, and Mrs. Hilda Cooper, whose preparation of this manuscript was truly superb. Finally, I would like to thank my wife, Carol, without whose support this work would never have been possible.

Brussels
November 1989

ABBREVIATIONS

BLNP D. Nauta, *et al.* (eds.), *Biografisch Lexicon voor de geschie-denis van het Nederlandse Protestantisme* (Kampen, 1978–1988)

BWN A. J. van der Aa (ed.), *Biographische woordenboek der Ne-derlanden* (Haarlem, 1852–1878)

BWPG J. P. de Bie, J. Loosjes, *et al., Biographisch Woordenboek van Protestantsche godgeelerden in Nederland* (The Hague, 1903–1949)

CE Charles Herbermann, *et al.* (eds.), *The Catholic Encyclopedia* (New York, 1911)

EB *Encyclopaedia Britannica*, eleventh edition (New York, 1910)

EP Paul Edwards (ed.), *The Encyclopaedia of Philosophy* (New York, 1972)

ME M. Gingerich, C. Krahn and O. Harms (eds.), *The Mennonite Encyclopedia* (Scottsdale, AZ, 1969–1973)

NNBW P. C. Molhuysen and P. J. Blok (eds.), *Nieuwe Nederlandsch biografisch woordenboek* (Leiden, 1911–1937)

All translations have been made by the author.

The Secularizing Trend in Collegiant Thought

Chapter One

THE COLLEGIANTS IN THE EARLY ENLIGHTENMENT

I don't claim that I have found the best
philosophy, but I do know that I understand
the true one.
—Benedict Spinoza

THE SECOND half of the seventeenth century was a period of turbulent transition in European intellectual life. In the years between 1650 and 1700 an intellectual transformation of fundamental and far-reaching importance changed the very nature of the assumptions and attitudes upon which European thought had been based for centuries, and in so doing changed the intellectual framework with which educated Europeans understood themselves and their world. During these years the traditional providential religious worldview began to be displaced by a new, secular worldview based largely on the foundation of human reason. The result was a broad-ranging transformation not only of ideas but also of perceptions, attitudes, and beliefs. This study will examine a specific example of this great intellectual transformation in the thought of a group of radical Dutch religious thinkers called the Collegiants.

The Collegiants were a small group of Protestant thinkers who underwent a profound intellectual transformation between 1620 and 1690. After beginning as a spiritualistic and millenarian religious sect influenced by the ideas of the sixteenth-century Radical Reformation and by Dutch Arminianism, the Collegiants gradually became a rationalistically inclined group of thinkers who passed through a stage of rational religion before arriving at a secularized philosophical rationalism that found its ultimate expression in the philosophy of Benedict Spinoza. By examining each phase of Collegiant intellectual evolution from millenarianism to rationalism, this study will attempt to describe a complex process of intellectual transformation as well as its religious and cultural roots. By making an in-depth analysis of the changing structure of Collegiant thought, this study seeks to illuminate the inner workings and the very mechanisms of a complex process of intellectual change.

During the second half of the seventeenth century the full complement of intellectual equipment with which educated people thought about themselves and their world underwent a radical change. A transformation of such monumental proportions could not take place suddenly or without preparation, of course, nor could it be brought to completion within a limited span of time. The period 1650-1700 witnessed a crucial stage in a long process of evolutionary change in European thought that had its beginnings many years earlier and that continued for years afterward. It was during these years that the outlines, nature, and profound importance of this epochal intellectual transformation first became clearly apparent to many Europeans.

As the terror of the Thirty Years War finally came to an end at midcentury, the violent confessional passions engendered by the age of religious conflict began to die down, and in their place a more tolerant attitude began to develop among the educated classes of Europe. Basic advances in mathematics and scientific method combined with the pioneering theories of Descartes, Galileo, Locke, and Newton to create an intellectual atmosphere in which the powers of human reason were valued ever more highly. It was during this period that the wave of epistemological skepticism spawned by the Reformation began to be turned back by the growing confidence in human reason that was so essential a part of the Scientific Revolution. It was also in these years that faith in special divine providence and the direct operation of God's will in the temporal world began to be replaced by a secularized view that placed the divine presence outside of the immediate sphere of human and natural activity. This great intellectual transition from faith to reason formed the intellectual foundation for the eighteenth-century Enlightenment and prepared the way for the later development of European thought.

In his classic study of intellectual change, *La crise de la conscience européenne* (1935), Paul Hazard described this transition from faith to reason in the following terms:

> Never was there a greater contrast, never a more sudden transition than this! An hierarchical system ensured by authority; life firmly based on dogmatic principle—such were the things held dear by the people of the seventeenth century; but these—controls, authority, dogmas and the like, were the very things that their immediate successors of the eighteenth century held in cordial detestation. The former were upholders of Christianity; the latter were its foes. The former believed in the laws of God; the latter in the laws of nature; the former lived contentedly enough in a world composed of unequal social grades; of the latter the one absorbing dream was equality. It was a revolution.[1]

[1] Paul Hazard, *The European Mind, 1680–1715* (Cleveland, 1964), p. xv. See also Margaret Jacob, "The Crisis of the European Mind: Hazard Revisited," in P. Mack and

While Hazard perhaps exaggerated the suddenness of this intellectual transformation, his dramatic prose conveys a sense of the epoch-making importance of the transition of worldviews. He went on to draw attention to the period that he called the early Enlightenment (1680–1715) as the most crucial time of intellectual change, a period of a great "crisis of the European conscience."[2] Other historians have recognized that the birth of the Enlightenment worldview was to be found in the last years of the seventeenth century. Alfred Cobban wrote: "We can legitimately concentrate on the eighteenth century as 'le siècle des lumières' and give the Enlightenment that title, but at the risk of forgetting that practically all of its essential ideas were inherited from the previous century."[3] Ernst Cassirer, in his brilliant study of Enlightenment philosophy, most clearly drew the connection between eighteenth-century thought and its seventeenth-century origins. According to Cassirer, seventeenth-century thought was involved in the construction of rationalist philosophical systems based on deductive logic, while the eighteenth century developed a philosophy based on the empirical methods of the natural sciences, but the central element binding together the thought of both centuries was reason. In Cassirer's view, the power and self-confidence of natural human reason formed the philosophical foundation of Enlightenment thought.[4]

Few transformations of worldview have been as decisive and influential as that which changed the religious worldview of traditional Europe into the rational and secular worldview of modern Europe. Among the educated elite of European society, the distance separating the way in which sixteenth-century people viewed their world from the way in which a person of the nineteenth century viewed the world was very great indeed—much greater, in fact, than the distance separating the educated from the uneducated during the Reformation era. During the sixteenth century the university-trained professional would have had a background in classical studies, a knowledge of Latin and perhaps of Greek, an appreciation for history and the natural sciences, and reading and writing skills that would have set him or her far apart from the average peasant or tradesman raised on folktales and devotional literature. The fundamental ways in

---

M. Jacob, eds., *Politics and Culture in Early Modern Europe* (Cambridge, England, 1987), pp. 251–271.

[2] Hazard, pp. xv–xvi.

[3] Alfred Cobban, *In Search of Humanity: The Role of the Enlightenment in Modern History* (London, 1960), p. 7. On the early Enlightenment, see also Alan C. Kors and Paul J. Korshin, eds., *Anticipations of the Enlightenment in England, France, and Germany* (Philadelphia, 1987).

[4] Ernst Cassirer, *The Philosophy of the Enlightenment* (Princeton, 1951), pp. 6–22.

which these two otherwise quite different people viewed the world, however, would have been remarkably similar. They were both participants in the providential Christian worldview that had provided the basic framework for European thought since the coming of Christianity a millennium earlier.

The traditional providential Christian worldview was based on the assumption of God's foresight, direction, and care for the temporal world. God was seen as a loving father who nourished his children and provided for them through his active governance of the world. For Christians, life was the working-out of God's purposes. God was believed to be constantly active in the temporal realm, guiding the course of worldly events according to his wishes both indirectly, through the ordinary laws of nature, and directly, through supernatural miracles, revelation, and inspiration. While God's governance of the world through the laws of nature was explained by theologians in the doctrine of general providence, the idea that God directed worldly affairs through miracles or supernatural revelations that suspended, abrogated, or violated the laws of nature was contained in the doctrine of extraordinary or special providence. The Bible showed that God had made the sun stand still and could interrupt the course of nature at will. God could also intervene in nature to produce earthquakes, floods, and other extraordinary natural events, striking accidents or amazing coincidences as signs for humankind. While these events did not actually violate the laws of nature, they were so unusual that they too were considered special or exceptional providences with specific meanings.[5] Ideas like these presupposed a certain linkage between heaven and earth because God was thought to favor the world with his revelations and direction, making the temporal world a realm of divine activity much as was heaven. As late as the mid-seventeenth century, supernatural interventions in daily life were taken for granted. In a world in which it was assumed that God and the devil intervened daily, it was not thought unusual for God to take direct and drastic action to punish sinners or to reward the virtuous.[6]

For humankind, the only path to follow in such a world was that of faith. Faith in God's providence and trust in divine guidance went side by side with belief in the divine truths revealed by God in Scripture. Belief in divine inspiration and faith in divine providence were the intellectual and emotional components of an assent to God's authority that bound peasant and professor alike in the sixteenth century. In his classic study of the religion of Rabelais, Lucien Febvre eloquently described the place of faith

[5] Keith Thomas, *Religion and the Decline of Magic* (New York, 1971), pp. 79–80.

[6] Christopher Hill, *The World Turned Upside Down: Radical Ideas during the English Revolution* (London, 1972), pp. 87–88.

in the lives of the people of that century: religion dominated people so completely and so totally that it was like the mantle of the Madonna of mercy, sheltering people of all estates in its maternal folds.[7] This religious belief rested firmly on the fundamental assumption of the presence and operation of God in the world.

Even in the sixteenth century, however, there was some debate among intellectuals over the question of whether God operated above nature or only through it. While few people doubted the miracles and other supernatural events reported in the Bible, some thinkers believed that such miracles no longer took place.[8] Still other intellectuals insisted, however, that supernatural miracles had by no means ceased, and few dared to suggest that divine control of the world was only remote. It was the seventeenth century that was the real turning point for belief in divine providence.

It has long been accepted that the great discoveries of the Scientific Revolution of the seventeenth century played a major role in the gradual displacement of the traditional European religious worldview by an outlook based on reason and secularism. The stress on rational and empirical explanation that was an essential part of the new scientific method greatly weakened belief in witchcraft, miracles, astrology, and many traditional Christian doctrines.[9] At the same time, the attack on Aristotelianism brought about by the physical theories of Galileo and Kepler, the empiricism of Francis Bacon, and the mechanistic cosmology of Descartes encouraged a rejection of the principle of intellectual authority in favor of free and rational inquiry and set off a massive cultural and intellectual transformation. The attempt to understand the physical world in terms of reason was followed closely by a desire to understand humankind's relationship to nature, society, and God in similar rational terms.[10] The demonstrated power of human reason to discover the fundamental natural laws governing the operation of the physical universe awakened in people a great confidence in the ability of reason to provide humankind with knowledge of other vital aspects of human experience as well. In addition, the emerging picture of the regular and mechanistic operation of the physical universe that culminated in the work of Boyle and Newton promoted the conception of a world regulated by natural laws and largely

[7] Lucien Febvre, *The Problem of Unbelief in the Sixteenth Century: The Religion of Rabelais*, trans. Beatrice Gottlieb (Cambridge, Mass., 1982), p. 351.

[8] See, for example, Jeffrey Burton Russell, *Mephistopheles: The Devil in the Modern World* (Ithaca, N.Y., 1986), p. 78.

[9] Alan G. R. Smith, *Science and Society in the Sixteenth and Seventeenth Centuries* (London, 1972), p. 176; Russell, pp. 78–127.

[10] Edward Kearns, *Ideas in Seventeenth-Century France* (Manchester, 1979), pp. 11–13. See also Hazard, pp. 304–318; and J. Bronowski and Bruce Mazlish, *The Western Intellectual Tradition* (New York, 1962), pp. 107–126.

undisturbed by supernatural influences. As R. S. Westfall noted in his book on science and religion in the seventeenth century, the birth of modern science brought the end of the age of faith in European thought.[11]

The mechanical philosophy of the later seventeenth century created much doubt about the doctrine of special providence. As belief in extraordinary providence waned, many intellectuals came to see God's providence as limited to the original act of creation, after which the world operated mechanically, like a great watch wound up and left to run by its maker.[12] Febvre described how the rise of modern science and the accompanying concept of natural law undermined belief in providence:

> Armed with the mighty concept of law, [science] gradually strove to reduce the powers of God. In the first place it strove to establish that, if it was strictly possible to admit the original intervention of a primum movens, an initial divine motor, there was in any case no longer room, once the machine was started, for an interventionist God, for his miracles, or even, quite simply, for his Providence.[13]

While belief in special providence declined, belief in general providence continued into the eighteenth and even the nineteenth centuries. Yet many intellectuals who dropped belief in special providence while continuing to insist on general providence simply refused to face the ultimate implications of their position. The increasing sense of separation between the temporal world and God that gave rise to doubts about special providence would inevitably undermine belief in general providence as well.

As early as the second half of the seventeenth century, the realms of heaven and earth were beginning to move apart in the minds of many people. Some late-seventeenth-century and early-eighteenth-century thinkers vigorously resisted this secularizing trend. The scientists Boyle and Newton firmly believed in general providence and, despite their physical theories, hesitated to reject the miracles of the Bible or the role of providence in everyday life.[14] But while many English Newtonians did not openly reject special providence, neither did they emphasize direct divine intervention in the natural world. They did not believe that extraordinary natural occurrences were necessarily signs from God, because for them providence did not operate in nature by means of dramatic events like comets or earthquakes but rather through the imposition of

[11] Richard S. Westfall, *Science and Religion in Seventeenth-Century England* (New Haven, 1958), p. 220. See also Russell, p. 80.

[12] Thomas, p. 80.

[13] Febvre, p. 459. See also P. M. Mitchell, "The Pattern is Perceived and the Seed is Sown," in Kors and Korshin, pp. 218–231.

[14] Thomas, p. 80; Westfall, pp. 70–105.

order and harmony by natural law.[15] Once the growing sense of separation between man and God had introduced the corrosive force of doubt into peoples' belief in direct divine intervention in the temporal world, however, it would not be long before this acid attacked the foundations of belief in indirect divine control of the world as well. Pious intellectuals like the Cambridge Platonists realized this danger clearly enough, and this was one reason for their great fear of the pantheism of Spinoza, which they saw as leading to atheism.[16]

The transformation of European thought during the second half of the seventeenth century was described by the historian of science Herbert Butterfield as "a colossal secularization of thought in every possible realm of ideas at the same time." While Butterfield believed that the rise of a rational and secular outlook during the late seventeenth century was in important measure the result of the Scientific Revolution, he recognized that the birth of modern science was not the only cause of this great intellectual transformation. He pointed to a parallel but largely independent crisis in religious belief, what he called a "decline of Christianity," as a second major cause of the secularization of European thought during the later seventeenth century.[17]

The crisis within European religious thought that played so vital a role in the seventeenth-century transition from faith to reason has been explained by Richard Popkin as the result of a challenge to traditional religious authority produced by the Protestant Reformation. According to Popkin, the influence of the turbulent period of intellectual confusion that resulted from the Reformation's rejection of traditional religious authority was an essential factor in the formation of seventeenth-century rationalism. The philosophies of Descartes and Spinoza were in part a response to the crisis of skepticism that engulfed the intellectual life of Europe during the sixteenth and seventeenth centuries. This skeptical crisis was caused, in Popkin's view, by a fateful coincidence of two important events: the rediscovery in the sixteenth century of the works of the Greek Pyrrhonist Sextus Empiricus, preceded by Luther's challenge to the Catholic church, which produced an intellectual dispute over the proper criterion for religious truth.

For centuries the Catholic church had maintained that the only criterion of truth for a religious proposition was the authority of church tra-

---

[15] Margaret Jacob, *The Newtonians and the English Revolution* (Ithaca, N.Y., 1976), pp. 61–107.

[16] See Margaret Jacob, *The Radical Enlightenment* (London, 1981); and Rossalie Colie, *Light and Enlightenment: A Study of the Cambridge Platonists and Dutch Arminians* (Cambridge, England, 1957).

[17] Herbert Butterfield, *The Origins of Modern Science* (New York, 1957), pp. 194–196.

dition, pope, and councils. Luther proposed a radical new standard for religious truth at the Diet of Worms in 1521 when he maintained that whatever his conscience was compelled to believe when he read Scripture was religious truth. Pressed by the imperial examiner to repudiate his books and the ideas they contained, Luther replied: "Unless I am convinced by Scripture and plain reason—I do not accept the authority of popes and councils, for they have contradicted each other—my conscience is captive to the Word of God. I cannot and I will not recant anything, for to go against conscience is neither right nor safe."[18] By dramatically rejecting the authority of the church and replacing it with the interpretation of the Bible by the individual conscience of the believer, Luther started an epistemological revolution in European thought. As Popkin explains, to raise the possibility that the traditional criterion of truth was faulty necessitated the substitution of another criterion by which the traditional criterion could be judged. Once the original criterion had been brought into question, however, it was impossible to determine which of the alternative criteria should be adopted in its place because there was no standard upon which to base such a judgment. Luther's rejection of the traditional standard of Christian orthodoxy destroyed the accepted foundation for religious knowledge and opened up an abyss of doubt concerning religious truth, an abyss in which many competing religious doctrines vied with one another to become the new orthodoxy. With the rediscovery of the skeptical philosophy of Sextus Empiricus later in the century, this crisis of religious doubt spread into all fields of knowledge and produced a crisis of epistemological uncertainty that was only resolved when Descartes and Spinoza established natural reason as the new criterion for truth in all human knowledge.[19]

Luther's challenge to traditional religious authority had monumental consequences for the history of European thought. As this study will show, the doctrine of the individual conscience that Luther outlined at Worms, which soon became an important part of Protestant thought especially among the more radical sects, opened the door for epistemological subjectivism, radical spiritualism, the religion of the inner light, and finally also for the development of philosophical rationalism. Luther himself gradually backed away from his stand of 1521 when he came to realize the revolutionary implications of such a doctrine. When the individual conscience was accepted as the only true interpreter of Scripture and thus as the individual's primary guide to religious truth, the next step was to ask how this individual conscience operated. Upon what basis did its

---

[18] Roland Bainton, *The Reformation of the Sixteenth Century* (Boston, 1957), p. 61.

[19] Richard Popkin, *The History of Scepticism from Erasmus to Spinoza* (Berkeley, 1979), pp. 1–3.

epistemological authority rest? Many reformers and spiritualistic theologians maintained that the individual conscience was directly inspired by God with religious truth or with the divine power to correctly understand biblical revelation. Sebastian Castellio, on the other hand, held that the individual conscience operated on the basis of a weak and fallible human reason that could not penetrate to the core of religious mysteries. The Cambridge Platonists and other seventeenth-century theologians believed that the individual conscience was irradiated by a "divine reason" that provided religious truth as well as natural knowledge. Rationalistic philosophers, finally, saw the individual conscience as operating by a natural human reason that was a source of truth as infallible in its prescriptions as the divine inspiration of the earlier spiritualists. In this changing conception of the individual conscience, one can see in microcosm the larger transformation of the European worldview that took place during the course of the seventeenth century. By investigating the changing idea of the individual conscience in Collegiant thought between 1620 and 1690, it will perhaps be possible to arrive at a deeper understanding of the nature and causes of the larger European intellectual transition from faith to reason.

The Collegiants were profoundly affected by the religious controversies of the late sixteenth and early seventeenth centuries. The period of religious conflict that made up the Reformation, the confessional age, and the era of religious wars had a tremendous effect on European thought in general and on religious thought in particular. The experience of these years formed Collegiant thought. The troubled course of the Protestant Reformation and the bloody effects of the age of religious wars convinced some people that God no longer chose to involve himself in human affairs. The mutually exclusive truth claims of the competing churches, combined with the great differences among their doctrines and the immense hostility with which they rejected all competing ideas, led some people to doubt the possibility of arriving at religious truth at all. This doubt cast a shadow over the ideas of divine providence and divine inspiration in the temporal world. In despair some thinkers came to see the world as primarily a sphere of human activity where divine inspiration and revelation no longer operated. These thinkers, among whom the Collegiants played a leading role, began to turn to human reason almost by default as their only remaining guide to truth and action. Thus, a trend toward secularism and rationalism developed out of religious despair and accelerated as the wars of religion drew to a close in 1648.

One result of this process was a transformation of religious thought in the second half of the seventeenth century. As Robert K. Merton pointed out in his seminal study of the relationship between Puritanism and modern science, an important step in the process of secularization that was under way in European thought during the second half of the seventeenth century was the growing belief in reason as an independent means of arriving at religious truth.[20] The years after 1650 saw the rapid progress of reason within religious thought, especially in England, where quarrels among Protestant groups over doctrine and scriptural interpretation led some Anglican churchmen to stress reason over authority in matters of religion. These liberal Anglicans promoted a comprehensive church and defended it by expanding the role of reason in religious discussion and by developing the doctrine of the adiaphora: the idea that certain doctrines and rituals could not be considered essentials of Christian faith. On these points, diversity of opinion was to be tolerated.[21]

During the Restoration period in England a dominant theme of Anglican religious thought was the search for a natural theology, a set of religious beliefs founded on reason. This search was in response to the strict Calvinism of the Puritans, the rise of enthusiast religious sects that denigrated the use of reason in favor of illumination and private revelation, and the threat of atheism that many Angelicans perceived in the thought of materialists and atomists like Hobbes. Although this natural theology led ultimately to deism and secularism, the Protestant theologians who developed it during the second half of the seventeenth century intended to put Christianity on a rational basis in order to defeat the arguments of atheists, enthusiasts, Calvinists, and Catholics. These Anglican thinkers insisted on the rationality of revelation and on the harmony of natural and revealed religion, and many tried to prove the rationality of the Christian religion as it was revealed in Scripture.[22]

The Cambridge Platonists used the appeal to a rational religion to combat rigid Calvinism with its doctrine of predestination. Thinkers such as Henry More, Ralph Cudworth, Benjamin Whichcote, and John Smith saw the exercise of reason as humanity's distinctive quality, and thus they held that reason should not be fettered by religious doctrines. For the Platonists, the true seat of authority in religion was the individual conscience, governed by reason and illuminated by a revelation that could not be inconsistent with reason itself. Reason was the divine governor of human life and the very voice of God, and for this reason the Platonists saw no conflict between faith and reason. Revelation never contradicted

[20] Robert K. Merton, *Science, Technology, and Society in Seventeenth-Century England* (New York, 1970), p. 98.

[21] Barbara J. Shapiro, *Probability and Certainty in Seventeenth-Century England: A Study of the Relationships between Natural Science, Religion, History, Law, and Literature* (Princeton, 1983), p. 78.

[22] Gerald R. Cragg, *From Puritanism to the Age of Reason: A Study of Changes in Religious Thought within the Church of England, 1660 to 1700* (Cambridge, England, 1950), pp. 13–21; Shapiro, pp. 83–94.

reason, but it was a necessary supplement to rational knowledge. The Platonists further believed that people possessed an innate knowledge of God and virtue that formed the basis for a religion clearly and distinctly understood.[23]

From the thought of the Cambridge Platonists flowed a broad stream of religious latitudinarianism, natural theology, and rational Christianity. Many of the English latitudinarians were taught by Smith, Cudworth, or More at Cambridge, and as a result they hated religious fanaticism, enthusiasm, and unregulated inspiration. They proclaimed the authority of reason in religion, stressed ethics over theology, and distinguished between the fundamentals and the nonfundamentals of religion. For the latitudinarians, the fundamentals included the precepts of natural religion and the basic principles of morality, while ceremonies, vestments, and most theological doctrines were counted among the nonessential points of religion. On these nonfundamental points a variety of opinions could be tolerated.[24]

Latitudinarian thinkers such as Edward Stillingfleet, John Tillotson, John Wilkins, and Joseph Glanville believed that human reason could grasp the essentials of religion without any need of external authority, but they also believed that natural reason needed the supplement of revelation. The latitudinarians held that rational, natural religion accorded closely with Christian revelation, and they also believed that revelation could be adequately defended by an appeal to reason. Despite their great faith in reason, however, the latitudinarians held the authority of revelation to be higher than that of reason. While reason supported revelation, it did not prove it. Revelation could be proved only by miracles, and a person who claimed divine authority could only be believed if he supported his claim with miracles. Furthermore, while the latitudinarians maintained that religious belief was reasonable, they also held that there were certain truths beyond the reach of reason that could only be known through revelation.[25]

Many latitudinarians sought to demonstrate the rationality of Christianity as it was revealed in Scripture. Stillingfleet tried to establish a rational basis for biblical accounts of the creation in his *Origines sacre* (1662), and a similar effort was made by Matthew Hale in his *Primitive Origination of Mankind* (1677). Stillingfleet, Tillotson, and other latitudinarians argued for a rational interpretation of Scripture against the authority of the Catholic oral tradition. In *A Rational Account of the Grounds of the Protestant Religion* (1665), Stillingfleet argued that reli-

[23] Cragg, pp. 42–59; Shapiro, pp. 106–107.
[24] Shapiro, pp. 104–108.
[25] Cragg, pp. 64–70.

gious faith was a rational assent based on evidence. In his *Rule of Faith* (1666), Tillotson again stressed the reasonableness of belief in Scripture. In a similar work, Isaac Barrow even suggested that religious belief was not very different from inferences made by reason.

Other latitudinarian thinkers sought to prove the existence of God by reason. In his *Principles and Duties of Natural Religion* (1675), John Wilkins proved God's existence by reasoning from effects to cause: the wonderful construction of nature itself was proof of its divine creator. Similarly, in *The Wisdom of God* (1691) John Ray proved God's existence from the effects and operations of nature. The latitudinarians believed that God revealed himself both in the book of revelation and in the book of nature.[26]

Many latitudinarians were active in the rise of modern science, in part as a result of their belief in the book of nature. Wilkins helped to found the Royal Society, in which Glanville and Thomas Sprat were also active. Latitudinarian efforts to prove God's existence through an examination of His creation encouraged the study of nature, and both latitudinarians and scientists rejected the principle of authority in favor of the operation of individual reason. Most latitudinarians believed that religion and science complemented each other and that any separation of the two would harm both.[27]

In many ways John Locke most epitomized the rational approach to religion that developed in late-seventeenth-century England. In *The Reasonableness of Christianity* (1695), Locke maintained that Christianity rested primarily on revelation and that reason could certify and interpret revelation. Locke reaffirmed the importance of reason in religion and explained how it worked by giving a rational account of the origins of the idea of God. He saw reason as a natural revelation by means of which one obtains that portion of truth that God had placed within one's reach, and he saw revelation as an enlargement of reason that provided truths communicated directly by God. For Locke, it was the duty of reason to verify the truth of revelation by showing that it came from God. Revelation was a supplement to rational truth that could not be contradicted by reason, but which was at the same time subject to the scrutiny of reason.[28]

The thought of the English deists developed under the influence of Locke's ideas. In 1696 John Toland published his *Christianity Not Mysterious*, in which he applied Locke's ideas on reason to religion. Toland went far beyond Locke by claiming that nothing contrary to or above reason could be accepted as part of Christianity. He went to great lengths

[26] Shapiro, pp. 88–102.
[27] Cragg, pp. 73–73; Shapiro, pp. 113–115.
[28] Cragg, pp. 115–130.

to show that Christianity conformed in all of its aspects to reason, which he called "the only foundation of all certitude." Unlike later deists, however, Toland neither denied nor disparaged divine revelation. For him, revelation provided part of the content of knowledge upon which reason operated, but revelation never disagreed with reason. Toland in effect altered the status of revelation by forcing it to conform in its entirety to reason. He saw religious faith as little more than a reasoned persuasion or conviction, and for him even miracles had to be understood by reason. While Toland and other deists did not deny the possibility of miracles, they regarded them as largely superfluous since they believed that the validity of revelation could be judged by reason.[29]

With the deists the progress of reason within English religious thought reached its seventeenth-century apogee. In the years after 1650 a similar transformation of religious thought was also taking place across the channel in the Netherlands. In the Dutch republic, the rational religious thought of the Cambridge Platonists and latitudinarians was echoed in the ideas of the Dutch Arminians and Collegiants. The Arminians, or Remonstrants, a liberal outgrowth of the Dutch Reformed church, about which more will be said in subsequent chapters, shared the rational approach to religion and the opposition to materialism and atheism that was found among the Cambridge Platonists. Like the Platonists, the Arminians used reason in defense of Christianity. The leader of the Dutch Arminians was the theologian Philip van Limborch, a thinker who was influenced by Cartesianism and who dedicated his life to arguing for reason and toleration in religion. Van Limborch corresponded with Locke, Stillingfleet, Tillotson, More, and Cudworth in England. His colleague Jean LeClerc, a teacher at the Arminian seminary in Amsterdam, was also influenced by Cartesianism and wrote often to Locke, the earl of Shaftesbury, and Gilbert Burnet.[30]

Like the Cambridge Platonists, the Dutch Arminians opposed strict Calvinism as well as enthusiast spiritualism in favor of a religion of reason and toleration. Van Limborch corresponded with Henry More from 1667 to 1687, and like More he gradually moved away from Cartesianism after 1669 because he came to feel that Cartesian dualism and the mechanical philosophy could lead to atheism. Both the Cambridge Platonists and the Dutch Arminians feared the materialism of Hobbes and were angered by Hobbes's rejection of the authenticity of some biblical books. The pantheism of the Dutch philosopher Benedict Spinoza, however, was seen as the greatest threat to Christianity by both More and van Limborch.

[29] Ibid., pp. 143–153.
[30] Colie, pp. 4–35.

Spinoza carried Cartesian ideas far beyond what More and van Limborch could accept, and for this reason he was seen by Platonist and Arminian alike as a materialist, mechanist, and atheist. Because both the Platonists and the Arminians combined reason and religion in their thought, they were much opposed to Spinoza's separation of rational philosophy from revealed religion in his *Theologico-Political Treatise* (1670). By drawing a sharp distinction between philosophy and religion, Spinoza developed a secular and rationalistic philosophy with little room for revelation or supernatural miracles. Van Limborch and the Arminians felt that Spinoza placed far too much importance on human reason and too little importance on biblical revelation.

Van Limborch also criticized the ideas of the Dutch philosopher Jan Bredenburg, a follower of Spinoza. Bredenburg, who was an important member of the Collegiants, published a work entitled *Enervatio tractatus theologici-politici* in 1675. Although the *Enervatio* was critical of Spinoza at several points, it showed Bredenburg's own philosophy to be very close to the ideas of Spinoza.[31] Bredenburg spent much of his career studying the ideas of Spinoza, who was involved in Collegiant circles in Amsterdam and Rijnsburg during the 1660s and 1670s. Along with Bredenburg, a number of other Collegiants were deeply influenced by Spinoza's rationalism.

In part as a result of Spinoza's influence, from 1650 to 1690 Collegiant thought evolved in a rationalistic direction that in many ways paralleled the development of the ideas of the Cambridge Platonists, latitudinarians, and deists in England. The present study will investigate the growing importance of reason within the religious thought of the Collegiants during the seventeenth century, and thus it will chronicle the dramatic transformation of Collegiant thought in that period. During the later years of the century Collegiant thought moved away from the millenarian spiritualism that was its birthright in the direction of an increasingly secularized and rationalistic philosophy that reached its maturity in a set of ideas similar to the philosophy of Spinoza. In Collegiant writings concerning religion and the condition of the Christian churches of seventeenth-century Europe there is a concrete example of the developing sense of separation between heaven and earth that culminated in the idea that the temporal world was essentially cut off from divine inspiration. The first part of this study will concentrate on the origin and development of this secularizing trend in Collegiant thought. The second part will show how this secularizing trend transformed the Collegiant's conception of the individ-

[31] Ibid., pp. 35–97. See also Wiep van Bunge, "Johannes Bredenburg and the Korte Verhandeling," *Studia Spinoziana* 4 (1988), pp. 321–328.

ual conscience and thus led the group to the brink of philosophical rationalism.

Today the ideas and writings of the Dutch Collegiants are almost entirely
unknown outside of a small circle of specialists. Although J. C. van Slee
wrote the history of Collegiantism in the last century and other historians
such as C. B. Hylkema, Rufus Jones, Cornelia W. Roldanus, Johannes
Lindeboom, S.B.J. Zilverberg, and K. O. Meinsma have dealt briefly with
the ideas of a few individual Collegiants, there has never been a detailed
study of the development of Collegiant thought as a whole. The reasons
for this neglect are not difficult to determine. The Collegiants were not
great philosophers or theologians, and none among them could match the
intellectual power and originality of Bayle, Malebranche, Simon, Locke,
and others one meets in the pages of Hazard. Historians interested in the
development of seventeenth-century thought have traditionally focused
on the systems and theories of the great thinkers of the age to the neglect
of lesser figures like the Collegiants. In the great philosophical and theological systems historians have seen powerful expressions of worldviews
new and old, and by comparing these systems they have sought to understand the intellectual transition between them. Among the Collegiants
one does not find such systems; rather, one finds the written record of
intellectual transition itself: the struggles, the give and take, the contradictions, the difficult process of disillusionment and adjustment that
marked the intellectual journey of a group of intensely serious and deeply
pious thinkers toward a new conception of religious truth. By focusing
on Collegiant thought one focuses on the process of intellectual change
itself. The lines of intellectual development among the Collegiants were
not always direct, clear, or simple. Yet the process of transformation that
took place in Collegiant thought through a dialectic of discussion, mistake, and improvisation provides the historian with a unique window to
the inner workings of historical change in the realm of ideas. The writings
of the Collegiants are not great monuments of European thought, but
they are revealing documents of intellectual history.

The Collegiants were what might be termed middle-level intellectuals.
They were educated and well-read professional people who maintained a
serious interest in intellectual and religious developments as well as an
intense religious piety and moral seriousness. They were not men of outstanding intellectual talent, creativity, or originality. As thinkers they
were located in that broad stratum of intellectual society below leading
figures such as Grotius, Huygens, Vondel, and Leeuwenhoek (described
by Westfall as a giant even among heroes), below even less imposing figures such as Arminius, van Limborch, and Coornhert, but well above the
great mass of uneducated or semieducated people who attended religious

services but gave little thought to intellectual issues. There are definite advantages to studying intellectual transformation within such a group of thinkers. The Collegiants did not create intellectual trends but they were sensitive to them, and thus their thought reflected the larger intellectual currents swirling about them. The Collegiants were a very broad-minded and intellectually tolerant group of thinkers living in the most open and tolerant society in seventeenth-century Europe, and thus their writings provide an exceptionally sensitive barometer for measuring changes in the intellectual atmosphere of the Dutch republic and Europe as a whole in this period. Furthermore, while the philosophical masterpieces of great thinkers seldom reveal the intellectual struggle behind their creation, the works of the Collegiants reflect the difficult process of thought that gave them birth. For this reason the course of intellectual transition can be studied revealingly in the writings of lesser thinkers like the Collegiants, who inconsistently combined both old and new and lived with contradictions they could not overcome.

The idea that intellectual history consists of an uninterrupted succession of great minds, each forging ideas in the burning fire of genius, is a myth propagated by great thinkers themselves and adopted by some historians, but it is a myth that does not enjoy much currency today. As the traditional history of ideas has given way to a broader and more contextual approach to intellectual and cultural history, to the history of mentalities and collective psychology, and to the study of popular culture, historians of thought have accepted the challenge of a multidimensional and multileveled approach to the examination of human intellectual activity. This challenge imposes on the historian a duty to fill in all the pieces of a very large and complex puzzle and to consider "lesser" thinkers and their ideas on a level once reserved for the great. One reason for this approach is to understand great thinkers and ideas within the historical and intellectual context provided by smaller thinkers and less-developed ideas.

By bringing the ideas of thinkers like the Collegiants into the mainstream of intellectual history we provide ourselves with a more complete picture of the rich fabric of intellectual life and we supply a fascinating new perspective on the genius of a thinker like Spinoza. In this particular case we also provide ourselves with a unique window to the troubled minds of people living in a crucial period of intellectual change. When one considers the development of the modern worldview, the important roles of leading figures such as Descartes, Spinoza, Locke, and Newton cannot, of course, be overlooked. But for a worldview to impose itself upon the common consciousness of a generation or an era it must have followers, a public, as well as leaders. The story of Collegiant thought is the story of how the modern rational and secular worldview gained a following among the educated public of the United Provinces.

It has been argued that the creation of the secular and rational worldview of the Enlightenment during the last years of the seventeenth century was part of a longer process of cultural bifurcation that began as early as 1500 and continued through the early nineteenth century. In this process the educated upper classes of Europe—the clergy, nobility, merchants, and professionals—first attempted to reform popular culture and then abandoned it to the lower classes, establishing for themselves a new elite culture and a new worldview based on reason and secularism. The development of Collegiant thought can be seen as an example of this process.

Beginning in the sixteenth century, a systematic attempt was made on the part of the educated classes of Europe, and in particular the clergy, to reform or change the attitudes and values of the rest of the population. Protestant and Catholic reformers endeavored to spread their religious ideas and practices among the lower classes, and in the process they attempted to suppress many aspects of traditional popular culture. Peter Burke has suggested that these religious reformers can be seen as "puritans" because they sought to purify the beliefs of the lower classes from popular superstitions and pagan survivals. This clerical campaign against popular culture made swiftest progress in urban areas and in Protestant regions of Europe, although Catholic areas were also affected, if somewhat later.

In Protestant areas, this campaign against popular culture has been described as a reformation within the Reformation because it involved a shift of emphasis away from the reform of ritual and belief to a new stress on inner moral reform. The German Pietist movement of Philipp Jakob Spener was a part of this reformation within the Reformation, and so, I will argue, were the Dutch Collegiants.

During the seventeenth century the effort to reform popular culture began to involve more of the laity, especially lay preachers who preached against folk songs, folktales, and folk dances in favor of godliness. Also during the seventeenth century, secular arguments came to play a more important role in the attack on popular culture. Witchcraft and magic were rejected as irrational, and the skepticism of the upper classes led to a gradual rejection of popular belief in prophecy. Nonbiblical prophecies like the oracles of the ancient world and the popular prophecies of the "Marvellous Merlin" were rejected by the educated classes, but by the late seventeenth century even biblical prophecies of the Apocalypse and the millennium were increasingly questioned. Indeed, after 1650 the educated classes rejected not just the festivals and practices of the lower classes, but their entire worldview. The Collegiants provide a fascinating example of this process.

The effort to reform popular culture did not succeed in transforming the beliefs of the masses, but it did lead to a widening gulf between elite and popular culture. The reforms affected the upper classes much more quickly and thoroughly than the masses, and thus the reform movement created a purified, secularized, and rational elite culture that separated itself from popular beliefs. Learned culture underwent rapid change from 1500 to 1800 as it was affected by the movements of humanism, Protestantism, the Scientific Revolution, and the Enlightenment, and this rapid pace of change helped to create an elite culture that was largely isolated from the beliefs of the masses. The Enlightenment worldview of reason and secularism was a manifestation of this elite culture.[32]

The evolution of Collegiant thought during the seventeenth century provides an excellent case study in the development of elite culture. Collegiantism was a movement dominated by educated, upper-class intellectuals, merchants, and professionals, and in its stress on inner spiritual regeneration it was very much a part of the reformation within seventeenth-century Protestantism. Within the Collegiant movement, traditional religious ideas mixed with humanism, Protestantism, and rationalism. As the Collegiants moved away from their original millenarian spiritualism, their conception of prophecy and their entire worldview underwent a fundamental change. The first Collegiants held religious beliefs that would have been fully understandable to ordinary people of the 1620s, but the rationalistic philosophy of Jan Bredenburg and other Collegiants of the 1680s could hardly have been farther removed from the beliefs of common people. Collegiantism thus provides eloquent testimony to the growing cultural bifurcation of European society that gave rise to the Enlightenment worldview.

There is yet another reason why the study of the Collegiants provides the historian with a unique view of intellectual transition. The study of intellectual evolution is a study of continuity as well as change. For this reason, the study of intellectual transition can be done with greater effectiveness within the context of a single group, institution, or other clearly defined unit. The examination of intellectual change involves a close scrutiny of the interactions and interrelationships among people and ideas, and this scrutiny can best be carried out within a consistent and well-established framework that provides a common context for intellectual development. In this way, both external and internal influences can be clearly recognized and their impact on intellectual change assessed. The great thinkers discussed by Hazard had in common only the originality of their ideas. They were not united by any single institutional or social

---

[32] Peter Burke, *Popular Culture in Early Modern Europe* (New York, 1978), pp. 207–281.

context, and this fact made it difficult for Hazard to assess accurately the influence of social and political factors on the overall development of European thought in the late seventeenth century. The Dutch Collegiants, however, provide an opportunity for the study of intellectual change within a defined social and institutional framework. The Collegiants were a relatively small and closely knit group of thinkers united by a common organizational structure as well as by common meetings, practices, and principles. Many Collegiants were linked to each other by additional bonds of friendship and family relations. Within such a well-defined and closely knit group, the factors influencing intellectual change can be more clearly identified and the lines of ideological transition can be more easily traced than is possible when one is dealing with a series of largely unconnected individual thinkers.

A final advantage of studying the Collegiants is provided by their location in the United Provinces. The Dutch republic was one of the foremost centers of European intellectual life during the second half of the seventeenth century and one of the primary birthplaces of the modern worldview. An important reason for this was the unparalleled religious and intellectual toleration that prevailed in Dutch society, especially in the large urban centers of Holland.[33] Dutch religious and intellectual life was characterized by a remarkable pluralism that saw the official Reformed church coexist with Mennonites, Catholics, Lutherans, and many smaller sects, while philosophical currents old and new vied with each other for preeminence within the great universities and a host of printing presses supplied reading material to the highly literate public of urban Holland. This atmosphere of pluralism and toleration gave rise to an extraordinary measure of freedom of thought, expression, and publication that attracted to the United Provinces many of the best minds of Europe. In the cosmopolitan cities of Holland thinkers from all over the Continent met in fruitful dialogue with each other and with important Dutch intellectuals. Here Descartes worked on his revolutionary philosophy, Locke and van Limborch discussed religious toleration, Bayle and LeClerc published their pioneering journals, Comenius found an audience for his ecumenical and educational projects, Spinoza corresponded with Oldenburg and Leibniz while perfecting his monistic rationalism, Leeuwenhoek made giant strides in microscopy, Socinians found refuge from persecution in Poland, Quakers spread their spiritualistic message, German followers of Jacob Böhme published his mystical writings, and prophets such as Antoinette Bourignon and Johannes Rothe predicted the immi-

---

[33] See, for example, H. A. Enno van Gelder, *Getemperde Vrijheid: Een verhandeling over de verhouding van kerk en Staat in de Republiek der Verenigde Nederlanden en de Vrijheid van meningsuiting in zake godsdienst, drukpers, en onderwijs, gedurende de 17e eeuw* (Groningen, 1972), pp. 1–7.

nent end of the world. In this atmosphere of intellectual freedom ideas were exchanged, debated, modified, and transformed with an ease unknown elsewhere, and out of this intellectual ferment a new worldview was emerging. In this milieu of exciting intellectual growth, the Collegiants were one of many important centers for the exchange, debate, and transformation of ideas. To study the evolution of Collegiant thought during the years 1620 to 1690 is to put a finger on the pulse of change in the most dynamic intellectual society in late-seventeenth-century Europe.

Chapter Two

THE COLLEGIANT MOVEMENT

Alas, if all men were but wise,
and would be good as well,
The earth would be a paradise,
where now 'tis mostly hell.
—D. R. Camphuysen
*(verse inscribed in the rear gable of Spinoza's house in
Rijnsburg)*

THE COLLEGIANTS were a group of religious dissenters in Holland who
began their meetings in 1620 after breaking with the Dutch Reformed
church. In their early years the Collegiants were heavily influenced by
Arminian ideas as well as by many of the beliefs and practices of the Anabaptists and spiritualists who made up an important part of the radical
wing of the sixteenth-century Protestant Reformation. The early Collegiants based their worldview on a firm belief in divine providence, revelation, and inspiration as well as on an ardent expectation of the imminent coming of the millennium of Christ. By the end of the seventeenth
century, however, many Collegiants believed that the only way man could
understand himself and his religious duty was through the use of human
reason. A spiritualistic and chiliastic religious sect thus evolved into what
was essentially an outpost of philosophical rationalism by 1690. The intellectual history of the Collegiants from 1620 to 1690 is the story of a
stormy spiritual journey from faith to reason. An understanding of the
dramatic transformation of Collegiant thought will shed important light
on some of the key mechanisms at work in the broader European intellectual transition that was under way during the seventeenth century.

The Collegiant movement occupied a central position in the intellectual
geography of seventeenth-century Holland, representing a point of intersection for a number of intellectual traditions and movements that were
important to both the past and the future of European thought. The Collegiants and their thought formed a bridge between the providential
Christian worldview of the Reformation era and the rational and secular
outlook of the early Enlightenment. In its origins and early development,
Collegiantism represented both a continuation of many of the ideas of the
sixteenth-century Radical Reformation and a late phase of a native Dutch

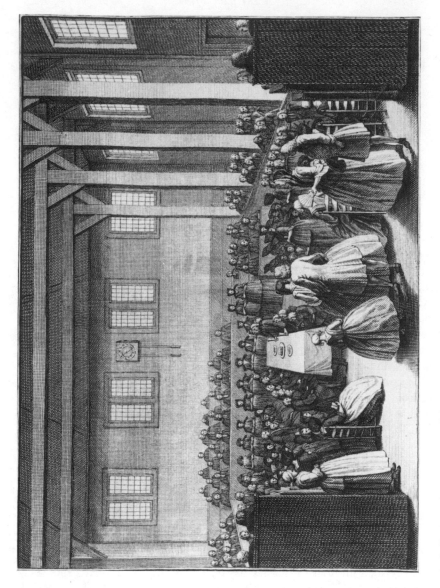

1. Collegiant Communion Celebration at Rijnsburg

reform movement that had roots reaching back well before the time of Erasmus. The Collegiants also formed an important part of a new and vigorous movement for a renewed reform and purification of religious life that swept through the Protestant communities of northern Europe during the seventeenth century to create English Puritanism and Quakerism, German Pietism and related forms of religious dissent. This new reform movement has been called by Leszek Kolakowski the Second Reformation of the seventeenth century. With these ties to the Protestant Reformation of the sixteenth century as well as to important reforming tendencies within seventeenth-century Protestantism, the Collegiants were an integral part of Dutch religious and intellectual life in the years after 1620. Collegiantism also had important connections with both the humanistic rationalism of the Renaissance and with the developing school of seventeenth-century philosophical rationalism. The Collegiants counted among their members many exiled Polish Socinians who were heirs of the evangelical rationalist tradition of late Italian humanism, as well as the outcast Jew and Cartesian philosopher Benedict Spinoza. In the investigation of the origins and early development of the Collegiant movement that follows, this intricate web of intellectual relationships will be sketched out in greater detail. In both the Dutch and the wider European intellectual context, Collegiantism was a vital nexus in a complex process of intellectual evolution.

Collegiantism represented a late phase in a movement for religious reform in the Netherlands that had roots stretching back as far as the late fourteenth century. Only within the context of this native Dutch reform tradition can the origin, ideals, and goals of the Collegiant movement be properly understood. Reform tendencies began within the Catholic church of the Netherlands during the fourteenth and fifteenth centuries with that particularly Dutch expression of late medieval piety known as the Devotio Moderna, or the Brethren of the Common Life, a movement joining clergy and laymen together in a life of ascetic spiritualism and devotional simplicity. By the early sixteenth century the biblical humanism of Erasmus, inspired in part by the ideals of the Devotio Moderna, called for a religious renewal within the established church modeled on the principles of apostolic simplicity and toleration.[1] After 1520 the Lutheran Reformation entered the Low Countries from northern Germany, but while Lutheranism had some impact among the Dutch regular clergy it failed to attract great popular support. A more important part of the

---

[1] S.B.J. Zilverberg, *Geloof en geweten in de zeventiende eeuw* (Bussum, 1971), pp. 7–8; George Hunston Williams, *The Radical Reformation* (Philadelphia, 1962), pp. 36–37, 344–350.

early Dutch Reformation was a native evangelical movement known as Sacramentarianism. Inspired by biblical humanism and by the example of the Brethren of the Common Life, the Sacramentarians (led by Cornelis Hoen, d. 1524) rejected the doctrine of transubstantiation as unbiblical and put forward a religious program calling for apostolic simplicity of life, purity in doctrine and conduct, and an undogmatic and individualistic piety that downplayed religious ceremony. Both the Sacramentarians and the biblical humanists represented an indigenous Dutch religious reform movement that did not break openly with the established church. Although this native reform movement was soon overcome by more radical Protestant influences entering the Low Countries from abroad, its spirit of toleration, devotional simplicity, and spiritualism later became an integral part of the Remonstrant and Collegiant movements.[2]

While many of the early Dutch reformers were influenced by the peaceful and moderate ideas of men like Erasmus and Sebastian Castellio, this moderate Dutch reform movement soon gave way to the militant preachings of Anabaptism, radical spiritualism, and Socinianism, the three main branches of what George Hunston Williams called the Radical Reformation. As these more extreme reformist currents flowed into the Low Countries from abroad a major change in the direction of the Dutch reform movement took place. This change was aptly represented by the radical preaching of the Anabaptist Melchior Hoffman (1495–1543), who came to the Low Countries in 1530 to proclaim the imminent arrival of the thousand-year kingdom of Christ on earth.[3]

Anabaptism was born in Huldrych Zwingli's Zurich in 1523 but it was soon widely spread over Germany, Switzerland, and the Low Countries. By the end of 1530, Anabaptist congregations had been established in the Dutch cities of Amsterdam and Leeuwarden. The Anabaptists sought to restore the spiritual purity of primitive Christianity to the sixteenth-century church through a strict adherence to the Bible, great moral rigor, separation of church and state, and rejection of infant baptism. Hoffman, who was the leader of the movement in north Germany and the Low Countries, added a radical millenarianism to other Anabaptist ideas, a doctrine that found its most tragic expression in the ill-fated kingdom of Münster in 1534–1535. The Münster disaster was accompanied in Holland by an equally ill-fated attempt by radical Anabaptists to seize control of the government of Amsterdam. After these tragic events the Anabaptists, who had long been persecuted by Catholics and Protestants alike as

[2] G. J. Hoenderdaal, "Begin en beginsel" in G. J. Hoenderdaal and P. M. Luca, eds., *Staat in de vrijheid: geschiedenis van de Remonstranten* (Zutphen, 1982), pp. 9–11. See also Heiko Oberman, *Forerunners of the Reformation* (Philadelphia, 1981), pp. 53–120; and Williams, pp. 35–37, 347–360.

[3] Cornelia W. Roldanus, *Zeventiende eeuwse geestesbloei* (Utrecht, 1961), p. 13.

dangerous subverters of civil and religious order, experienced intensified pressure from authorities in Germany and the Netherlands. Many Dutch Anabaptists became martyrs at the hands of Spanish authorities, and the remnants of the movement in the Low Countries sought to evade further persecution and thus to survive by adopting strict pacifism under the leadership of Menno Simons (1496–1561). Many of these Dutch Anabaptists, who were soon to be called Mennonites, sought refuge in the great cities of the province of Holland, where commercially minded civil authorities were reluctant to sanction religious persecution without the most serious provocation. After a brief period of tension immediately following the Münsterite and Amsterdam uprisings, the Mennonites were generally left to practice their religion in peaceful privacy by the urban magistrates of Holland, many of whom were soon involved in the revolt against Spain. The Mennonites remained the most widespread Protestant group in the Netherlands until the coming of Calvinism after 1560.[4]

Although the Anabaptists were the most important of the radical Protestant sects that entered the Low Countries during the sixteenth century, they were not the only branch of the Radical Reformation to take root in Dutch soil. Both radical spiritualism and the evangelical rationalist movement known as Socinianism eventually found their way into the Low Countries. Radical spiritualism was a movement that began in Germany under the leadership of the reformers Sebastian Franck (1499–1543) and Kaspar Schwenkfeld (1489–1561). The spiritualists rejected the importance of all external religious institutions, sacraments, and ceremonies as well as the relevance of theological doctrine in favor of a religion based entirely upon the direct, sanctifying, and illuminating inspiration of the Holy Spirit in the individual soul of each believer. This inner inspiration they called the "inner light" or "inner word," and they felt that it would bring the believer perfect religious knowledge as a means of preparing his soul to receive God's saving grace. The immediate contact with God that was the central feature of spiritualism made the visible church and external religion unnecessary, and even Scripture was considered to be of secondary importance. Most spiritualists insisted on the absolute separation of word and spirit as well as of church and state. Franck and Schwenkfeld spread this subjectivistic creed in southern Germany during the second quarter of the sixteenth century. Hounded from city to city by suspicious civil authorities, these lonely prophets of inner religion established small cells of disciples in various locations in south Germany, but when they died they left behind no large body of followers. Their ideas found greater circulation during the later sixteenth and early seventeenth centuries in the Netherlands, where the writings of Franck were translated into Dutch

---

[4] Zilverberg, p. 8; Williams, pp. 355–360, 387–400.

and printed several times after 1560. Franck's thought was so popular among Dutch Protestants, especially among the Mennonites, that later writers believed (probably incorrectly) that Franck himself had journeyed to the Low Countries shortly before his death.[5] Schwenkfeld's ideas, although less influential in the Netherlands than Franck's thought, nevertheless found favor with the radical Anabaptist David Joris (ca. 1501–1556) and his followers, as well as with later Mennonites such as Pieter Jansz. Twisck (1565–1636) and Hans de Ries (1553–1638). The mystical physician Justus Velsius Haganus (1505–1581), the spiritualist poet Daniel Suderman (1550–1631), the Lutheran mystic Christian Hohburg (1607–1675), and the statesman and political theorist Aggaeus van Albada (ca. 1525–1587) were among other Dutch thinkers who were influenced by Schwenkfeld's ideas. Albada spread Schwenkfeld's ideas and made translations of his works, although these were probably not published. The chief Dutch proponent of the ideas of both Schwenkfeld and Franck was the influential humanist and ecumenicist Dirk Volckertsz. Coornhert (1522–1590), whose ideas were important for many of the principal religious thinkers in the Netherlands during the later sixteenth and seventeenth centuries—including many prominent Collegiants.[6]

Socinianism, the third branch of the Radical Reformation, was founded by Laelius (1525–1562) and Faustus (1539–1604) Socinus, natives of Siena who were under the influence of Italian humanism and its rationalistic biblical scholarship. The Socinians' rejection of the traditional Christian doctrines of the Trinity, the divinity of Christ, and Christ's satisfaction sprang from a criticism of Christian dogma that was based both on an extreme biblical literalism and a commonsense rationalism inherited from humanism.[7] These ideas made the Socinians un-

---

[5] Bruno Becker, "Nederlandsch vertalingen van Sebastian Francks geschriften," *Nederlandsch Archief voor Kerkgeschiedenis* 21 (1928), pp. 149–160; Gerald Strauss, *Sixteenth Century Germany: Its Topography and Topographers* (Madison, 1959), p. 113. On Franck, see also Siegfried Wollgast, *Der deutsche Pantheismus im 16. Jahrhundert* (Berlin, 1972); and Johannes Lindeboom, *Een Franc-tireur der Reformatie: Sebastiaan Franck* (Arnhem, 1952).

[6] Wiebe Bergsma, "Aggaeus van Albada (c.1527–1587), Schwenckfeldiaan, staatsman en strijder voor verdraagzaamheid" (dissertation, University of Groningen, 1983), pp. 58–66. On Schwenkfeld, see also R. Emmet McLaughlin, *Caspar Schwenkfeld, Reluctant Radical* (New Haven, 1986); Peter Erb, ed., *Schwenkfeld and Early Schwenkfeldians: Papers Presented at the Colloquium on Schwenkfeld and the Schwenkfelders, Pennsburg, Pa., September 17–22, 1984* (Pennsburg, Penn., 1984); Gottfried Maron, *Individualismus und Gemeinschaft bei Caspar von Schwenkfeld* (Stuttgart, 1961); and Joachim Seyppel, *Schwenkfeld: Knight of Faith* (Pennsburg, Penn., 1961). On Coornhert, see H. Bonger, *Leven en werken van D. V. Coornhert* (Amsterdam, 1978); and F.D.J. Moorrees, *D. V. Coornhert de libertijn* (Schoonhoven, 1887).

[7] On the Socinians, see W. J. Kühler, *Het Socinianisme in Nederland* (Leiden, 1912; reprint Leeuwarden, 1980).

welcome in Catholic Italy and Protestant Germany alike, but they flourished in relatively tolerant Poland during the last years of the sixteenth century. In the years immediately following the arrival of Faustus Socinus in Krakow in 1580 the Polish monarchy was disorganized and weak and the Polish Catholic church was occupied by the challenge of Calvinism. After 1600, however, the Counter-Reformation reinvigorated both church and monarchy in Poland, and the crown, with Jesuit prompting, undertook an energetic attack on the Socinians. There followed a mass exodus of Socinians from Poland, with many going to East Prussia or the Rhineland but most ending up in tolerant Holland, especially in Amsterdam. During the seventeenth century Socinianism became a predominantly Dutch movement.[8]

Despite the impact made on Dutch religious life by the various branches of the Radical Reformation that penetrated Holland during the sixteenth and early seventeenth centuries, the single most important turning point for the Dutch Reformation occurred around the year 1560 when Calvinism first reached the northern Netherlands. Calvinism came to the northern Netherlands from France by way of the French-speaking areas of the southern Netherlands. Unlike the pacifist Mennonites, who denied Christians the right of opposition to an ungodly prince, Calvinism granted Christians this right. Thus, the new religion offered the Dutch a religious justification for revolt against their Spanish Catholic overlord in the same way that it offered such legitimacy to the revolt of French Protestants against their Catholic monarch. Partly for this reason, Calvinism assumed a commanding position within Dutch Protestantism shortly after the outbreak of the Dutch revolt.[9]

The progress of Calvinism in the northern Netherlands was aided greatly by the uprising of the provinces against the rule of Philip II, who had inherited the Low Countries from his father, the Emperor Charles V. Philip's reorganization of the Dutch church and his vigorous prosecution of the edicts against Protestantism aroused great opposition among the Dutch and provoked a wave of iconoclasm in 1566. The king attempted to crush all opposition with military force and the public execution of Protestants, but this led to the outbreak of organized rebellion in 1572. Uprisings against Spanish authority swept through the towns of the north with Calvinists playing a key role in the revolt, fired by their desires for both religious and political freedom. In 1579 the seven northern provinces united in the Union of Utrecht, and by the 1590s the Dutch republic

---

[8] See Earl M. Wilbur, *A History of Unitarianism: Socinianism and its Antecedents* (Cambridge, Mass., 1946).

[9] Zilverberg, p. 14.

had established its control as far south as Flanders. Calvinism became firmly entrenched in the north.

The first Calvinism in the northern Netherlands was neither as strict nor as confessional as it was later to become. During the late sixteenth century, Calvinist ideas mixed freely with the spirit of the indigenous Dutch Reformation, with its biblical piety, irenic spirit, and distaste for extremism in theology. The result was a moderate and tolerant Protestantism closely allied to the peaceful attitude of many of the urban magistrates of Holland. By the last two decades of the century, however, there arose a growing tension between this moderate Protestantism and an increasingly influential group of strict Calvinists, recent immigrants from the southern Netherlands, who represented a confessional and Geneva-oriented point of view. These strict Calvinists, known as *preciezen*, favored a rigorous interpretation of the doctrine of predestination, rigid church discipline, and intolerance of dissent.[10] After 1600 the influence of the *preciezen* was on the rise in the Dutch Reformed church, leading to an increasing adherence to the importance of confessions in religious life and to a growing trend toward doctrinal rigidity among Dutch Calvinists. The tension between the *preciezen* and the older and more moderate branch of Dutch Protestantism gave rise to a great dispute within the Reformed church during the first two decades of the seventeenth century.[11] This struggle, known as the Arminian controversy, not only determined the nature and character of the Dutch Reformed church for the remainder of the seventeenth century, but it also gave birth to two new religious movements: the Remonstrants and the Collegiants.

This great controversy took its name from Jacob Arminius (1560–1609), one of three professors of theology at Leiden University and a spokesman for the moderate reform movement in the Dutch republic. Arminius was born in the town of Oudewater in 1560, and he was studying abroad in 1575 when Spanish troops seeking to quell the Dutch revolt destroyed his hometown and murdered his family. After a brief stay with the family of the Reformed pastor Pieter de Bert in Rotterdam, Arminius enrolled in Leiden University in 1576 to begin preparation for the ministry. Upon the completion of his studies at Leiden in 1581, Arminius was still too young to take up the office of pastor, so with financial support from an Amsterdam merchant guild he traveled to Geneva to study theology under Theodore Beza. In 1587 he returned to Amsterdam and took up his duties as a Reformed pastor.

---

[10] Carl Bangs, *Arminius, A Study in the Dutch Reformation* (Nashville, 1971), p. 54; G. J. Heering, "Het godsdienstig beginsel der Remonstranten tegenover dat der Calvinisten" in G. J. Heering (ed.), *De Remonstranten: gedenkboek bij het 300-jarig bestaan der Remonstrantsche Broederschap* (Leiden, 1919), p. 22.

[11] Roldanus, *Zeventiende eeuwse geestesbloei*, p. 38.

By the late 1580s tension was already building within the Amsterdam church between the *preciezen*, led by the pastor Petrus Plancius, a firm believer in the doctrine of predestination, and more moderate Protestants. As soon as Arminius assumed his position in Amsterdam, the *preciezen* began to suspect that he disagreed with Beza's doctrine of predestination. By 1591 Arminius's sermons had confirmed these suspicions, and Plancius accused him of Pelagianism. Arminius denied that his views differed from those contained in the Belgic Confession and the Heidelberg Catechism, the official standards of Dutch Reformed belief, but he refused to discuss publicly the doctrine of predestination. The Amsterdam city fathers did not favor a strict interpretation of the doctrine of predestination, and thus they defended Arminius against the attacks of the *preciezen*. By 1593, however, the dispute grew more heated and parties began to form around Arminius and Plancius.[12]

Arminius was deeply troubled by the deterministic idea of election and damnation contained in the doctrine of predestination held by Beza in Geneva and by the Dutch *preciezen*. To Arminius this doctrine seemed to make God the author of sin. Arminius maintained that God had predestined sinners as a group to be damned, but he also insisted that each individual made the choice to sin by his own free will and thus freely joined the circle of the damned. Likewise, Arminius believed that God had predestined all people who sought salvation through faith to be saved, but Arminius did not see free will as instrumental to salvation. Rather, he held that it was God's grace that actualized the individual's potential free will and made it possible to choose faith. With these ideas Arminius sought to preserve human free will from the threat of Calvinist determinism.[13]

Despite the protests of the strict Calvinists, Arminius's theological star continued to rise when in 1603 he was appointed one of three professors of theology at Leiden University. Questions about his views on predestination followed Arminius to Leiden, where he was opposed by his colleague in theology, Franciscus Gomarus (1563–1611). In a public disputation in 1604 Arminius maintained that original sin had been contingent on free will, not determined by predestination as many *preciezen* believed. In response to these ideas Gomarus held his own disputation later that year in which he condemned Arminius's views and supported the doctrines of Beza. By 1606 the question of predestination had developed into a major controversy in Leiden and the *preciezen* accused Arminius of favoring a return to Catholic works piety.

---

[12] Bangs, pp. 52–147; Hoenderdaal, in Hoenderdaal and Luca, eds., p. 33; H. Y. Groenewegen, "Arminius en de Remonstrantie," in Heering, ed., *De Remonstranten*, pp. 61–67.

[13] Hoenderdaal, in Hoenderdaal and Luca, eds., p. 15; Heering, p. 22; Bangs, pp. 195–216.

Arminius and Gomarus also clashed over the issue of confessionalism. The *preciezen* considered the Belgic Confession and Heidelberg Catechism to be of such great authority in matters of doctrine that in certain instances they were as important as the Bible itself for determining true belief. While this attitude can be seen in retrospect as part of a general trend toward doctrinal conservatism within European Protestantism as a whole during the last quarter of the sixteenth century, such dogmatization of religious belief was directly contrary to the spirit of the indigenous Dutch Reformation. Arminius was in many ways a spokesman for that impulse toward practical piety following the apostolic example that had found expression in earlier movements such as the Devotio Moderna, Sacramentarianism, and biblical humanism, and as heir to this native reform tradition he took up the battle against confessionalism. Following in the tradition of Erasmus, Arminius called for unity of belief in a few fundamental doctrines of Christianity, toleration with regard to all other doctrines, and a recognition of the supreme authority of the Bible in theological questions. These ideas became central Collegiant beliefs.

The dispute between Arminius and Gomarus reached a climax in 1608. Angered by the attacks of the *preciezen*, Arminius made a public declaration of his beliefs before the States of Holland. In this declaration he vigorously rejected the doctrine of predestination as held by Beza, Plancius, and Gomarus. Arminius claimed that strict predestination was contrary to the wisdom, justice, and goodness of God; contrary to the nature of sin as disobedience meriting damnation; and contrary as well to the nature of man, who was created in God's image with the freedom and aptitude for eternal life. According to Arminius, the doctrine of predestination subverted the very foundations of true religion and had never been approved by the church fathers (including Augustine) or by church councils. Arminius also declared that the Belgic Confession and Heidelberg Cathechism were merely human documents liable to error and thus they were inferior in authority to the Holy Scripture in all matters of doctrine.[14]

Early in February 1609 Arminius suffered an illness that completely incapacitated him for a time. Although he recovered sufficiently to resume the struggle against his opponents, his condition worsened as the year went by, and by September he was gravely ill with consumption. Arminius died on 19 October, 1609, surrounded by family and friends. He left behind a body of ideas that continued to find powerful support both inside and outside of the Dutch Reformed church throughout the seventeenth century. Many of these ideas, along with Arminius's tolerant spirit, later became integral parts of the Collegiant movement.

[14] Hoenderdaal, in Hoenderdaal and Luca, eds., p. 24; Bangs, pp. 308–315.

In 1610 the party of supporters that had formed around Arminius served a formal remonstrance upon the States of Holland pleading for toleration of their views and asking for protection from orthodox persecution. The remonstrance summarized the essential points of Arminian belief and denied the charge that such views entailed a change in Dutch Reformed doctrine. With this plea the party henceforth known as the Remonstrants put forth its principles of anticonfessionalism, anticlericalism, and freedom of conscience. Calvinist dogmatism had put too much emphasis on the intellectual side of religion, the Remonstrants felt, at the expense not only of free thought but also of moral responsibility.[15] Against Calvinist confessionalism the party of Arminius put forward an evangelical and Erasmian piety in the spirit of the first Dutch reformers.

During the sixteenth and seventeenth centuries, religious controversies of all kinds were intricately interwoven into the complex fabric of social and political conflict that formed the texture of life in early modern society. The Arminian dispute was no different in this regard. In the Dutch republic during the truce with Spain, which lasted from 1609 to 1621, the political and social situation was extremely volatile. Tensions resulting from the unique nature of power relationships within the young republic soon brought the religious controversy to a crisis point. The years of peace with Spain provided opposing parties in the republic with the opportunity to quarrel over the question of where sovereignty should be located in the new state. Count Maurice of Nassau (1567–1625), the powerful stadtholder of the provinces of Holland, Zeeland, Utrecht, Gelderland, and Overijssel, joined with the States General of the United Provinces in an effort to mold a powerful central government for the nation under the leadership of the house of Orange. Maurice and the States General were supported by the Dutch nobility, which favored a centralized state under the house of Orange; by the largely agricultural provinces of Utrecht, Groningen, Gelderland, and Overijssel, which resented the dominant position within the republic assumed by the maritime provinces of Holland and Zeeland; and by the strict Calvinists, who favored a strong central government that could eject Catholic Spain from the Low Countries. Opposing this powerful coalition was Johan van Oldenbarnevelt (1547–1619), land's advocate of Holland and thus minister to the States of Holland. Oldenbarnevelt and the States of Holland favored a loose, federal arrangement for the United Provinces because such a government would easily be dominated by the economically powerful province of Holland. Oldenbarnevelt's policy was backed by many of the regents, members of the municipal and provincial governments of Holland and Zeeland. The regents were chiefly concerned with commercial affairs

---

[15] Hoenderdaal, in Hoenderdaal and Luca, eds., p. 16; Groenewegen, pp. 70–71, 73.

and they therefore opposed the desires of the nobility and the Calvinist clergy for renewed war with Spain when the truce expired in 1621. The Remonstrants sought protection from the party of Oldenbarnevelt, which tended toward Erastian views and was more tolerant of differences within the church than was the party of Maurice. The population at large, however, tended to side with Maurice and the Calvinist *preciezen*—after 1610 known as the Contra-Remonstrants. A large segment of the middle and lower classes of the United Provinces viewed the Remonstrants as dangerous troublemakers that the republic could ill afford in the face of the continuing Spanish threat.[16]

With so many volatile ingredients, this complex mixture of social, political, economic, and religious tensions began to heat up rapidly as the end of the truce with Spain approached. Although the States of Holland had attempted to grant the Remonstrant petitioners of 1610 the protection they sought in the form of a general admonishment for religious peace directed especially at the Contra-Remonstrants, agitation between the two sides continued undiminished. In 1611 the States organized a peace conference between the two parties in The Hague, but no agreement was reached. The Contra-Remonstrants favored the calling of a national synod of the Reformed church to settle the religious dispute, but the States of Holland blocked the calling of a synod because of their fear that it would be dominated by Contra-Remonstrant clergy, who were in a majority outside of the province of Holland. As tensions increased, the Remonstrants' opponents accused them of being agents of Spain working for the return of Catholicism to the northern Netherlands, while the internationally renowned historian and jurist Hugo Grotius eloquently defended Oldenbarnevelt and his party. In many of the important towns of Holland the Contra-Remonstrant populace struggled with municipal governments that favored the Arminians. In Amsterdam, where the local government was by now not Arminian, the populace often broke up Remonstrant meetings. In February 1617 a hostile crowd invaded and ransacked the Amsterdam home of a prominent Remonstrant citizen, Rem Bisschop. During the summer of 1617 the States General of the United Provinces overrode the objections of Holland and voted to summon a national synod of the Reformed church for the following year to settle the religious dispute. Tensions between the two parties continued to increase, and in August 1617 Oldenbarnevelt convinced the States of Holland to pass a resolution empowering municipal governments to raise local militias to preserve order. Maurice saw these militias as a direct threat to his military power as well as to the unity of the republic, and thus he decided to take action against Oldenbarnevelt's party. In January 1618 Maurice

[16] Hoenderdaal, in Hoenderdaal and Luca, eds., pp. 20–21.

used his army to overturn the Remonstrant governments of Nijmegen and Overijssel, and he followed these actions with a similar coup in Utrecht during the summer. In July 1618 Maurice, now prince of Orange following the death of his elder brother Philip William, convinced the States General to pass a resolution disbanding the militias. In August he used his army to arrest Oldenbarnevelt, Grotius, and other leading members of the opposition. Maurice then consolidated his grip on political power by transferring all of the municipal governments of Holland from Remonstrant to Contra-Remonstrant control.[17] Having thus effectively seized political power, Maurice left it to the national synod of the Reformed church, meeting later that year in Dordrecht, to settle matters in religion.

When the Synod of Dordrecht (or Dort) convened in November 1618 it was dominated by the Contra-Remonstrant party. The Remonstrants were called to the meeting not as fellow participants but rather as defendants before a tribunal. In view of the political victory of the Orangists, the Remonstrants had little choice but to submit themselves to the judgment of the synod. The Remonstrants were led during the difficult sessions of November and December by Simon Episcopius (1583–1643), the brother of Rem Bisschop and a brilliant theologian who had studied under Arminius in Leiden, where he had succeeded his teacher as professor of theology. Certain of eventual condemnation, the Remonstrants tried to clog the synod's proceedings with long speeches, but they were rewarded for their efforts with ejection from the meetings followed by condemnation in absentia. The decrees issued by the synod officially condemned many Arminian beliefs and permanently deposed all Remonstrant preachers, who were given the choice of signing a pledge never to preach again or of being banned from the country. Most chose exile. The synod also adopted the Heidelberg Catechism and a revised Belgic Confession as obligatory rules of belief for the Reformed church. After many long, difficult, and stormy sessions, the Synod of Dordrecht ended with a sweeping victory for the strict Calvinists. To enforce the decrees of the synod, civil authorities purged Leiden University of Remonstrant sympathizers and issued an edict forbidding Remonstrant conventicles and putting a price on the head of any Arminian who attempted to preach. The victory of the Contra-Remonstrant party appeared to be complete.[18]

While the events in Dordrecht temporarily ended the debate within the

[17] Ibid., p. 38; Zilverberg, pp. 23–25; Pieter Geyl, *The Netherlands in the Seventeenth Century* (New York, 1961), vol. 1, pp. 47–61.

[18] S.B.J. Zilverberg, "Van gedulde tot erkende geloofs-gemeenschap," in Hoenderdaal and Luca, eds., pp. 38–44; L. Knappert, "Episcopius en de Synode," in Heering, ed., *De Remonstranten*, pp. 84–88; Geyl, pp. 70–72.

Reformed church, the synod did not succeed in destroying the Remonstrant party. After their condemnation by the synod most Remonstrant leaders sought refuge in Antwerp, ironically enough under Spanish protection. There, on 30 September 1619, the Remonstrant Brotherhood was founded as a church in exile. Episcopius, Johannes Uytenbogaert (1557–1644), and Nicolaas Grevinkhoven (1570–1632) were named directors and made responsible for the organization of the new church. The Brotherhood did not intend, however, to be satisfied with permanent exile from the land that Arminius had tried so hard to save from religious intolerance. The pastors Carolus Niellius and Eduardus Poppius were appointed directors of covert operations in the northern provinces, where many Remonstrant preachers continued to serve their congregations secretly and illegally, at the risk of prison or even death. Many heroic chapters were written into the history of the young Brotherhood by such secret pastors who preached to their congregations only a few feet from wagons readied for their escape from authorities. These preachers were often hidden from local officials in the homes of their courageous flocks.[19]

Johannes Uytenbogaert played the major role in the organization and building of the Remonstrant Brotherhood. A compatriot of Arminius during their student days in Geneva, Uytenbogaert later became the influential court preacher to Prince Maurice and an intimate advisor of Oldenbarnevelt. Like Arminius, Uytenbogaert was a great advocate of toleration and a fiery foe of clericalism and confessionalism, but it was his great gift as an administrator that served his coreligionists best in the early days of the Brotherhood. Conditions in the Dutch republic became more favorable for the Remonstrants in 1625 when Prince Maurice died and was succeeded by his brother Frederick Henry, who was sympathetic to the Remonstrants without directly offending the Contra-Remonstrants. Under these circumstances Uytenbogaert returned to The Hague, where growing toleration allowed him to preach again in 1632.[20]

After 1630 toleration began to increase rapidly in the republic. The Remonstrant Brotherhood was soon able to establish itself in the United Provinces, leading a semipublic life as an unofficially tolerated church, much like the Mennonites. In 1631 the first Remonstrant national synod was held to complete organizational details. Because the Brotherhood was still hopeful of an eventual reunion with the Reformed church, the synod took no further steps away from Calvinist belief and practice. In 1634 the Remonstrant Seminary was opened in Amsterdam, where toleration was greatest, with Episcopius as its first head. He was followed in

[19] Zilverberg, in Hoenderdaal and Luca, eds., pp. 44–45.

[20] A. H. Haentjens, "Johanns Wtenbogaert en de stichting der Remonstrantsche Broederschap," in Heering, ed., *De Remonstranten*, pp. 110–136.

that position by the Cartesian Etienne de Courcelles, and then from 1668 to 1712 by Philip van Limborch, greatest of Remonstrant theologians, whose international scholarly reputation brought the Brotherhood esteem throughout Protestant Europe.[21] In 1671 the first volume of the Remonstrant historian Gerard Brandt's *Historie der Reformatie* was published. This great work of historical scholarship and religious apologetics set the seal on a century and a half of Dutch religious reform based on practical moral piety and humanistic scholarship. Intended as a work of justification for the Remonstrants, the *Historie* traced the roots of the Brotherhood back to the beginnings of the Dutch Reformation, and it presented the Remonstrants as standing in the main line of reform stretching from the Devotio Moderna through Erasmus to Arminius. Calvinism was portrayed as a foreign import.[22] With Brandt's work the Remonstrants laid claim to a prominent place in seventeenth-century Dutch religious life only fifty years after the official church had rejected them as heretics.

The Collegiants were born, of Remonstrant parentage, into this world of religious turmoil. In 1618 the provincial synod of the Reformed church of Holland, meeting at Delft in order to prepare for the national synod in Dordrecht, suspended all Remonstrant preachers in the province from their posts. Among the pastors suspended was Christian Sopingius, minister to a congregation in the village of Warmond, near Leiden. In 1619 Sopingius was formally deposed as pastor of the Warmond congregation by decree of the Synod of Dordrecht. The congregation, however, refused to accept the appointment of a Contra-Remonstrant pastor to replace him. Faced with imminent dissolution in the absence of a preacher, the congregation turned for help to a former elder named Gijsbert van der Kodde. Gijsbert suggested that the congregation continue to meet without a preacher in order to pray, read Scripture, and hold free religious discussion. The congregation thus continued to meet each Sunday evening after the new moon, in secret locations because of the threat of persecution from the Reformed.[23] These meetings were in effect the first Collegiant assemblies.

The term "college" had been in use in the Netherlands at least since the late sixteenth century to refer to informal gatherings of Protestants held for the purposes of Bible reading and religious education. The evangelical

[21] Zilverberg, in Hoenderdaal and Luca, eds., pp. 48–55.

[22] R. B. Evenhuis, *Ook dat was Amsterdam: de kerk der Hervorming in de tweede helft van de zeventiende eeuw: nabloei en inzinking* (Amsterdam, 1971), vol. 3, pp. 85–87. On Brandt, see also *BLNP*, vol. 2, pp. 93–95.

[23] J. C. van Slee, *De Rijnsburger Collegianten* (Haarlem, 1895; reprint Utrecht, 1980), pp. 16–37.

emphasis of the Reformation created a growing need for scriptural knowledge among both clergy and laity, and the new Protestant churches, including the Dutch Reformed church, encouraged the holding of educational meetings. It is unclear how early the name college was given to the gatherings in Warmond. When these meetings later grew into a religious movement that expanded far beyond the borders of the tiny village, both participants and observers came to apply the name Collegiant to those who followed the religious principles and practices that developed out of the meetings of the Warmond college.

The founder of the Collegiant movement, Gijsbert van der Kodde, came from a long line of religious radicals. His father and grandfather had both been secret Protestants, his elder brother Jan sheltered Remonstrant preachers in his home, and his younger brother—also called Jan— claimed to have the indwelling of the Holy Spirit as strongly as had the apostles.[24] Gijsbert himself read widely, including such writers as Sebastian Castellio and the Dutch humanist Dirk Volkertsz. Coornhert.[25] It was, nevertheless, from the press of circumstance rather than on point of principle that the first college was founded in Warmond.

If the birth of the Collegiant movement can be said to have been somewhat fortuitous, its first year of life witnessed a difficult struggle for survival during which the movement evolved its basic principles and developed the sense of purpose that was to characterize later Collegiantism. Almost immediately after its creation the college faced a crisis that threatened its very existence. The newly organized Remonstrant Brotherhood wanted to retain the Warmond congregation in its fold, and for this purpose the Remonstrants appointed Hendrik van Holten as Warmond's secret preacher in 1620. When Holten arrived in Warmond he was received not with rejoicing but with apprehension by Gijsbert, who claimed that Holten's presence was dangerous and assured him that the congregation was doing well without a pastor. After Holten's departure, several members of the congregation criticized van der Kodde for his dismissal of the Remonstrant minister, and in reply Gijsbert appealed to religious principle for the first time in defense of the congregation's right to worship without a preacher. Van der Kodde argued that by meeting without a preacher and giving each member the freedom to speak during the service, the college was conforming more closely to apostolic Christian practices than did the services of the established churches. Thus, Gijsbert found theoretical justification for his rejection of Remonstrant efforts to reincorporate the Warmond congregation into a traditional church structure.

[24] Ibid., pp. 26–27.
[25] Johannes Lindeboom, *Stiefkinderen van het Christendom* (The Hague, 1929; reprint Arnhem, 1973), p. 340.

By arguing that college free-speech services were closer to apostolic Christian practice than traditional religious services conducted by a preacher, van der Kodde defended the college's right to exist and worship as an independent body. The idea of free speech, perhaps taken by Gijsbert from his reading of Coornhert, became the guiding principle of the Collegiant movement.

The Remonstrants did not give up their efforts to reincorporate the Warmond congregation when Holten was rejected. Later in 1620 the Brotherhood appointed another pastor, Wouter Cornelisz. van Waarder, as head of the Warmond flock. Van Waarder managed to establish himself in Warmond and actually held services that were attended by some members of the congregation. Gijsbert, however, stayed away from these services and objected in principle to religious meetings where only the pastor was free to speak. As a result, the Warmond congregation was divided between supporters of Gijsbert's ideas and those members who were reluctant to reject the traditional structure of the Remonstrant service. When van Waarder proved unable to heal this division, the Remonstrants appointed the talented preacher Paschier de Fijne to the Warmond post in a last effort to bring the entire congregation back to Remonstrant principles. Gijsbert and his followers, however, continued to insist on free discussion in place of a pastoral sermon in the religious service. Paschier recognized that the Collegiant position was winning over many of the still-wavering members of the congregation, and in order to stop this erosion of support he proposed several compromise arrangements designed to maintain Remonstrant influence over the congregation. He suggested that congregational meetings consist of both a sermon and free discussion of religious questions, or that alternate meetings be devoted entirely to a sermon or free speech. To these suggestions Gijsbert simply replied that it was the absolute right of each individual to speak in any religious meeting whenever the spirit moved him to do so. This position made schism inevitable. Before the end of 1620 Gijsbert and his followers moved to a separate location in Warmond for meetings of the free-speech assembly.[26] The crisis had passed and a new religious movement was beginning to gain momentum.

In 1621 Gijsbert moved the free-speech assembly (or college) from Warmond to the neighboring village of Rijnsburg in order to escape Paschier's continued efforts for a reunion of the two groups of worshippers. In Rijnsburg, Gijsbert instituted separate communion and baptism.[27] The college at Rijnsburg, having been instituted in order to preserve the principle of individual free speech—or, as it came to be called, "free proph-

---

[26] Van Slee, De Rijnsburger Collegianten, pp. 38–41, 42–45.
[27] Lindeboom, Stiefkinderen van het Christendom, p. 340.

ecy"—continued to organize its meetings around this practice. Meetings were held once a month and consisted primarily of the reading aloud of several chapters of Scripture, followed by a series of addresses by anyone who felt moved by the Spirit to interpret the scriptural passages for the edification of the group. The meetings could often be lengthy; in cases where there was much to say they stretched far into the night. To avoid any suggestion of clerical authority, no podium was used. Each speaker addressed the meeting from his seat among the congregation. The meetings usually closed with prayer and song.[28]

The college grew and prospered in Rijnsburg. In later years, when the Collegiant movement had spread all over the United Provinces, the Collegiants were still often referred to as "Rijnsburgers." During the years 1630 to 1650 Gijsbert was followed as leader of the Rijnsburg college by Frans Joachimsz, Oudaan, father of Joachim Oudaan, the poet and Collegiant leader in Rotterdam.[29] During these years the college often met in the Oudaan home. The reputation of these meetings spread far beyond the boundaries of the tiny village, and converts from all over the country soon began to come to Rijnsburg. Among these early converts the poet Dirk R. Camphuysen was typical. In 1619 Camphuysen was removed from office as a Reformed preacher in Vleuten, near Utrecht, because of his Remonstrant sympathies. After hiding for a time in Amsterdam he left Holland in 1620, going to Norden in East Friesland, where he opened a printing shop. After living briefly in Harlingen and Ameland, Camphuysen settled in Dokkum in 1623. In 1625 he traveled to Delft at the invitation of the painter van Mierevelt, and it was during this journey that Camphuysen visited Rijnsburg and associated with the Collegiants. In Rijnsburg, Camphuysen became a vigorous advocate of free prophecy and other Collegiant ideals, and following his return to Dokkum he wrote poems in praise of religious freedom. He died in Dokkum in 1626.[30]

The origins and early development of the Collegiant movement in Warmond and Rijnsburg from 1620 to 1640 made up the first phase of the history of Dutch Collegiantism. After 1640 the movement began to expand rapidly, spreading its reach to set up colleges in most of the major cities of Holland as well as in many other locations throughout the United Provinces. At first the colleges were made up largely of former Remonstrants seeking greater toleration and a means of expression for their undogmatic piety. The Rotterdam college was founded by the Remonstrant

---

[28] Van Slee, *De Rijnsburger Collegianten*, p. 46.

[29] H. W. Meihuizen, "Collegianten en Doopsgezinden," in S. Groenveld, ed., *Daar de Orangie-appel in de gevel staat: in en om het weeshuis der Doopsgezinde Collegianten 1675–1975* (Amsterdam, 1975), p. 89.

[30] Van Slee, *De Rijnsburger Collegianten*, pp. 67–70. On Camphuysen, see also H. G. van den Doel, *Daar moet veel strijds gestreden zijn. Het leven van Dirk Rafaelsz. Camphuysen* (Meppel, 1967).

pastors Peter Cupus and Samuel Lansbergen, and it was led for many years by the Remonstrant poet and classical scholar Frans Joachim Oudaan (1628–1692). The Amsterdam college was founded by the former Remonstrant Daniel de Breen (1594–1664), along with the spiritualist Adam Boreel (1602–1665). As a result of these Remonstrant origins, the Collegiant movement incorporated into its religious thought the chief Arminian criticisms of the Reformed church. The Collegiants rejected predestination, confessionalism, and doctrinal rigidity in favor of a theologically tolerant and morally upright religion. Because of its opposition to the official Reformed church, the Collegiant movement acted as a magnet, drawing to itself the scattered groups of radical Protestants who had come to settle in the Netherlands since the sixteenth century.[31] Like the Collegiants, these radical groups had little sympathy for the doctrinaire and intolerant established church. As these older forms of Protestant radicalism mixed with Remonstrant elements already present in the colleges, a unique brand of religious reformism evolved that incorporated Arminianism, spiritualism, chiliasm, and rationalism.

Among the Dutch descendents of the sixteenth-century Radical Reformation, the Anabaptist Mennonites were the first group to be attracted in large numbers to the colleges. In Rotterdam the college gained many members from the local congregation of Waterlander Mennonites, and in Haarlem the college was heavily Mennonite. The Haarlem college was greatly influenced by the ideas of the Mennonite pastor Pieter Langedult (1640–1677), while in Leiden the college was led by another Mennonite, Dr. Laurens Klinkhamer (1626–1687). In Amsterdam after 1650 the leadership of the college passed into the hands of the eloquent Mennonite pastor Galenus Abrahamsz. (1622–1706), one of the principal moving forces behind Dutch Collegiantism in the second half of the seventeenth century.[32] By midcentury Mennonites made up a substantial portion of the Collegiant membership, and with the Mennonites came Anabaptist ideas. The Collegiants practiced adult baptism (or rebaptism) and were deeply influenced by pacifism and millenarianism, ideas that were integral parts of Mennonite belief. In addition, the traditional Anabaptist view of the established Protestant churches as having compromised true Christian principles for worldly gain had an important influence on the development of Collegiant thought.

Radical spiritualism as propounded by Sebastian Franck and Kaspar Schwenkfeld also found a place within Collegiantism after 1640. In Amsterdam, Adam Boreel, cofounder of the college and an important influence on its early development, was a devoted follower of the ideas of Franck, which he had encountered in the writings of the humanist Coorn-

[31] Van Slee, De Rijnsburger Collegianten, pp. 95–114.
[32] Ibid., pp. 95–114, 142–144, 162–165, 178–180, 184–186.

hert. Boreel was strongly influenced by Franck's rejection of the sacraments and ceremonies of all established churches. From Boreel, Galenus Abrahamsz. adopted certain elements of Radical Reformation spiritualism and passed these ideas along to his followers Pieter Balling and Jarig Jelles.[33] The spiritualists' rejection of all established churches and their guiding principle of the inner light fit well with the Collegiants' critique of confessional, institutional religion.

By the mid-seventeenth century Socinianism also had become a part of the Rijnsburger movement. When Polish Socinian refugees arrived in the United Provinces after 1660 even the tolerant Dutch authorities were unwilling to grant them the right to worship openly. Although their antitrinitarianism found no sympathy among the civil authorities and met with bitter hostility from the Reformed church, the Socinians were welcomed into Collegiant meetings, where they were permitted free expression of their ideas through the practice of free prophecy. An atmosphere of extreme toleration prevailed in the colleges because the Rijnsburgers believed such toleration to be an aspect of the pristine spirituality of the primitive church that they hoped to revive. No one was censured for their beliefs in college meetings, and even Socinian antitrinitarianism provoked little opposition among the Collegiants. Although the Socinians made few real converts among the Rijnsburgers, many of their ideas did influence the development of Collegiant thought. It was not Socinian antitrinitarianism, however, that most influenced Collegiant ideas. Rather, it was the Socinians' uniquely rational approach to biblical interpretation, an approach inherited from Italian humanism, that left its mark in the colleges. Socinian ideas influenced several important figures in the Collegiant movement, including Johannes Becius (1626–1680), a member of the Rotterdam college, and Frans Kuyper (1629–1692), a former Remonstrant who was active in both Rotterdam and Amsterdam.[34]

The influx of new members and new ideas from among the descendents of the earlier Radical Reformation made the years 1650 to 1700 a period of great growth, intellectual activity, and prosperity for the Collegiants. During this golden age the Collegiants, who had begun life as a tiny group of independent-minded believers meeting in an isolated village near Leiden, grew into one of the most important and influential religious forces in seventeenth-century Holland.

Between 1640 and 1650 Collegiantism rapidly spread its influence beyond Rijnsburg with the founding of colleges in most major Dutch cities.

---

[33] Walter Schneider, *Adam Boreel: Sein Leben und Seine Schriften* (Giessen, 1911), pp. 32–40; Herman Vekeman, *Toelichting over Galenus Korte verhandeling* (Cologne, 1983), pp. 29–34.

[34] Van Slee, *De Rijnsburger Collegianten*, p. 378; Kühler, pp. 134–147; *BWPG*, vol. 1, pp. 365–368; *BLNP*, vol. 1, p. 99.

The speed and seeming ease with which the Collegiants expanded can be explained in part by the fact that the Rijnsburgers were able to take advantage of growing tensions and divisions within Mennonite and Remonstrant congregations in these cities to recruit members for their own movement. In addition, the fact that there were precedents for the Collegiant form of religious organization within these very congregations made it easier for Mennonites and Remonstrants to become Collegiants.

Collegiant meetings were organized around the principle that meetings of laymen could undertake mutual religious education without clerical supervision. The use of lay meetings for religious education was in fact not an uncommon practice in Dutch cities during the second quarter of the seventeenth century, and this fact helped to make it easier for the Rijnsburgers to establish their own cells in most large cities. As early as the end of the sixteenth century the Dutch Reformed church had endorsed the idea of organizing lay meetings or "colleges" within its congregations for the purpose of biblical and doctrinal study. Despite the urgings of Calvinist clergymen, however, religious self-education never became a very popular activity among the Reformed faithful. Such lay religious meetings did become prevalent among Mennonites, Remonstrants, and other dissenters from the established faith during the first half of the seventeenth century, and it was the gradual orientation of these lay meetings around Rijnsburger principles that provided the mechanism by which the Collegiant movement established itself in the major urban centers of the Dutch republic.[35]

A growing tide of discontent over clerical regulation of religious life swept over many dissenting congregations in the big Dutch cities during the 1640s, and it was this discontent that provided the opening for Collegiant influence among Remonstrant and Mennonite groups. It was often the younger members of the congregations who most resented what they saw as an increasing tendency toward doctrinal conservatism and clerical control of religious life in their churches. This dissatisfaction frequently led the unhappy members to hold separate worship or educational meetings in the congregational chapel or in a private home. These meetings were characterized by an atmosphere of free discussion and a spirit of self-education emphasizing the ability of laymen to obtain a degree of religious knowledge without the aid of the clergy. Conservative church members and the clergy themselves soon came to oppose these meetings because of the very spirit of freedom that attracted younger members to them. The resulting split between the conservatives and the young dissenters usually grew rapidly in a spirit of bitterness on both sides, and in this atmosphere Rijnsburger ideas of freedom and spiritual independence held great appeal for the young members. It was in many

---

[35] Rolandus, *Zeventiede eeuwse geestesbloei*, p. 97.

cases not long before the young dissenters began to question their confessional ties and to bring their meetings into the mainstream of the Collegiant movement.[36]

An example of this process can be found in Rotterdam, where around the year 1630 a college or lay meeting came to be held on Friday evenings at the Remonstrant church. The first leaders of these meetings were two Remonstrant preachers, Peter Cupus and Samuel Lansbergen. Free discussion of Scripture was the main activity of these meetings, but the gathering of 1630 was not yet a Rijnsburger college. Not long after the start of these meetings, however, Frans Joachim Oudaan, leader of the college in Rijnsburg, appeared on the scene. The Oudaan family had Rotterdam roots and a Remonstrant religious background, and Frans made frequent trips to the city to meet friends and discuss business. It was Oudaan who first introduced Rijnsburger ideas of free prophecy and anticlericalism into the circle of young Remonstrants meeting in the Friday college. These ideas received an immediate and enthusiastic reception from such men as Adrian Paets, Jan Dionysius Verburg, and Joan (Johan) Hartigveldt. These first Rijnsburger disciples in Rotterdam were later to play influential roles not only in local Collegiantism but in the development of the movement as a whole.

In the same years that the Remonstrant college was active another college was held on Wednesday evenings in the Rotterdam church of the Waterland Mennonites. That college was led by the physician Jacob Ostens (1630–1678) and there too Rijnsburger influences began to creep in, partly because of the participation of several members of the Remonstrant college. When Collegiant ideas began to obtain a large following among the Waterlander congregation a bitter fight erupted in which conservative members threatened to force the closing of the Wednesday college. Meanwhile, events in the Remonstrant congregation had taken a similar turn. After a long struggle, Remonstrant conservatives succeeded in having the Friday college closed in 1654. Undaunted, Verburg, Hartigveldt, and Paets founded an independent Rijnsburger college, meeting in a private home. This college quickly gained additional members from the Waterlander congregation (including Ostens), and the Collegiant movement in Rotterdam was born.[37]

In 1646 the Collegiant movement took another important step forward when a college was established in Amsterdam by Adam Boreel and Daniel De Breen. This gathering was not at first a true Rijnsburger college, but

[36] C. B. Hylkema, *Reformateurs* (Haarlem, 1900; reprint Groningen and Amsterdam, 1978), vol. 1, pp. 5–6.

[37] Van Slee, *De Rijnsburger Collegianten*, pp. 95–114; Zilverberg, pp. 33–34; Wiep van Bunge, "A Tragic Idealist: Jacob Ostens (1630–1678)," *Studia Spinoziana* 4 (1988), pp. 265–267.

rather one of a series of colleges founded in various locations around the Netherlands by Boreel, a spiritualist and nonconfessional theologian. These "Boreelist colleges" were modeled on the spiritualist cells established by Franck and Schwenkfeld in South Germany during the preceding century, and their object was the dissemination of Boreel's own radical spiritualistic ideas. Most of the Boreelist colleges were short-lived, but Boreel's college in Amsterdam had the advantage of the early support of De Breen, a Leiden-educated Remonstrant theologian who had served as secretary to Episcopius at the Synod of Dordrecht. After the synod De Breen had split with the Remonstrants to become a Rijnsburger, and it was through De Breen that Rijnsburger ideas infiltrated the Amsterdam college, blending there with Boreel's spiritualism. By 1650 the Amsterdam college was completely oriented around Rijnsburger principles. Also in 1650 the Amsterdam college gained its most important convert: Galenus Abrahamsz., the eloquent young pastor of the United Mennonite congregation. This young man had become a Mennonite leader only two years earlier, but by 1650 he was undergoing a difficult intellectual and spiritual trial as a result of events within the Mennonite congregation. Under these circumstances Galenus met Boreel, and the impact of Boreelist and Rijnsburger ideas on the young Mennonite was decisive. Galenus not only joined the Rijnsburger college but became its most dynamic and influential leader in the years after 1650. Under his spell, many disenchanted Mennonites swelled the ranks of the Amsterdam college.

At first the Amsterdam college held its meetings on Sunday evenings in a private home on the Lindengracht. Right away, however, the Reformed clergy began to complain to the municipal authorities that the college was in fact a meeting of those most dreaded of heretics, the Socinians. This accusation was not entirely false. A number of Socinians did indeed attend college meetings, and this fact was well known in government circles. For the tolerant regent administration of Amsterdam the mere presence of the Socinians was no cause for alarm, but the conspicuousness with which the Socinians frequented college meetings did disturb the city fathers. Such indiscretion by an officially banned sect inevitably led to agitation on the part of the Calvinist clergy, and this clerical agitation created unrest among the people. The spectacle of popular unrest was very unsettling for the authorities, and thus for the sake of public peace they ordered the college to close in 1652. At the same time that they officially ordered the college to close, however, the authorities secretly gave the Rijnsburgers permission to resume their meetings in a more secluded location. This the Collegiants did, but more trouble arose in 1653. In that year the States General of the United Provinces issued a general decree forbidding all Socinian books and meetings in the republic. Under intense pressure from both the government and the Reformed church, the Amsterdam college was forced to suspend operations for all of the year 1654.[38]

This general pattern of events continued for several more years. In 1655 the new leader of the college, Galenus Abrahamsz., attempted to give its meetings an aura of greater respectability by moving them into the Mennonite chapel. This attempt met with fierce opposition from conservative Mennonites and the college was forced to move yet again. In 1656 came another official ban on Collegiant meetings and yet another retreat into hiding.[39] After 1660 the pressure at last began to ease, and the college was able to meet openly in a building on the Rokin from 1660 to 1667. During the years 1668 to 1675 the college held its meetings in the Mennonite church on the Singel Canal, then it moved to the newly constructed Collegiant orphanage Het Orangje-Appel ("The Orange Apple," named for its colorful gable decoration). This nomadic existence did not detract in the least from the intellectual and spiritual vitality of Collegiant meetings. The Amsterdam college was always well attended, peaking at an attendance of approximately two hundred in the mid-1660s, and it was a source for many of the most important intellectual developments within Collegiantism from 1650 to 1690.[40]

Other Rijnsburger colleges sprang up all over the Netherlands around midcentury. At Leiden a college was founded by Quirijn van Vissendiep and led by the distinguished Mennonite physician Laurens Klinkhamer, a great champion of free prophecy and individual conscience. In 1662 a college was established in Haarlem, where it drew the bulk of its membership from the Flemish and Waterlander Mennonite congregations. Other colleges were established in Hoorn, Krommenie, Wormerveer, Zaandam, Alkmaar, Enkhuizen, Leeuwarden, Harlingen, Grouw, Knijpe, Oldenboorn, and Groningen. These colleges were smaller and less influential than the big colleges of Holland, and little information on their activities is available. All of these local colleges were united by Rijnsburger principles and practices, and in addition they all came together twice yearly in the village of Rijnsburg for general meetings. At these general meetings the Collegiants held common communion services, which for them signified not membership in a particular church or sect but simply

[38] Van Slee, De Rijnsburger Collegianten, pp. 142–144; K. O. Meinsma, Spinoza und Sein kreis (Berlin, 1909), pp. 188–189. This is a translation of the original Dutch Spinoza en zijn kring (The Hague, 1896, reprint Utrecht, 1980). I used the German translation in this instance because the original was unavailable. The pagination of the two editions varies slightly.

[39] Meinsma, pp. 192–195, 205.

[40] Van Slee, De Rijnsburger Collegianten, pp. 162–165; Wilhelm Goeters, Die Vorbereitung des Pietismus (Leipzig, 1911), p. 48.

mutual Christian brotherhood. Free prophecy, the most fundamental of Collegiant principles and practices, played a central role even in the communion services. These general meetings and communion services were held on the first Whitsunday and the last Sunday in August of every year at a large meeting house called the Vergaderplaats, on the east end of Rijnsburg.[41] Collegiants traveled from all over the United Provinces to attend these meetings, and in the fellowship of the general gathering they became acquainted with the ideas, feelings, beliefs, and activities of their brothers from far and wide.

The many local colleges were bound together by a common set of beliefs and principles that made the Collegiants a unique group in Dutch religious life. The Rijnsburgers nourished a strong aversion to clergy, church dogma, confessions, creeds, and ceremonies while putting great stress on toleration and individual freedom of conscience in religion. College membership was open to all Christians, and Rijnsburgers were free to retain membership in other churches. Communion in the colleges was likewise open, and adult baptism by immersion was practiced as a sign of an individual's mature confession of belief in Christ as savior. Free prophecy—the complete freedom of any college member to express views on any matter of Scripture or religion—was the centerpiece of all college meetings. Beyond these basic principles, Collegiant toleration allowed for a wide variety of opinions on the minutiae of doctrine, which the Collegiants regarded as the adiaphora of religion. Despite such differences of detail, however, the Rijnsburgers never lost their sense of being members of a unified and distinctive brotherhood of kindred spirits. As they demonstrated by their biannual Rijnsburg meetings and as they repeatedly expressed in their writings, Collegiants from all of the many local colleges considered themselves to be members of a unified and distinctive religious movement founded on a set of fundamental principles that they believed to be the basis of true Christianity.

The membership of the colleges was truly varied. There were Remonstrant and Mennonite preachers, statesmen and municipal authorities, merchants and shopkeepers, physicians and theologians, poets and printers. Many Collegiants were university educated (almost all at Leiden), but even those who were not were exceptionally well read and demonstrated active interest in intellectual and spiritual pursuits.[42] It would not have been unusual to hear a discussion at a college meeting between, for example, a university-trained theologian like Daniel de Breen and a humble

---

[41] Van Slee, De Rijnsburger Collegianten, pp. 178–180, 288–293.

[42] Zilverberg, p. 30; Van Slee, De Rijnsburger Collegianten, p. 76. For an interesting occupational survey of Collegiants in the eighteenth century, see Marieke Quak, "De sociale status van Amsterdamse doopsgezinde Collegianten in de 18e eeuw," Doopsgezinde Bijdragen, n.s. 11 (1985), pp. 109–117.

grocer like Jarig Jelles, who was self-educated in Cartesian philosophy. A great deal of intellectual cross-fertilization took place at such meetings, not in the least because a wide variety of spiritual directions was represented among the Rijnsburgers. Among the most active Collegiants were Mennonites and Remonstrants who stressed pietistic values and practical morality, nonconfessional theologians of a spiritualistic bent, Socinians who were influenced by humanistic rationalism, millenarians and others inclined toward prophecy, adherents of the emerging philosophies of Descartes and Spinoza, and many people who combined several of these influences in their thought.[43] These many different intellectual interests were held together by the Collegiant demand for freedom, toleration, and simple lay piety without ecclesiastical authority or dogma. In developing and maintaining their independent-minded spiritual life in opposition to the rigid and authoritarian structure of the Dutch Reformed church, the Collegiants produced a body of thought concerning the nature of religion and man's relationship to God that bridged the gap between the traditional worldview of faith and the emerging creed of reason.

Despite the unifying elements within the Collegiant movement, the rapid growth of the local colleges after 1640 created some noticeable differences between the first period of Collegiantism at Rijnsburg and the flowering of the movement during the years 1650–1700. At Rijnsburg simple men were inspired by a few basic principles of apostolic Christianity. In the colleges of Amsterdam, Rotterdam, Haarlem, and Leiden, however, intellectual curiosity was greater, the scope of religious discussion much broader, and plans for a total reformation of universal Christianity were often debated. Whether such plans were based on spiritualistic fervor or rationalistic toleration, they always aimed at the overall goal of universal moral regeneration.[44] With these reform plans expressing their ideal of a regenerated universal Christian church, the Collegiants were part of a larger movement of religious reform within seventeenth-century Protestantism that has been called the Second Reformation of the seventeenth century.

According to Leszek Kolakowski, the Second Reformation of the seventeenth century was a movement for religious renewal made up of a diverse collection of religious groups that grew out of the main Protestant churches of the Reformation era. This new reform movement criticized the established Protestant churches for carrying out only a very incomplete reform of religious life. The Second Reformation groups accused the established churches of abandoning spiritual principles and compromis-

---

[43] Roldanus, p. 98.

[44] Zilverberg, p. 31; Lindeboom, *Stiefkinderen van het Christendom*, p. 311; Hylkema, p. 11.

ing with the secular world on important matters of theology, morality, religious life, and political involvement.[45] This new wave of reforming zeal developed in several independent but largely parallel forms both within the established Protestant churches and outside of these churches in small independent sects and among individual reformers. Not unlike the Radical Reformation of the previous century, the Second Reformation accused the institutional Protestant churches of not having gone far enough toward the original Protestant reform goals, and thus the new reformers called for a second and more thoroughgoing reformation of religious life. They wanted to eliminate the ceremonialism and confessionalism of the established churches, which they saw as signs of religious decay, and to establish a new form of Protestant Christianity based on spiritual zeal and ethical purity in individual religious life.

While almost all of the proponents of the Second Reformation recognized themselves as products of the first Protestant Reformation, the attitudes of the new reformers toward the original Reformation and the Protestant churches that it produced varied widely. The more moderate among the new reformers saw themselves as carrying the work of the first Reformation to its logical conclusion by working within the established churches to purify and perfect them. Other more radical reformers, however, considered the Reformation of Luther and Calvin to have been a disappointing failure. They completely rejected the churches of the first Reformation in favor of a radically individualistic, nonconfessional, anticlerical, and even antiecclesiastical reform of religious life. Regardless of their attitudes toward the first Reformation and its churches, however, the common goal of all of the new reformers was to carry the Protestant purification of religion a step further, beyond the stage reached by the established churches, to an individually experienced inner piety within the heart of each believer.

The moderate wing of the Second Reformation was represented in the Netherlands by a movement within the Dutch Reformed church that historians have called the *Nadere Reformatie* (Further Reformation). Partly as a result of the influence of English Puritanism, this movement developed within the official church during the 1620s under the leadership of men such as Willem Teellinck, Jacobus Koelman, and Gisbertus Voetius. Reacting against what they considered to be the dead orthodoxy, poor preaching, lax discipline, and worldliness that had become common in the Reformed church in the years after the Synod of Dordrecht, the men of the *Nadere Reformatie* called for a spiritual regeneration of the established church. Teellinck and his followers attempted to purify Calvinist

---

[45] Leszek Kolakowski, *Chrétiens sans église: la conscience religieuse et le lien confessionnel au XVIIe siècle* (Paris, 1969), pp. 9–10.

religious life from within by working for a renewal of the Reformed church along ethical and spiritual lines, using fiery penitential preaching as their main weapon. These men called for a second (or further) reformation to follow upon and complete the work of the first reformation by making the Reformed church a body of ethically upright, spiritually pure, and personally regenerate believers whose faith was individually experienced and active in everyday life. When they were unable to win over the majority of Reformed believers, Teellinck and his followers met together in conventicles to practice their form of piety. Although the *Nadere Reformatie* did not succeed in revitalizing the entire Reformed church, it was nevertheless a significant force in Dutch religious life during the seventeenth century. It also had an important place within the wider movement of the Second Reformation. Indeed, the Second Reformation was a movement truly international in scope, encompassing other groups such as the English Puritans and the north German Pietists of the eighteenth century. The Historian Wilhelm Goeters considered Teellinck's *Nadere Reformatie* an important forerunner of later German Pietism.[46]

The radical wing of the Second Reformation in Holland consisted of a group of reformers called by Kolakowski "nonconfessional Christians," referred to by Lindeboom as *"Stiefkinderen van het Christendom"* (stepchildren of Christianity), and called by C. B. Hylkema *"Reformateurs."* While the *Nadere Reformatie* worked for a renewal within the established Reformed church, the small sects and individual reformers who made up the radical Second Reformation wanted a total and immediate restoration of apostolic Christianity in all of its forms, even if this meant a rejection of all established churches. The radicals did not call for a rebirth of the church alone, they demanded a total rebirth of society as a whole along ethical and spiritual lines. These radical reformers often saw a fundamental conflict between basic Christian values and the temporal organization of ecclesiastical institutions, and for this reason they opposed all religious life organized around rituals, ceremonies, sacraments,

---

[46] Evenhuis, pp. 207–208. See also W. J. Op't Hof, *De visie op de Joden in de Nadere Reformatie tijdens het eerste kwart van de zeventiende eeuw* (Amsterdam, 1984); T. Brienen et al., *De Nadere Reformatie: Beschrijving van haar voornaamste vertegenwoordigers* (The Hague, 1986); and Goeters. Kolakowski refers to the *Nadere Reformatie* of Voetius and his followers as the "Calvinist Counter Reformation" because the movement was in part a reaction against Arminianism within the Dutch church. Kolakowski does not specifically include this movement in his conception of the Second Reformation, which he sees as a nonconfessional movement. Thomas A. McGahagan follows this use of terminology in "Cartesianism in The Netherlands, 1636–1676: The New Science and the Calvinist Counter-Reformation" (dissertation, University of Pennsylvania, 1976). I believe, however, that the great similarity both in motivation and in goals between the proponents of the *Nadere Reformatie* and other groups in the Second Reformation justifies including the *Nadere Reformatie* as a moderate and confessional branch of the larger Second Reformation.

and confessions. The radicals tended to see the first Protestant Reformation as a disappointing failure, and thus they rejected the churches produced by it as lacking in holy life and power. In place of the established congregations they proposed a Christianity without formal church structures, a universal Christianity above doctrinal divisions and a regeneration of religious life through individual piety and moral purity.[47]

The radical wing of the Second Reformation was also international in scope, but it flourished especially in the Netherlands, where great religious toleration prevailed. In the United Provinces millenarian prophets such as Johannes Rothe, Quirinius Kuhlman, and Antoinette Bourignon predicted the second coming of Christ to purify the world of sinners, while ascetic spiritualists like Jean de Labadie and mystic followers of Jacob Böhme such as Johannes Gichtel and Alhardt De Raedt spread their radical reform ideas.[48] The Collegiants were the largest and most organized branch of the radical Second Reformation in the Netherlands. The central characteristic of the Collegiant movement was its opposition to ecclesiastical authority and its desire for individual liberty and equality in religious life. In their desire for a religion without the constraints of clergy or institutional authority, the Rijnsburgers based their movement on the dual principles of anticlericalism and freedom of speech.[49] The Collegiants also acted as a conduit by way of which many of the ideas of the sixteenth-century Radical Reformation entered the ideology of the Second Reformation of the seventeenth century. These ideas led the Collegiants to formulate a critique of the established Protestant churches that was among the most radical of all of the Second Reformation programs for religious renewal. As part of the great second wave of reforming zeal that swept over the Protestant world during the seventeenth century, the Collegiants can be grouped with Puritans, Pietists, Quakers, and the *Nadere Reformatie* as well as with mystics, chiliasts, and prophets of various stripes. For the Collegiants, however, the ideas and goals of this Second Reformation were only a beginning point for the development of a worldview that would, in the end, merge into the rational and secular outlook of the early Enlightenment.

Even as the scope of college discussions and the range of ideas debated expanded greatly during the later years of the seventeenth century to include plans for the universal reform of Christianity, the Collegiants continued to follow the central principles and practices of the original Rijnsburg meetings. Colleges generally met two or three times a week in a church or private home, where the members prayed, sang hymns, read,

[47] Evenhuis, pp. 311–312; Kolakowski, p. 10; Hylkema, pp. 101–108.

[48] For these interesting figures see Roldanus, *Zeventiende eeuwse geestesbloei*, and Lindeboom, *Stiefkinderen van het Christendom*, as well as Kolakowski and Hylkema.

[49] Kolakowski, pp. 168–176.

and discussed Scripture and debated religious reform. Many different opinions were expressed with complete freedom in college meetings. At regular college gatherings discussions were usually confined to practical Bible explication along with explanations of Collegiant religious principles and plans. The hymns sung at these meetings were often verses by Camphuysen set to music.[50] In addition to these regular meetings, however, the Collegiants often held separate and less formal gatherings for discussion of a wide variety of religious, moral, and philosophical topics. At these meetings the most controversial questions of the day were addressed. In Amsterdam such meetings were frequently held in the shop of the Collegiant bookseller and publisher Jan Rieuwertsz., where members listened with great interest to the divergent ideas of such thinkers as the exiled Moravian ecumenicist and pedagogue John Amos Comenius and the excommunicated Jew Benedict Spinoza. Out of such gatherings, in which Comenius described his plans for a universal reformation of religion, learning, and society while Spinoza discussed the Cartesian philosophy in which he was fast becoming an expert, it is not surprising to see the emergence of Collegiant plans for a reformation of religious life based on reason and toleration.[51]

A movement such as Collegiantism, which was regularly and more or less publicly engaged in discussions of highly controversial questions of religion and morality, probably could not have thrived outside of the Dutch republic during the seventeenth century. The society in which the Collegiants lived was marked by frequent and tumultuous religious disputes that were in part the product of a freedom of thought and expression unique to the United Provinces. This great freedom gave tremendous scope to inventive minds and favored the emergence of novel and radical ideas, but it also produced a situation in which intellectual warfare among the various groups was endemic and self-defense on the intellectual plane essential.

The unusual measure of intellectual freedom present in the United Provinces was a direct result of a very considerable degree of religious freedom, and this religious freedom was itself in turn produced by a very ambiguous relationship between the official Reformed church and the government of the Dutch republic. As a result of the Dutch revolt against Spain, the relationship between church and state in the United Provinces

[50] Hylkema, pp. 13–14; Van Slee, *De Rijnsburger Collegianten*, p. 56, 348–352, 362.

[51] On Spinoza and the Collegiants, see Meinsma, chap. 4. On Comenius and the Collegiants, see Wilhelmus Rood, *Comenius and the Low Countries* (Amsterdam, 1970), p. 204. On Comenius, see also G. H. Turnbull, *Hartlib, Dury, and Comenius* (London, 1947); Matthew Spinka, *John Amos Comenius: That Incomparable Moravian* (New York, 1967); and Robert Young, *Comenius in England* (London, 1947).

had been greatly altered. Catholicism was dethroned as the official religion and Dutch citizens were free to join any church that they desired. Although there was no mandatory state religion, the Reformed church was considered the official church and thus received government financial support and protection. Other religions were not officially recognized but they were in practice tolerated.[52] Following the Synod of Dordrecht, the States General of the United Provinces considered it to be the government's duty to further the interests of the Reformed church, but this policy was short-lived because many regents disagreed with it and because town magistrates who were not Contra-Remonstrants did not implement it.

The history of free thought in the Dutch republic during the seventeenth century was in large part the story of a constant struggle between the Calvinist clergy and the regents. The clergy demanded closer ties between church and state that would have amounted to clerical control of the government in many areas. The regents, however, favored a much looser relationship between church and state because they had no desire to strengthen the clergy politically and see a militant church compete with them for power in the republic.[53] As a result of the position of the regents, the generation after the Synod of Dordrecht witnessed not the realization of Calvinist hopes for a Geneva-style theocracy but rather an unprecedented spread of toleration in Dutch society. This trend accelerated after 1625, when Prince Maurice was succeeded as stadtholder by Frederik Henry. Especially in the province of Holland after the death of Stadtholder William II in 1650 and the rise to power of Jan de Witt as councilor-pensionary in 1653, the government actively sought a reconciliation among all of the various religious and political groups within society. The result was a period of increasing freedom of conscience. Only the troublesome Jesuits, who were seen as foreign conspirators, and the Socinians, who were branded as atheists, were beyond the pale of government toleration.[54] Religious freedom was so great in the province of Holland that there were not even laws compelling church attendance or excluding the non-Reformed from government office.[55] The religious constraints on freedom of thought that were so apparent in other European societies of the day had largely disappeared from intellectual life in many areas of the United Provinces by 1660, much to the chagrin of the Reformed church establishment. This atmosphere of freedom was conducive to the birth of

[52] H. A. Enno van Gelder, pp. 2–5. See also Joseph Lecler, *Histoire de la tolérance au siècle de la Réforme* (Paris, 1955), vol. 2, pp. 161–279.

[53] Ibid., pp. 6–12.

[54] Rolandus, *Zeventiede eeuwse geestesbloei*, pp. 32, 51. See also Herbert Rowen, *John de Witt, Grand Pensionary of Holland, 1625–1672* (Princeton, 1978), chaps. 20 and 21.

[55] Van Gelder, pp. 150–162.

new ideas, but it also created an intense competition among ideas and
their defenders that often led to the intrusion of rancorous personal feuds
into the intellectual realm.

Like freedom of thought, freedom of the press was greater in the United
Provinces than elsewhere in Europe. Many books were printed in Amsterdam that could be published nowhere else. There were in theory laws
and regulations applying to the press, but in practice there was full freedom. Government censors acted only to avoid disturbance of public order
by irresponsible or inflammatory tracts, and political works undermining
state authority were also banned. Fewer than 150 books were officially
banned in the United Provinces during the entire seventeenth century, and
even these infrequent prohibitions were ineffective. Spinoza's books were
banned as immoral, but they were nevertheless widely read in intellectual
circles. Following the Synod of Dordrecht the works of the Remonstrant
leader Uytenbogaert were banned—and as a result they were reprinted
four times. Socinian books were banned, of course, but this did not prevent Amsterdam from becoming the foremost European center for the
printing and distribution of Socinian works. Members of the municipal
government of Amsterdam regularly warned printers of impending
searches by the sheriff.[56]

Freedom of thought extended even into the Dutch universities, which
in most seventeenth-century societies were bastions of intellectual conservatism. In the United Provinces, as elsewhere, the universities were officially enjoined to teach only Aristotelian philosophy. Despite this stric-
ture, Cartesianism found a home in the Dutch universities earlier than
elsewhere in Europe. Although Dutch university Cartesians were eclectic
thinkers who often tended to misinterpret the thought of Descartes, the
spread of Cartesian-inspired ideas was an event of the first importance for
university intellectual life and for Dutch culture as a whole. The University of Utrecht was the first institution of higher learning in the Netherlands to unofficially open its doors to the new philosophy. At Utrecht,
Henricus Regius, a professor of medicine, and Frans Burman, professor
of theology, were the leading Cartesians. A little later Cartesianism also
came to Leiden University, where quarrels between Cartesians and Aris-
totelians immediately broke out and became so fierce that the new philosophy was banned from the university for a short time in 1648. At Leiden,
Abraham Heidanus held the banner of Descartes high. Similar Cartesian
penetration also occurred at the universities in Groningen, Franeker, and
Harderwijk. Especially after 1650, university officials in all of these cities
had to walk a very fine line between the intellectual peril of stifling new

---

[56] Zilverberg, p. 15; Van Gelder, pp. 150–162, 175–179.

ideas and the political danger of unwisely offending the influential Calvinist party.[57]

In Dutch religious life such freedom of thought and toleration was not so much the cause as the result of pluralism. In a society that was deeply and fundamentally divided, compromise and consensus were vital for national survival. In many respects the seemingly dominant position of the Reformed church was an illusion. After the Synod of Dordrecht, the official church was quickly put on the defensive by the Second Reformation, while the church's demands for greater power and influence in state affairs were turned down by a burger aristocracy for whom considerations of trade demanded toleration, peace, and freedom.[58] Because of its ties to the state, the Reformed church was in fact less free than the other, unofficially tolerated churches. Local and municipal governments had considerable influence in the choosing of Reformed preachers, owned all church property, and provided the church's primary financial support. Because governmental authorities wanted peace in religious life, they often used state power over the church to limit Reformed agitation against the other religious groups in Dutch society. The Remonstrants, meanwhile, became perhaps the most influential of the tolerated churches after the accession of Frederik Henry in 1625. Through the Remonstrant Seminary in Amsterdam, Arminian ideas continued to play an important role in Dutch religious thought throughout the seventeenth century.[59] The Mennonites, who gradually split into many factions, of which the Waterlanders, Flemings, High Germans, and Friesians were only the most important, continued to be an influential force in Dutch religious life throughout the century. Although the Calvinist clergy carried on persistent agitation against Mennonite ideas on pacifism, baptism, and the swearing of oaths, the Mennonites found widespread popular toleration, especially in Amsterdam and Haarlem. In almost all of the major cities of the Dutch republic, the Mennonites held their meetings undisturbed in private homes, warehouses, and even barns.[60] Lutherans were also present within the Dutch

[57] Van Gelder, pp. 218–232. On Dutch Cartesianism, see C. L. Thijssen-Schoute, *Nederlands Cartesianisme* (Amsterdam, 1954); E. J. Dijksterhuis, C. Serrurier, P. Dibon, *Descartes et le Cartesianisme Hollandais* (Amsterdam, 1951); McGahagan; Ferdinand Sassen, "Adrian Heereboord. De opkomst van het Cartesianisme te Leiden," *Algemeen Nederlands Tijdschrift voor Wijsbegeerte en Psychologie* 36 (1942–1943), and "Henricus Renerius, de eerste 'Cartesiaansche' hoogleerar te Utrecht," *Medeelingen van de Koninklijke Nederlandsche Akademie van Wetenschappen*, Afd. Letterkunde, n.s. 4, no. 20 (1941), pp. 853–902.

[58] Roldanus, *Zeventiede eeuwse geestesbloei*, pp. 50–57.

[59] Van Gelder, pp. 19, 32–33, 59, 10–12, 82–83.

[60] Ibid., pp. 92–96; Zilverberg, pp. 21–22. By law the Reformed church occupied all official church buildings in the republic. Other congregations met in homes, shops, and elsewhere.

religious community, although in smaller numbers than the Mennonites and Remonstrants. The Lutherans tended to have better relations with the Reformed church than either of the other two tolerated churches, perhaps in part because of the efforts of John Dury, the ecumenicist who sought a union between Lutherans and Calvinists and who lived much of his life in Amsterdam.[61]

Although Catholicism was officially banned in the United Provinces, Catholics too found a considerable degree of toleration in Dutch society. Holding their services in so-called *schuilkerken* (churches in concealment), Catholics were usually left more or less in peace as long as the proper bribe money was paid to the local sheriff. In Amsterdam there was also a large and wealthy Jewish community living apart from the rest of the population and enjoying considerable privileges granted by the municipal government.[62] Completing the religious spectrum of seventeenth-century Holland were the Collegiants and other members of the radical wing of the Second Reformation. Called *Reformateurs, Chrétiens sans église*, or *Stiefkinderen van het Christendom* by later historians, these splintered groups of believers made up the extreme left wing of Dutch religious life.[63] Among these radicals the ferment of reform in both spiritualist and rationalist directions was strong by the middle of the seventeenth century. It is on this distant edge of the Dutch Reformation that we find the Collegiants building an intellectual bridge to the Enlightenment.

---

[61] Evenhuis, pp. 110–113. See also Turnbull.

[62] Evenhuis, pp. 69, 88–89; Roldanus, *Zeventiende eeuwse geestesbloei*, p. 29.

[63] Kolakowski, pp. 9–10. A very interesting recent interpretation of Dutch culture during the seventeenth century is Simon Schama, *The Embarrassment of Riches: An Interpretation of Dutch Culture in the Golden Age* (New York, 1987). Other useful works on Dutch Golden Age culture include J. L. Price, *Culture and Society in the Dutch Republic during the Seventeenth Century* (London, 1974); and John J. Murray, *Amsterdam in the Age of Rembrandt* (Norman, Okla., 1967). Excellent general histories of the republic in these years are Charles Wilson, *The Dutch Republic* (London, 1968); K.H.D. Haley, *The Dutch in the Seventeenth Century* (London, 1972); and Geyl.

Chapter Three

A PROPHETIC LIGHT IN THE DARKNESS SHINING: COLLEGIANT CHILIASM

Nevertheless we, according to his promise,
look for new heavens and a new earth,
wherein dwelleth righteousness.
—2 Pet. 3:13

FROM THEIR earliest beginnings the Dutch Collegiants found themselves attracted to the doctrines of millenarianism or chiliasm. Collegiant millenarian writings advanced the idea of the imminent return of Christ to earth and the establishment of a thousand-year temporal paradise in which God's elect would rule the world while enjoying all of the rewards of their faith. In this belief the Collegiants were no different from countless other individuals and sects throughout Christian history who have been attracted by the vision of the millennium. The special emphasis that the Collegiants gave to certain aspects of chiliastic doctrine and the role played by chiliasm within the overall body of Collegiant thought changed Collegiant chiliasm from a traditional Christian doctrine into the beginning point for a secular view of the world.

Christian chiliastic writings traditionally focused on the temporal paradise to be expected upon Christ's return to earth, but traditional doctrines also maintained that the paradise would be preceded by a long period of spiritual decay and deprivation in the natural world. Collegiant writers on the millennium put a great deal of stress on the corrupt and sinful condition of the world prior to the coming of the millennium in order to acentuate the great transformation that would take place in the world when Christ returned. Although many other writers on the millennium both before and after the Collegiants gave considerable attention to the sad condition of the world before the return of Christ, in Rijnsberger thought these chiliastic ideas of premillennial corruption came to occupy an especially prominent place. This pessimistic assessment of the condition of the temporal world prior to the millennium had a significant influence on the overall shape and direction of Collegiant thought, as the Rijnsburgers came to see the premillennial world—their world—as hopelessly sinful and decayed. This conception of a decadent world had pro-

Wat maelt Oudaen zoo levend voor 't gezicht,
Als zyne kracht van tael, in maetgedicht,
In ondicht ook uitblinkende in zyn boeken,
Daer toont hy zich als d'eer der letterkloeken,
En schryveren, daer Neêrlant roem op draegt,
Terwyl de faem van zynen lof gewaegt.
                                    D. van Hoogstraten.

2. Joachim Fransz. Oudaan

found implications for the Collegiants' view of the condition of the Christian churches of the seventeenth century and thus for Rijnsburger plans for religious reform. This pessimistic view of the world also had a significant influence on the evolution of the Collegiant worldview, especially when the millennium repeatedly failed to arrive on the dates assigned for it. A brief survey of the history of Christian millenarianism will provide a useful background to the function of chiliastic ideas within Collegiant thought.

Chiliasm and millenarianism are the terms usually applied to an age-old body of Christian thought that maintained that Christ would return to earth before the Last Judgment, resurrect the saints, and rule with them over a glorious temporal kingdom for a thousand years. Basing itself in part on an interpretation of the twentieth chapter of the Book of Revelation (verses 1–5), this body of thought portrayed the millennium as an interval in the bitter war between God and Satan that formed the pattern of all history. According to this interpretation of history, after a long and bitter struggle between God and Satan the stronghold of evil would finally fall and an angel of God would descend from heaven to put an end to Satan's persecution of the holy people by imprisoning him in hell for a thousand years. There would then follow a glorious millennium in which Christ and the resurrected saints would reign over a temporal paradise of physical and spiritual pleasures. At the end of the millennium Satan would return to renew the battle against God, but the forces of evil would be defeated at the final battle of Armageddon, after which the Last Judgment would take place and an eternal heavenly state—"a new heaven and a new earth"—would be established. Interpretations of the nature and advent of the millennium varied greatly throughout the history of chiliasm, but the core idea remained constant: the kingdom of Christ would be a temporal paradise dawning after a time of great turmoil.[1]

Christian millenarianism had its roots in the Jewish apocalyptic tradition, which predicted that a messianic deliverer would lead the armies of the chosen people in the annihilation of their enemies. In the later Jewish tradition it was predicted that this messianic leader would come to reign over the entire world. During the decades immediately surrounding the founding of the Christian church the Jewish world was permeated by messianic expectations, and for this reason it is not surprising that the early Christians, many of whom were converted Jews, were strongly attracted to millenarian ideas.[2] Cerinthus (fl.ca. 100), an early Christian

---

[1] E. R. Chamberlain, *Antichrist and the Millennium* (New York, 1975), pp. ix–x; Ernest Tuveson, "Millennnarianism," in *Dictionary of the History of Ideas*, vol. 3 (New York, 1973), pp. 223–225.

[2] Tuveson, p. 224.

theologian who the apostle John accused of holding heretical ideas, was one of the first Christian millenarians.[3] Among the followers of the heavily persecuted early church many placed their hopes in an imminent return of the Lord. Justin Martyr, Commodianus, and the Greek church father Irenaeus all expected the speedy advent of the millennium. Lactantius (250–330) predicted that the earthly paradise of Christ would follow only after a long period of sorrow and evil on earth during which the wicked would prey on the good and Christians would be persecuted by pagans. Others among the early church fathers gave even greater emphasis to the period of grief and disaster that would precede the coming of the millennium. Cyprian (200–258) wrote that nature was declining in its old age, that the earth was becoming exhausted and its moral order subverted as the end of time drew near.[4]

The doctrine of the millennium gradually began to lose its central importance within Christian thought late in the reign of the emperor Constantine (d. 337). By this time Christianity was no longer a persecuted religion forced to pin its hopes on a divine transformation of the world. Moreover, the failure of the millennium to arrive encouraged a new, allegorical interpretation of the relevant passages in the Book of Revelation by the great Christian theologian Augustine of Hippo (354–430). Augustine saw religion as primarily a personal experience of the individual soul, not as the rise and fall of a divine kingdom on earth. Rather than interpreting the predictions in the Book of Revelation literally, as foretelling the pattern of future earthly events, Augustine saw in these verses an allegory of the soul rising from the bonds of sin. Augustine believed the biblical story of the millennium to be an allegory of the last stage of human redemption, because in his view the paradise of the holy would not be found on earth, but rather in heaven. Augustine's allegorical interpretation of Revelation carried such doctrinal authority during the Middle Ages that the idea of the millennium as a temporal utopia virtually disappeared from official church doctrine in this period.[5]

Even though the medieval church largely adhered to the Augustinian allegorical interpretation of the Book of Revelation, the idea of Christ's temporal kingdom lived on during the Middle Ages as a means by which people made sense of the world in which they lived by seeing it in the context of a transcendent scheme of world history. Millenarianism was especially important in the thought of the Italian mystic Joachim á Fiore

---

[3] On Cerinthus, see J. H. Alsted, *The Beloved City or The Saints Reign on Earth a Thousand Years* (London, 1643), p. 70, marginal note. This is an English translation by William Burton of Alsted's original Latin text.

[4] Ernest Tuveson, *Millennium and Utopia: A Study in the Background of the Idea of Progress* (Berkeley, 1949), pp. 12–14.

[5] Ibid., pp. 15–21.

(1135–1202), a former Cistercian abbot who believed himself to possess the gift of "spiritual intelligence" enabling him to understand the inner spiritual meaning of history. In his prophecies Joachim divided the history of the world into three eras: the period of the Father (the law), the period of the Son (the gospel), and the period of the Holy Spirit. These eras he considered roughly equivalent to the historical ages of the Old Testament, the New Testament, and a third millennium-like spiritual age of prayer, contemplation, and purification of the church that would be the culmination of all history. The beginning of the millennial age of the Holy Spirit Joachim predicted for the year 1260. Joachimite chiliastic ideas had considerable influence in the later Middle Ages, especially among the rigorist reformers of the Franciscan order known as the Spirituals. These men believed that St. Francis had been the initiator of Joachim's age of the Holy Spirit, an age in which the ascetic reform ideals of the Spirituals would be realized.

With the religious, social, and political upheavals of the fourteenth, fifteenth, and sixteenth centuries, apocalyptic visions of the imminent end of the world became even more prominent a part of the Christian consciousness. Most apocalyptic systems of thought stressed the rapid decline of a corrupt and sinful world nearing its end. While many apocalyptic visions expected the end of the world to be followed immediately by the Last Judgment and a heavenly reward for the holy, millenarianism became an increasingly popular variant of apocalypticism because it predicted the transformation of the sinful world into a temporal paradise before the final end. Especially in Germany during the second half of the fifteenth century, apocalyptic and millenarian ideas were increasingly used in popular literature to explain the widespread social and political turmoil resulting from the fragmentation of the Holy Roman Empire and the gradual dissolution of medieval society. The progressive decline of law and order in the empire, the depredations of emerging capitalism upon the traditional artisan economy, and the ever-present scourges of war and pestilence combined with other factors to produce an erosion of the traditional social structure that was explained by popular writers and preachers in terms of the decay and corruption of the earth that apocalyptic theories predicted would precede the end of the world.

While the apocalyptic idea of the nearing end provided ordinary people with a familiar frame of reference within which to place the disastrous and unfamiliar events of their own day, the chiliastic vision of a millennial paradise on earth gave them hope for better times. Much popular millenarian literature contained predictions of the advent of a redeemer figure who would bring an abrupt end to the suffering and privation of society and usher in a new and blessed regime based on some ideal vision of a past golden age. The *Book of a Hundred Chapters*, influential in Germany in the early sixteenth century, predicted the resurrection of the Emperor Frederick I, "The Emperor from the Black Forest," who would save the German people from their troubles. Whatever wonderful promises of an approaching paradise were made in chiliastic literature, however, the prospect for the immediate future was always gloomily cast in terms of increasing turmoil and disintegration as the world rushed to its inevitable end. Among the many examples of this wave of popular apocalyptic and chiliastic fervor in Germany during the fifteenth and early sixteenth centuries were the sermons of the lay preacher Hans Böhm, called the "drummer of Niklashausen" (fl.ca. 1476), and the prophecy concerning the redeemer Frederick of Lantneuen contained in the final sections of the *Reformatio Sigismundi* (ca. 1438). Without exception, these chiliastic prophecies were of a dual nature, stressing both the corrupt decline of the premillennial world and its ultimate regeneration in the millennium.[6]

During the Protestant Reformation apocalyptic ideas gained great intellectual currency in Germany and northern Europe due to the important role played by these ideas in the emerging tradition of Protestant religious thought. Both simple apocalypticism and its variant millenarianism functioned as important explanatory paradigms that were used by the Protestants to justify their place in Christian history. Beginning with Luther's attack on the papacy, the Protestant movement claimed that the Catholic church represented a corrupt perversion of the true religion and that God had inspired the Protestants to purify religion by preaching the true word of God. Having made this argument the Protestants were faced with a troubling question: How could a good and merciful God have allowed the medieval church to become so corrupt that it was in need of such a drastic purification? Many Protestant thinkers answered this question, and in so doing justified the actions of the reformers, by appealing to an apocalyptic vision of Christian history. They saw the papacy as the earthly incarnation of Satan or Antichrist, whose persecution of God's people was a necessary prelude to the coming of the millennium and the Last Judgment. The period of Christian history between the death of the apostles and the Protestant Reformation represented the period of premillennial decay predicted by prophecy, and the coming of the reformers to restore true religion signaled the end of the sinful world and presaged the coming of the millennium. Thus, Protestantism represented not an unnatural break in the history of the universal church but a prophesied and inevitable stage in Christian history.

Some Protestant chiliasts, such as the Anabaptists of Münster, saw

[6] For the millenarian tradition in fifteenth–century Germany, see Gerald Strauss, *Manifestations of Discontent in Germany on the Eve of the Reformation* (Bloomington, Ind., 1971), pp. xviii–xxi, 30–31, 218–222, 233–247. For the distinction between millenarianism and apocalypticism, see Bernard McGinn, *Visions of the End: Apocalyptic Traditions in the Middle Ages* (New York, 1979), pp. 28–36.

their movement as ushering in the millennium itself. For more moderate Protestants, apocalyptic ideas helped to explain the social and spiritual chaos brought by the Reformation's religious disputes. Biblical prophecies had predicted that the last days of the earth would be filled with sorrow, decay, war, and sin, and this prophecy seemed to be unfolding into reality during the sixteenth century. Belief in the imminent dissolution of the natural world became widespread among Protestants who were themselves repeatedly faced with the threat of annihilation at the hands of Catholic powers such as Spain, France, and the Holy Roman Empire. This Protestant conception of Christian history gave new life to apocalyptic ideas and especially to that part of chiliasm that stressed premillennial decline.[7]

The radical wing of the Protestant movement especially incorporated millenarian ideas into its program of religious reform. As early as 1521 the radical reformer Thomas Müntzer began to give chiliastic form to his calls for a total reform of church and society. Müntzer drew on the rich tradition of popular millenarianism already present in Germany as well as on the chiliastic ideas of the Taborites, a radical branch of the Hussite reform movement in fifteenth-century Bohemia. The desire for a ground-up transformation of the Christian church that had inspired the Taborites moved Müntzer and the radical wing of the sixteenth-century Reformation as well, and it was this obsession with universal reform that acted as a vehicle for the introduction of chiliastic ideas into religious life on a broad scale by the radicals. Such millenarian-inspired reform expectations tended to center on the idea that the coming of the Protestant Reformation represented a prelude to the final universal reformation that would take place with Christ's return to earth. With Müntzer and his followers these ideas took on a violent color. Müntzer held that it was the duty of God's elect, once they had been inwardly transformed in the image of Christ, to take up arms and do battle with the evil world in order to destroy the enemies of God and institute universal reformation.[8] These violent ideas were later adopted by the Anabaptists of Münster and through them became the unwanted heritage of the Dutch Mennonites, whose rejection of violence had important consequences for their own conception of the church during the seventeenth century.

Many of the more moderate Protestant reformers resisted the extreme chiliasm of the radicals in favor of simple apocalypticism, but they could not escape millenarian influences altogether. Martin Luther believed the pope to be the Antichrist and the world to be in its last days, but Luther

---

[7] B. S. Capp, *The Fifth Monarchy Men: A Study in Seventeenth-Century English Millenarianism* (Totowa, N.J., 1972), pp. 24–25.

[8] Reinhard Schwarz, *Die apokalyptische Theologie Thomas Müntzers und der Taboriten* (Tübingen, 1977), pp. 2–9, 58–59; and Williams, pp. 44–58. For another view of Müntzer, see Günther List, *Chiliastiche Utopie and Radicale Reformation* (Munich, 1973).

saw the millennium as existing in the past rather than the future. Although Luther considered various historical interpretations of the millennium, he tended to believe that the period of the establishment and early growth of the church, from the coming of Christ to about the year 1000, had in fact been the prophesied millennium of prosperity for God's people. He believed that during the High Middle Ages the tyranny of the papacy over the church had brought an end to this golden age of Christianity, and thus he maintained that the world of his day was in the predicted period of renewed persecution by the Antichrist immediately preceding the Last Judgment. Luther saw these trials as a purification of God's chosen people that would cease only at the end of the world.[9]

During the sixteenth and seventeenth centuries there was considerable discussion among reformers about whether the millennium should be placed in the past or in the future. Some followed Luther in placing it in the past, thus holding out little hope for an improvement of temporal life before the Last Judgment. Others argued that, in view of the corruption of the Roman church even during its early growth period, the millennium could only be considered as an event still to come. This latter position was generally held by the radical reformers, whose rejection of the Catholic tradition was more total than that of the moderate Lutherans and Calvinists and whose reform plans were thus more far reaching. Regardless of whether they saw the kingdom of Christ in the past or the future, however, most Protestant apocalyptic thinkers were united in the belief that their own day was one of corruption and decay.[10]

Seventeenth-century Protestant chiliasm was in many ways a continuation of ideas popular during the Reformation. This century saw a flourishing of millennial expectation, which often tended to be paired with spiritualistic or mystical ideas. In northern Germany one of the most important writers on the millennium during the seventeenth century was Johannes Alsted (1588–1638), Calvinist professor of philosophy at the University of Herborn. Alsted envisioned the coming holy kingdom, whose advent he set for the year 1694, as a sudden and total transformation of the world during which the saints would rise from their graves to rule the earth. He went to great lengths to refute the suggestion of some moderate reformers that the millennium had already occurred. In England the so-called Fifth Monarchy Men and other radical sects drew heavily on the writings of Alsted when they applied chiliastic ideas to the problems of the civil war years.[11]

Millenarianism entered the Dutch republic from both England and Germany during the seventeenth century. John Archer, pastor of the En-

---

[9] Tuveson, *Millennium and Utopia*, pp. 29–30.

[10] Ibid., pp. 23–24; Cornelia Roldanus, *Zeventiende eeuwse geestesbloei*, p. 171.

[11] Cornelia W. Roldanus, *Coenraad van Bueningen, staatsman en libertijn* (The Hague, 1931), pp. 179–180; Alsted, pp. 33, 36–37; Capp, p. 30.

glish Independent church meeting in exile at Arnhem, was a prominent chiliast. In 1641 he wrote that even though the people of his day suffered under all manner of ungodly tyranny and oppression, they could expect the imminent coming of a kingdom of heaven on earth that would destroy all temporal monarchies. The dawning of this age of holiness Archer set for the year 1666. The ideas of Alsted were brought into the United Provinces by such thinkers as John Amos Comenius (1592–1670), the exiled Moravian ecumenicist who was a former colleague of Alsted at Herborn. After 1656 Comenius lived in Amsterdam, where he frequented the college and engaged in bitter polemics in defense of chiliasm with the Groningen theologian Samuel Maresius.[12] The influence of imported English and German chiliastic ideas combined with a native Dutch millenarian tradition present at least since the preaching of Melchior Hoffman and his radical Anabaptist follower David Joris in the sixteenth century to make the Netherlands a hotbed of chiliastic speculation during the seventeenth century.

There were also many chiliasts in the Low Countries during these years who did not confine their millenarian activities to speculation. Johannes Rothe (1628–1702) preached the coming of Christ's kingdom in the streets of city and village alike. He believed himself to be Christ's appointed messenger charged with the mission of bringing this good news to God's people. Rothe was also in the habit of writing threatening letters to high government officials in which he admonished them to prepare themselves for the coming day of the Lord, and it was one such letter to the prince of Orange that landed Rothe in prison and ended his career.[13] Rothe's disciple Quirinus Kuhlmann called himself "the new inspired Jacob Böhme." After publishing many of Rothe's confused writings in Holland, Kuhlmann set out to find converts to his master's teachings abroad. Shortly after he embarked on this mission, however, he met an inglorious end by being committed to the fires in Moscow for proclaiming himself Jesus Christ.[14] Another follower of Rothe, Alhardt De Raedt (1645–1699), cooperated with the spiritualist Johannes Gichtel (1638–1710) in producting a new edition of the works of the German mystic Jacob Böhme. This edition was published in Amsterdam in 1684 with the financial backing of the Collegiant former mayor of that city Coenraad van Beuningen. The writings of Böhme were popular among Dutch radicals for many years.[15] Another unique figure from this period was Antoinette

---

[13] Zilverberg, pp. 62–63; M. G. de Boer, "Een unrustige geest: Johannes Rothe," *Tijdschrift voor Geschiedenis* 15 (1900), pp. 201–229.

[14] Lindeboom, *Stiefkinderen van het Christendom*, p. 356. On Kuhlmann, see also Jon Clark, "Immediacy and Experience: Institutional Change and Spiritual Expression in the Works of Quirinus Kuhlmann," (dissertation, University of California at Berkeley, 1986).

[15] Zilverberg, pp. 60–61. For Böhme in the Netherlands, see Michael J. Petry, "Behmen-

Bourignon (1616–1680), who her disciples called "the light of the world." This Walloon mystic, ascetic, and prophet was born in Lille and attracted many followers in the Low Countries, including Comenius and his fellow Collegiant Pieter Serrarius. Bourignon was active in Amsterdam during the 1660s and impressed Collegiant chiliasts with her zeal. She declared that the world was in the grips of the Antichrist and she called on the elect to make themselves known through lives of ascetic holiness.[16]

As with the earlier Protestant apocalyptic tradition, many seventeenth-century Protestant millenarians held a very pessimistic view of the world in which they lived. Especially among the more radical Protestant reformers who felt alienated from the churches of their day, it was believed that the coming of the millennium was to be a dramatic change from a thoroughly decayed world. As B. S. Capp has noted in his book on the Fifth Monarchy Men, "Despite the pleasure with which it anticipated the punishment of God's enemies, the apocalyptic school was definitely pessimistic in outlook. There was no real hope of improvement before the end of the world." Indeed, in the seventeenth century much radical Protestant chiliastic thought expected the irreversible decay of the natural world to be ended only by ultimate divine intervention in the millennium. While many more moderate Calvinist millenarians of the seventeenth-century, such as the Englishmen Joseph Mede, Thomas Burnet, and William Whiston, tended to be more progressivist and even melioristic in outlook, the predominant trend in radical Protestant apocalyptic and millenarian thought during the seventeenth century was pessimistic, stressing the increasing corruption of the temporal world leading up to a final and dramatic change.[17]

Collegiant chiliasm was an outgrowth of the radical Protestant millenarian tradition and thus shared in its pessimistic appraisal of the temporal

---

ism and Spinozism in the Religious Culture of The Netherlands, 1660–1730," in Karlfried Gründer and Wilhelm Schmidt-Biggeman, eds., *Spinoza in der Frühzeit Seiner Religiösen Wirkung* (Heidelberg, 1984). See also Clasina Manusov, *Pelgrims en Profeten: Bunyan's "The Pilgrim's Progress" in de Mystieke denkwereld van Jacob Böhme* (Utrecht, 1985).

[16] Lindeboom, *Stiefkinderen van het Christendom*, pp. 362–369. See also A. van der Linde, *Antoinette Bourignon, das Licht der Welt* (Leiden, 1895); and the more recent work by Marthe van der Does, *Antoinette Bourignon sa vie (1616–1680), son oeuvre* (Groningen, 1974).

[17] Capp, p. 27. For the differences between progressivist Calvinist apocalypticism and the more pessimistic outlook, see Robin B. Barnes, *Prophecy and Gnosis: Apocalypticism in the Wake of the Lutheran Reformation* (Stanford, 1988), pp. 30–36; M. H. Abrams, "Apocalypse: Theme and Variations," in C. A. Patrides and Joseph Wittreich, eds., *The Apocalypse in English Renaissance Thought and Literature* (Ithaca, N.Y., 1984), pp. 342–368; Tuveson, *Millennium and Utopia*; and Jacob, *The Newtonians and the English Revolution*, p. 139.

world. Coenraad van Beuningen (1622–1693) was one of the most visible of Collegiant chiliasts because of his important position as mayor and leading citizen of Amsterdam. Coming from a Remonstrant background, van Beuningen was classically educated and fed by the spirit of the Dutch humanists Erasmus, Coornhert, and Grotius. Like them he was inclined toward a primarily eithical view of religion, and he read widely in history and philosophy. For many years he was a powerful mayor of the city on the Ij, and in this position he acted as patron and protector of the Collegiants, among whom he was an active member. Van Beuningen was influenced by both spiritualistic and chiliastic ideas. At first he confined himself to supporting these ideas as a patron by financing the De Raedt edition of Böhme and by supporting other chiliasts with funding in times of need. In 1688 he began to write spiritualistic and millenarian works, proclaiming the nearing kingdom of Christ on earth and describing it not as a carnal paradise but as a spiritual kingdom in which the inner word of the Lord would enlighten his holy people. In the biblical prophecies concerning the millennium, Van Beuningen saw a condemnation of the external, worldly churches. Although he moved in important intellectual circles both within the Amsterdam college and without (he was a friend of the humanists Nicolass Heinsius and Gerardus Vossius, while among the Collegiants he knew most men of intellectual talent, including Spinoza), Van Beuningen was most influenced in his own work by the Collegiant chiliast Daniel De Breen.[18]

De Breen (1594–1664), cofounder of the Amsterdam college with Adam Boreel, was the most important of Collegiant writers on the millennium. Born in Haarlem, he was educated as a grant holder at the States College of Leiden University, where the republic trained its future pastors. At Leiden, De Breen was a student of Arminius's successor Simon Episcopius, and in the years before the Synod of Dordrecht he became a strong advocate of the Remonstrant cause. When Episcopius took over the leadership of the Remonstrant party at the synod, De Breen became his secretary and thus was able to observe that entire sad drama from close at hand. After the synod De Breen did not return to Leiden, knowing full well that all Remonstrant sympathizers were soon to be purged from the States College. Instead he traveled to Germany, and in Strasbourg he met some followers of the spiritualist Kaspar Schwenckfeld, who impressed him greatly with their millenarian ideas. In 1621 De Breen returned home to Haarlem, where he was immediately arrested in a raid by city officials on an illegal Remonstrant meeting. Put in the municipal prison, De Breen was repeatedly interrogated about the identity of others at the meeting. When he obstinately refused to answer he was released with a warning never again to attend such heretical gatherings. As was

[18] Roldanus, *Coenraad van Beuningen*, pp. 140–151, 185–187, 159–160.

soon to become apparent, however, De Breen already nourished ideas far more radical than those of the Remonstrants.

Shortly after his release from jail De Breen moved to Amsterdam, where he became an advocate of Collegiant ideas. As early as 1620 he had disagreed in writing with his teacher Episcopius over the issue of Christians holding government office, and in 1638 he became involved in another dispute with the Collegiants' old adversary Paschier De Fijne. Against De Fijne, De Breen upheld the Collegiant belief that all religious creeds and cofessions were undue restraints on the individual conscience and he condemned the Remonstrants for adopting such a confession of faith. In 1646 De Breen helped to organize the Amsterdam college, and in the following years he had many dealings with Adam Boreel and Galenus Abrahamsz. By and large, however, De Breen tended to remain in the background of Collegiant affairs. Not by nature an administrator, De Breen exercised much greater influence on the Rijnsburger movement through his writings.[19]

In his religious thought De Breen was an advocate of toleration, declaring that doctrinal differences did not belong to the essentials of religion. He also formulated rules for biblical interpretation that stressed the use of reason to understand Scripture. He maintained that Christianity imposed no obligation on people that did not accord with reason, and he even went so far as to declare that a Christian should accept no interpretation of Scripture that was contrary to reason or external experience. But De Breen did not apply these rules in his own work with the Bible, a fact that led Leszek Kolakowski to conclude that De Breen's rationalism went little deeper than mere phraseology.[20] In any case, the main body of De Breen's work dealt not with rationalistic scriptural interpretation but with chiliastic dreams of the establishment of Christ's kingdom on earth.

In his important work *Van 't geestelyk triumpherende ryck onses heeren Jesu Christi* (On the spiritually triumphant empire of Our Lord Jesus Christ), which was published in Amsterdam in 1653, De Breen put forth views on the millennium that were to have great currency among the Collegiants. In the introduction to his treatise, De Breen took on those critics who discounted chiliasm as an unimportant and even heretical doctrine by reminding his readers of the antiquity of chiliastic ideas. As evidence for this he pointed to fathers of the early church such as Justin, Irenaeus, Melito, and Tertullian who had held millenarian ideas. God promised that a kingdom of Christ would be erected on earth before the final destruction of the world, De Breen declared, adding that the holy people

---

[19] *BWPG*, vol.1, pp. 604–605; Zilverberg, p. 29; *BWN*, vol. 1, pp. 391–392; Van Slee, *De Rijnsburger Collegiantan* pp. 135–138.

[20] Kolakowski, *Chrétiens sans église*, pp. 200–201.

would rule in this kingdom for a thousand years with all necessary power, justice, spiritual wisdom, and strength. But De Breen pointed out that this glorious reign of the saints would come only after the total destruction of all the enemies of God's people. The worldly kingdoms under which God's elect had so long been persecuted and oppressed would be reduced to ruin by the power of God, he declared. For De Breen, the chiliastic coin was dramatically two-sided: The coming paradise of the saints was necessarily set against the dark background of the prior annihilation of a world of evil. The stark contrast between the evil temporal world and the glories of the divine millennium was the central imagery of Collegiant chiliastic writing. In De Breen's eyes, the holy people included all true, sincerely believing Christians, but their enemies were legion: the papal Antichrist and his godless hordes who had so long persecuted true Christians; the "Roman" monarchy (Holy Roman Empire), which had acted as the right hand of the Antichrist in these persecutions; and all those people who confessed Christ in words but denied him in deeds.[21] In De Breen's mind the holy people must have seemed a very small minority indeed, faced with enemies so powerful that the victory of the elect would be impossible without divine intervention.

As evidence for the coming of the millennium, De Breen summoned the traditional collection of scriptural passages. From this discussion it is clear that Collegiant chiliastic thought grew out of an intense absorption in Scripture that gave the Rijnsburgers a very biblically oriented consciousness of both the past and the future. The second chapter of the Book of Daniel was for De Breen (as for other millenarians) a key source of chiliastic ideas. In this chapter King Nebuchadnezzar's dream was interpreted by his servant Daniel as foretelling a series of kingdoms that would rule the earth after the death of Nebuchadnezzar. Following the standard millenarian interpretation of Daniel's prophecy, De Breen wrote that Daniel referred to four future worldly empires: the Babylonian, Persian, Greek, and Roman.[22] The stone that in the king's dream shattered the image of these worldly kingdoms and then grew into a great mountain was interpreted by Daniel in verse 44: "And in the days of these kings shall the God of heaven set up a kingdom which shall never be destroyed . . . it shall break in pieces and consume all these kingdoms, and it shall stand forever."[23] For De Breen this stone was the symbol of Christ's kingdom on earth, which would destroy the fourth worldly monarchy—the

---

[21] Daniel De Breen, *Van 't geestelyk triumpherende ryck onses heeren Jesu Christi* (Amsterdam, 1653), pp. i–iii, 1–3.

[22] Ibid., pp. 13–21.

[23] This and following citations are from the Authorized (King James) version of the Bible (1611).

(Holy) Roman Empire—and rule the world until the arrival of the Last Judgment.

In his interpretation of Daniel, De Breen was quick to reject the Augustinian approach and to insist that the prophecy foretold actual world-historical events. He vigorously rejected the idea that Christ's holy fifth monarchy would be only an inner, spiritual kingdom in the hearts of men, insisting instead that Christ would rule an actual earthly kingdom that would sweep the enemies of God before it. While Christ's kingdom on earth would indeed be quite different in nature from the sinful worldly monarchy that it replaced, it would nevertheless be an external, visible, and tangible power whose victory over the corrupt world would be real for all to see.[24] This insistence on a visible, tangible, and even violent negation of the sinful world by the coming holy paradise was clearly important for De Breen. He lost no opportunity to assure his readers that the millennium would involve a total and dramatic transformation of the earth.

De Breen turned to the Gospel of Matthew for more evidence of the coming millennium, and there he found further examples of the great contrast between the sinful temporal world and the approaching paradise. In Matt. 5:5, Jesus promised the meek that they would inherit the earth. For De Breen this promise represented Christ's announcement of the coming of a millennial paradise in which the holy people would rule the world. He emphatically rejected the interpretation of this verse that held that Christ had promised the meek eternal life in heaven, not happiness on earth, and the reason that he gave for this rejection reveals much about his view of the temporal world. If such an interpretation was true, De Breen argued, it would mean that no limit would be placed upon the tyranny of the godless in this world. From this suggestion De Breen recoiled in horror and disbelief. He repeatedly insisted that all Scriptural evidence indicated that the oppression of God's people on earth would indeed end before the end of the world, and his revulsion from the idea that this might not happen clearly showed the extremely negative conception that he had of earthly life. He saw the premillennial world as a place where God's people were continually oppressed and killed by their evil and godless enemies, and he believed that Christians would escape this persecution only when Christ himself returned to earth to purify the world of evil.[25]

De Breen further believed that the corruption, decay, and sinfulness of earthly existence was itself necessary and certain proof for the imminent

[24] De Breen, *Van 't geestelyk triumpherende ryck*, pp. 35–40.

[25] Ibid., pp.80–85. De Breen discussed Matt. 25, Luke 17:20, Acts 1:6–7 and 3:19–21, and Rev. 20:1-11 to reinforce his argument.

coming of the millennium. In Matt. 24, the "little Apocalypse," Christ told the apostles about the end of the world and related to them the frightful signs that would precede the end. De Breen interpreted the words of Christ in Matt. 24 as describing the coming of the millennium and the signs that would portend this great transformation of the world, and he found all of these terrible signs present in his own day: false prophets, war and rumors of war, famine, pestilence, earthquakes, suppression of the holy people, cooling of love for God, and neglect of religion. All of these signs meant, for De Breen, that God's terrible judgment over the heathen earthly powers was near. God would use fire, hail, thunder, and lightning to devastate the papal Antichrist and the worldly empire—the Roman monarchy that had crucified Christ and persecuted his people. Christ would then send messenger angels to set up his kingdom on earth, which he would rule through the holy people, who would be given heavenly strength to serve as "stadtholders of God."[26]

In the final climactic section of *Van 't geestelyk triumpherende ryck* De Breen described the glorious characteristics of Christ's kingdom on earth. He presented a vision of a millennial utopia seen primarily in terms of its stark contrast with the condition of the world prior to the victory of the saints. In the millennium the church would be free at last from persecution and its majesty and glory would be great above all measure, De Breen wrote. In the coming earthly paradise all that the senses enjoy and all that the heart finds desirable would abound for the pleasure of God's people. There would be a total transformation and renewal of the world providing everything that people needed for happiness, including great peace and well-being, exceptional knowledge of God's secrets, abundant holiness, good bodily health, and long life. Belief, hope, and love would flourish. Paraphrasing the prophet Isaiah, De Breen exclaimed climactically: "I see a new heaven and a new earth, for the first heaven and the first earth have perished!"[27]

The contrast between this new earth and the old one was indeed striking, and De Breen meant it to be. His vision of a divine millennium set against the background of an unholy world was intended as a stinging criticism of the religion and society of his own day. True to the tradition of Protestant chiliasm, De Breen's work directed many of its sharpest criticisms at the pope and emperor, but his book was far more than a mere anti-Catholic polemic. It was a powerful polemic against the entire ungodly temporal world. In the face of sweeping worldly decay and corruption, Christians could place their hope only in the expectation of direct divine intervention effecting a total transformation of the world. Leszek

[26] De Breen, *Van 't geestelyk triumpherende ryck*, pp. 97–141, 371–378.
[27] Ibid., pp. 435–439.

Kolakowski pointed out the intrinsic function of De Breen's chiliasm as an instrument of Second Reformation religious dissent. *Van 't geestelyk triumpherende ryck* formulated a criticism of the established churches similar to that of other reformers, but set in the context of the future. For De Breen, to say that Christ would soon return to establish his kingdom on earth was to say that no existing church enjoyed Christ's favor and protection. For this reason the established churches feared chiliasm and the Second Reformation fostered it. In assessing De Breen's millenarianism Kolakowski wrote: "Here we have a Christian utopia. With regard to religious life it has the same function as secular utopias with regard to secular life: it expresses the negation of the existing state by means of a positive description of the ideal state."[28] De Breen's new earth was a product of his dissatisfaction with the old earth.

Van 't geestelyk triumpherende ryck was a seminal work within the Collegiant tradition in several respects. It was the first major work of Collegiant chiliasm and, appearing as it did in 1653, it stood at the beginning of the most productive period of Collegiant intellectual activity. The millenarian ideas contained in De Breen's book had a far-reaching influence on all of the Collegiant thought that followed. De Breen's first and most immediate impact was on the Amsterdam college that he helped to found. There his writings convinced the influential Collegiant-Mennonite leader Galenus Abrahamsz. to consider chiliastic ideas. The decade of the 1660s was a time of rising expectations and increasing interest in chiliastic ideas within the Amsterdam college, in part because many chiliasts predicted the advent of the millennium for the year 1666.[29] In the anticipation, the excitement, and ultimately the disappointment of this decade, many Collegiant ideas were formed. During these years Galenus often spoke with another prominent Collegiant chiliast, the one-time follower of Antoinette Bourignon, Pieter Serrarius.

Pieter Serrarius (1600–1669) was born to Walloon parents in London at the turn of the century. In 1620 he was admitted to the Walloon college at Leiden, where he prepared for the ministry. During the years 1624–1626 Serrarius served as an assistant in several Walloon churches in Zeeland before moving on to the congregation in Cologne. Because the Walloon church adhered strictly to Calvinist doctrine, the independent-minded Serrarius soon came to feel uncomfortable in its fold. In 1628 he was forced to leave the Cologne congregation under the suspicion of doctrinal errors, including mysticism. In later life Serrarius showed great

---

[28] Kolakowski, pp. 202–204. My translation.
[29] H. W. Meihuizen, "Collegianten en Doopsgezinden," in Groenveld, *Daar de Orangie-appel in de gevel staat*, p. 94.

fondness for the thought of the mystics Tauler, Ruysbroeck, Suso, and Thomas à Kempis, and for this reason it is possible that he already harbored mystical beliefs during his Cologne period. In any case, after leaving Cologne, Serrarius spent a brief time in Groningen, where he might have studied medicine, before he arrived in Amsterdam in 1630. There he was to spend the rest of his life.

Soon after his arrival in Amsterdam, Serrarius joined Galenus Abrahamsz.'s United Mennonite church, in which he eventually became a deacon. He also began to attend Collegiant meetings and soon became one of the leading Collegiants in Amsterdam. Serrarius was employed as a proofreader in an Amsterdam printer's shop for some time after his arrival, but in his later years he worked at this job only irregularly, spending most of his time writing and translating theological works. He translated the writings of the German mystic Johannes Tauler (1300–1361) as well as works of several lesser mystical thinkers, including Christian Entfelder and Josua Sprigge. For a time Serrarius maintained a close relationship with the mystic prophet Antoinette Bourignon, but a permanent parting of ways occurred between the two several years before Serrarius's death. Serrarius's broad and impressive circle of friends also included the Lutheran mystics Friedrich Breckling and Christian Hohburg; Johannes Gichtel, the editor of Böhme's works; the Pietist and chiliast Jean de Labadie; the mystical alchemist Franciscus Mercurius van Helmont; Henry Oldenburg, secretary of the Royal Society; the physicist and chemist Robert Boyle; the Amsterdam Rabbi Menasseh ben Israel; the expelled Jewish philosopher Benedict Spinoza; the pansophist pedagogue Jan Amos Comenius; the irenicist John Dury; and Samuel Hartlib, the great inspirer of intellectual projects. Serrarius held an important position in the circle of Hartlib, Dury, and Comenius, one of the most active intellectual networks of the time.[30] Exceptionally well connected even for a Collegiant, Serrarius was an important link between the Rijnsburgers and the broader intellectual world of the late seventeenth century.

In his religious thought Serrarius combined chiliasm, spiritualism, and irenicism in a truly Collegiant manner. Calling himself "a servant of God's universal church," Serrarius despised all religious confessions and creeds and worked untiringly toward the goal of universal Christian unity. He believed that his mystical chiliasm would provide the solution

---

[30] E.G.E. van der Wall, "De Hemelse takenen en het rijk van Christus op aarde: chiliasme en astrologie bij Petrus Serrarius (1660–1669)," *Kerkhistorische Studien* (1982), p. 46; J. van den Berg, "Quaker and Chiliast: The 'Countrary Thoughts' of William Ames and Petrus Serrarius," in R. Buick Knox, ed., *Reformation, Conformity, and Dissent: Essays in Honor of Geoffrey Nuttall* (London, 1977), p. 187; E.G.E. van der Wall, "De Mystieke Chiliast Petrus Serrarius (1660–1669) en zijn Wereld" (dissertation, Leiden University, 1987), pp. 624–626; See also Turnbull, *Hartlib, Dury, and Comenius*.

needed to effect a reunification of the many Christian sects, and he even hoped that it might also help to achieve a reconciliation between Christians and Jews. Serrarius was a truly spiritualistic theologian filled with the need for an inner faith. His thought combined the tradition of medieval German mysticism represented by Tauler with the mystical natural philosophy of Paracelsus and the spiritualism of Schwenkfeld and Franck. Above all, however, Serrarius was a passionate believer in the idea that the end of the world was near and that Christ was about to return to earth to found his millennial kingdom. He wrote numerous works in which he put forward his chiliastic ideas, including his treatise *Assertion du regne de mille ans* (1657), regarded by many scholars as an excellent example of seventeenth-century millenarian thought. In 1659 Serrarrius again took up his pen in defense of chiliasm when he refuted the arguments of conservative critics of his friend Galenus Abrahamsz. in his work *De vertredinge des heyligen stadts. . . .*[31] In a work entitled *Naerder Bericht Wegens die Groote Conjunctie* (Further report concerning the great conjunction), published in 1662 in Amsterdam, Serrarius most clearly presented his own ideas regarding the approaching transformation of the world.[32] This book played a very influential role in the surge of millenarian interest within the Amsterdam college during the 1660s.

The theme of premillennial worldly decay contrasted with the coming of a divine paradise was present in Serrarius's work just as in the earlier work of De Breen, but Serrarius took a slightly different approach to the topic. In the *Naeder Bericht* he employed traditional astrological speculations as well as chiliastic ideas to warn the sinful world of God's approaching wrath. Serrarius believed that the "science" of astrology testified to the harmony of heaven and earth, and for this reason he maintained that God's purpose could be read in either the Bible or the book of nature. Serrarius therefore utilized astrological phenomena as well as scriptural evidence, historical events, and prophetic signs to support his millenarian theories.[33] In the *Naeder Bericht* Serrarius proclaimed that a great conjunction of planets was due to occur in the year 1662, and he argued that such a great heavenly event was undoubtedly the sign of a monumental earthly happening: the coming of Christ's king-

[31] *BWN* vol. 1, p. 195; van den Berg, in knox, ed. *Reformation, Conformity and Dissent: Essays in Honor of Geoffrey Nuttall* (London, 1977), pp. 190–193; van der Wall, "De Mystieke Chiliast," pp. 623–629. For Serrarius's chiliastic work of 1659, *De vertredinge des heyligen stadts . . .* (Amsterdam, 1659), see chap. 4. Serrarius expounded on the argument of *De vertredinge* in *Antwoort op 't boeck in 't jaer 1659 uytgegeven* (Amsterdam, 1661).

[32] A contemporary Dutch translation of the Latin original entitled *Brevis dissertatio de fatali et admiranda illa omnium planetarium in uno eodemque signo . . . conjunctione die 1/11 dec. anno 1662 futura* (Amsterdam, 1662).

[33] Van der Wall, pp. 45–55.

dom. He further explained that because many people of his day ignored the operation of the planets and their influence on the world, he felt obliged to demonstrate how such heavenly signs did indeed foretell great earthly events. It was especially necessary, Serrarius felt, to explain to his readers in detail what the great conjunction of 1662 portended for the world.[34]

Serrarius first undertook to explain how it was that men could learn of future earthly events by observing the stars. He argued that just as the light of the sun created daylight for the benefit of people on earth, there was also another kind of heavenly light that was important for humankind. This light Serrarius called the "astral light," the light of the stars. It "descends from on high and is nourished from above," he wrote, and he described it somewhat curiously as "a rational light of discerning and clearness of understanding," from which "arts and sciences, negotiations and governments, both ecclesiastical and secular," were created. Serrarius further explained that God had created the stars for the purpose of revealing events that would take place on earth, and for this reason observation of the stars was a gift from God. The signs in the heavens were established by God to lead the heathen to know their creator, Serrarius argued, because, unlike Israel, these people had no better way to know God. But reading the stars was a difficult art, he warned, and even though people skillful in these matters could provide a few rules for use in observing the heavens, ordinary Christians had only one way to attain certainty in this, as in all other things; They had to pray for God's inspiration.[35]

Having explained how it was possible for people to learn of future events by observing the stars, Serrarius proceeded to explain what the great conjunction of 1662 meant for humankind. Following a long tradition of astrological prophecy, Serrarius wrote that of all the events observed in the heavens it had always been conjunctions of Saturn and Jupiter that foretold the most notable events on earth. Since the time of Adam there had been seven such conjunctions. The first preceded Adam's fall, the second foretold the anarchy of Enoch's day, the third heralded the flood of Noah's time, the fourth preceded Moses leading Israel out of Egypt, and the last three foretold the captivity of the tribes of Israel in Assyria, the birth of Christ, and the rise of Charlemagne's empire. The eighth great conjunction of Jupiter and Saturn would occur in 1662, Ser-

---

[34] Pieter Serrarius, *An Awakening Warning to the Woefull World, By a Voyce in Three Nations; Uttered in a brief Dissertation Concerning that Fatal, and to be admired Conjunction of all the Planets in one and the same sign of . . . Sagitarius, the last of the Fiery Triplicity, to come to pass the 11 day of December, Anno 1662* (Amsterdam 1662; the comtemporary English translation that I have used in my account of Serrarius's work), pp. 1–2.

[35] Ibid., pp. 3, 4–8.

rarius delcared, and it would foretell the greatest event of all: the establishment of the millennium.[36]

Having presented his astrological argument, Serrarius turned to other signs that he felt indicated the imminent coming of the kingdom of Christ. In this discussion his pessimistic attitude toward the temporal world became apparent. Like De Breen, Serrarius saw the corruption and decay of the temporal world as a necessary and certain proof of the coming of the millennium. For this reason, his argument focused on the same terrible signs of the end of the world that De Breen had discussed in his treatment of Matt. 24. Serrarius saw all of these tragic signs present in the disastrous events of his own time: the terrible wars among Germany, Poland, England, Sweden, and Denmark; the earthquakes that had destroyed entire cities in Italy and France; famines across Europe that Serrarius claimed had caused mothers to eat their children; the comets of 1618, 1652, and 1659; the sudden fire at Galata, near Constantinople, in which evil spirits were seen diving on the flames; and especially the repeated births of monsters and prodigies, such as the baby born in Tannum, Norway, who had been heard to cry out from its mother's womb: "woe to Denmark, woe to the whole world." These events left Serrarius with no doubt that the end of the sinful world was near. He found still further proof in the generally corrupt and decadent state of things that he observed around him. Society was pitifully torn and divided, just as David had predicted the last worldly monarchy would be. Christendom was splintered into many tiny sects, each disagreeing with and quarreling with the others, so that no one knew which way to turn. Catholics fought Catholics, Lutherans fought Lutherans, Reformed battled other Reformed, and Anabaptists fought other Anabaptists. The Bible predicted that in the last days many people would search for truth and righteousness but none would find it, Serrarius continued, and Scripture also predicted that many scoffers would appear who would say that the end was not near. Serrarius found in these gloomy predictions a perfect description of the world of his day—a world in which there were many contradictory opinions concerning the true knowledge of God and in which the churches and cloisters abounded with scoffers. He saw his world torn assunder by ignorance, hostility, and lack of faith.[37]

Against this background of temporal despair and suffering Serrarius placed the bright expectation of the coming millennium. Christ would soon wipe out the ungodly people and their works, while the holy people, so long trampled underfoot by the sinful world, would be clothed in power and glory. Thus, Serrarius ended his work as De Breen had ended

[36] Ibid., pp. 9–13. See also Barnes, chap. 4.
[37] Serrarius, pp. 20–21, 23–34.

his, with a vision of the drastic transformation of an evil world through direct divine intervention.[38]

Along with the prophecies contained in the books of Daniel and Matthew, Christian chiliastic thought relied heavily on the Book of Revelation for inspiration and support. One of the most important Collegiant commentaries on the Book of Revelation, and one of the most revealing examples of Rijnsburger thinking about the condition of the natural world in its last days, was written by the Rotterdam Collegiant poet and classical scholar Joachim Fransz. Oudaan (1628–1692).

Joachim was the son of Frans Joachimsz. Oudaan, an important leader of the college in Rijnsburg during the years 1630–1650. Joachim was born in Rijnsburg, the cradle of Collegiantism, in 1628. His maternal grandfather was Jan van der Kodde, a brother of Gijsbert and a co-founder of the Rijnsburg college. Joachim's father was a staunch ally of the van der Koddes and became the leader of the college after the deaths of Gijsbert and Jan. Joachim attended Latin school at age twelve in nearby Leiden, where he showed himself to be a brilliant pupil. Moving on to Leiden University, Oudaan studied under the classicist Petrus Scriverius (1576–1660), a disciple of Joseph Scaliger. Under the influence of Scriverius, Oudaan translated Agrippa von Nettesheim's *Declamatio de incertitudine scientiarium atque artium.* In 1646 Oudaan produced his first major poetic work, and in 1648 he wrote his first tragedy, *Johanna Grey.* During his Leiden years Oudaan concentrated on the study of the Greek and Roman classics and on numismatics, but much of his poetry from these years reflected a deep concern with religion. In his poetry Oudaan expressed an aversion to doctrinal intolerance and confessionalism that no doubt was a result of the influence of his father and the van der Koddes during his early years in Rijnsburg.

In 1656 Oudaan left Leiden and returned home to marry Ewoutje Stout. His new father-in-law set him up in business as a tile maker in Rotterdam, and his affairs so prospered in that great commercial city that he was soon chosen to head his guild. Despite his business success, however, Oudaan still found time for literature. He read the Collegiant poet Camphuysen and published a new edition of his works that became the standard, while in the bookshop of his friend François van Hoogstraten, Oudaan debated the ideas of Coornhert, Spiegel, and Hooft with all comers. Oudaan was an active Collegiant, attending college meetings regularly and contributing many of his own writings to the tradition of Rijnsburger religious thought.

One of the strongest intellectual influences on Oudaan's thought was

[38] Ibid., pp. 34–40.

the chiliasm of Daniel De Breen. Oudaan became a vigorous proponent of Millenarianism and devoted much effort to explaining chiliastic ideas in a series of lengthy writings. In 1666 he wrote an important chiliastic work in verse entitled *Het Zegepralende Rijk Onzes Heeren en Zaligmakers Jesu Christi op Aerden* (The victorious empire of Our Lord and Savior Jesus Christ on Earth) and in 1671 he produced a verse commentary on the Book of Job that was largely inspired by the work of De Breen. Oudaan's poetry was pensive, intellectural, and rhetorical but not deep in feeling or aesthetic quality, according to his biographer, J. Melles. In Melles's opinion, Oudaan's historical importance was not as a poet but rather as a representative of the seventeenth-century Rotterdam intelligentsia and as a historian, antiquarian, and Collegiant. The central role that Oudaan played in the Rotterdam college was in a sense symbolized by the marriage of his two sisters to the influential Collegiant leaders Jan Bredenburg and Jan Dionysius Verburg. Among the Rijnsburgers, family ties often accompanied bonds of intellectual relationship. In 1683 Oudaan was enriched by an inheritance that permitted him to lease his tile shop to an apprentice and retire to spend the last years of his life in full-time study.[39] During these years he wrote many scriptural commentaries, numerous works in which he championed the Rijnsburger principles of free thought and free speech, and several works on religious reform. In his commentary on the Book of Revelation, entitled *Bedenkelijke toepassing op eenige stukken in de Openbaringe* . . . (Thoughtful application of several parts of the Revelation . . . [1689]), Oudaan gave his most striking picture of the Collegiant view of the premillennial world.[40]

The *Bedenkelijke toepassing* was unlike the works of De Breen and Serrarius in that it focused almost entirely on the condition of the world before the millennium. Christ's earthly kingdom itself was never expressly discussed in the work, so that the *Bedenkelijke toepassing* can be seen as a work of simple apocalypticism. Like many other Collegiants, Oudaan considered biblical prophecy to be a vitally important source for man's knowledge of God and God's plans for the future of the world. Of all the prophetic books, Oudaan considered the most important to be the Book of Revelation, and thus he devoted a long commentary to explaining the predictions hidden within that book. He was concerned specifically with the prophecy of the seven seals contained in chapter 6, because in this prophecy Oudaan saw a clear exposition of the entire history of

---

[39] Van Slee, *De Rijnsburger Collegianten*, pp. 121–122; J. Melles, *Joachim Oudaan, heraut der verdraagzaamheid, 1628–1692* (Utrecht, 1958), pp. 1–42, 50–81. See also C. C. de Bruin, *Joachim Oudaan in de lijst van zijn tijd* (Groningen-Djakarta, 1955).

[40] Joachim Fransz. Oudaan, *Bedenkelijke toepassing op eenige stukken in de Openbaringe: ten proeve voorgestelt . . . met bijvoeging der brieven van Franciscus Morstinius en Samuel Pripkovski over het onverschillig oeffenen van den godsdienst* (Rotterdam, 1989).

Christianity from its beginning to its rapidly approaching end. In these few verses he believed the entire secret of divine revelation to be summarized. Even more importantly, Oudaan believed the story of the seals to be a prophecy that had come true.[41]

Oudaan began his commentary on chapter 6 by considering verses 1 and 2, in which the first seal was opened to reveal a white horse ridden by a crowned figure: "behold a white horse: and he that sat upon him had a bow, and a crown was given unto him; and he went forth conquering, and to conquer." This white horse Oudaan interpreted as a symbol of the purity of the early Christian church, and the conquest spoken of he believed to be the original proclaiming and spread of the Gospel by the members of the first church. With this line of explanation Oudaan followed many traditional commentaries on the Book of Revelation, but in his discussion of the following verses he made a dramatic break with previous interpretations. Orthodox writers had traditionally explained the violence and disorder that were introduced with the opening of the remaining seals as representing the punishment of the heathen by the victorious Christian church. Oudaan, however, rejected this idea. Instead he maintained that the remaining seals portrayed the steadily decaying condition of Christianity after the pristine spiritual purity of the first apostolic church was lost. In the remaining verses of chapter 6 Oudaan saw a sad story of the deviation of the church from its original principles and its continual decline into decay and corruption.[42] This view of Christian history as a story of steady decline was an idea that the Collegiants adopted from the Radical Reformation of the sixteenth century. Many Anabaptists believed that the first apostolic church had been spiritually pure because it had not been polluted by compromise with the sinful, secular world. This spiritual purity had ended, according to Anabaptist ideas, when the emperor Constantine allied the church with the secular state and compromised the church's spiritual principles for political purposes. The radical spiritualist Sebastian Franck placed the beginning of the church's spiritual decay even earlier, immediately after the death of the apostles. The history of Christianity from earliest times was thus viewed by the Anabaptists and radical spiritualists as a story of the ever-increasing worldly corruption of the church. Many Anabaptists sought to reestablish the pure, spiritual, apostolic church in their own communities by avoiding contact with the sinful world and by rejecting the authority of civil governments by refusing to pay taxes or perform military service. The influence exerted on Collegiant thought by the Anabaptist-Menno-

[41] Ibid., pp. v–ix, 2–4.
[42] Ibid., pp. 4–8.

nite tradition as well as by the writings of the spiritualists led the Rijnsburgers to adopt this pessimistic view of Christian history.

The remaining verses of chapter 6, according to Oudaan's interpretation told this grim story of the decline of the church. Verse 4 described
the opening of the second seal and the appearance of a red horse: "and
power was given to him that sat thereon to take peace from the earth, and
that they should kill one another: and there was given unto him a great
sword." To Oudaan this horse symbolized the fiery passions and disorders
caused by the many disputes that early Christians bishops had with opponents and schismatics, quarrels that began the disintegration of the
church. Oudaan gave several examples of such disputes, beginning with
the schism of 252 that was caused when both Novatianus and Kornelius
were elected bishop of Rome. This schism spread to Africa, divided the
entire church, and ended in mutual excommunication. To Oudaan's contemporaries the resemblance between this incident and the Great Schism
of 1378–1415 would have been obvious. Oudaan did not, however, re-
late these incidents with the glee of a Protestant polemicist intent on prov-
ing the sinfulness of the Roman church. His tone was rather one of sorrow and despair over the corruption of Christ's followers. He mentioned
with sadness the pitched battles fought in the streets of Rome in the year
362 between Damasus and Ursicinus for possession of the bishop's seat.
He also related the stories of the Arian controversy, the Eutychian heresy
of 444, and many similar cases of turmoil in the church.[43]

The opening of the third seal revealed a black horse, "and he that sat
on him had a pair of balances in his hand" (6:5). Oudaan preferred to
translate as "yoke" the Greek word usually rendered in this verse as
"scale" or "balance." Thus, he saw the black horse as symbolizing the
great yoke of darkness, confusion, and ignorance burdening Christianity.
According to Oudaan, this great darkness descended on the church in 529
when the Benedictine order was founded. He noted that the order's
founder, Benedict of Nursia, was born in Umbria—a "dark land." In the
cloisters the monks were bound to rules of blind obedience and superstition that smothered true religion, Oudaan argued. Following the death of
Pope Gregory I in 604 the little light left in the church went out, and
thereafter the yoke of papal supremacy was clamped ever tighter upon
Christianity. In Oudaan's view, the results of papal rule were that the fear
of God became mere appearance, religion was but superstition, monastic
poverty was really wealth, and the clergy became immoral and licentious.
God seemed to have forgotten his church. As a typical but horrifying example of the corruption of the church, Oudaan cited the canonization in
the year 975 of King Edgaard of England, a murderer and adulterer.[44]

[43] Ibid., pp. 9–15, 16, 19–32.
[44] Ibid., pp. 34–67.

The fourth seal opened to produce a pale horse, "and his name that sat on him was Death, and Hell followed with him. And power was given unto them over the fourth part of the earth, to kill with sword and hunger, and with death" (6:8). For Oudaan the pale horse represented the last desperate state of Christianity in his own day. In his interpretation, verse 8 foretold God's destruction of the worldly Roman Empire and its papal ally. When the Scripture said that the riders of this horse would kill a quarter of the earth, Oudaan took this to mean that God would destroy all who had not heeded his call. When the fifth seal was opened in verse 9 it revealed "under the altar the souls of them that were slain for the word of God, and for the testimony which they held." Oudaan proclaimed that this verse was meant to show that persecution and suffering were not yet over for Christians because, when heathen enemies ceased to punish them, fellow Christians took up the persecution. As proof of this he reminded his readers of the fate of the Albigensians, Waldensians, Hussites, and victims of the Roman Inquisition. But God would not forget the pious souls under the altar, Oudaan added. The Almighty was preparing his vengeance on those who had oppressed his people. With the opening of the sixth seal God's judgment over the unholy world was revealed: a great earthquake would destroy peoples, lands, and kingdoms. The seventh seal opened with silence, followed by the appearance of glorious angels sounding trumpets heralding the end of all things. The decline and final destruction of a world gone wrong was the climax of the prophecy of the seals as interpreted by Oudaan. He saw his world as a world unholy, destined for divine destruction. After such frightful predictions for the future of the world, Oudaan's advice to his readers in the beginning of his book must have had an even more piercing ring: "This prophetic word, which as a light has for a long time shined in a dark place, now lights up the day, and thus it binds and obligates persons of good will, now more than ever, to see to it that the coming Morningstar rises in their heart" ("dit Prophetisch Woord, als een licht nu een geruymen tijd geschenen hebbende in een duystere plaatse, den Dag doet aanlichten, zoo verbind en verplicht het den goedwilligen nu mede des te meer, datze zich bevlijtigen dat de voortkomende Morgenstarre mag opgaan in hun hert").[45]

In his book on English chiliastic thought in the seventeenth and eighteenth centuries, Ernst Tuveson found one of the roots of the Enlightenment idea of progress in the traditional belief in the coming of the millennium. Although he recognized that Protestant chiliasm during the sixteenth and early seventeenth centuries was based primarily on ideas of

---

[45] Ibid., pp. 2, 69–74, 77–87, 93–124.

temporal decay rather than progress, Tuveson detected a different emphasis in English millenarianism later in the seventeenth century. In the chiliastic thought of this period he saw arguments for earthly decay being
replaced by the progressivist idea that God was constantly improving the
world and that the course of human history leading up to the millennium
would be one of progress and growth.[46] Collegiant millenarianism during
the latter half of the seventeenth century stands in direct contrast to Tuveson's portrayal of English thought in that period. The Rijnsburgers were
part of a tradition of radical Protestant chiliastic thought that emphasized
the corrupt and decadent condition of the temporal world before the
coming of the millennium, and in their own writings the Collegiants retained this stress on worldly decay. For the Rijnsburgers, only a future
miraculous and divine intervention could change the course of world history from one of constant decline.

Collegiant chiliasm differed little from the rest of the radical Protestant
apocalyptic tradition in its emphasis on worldly corruption, but it was
the special function of chiliastic ideas within the overall system of Rijnsburger thought that gave Collegiant millenarianism its real significance.
Rijnsburger chiliastic writings offered a stark contrast between the glories
of the coming paradise and the hopeless decadence of the world prior to
the arrival of the millennium, a decadence that implied the absence of
God's guiding hand. In De Breen's work this contrast became a powerful
criticism of the condition of Christian society during the seventeenth century. Serrarius informed his comtemporaries that the great astral conjunction of 1662 presaged the coming of the glorious millennium, and as
proof of this contention he offered a frightening account of the tragic
events and sad condition of the world in which he lived. The Collegiants
took from chiliasm a view of the premillennial world as a corrupt and evil
place. This pessimistic outlook on the world sometimes overwhelmed the
hopeful message of the millennium. Such was the case with Oudaan's discussion of the prophecy of the seals, in which the primary focus was on
the steady decline of the Christian church leading up to the final destruction of the evil world. Despite this pessimistic conception of the premillennial world, however, the Collegiants generally maintained their hope
that Christ would soon return to earth and transform the world into a
temporal paradise. This hope meant that the Rijnsburgers did not have to
accept the corrupt, godless, and essentially secular state of the premillennial world as the final and permanent condition of human society. God

---

[46] Tuveson, pp. viii–xi. For the Puritan roots of this outlook, see Charles Webster, *The
Great Instauration* (New York, 1975), pp. 1–3. For a different view of English chiliasm in
this period, see Jacob, *The Newtonians and The English Revolution*, chap. 3.

might have forsaken the temporal world, but his influence over the earth would be renewed in the millennium.

Chiliasm thus made a profoundly pessimistic view of a corrupt and unholy world acceptable to the minds of sincerely religious people with the promise that this decadence was only a temporary state soon to be reversed in the millennium. The millennium, however, repeatedly failed to appear on the dates assigned for its arrival (1660, 1662, 1666, etc.). The impact of these disappointments on the hopeful attitudes of pious people cannot be underestimated. With each date's passing Rijnsburger expectations became more and more tenuous as the time for the millennium's arrival was placed farther and farther into a vague and distant future. As the greatly anticipated decade of the 1660s passed uneventfully, the Collegiants' hopes for a future transformation of the world dimmed as they faced the prospect that the corrupt premillennial world might in fact be a semipermanent or even a permanent state of affairs. In this way the pessimistic view of the temporal world derived from Collegiant chiliasm laid the foundations for the development within the colleges of a secularized view of the world that saw it separated from divine influence and control.

Chiliastic ideas prepared the way and provided a historical framework for the further development of Collegiant thought in secular directions. It was no mere coincidence that the decade of the 1660s and the years that followed were the most important period of intellectual ferment in the colleges, a period that saw the beginnings of Collegiant rationalism. But millenarianism was only a beginning point for the evolution of the Rijnsburger worldview. As Collegiant thinkers explored the implications of Chiliastic ideas for the condition of the Christian churches of the seventeenth century they developed a program of religious reform that would permit pious Christians to continue a devout life in a world unholy. With these ideas Rijnsburger thought moved beyond chiliasm to a new view of humanity, society, and religion. This extraordinary step was largely the work of an extraordinary man: Galenus Abrahamsz., leader of the Amsterdam college.

Chapter Four

GALENUS ABRAHAMSZ.: A CHURCH UNHOLY

Galenus, who no man to his own ideas would bind,
And who his own imperfections does gladly confess
Who no apostolic church in this day can find;
He is the vigilant cock against all unreasonableness.

(Galenus, die geen mensch aan zijns verstand wil binden,
En d'onvolmaakheid van zijn zelf, zeer graag belijdt
Die geen Apostelkerk, in deze tijd, kan vinden;
Die is de wakk're Haan, daar 't onverstand op bijt.)
—Jan Zoet

CHILIASTIC PESSIMISM concerning the state of the natural world contributed to the formation of a unique and radical Rijnsburger critique of the Christian churches of the seventeenth century. This Collegiant view of the church combined millenarian ideas with other ideas inherited from the Anabaptist and radical spiritualist traditions of the sixteenth century to produce a sweeping condemnation of all of the established Christian churches of the day, thus putting the Collegiants squarely in the vanguard of the Second Reformation of the seventeenth century. This view of the church, which was championed by the Amsterdam Collegiant leader Galenus Abrahamsz., also took the Rijnsburgers another step closer to a secularized worldview.

The Collegiants' conception of the premillennial world as corrupt and degenerate inevitably influenced their view of the Christian churches that existed in that world. By living in the decayed world these churches could not but share in the general corruption. This view fit well with the idea of the Christian church and its history that the Collegiants inherited from the Anabaptists and spiritualists. These radical reformers believed that the Christian church as a whole had been in irreversible decline ever since it had lost its pristine spirituality at a very early date, either immediately following the death of the apostles or under the emperor Constantine. The Collegiants followed many earlier radical reformers in rejecting all of the visible, institutional churches of their day as corrupt, worldly, and devoid of divine authority. The Collegiants furthermore condemned the Reformation of the sixteenth century not only for failing in its mission of

MICAT INTER OMNES.

GALENUS wezen leeft op 't velt van dit papier,
Zyn tong alleen is stom; kon die de banden breken,
Zy zou hier hemelval, en doctorakels spreken,
En herten blaken met een toorts van heilig vier.
In andre vintmen minst welsprekenheit en zeden,
Maer hier zyn bei volmaekt, de deugt en kracht van reden.

C. vander Sye excudit   J. Antonides.

3. Galenus Abrahamsz.

reforming the church, but also for actually making the religious situation worse by giving rise to factional quarreling and spiritual hatred. For the Rijnsburgers, the corruption of the Christian churches and the failure of the Reformation provided striking evidence of a widening separation from God. God apparently no longer gave divine inspiration and direction to people on earth, even to those involved in the important work of reforming the church. It seemed to many Collegiants that God had actually given up on both church and world.

Like the Anabaptists and spiritualists before them, the Collegiants still held out hope that pious Christians could continue to practice their religion despite the corruption of church and world. According to the Rijnsburgers, the few truly spiritual souls left in the midst of the decadent world made up an invisible church that was not corrupted by contact with worldly sin and evil. While this small community of believers could not alone reverse the general tide of decay in the world or rebuild the true visible church of Christ, these pious souls could meet together in small groups to pray, discuss religious questions, read the Bible, and help each other to lead spiritual lives despite the sinfulness of the surrounding world. The spirtualist Kaspar Schwenkfeld had considered the small conventicles of followers that he set up in south Germany during the sixteenth century as meeting places for the pious remnant in a world unholy, and this was also the function that Adam Boreel, Galenus Abrahamsz., and their followers envisioned for the Rijnsburger colleges.

The conception of an invisible church meeting temporarily in colleges formed the nucleus of Rijnsburger Second Reformation plans for the improvement of religious life in a corrupt secular world. Unlike the reformers of the previous century, however, the Rijnsburgers did not consider their colleges to be the one true church of Christ in exclusive possession of divine inspiration and revelation. The Collegiants concluded from the church's history of corruption, and especially from what they perceived as the failure of the Protestant Reformation, that God no longer gave his inspiration or revelation to anybody in the secular world. The Rijnsburgers thus became convinced that there was no true church of Christ in the corrupt premillennial world.

The Collegiant critique of the Christian churches of the seventeenth century was developed and popularized in the Amsterdam college by its leader, Galenus Abrahamsz. (1622–1706). Galenus's criticism of the visible churches had roots that stretched back deep into the Radical Reformation of the sixteenth century. The radical spiritualists Sebastian Franck and Kaspar Schwenkfeld first championed the idea of the corruption of all visible churches, and their ideas were transmitted into the Low Countries in their own writings and those of their disciples, especially the humanist Dirk Volckertsz. Coornhert. Coornhert's works were read by Adam Boreel (1602–1665), cofounder of the Amsterdam college, who adopted the spiritualist view of the church and passed it on to his own disciple Galenus Abrahamsz. Galenus and his follower Pieter Serrarius further developed the spiritualist critique of the church by combining it with Collegiant millenarian ideas, thus producing a potent fusion of concepts that had great appeal in the colleges. Because of the great influence that Galenus had not only in the Amsterdam college but throughout the entire Rijnsburger movement during the second half of the seventeenth century, the doctrine of church decay became a standard component of Collegiant thought after 1655.

The earliest roots of the Collegiant critique of the visible churches can be traced to the teachings of the spiritualists Franck and Schwenkfeld during the sixteenth century. For both men, the essential element of the true Christian religion was what they called the "inner light": the direct inspiration of the Holy Spirit in the soul of the individual believer. The inner light gave the believer religious truth in the form of God's direct revelation as well as the inner faith that insured individual salvation. For the spiritualists religion was an individual and inward experience, and for this reason they devalued the forms and practices of ecclesiastical institutions. According to Franck, the believer in possession of the inner light needed none of the external trappings of religion offered by the visible churches. If the believer did not have the inner light, however, all of the ceremonies, sacraments, confessions, and practices of the visible churches would be of no avail. Franck believed that none of the religious groups of his day possessed divine truth and therefore no visible church could claim to be the one, true church of God. Because Franck did not feel at home in any of the religious groups of his day, he set out to establish an invisible, spiritual church that would have no outward ceremonies or sacraments. This invisible church would be a collection of true believers gathered in the unity of the spirit and governed without external rules or regulations by God's eternal, invisible word.[1]

While Franck believed that true Christians no longer needed the visible churches, Schwenkfeld maintained that divine intervention would restore the true visible church of the apostles on earth at some future time. This restored church would be led by prophets inspired by the Holy Spirit. In his own day, however, Schwenkfeld saw no divinely inspired prophets who could lead the faithful to religious truth, and he denied that the Lutheran, Reformed, Anabaptist, Catholic, or any other visible church was the true church of Christ. True Christians were spread throughout the world in the many competing churches and sects, Schwenkfeld main-

[1] *ME*, vol. 1, pp. 363–364.

tained, and he urged these true believers to come together to form conventicles in order to console, exhort, and instruct each other in religious truth. These conventicles would not be churches, Schwenkfeld insisted, and their members would not abandon their memberships in the established churches. They would simply meet together in informal gatherings for fellowship and mutual support while they patiently awaited the future restoration of the true visible church by God. Schwenkfeld put his ideas into practice by setting up spiritualist conventicles in many cities and towns in his native Silesia and throughout southern Germany. In these conventicles believers met for sessions of prayer, prophecy, and Bible study. The members of Schwenkfeld's conventicles rejected any association with the secular state, used no external sacraments and practiced great toleration. Members of the conventicle in Strassbourg fasted prior to their meetings, in which they prayed and prophesied together.[2] In these sixteenth-century Schwenkfelder conventicles one can easily recognize a blueprint for the later Rijnsburger colleges.

The humanist Dirk Volckertsz. Coornhert, a disciple of Franck and Schwenkfeld, was one of the most important sources for the introduction of spiritualist ideas into Dutch religious life during the later sixteenth century.[3] Coornhert was born in Amsterdam, but he spent much of his youth abroad in Spain and Portugal. Upon his return to Amsterdam he married Cornelia Simons, a portionless gentlewoman, a marriage that so enraged his father that Coornhert was disinherited. Having thus to seek his own way in the world Coornhert settled in Haarlem, where he became an expert in copper-plate engraving and etching. After establishing himself in this vocation, Coornhert was seized by a desire to read the Bible and the church fathers in their original languages. Although well past the age of thirty, Coornhert taught himself Greek and Latin, becoming so proficient in these languages that he soon published translations of Cicero, Seneca, and Boethius. In 1562 Coornhert was appointed secretary to the city of Haarlem, and in his new position he took an active part in the Dutch struggle against Spain by drawing up a manifesto for William of Orange in which the prince declared himself in favor of religious toleration. Despite his patriotism, however, Coornhert was unwilling to take part in the military side of the rebellion. For this reason he spent most of his later years in voluntary exile in Cleves, where he still occasionally wrote tracts

---

[2] McLaughlin, *Caspar Schwenkfeld*, pp. 138–143. On the spiritualists, see also Rufus Jones, *Spiritual Reformers in the Sixteenth and Seventeenth Centuries* (London, 1914); and Williams, *The Radical Reformation*.

[3] Jones, p. 118; Bergsma, pp. 58–59. See also Wiebe Bergsma, "Schwenkfeld in the Netherlands: Aggaeus van Albada (c. 1525–1587)," in Erb, ed., *Schwenkfeld and Early Schwenkfeldians*.

in the service of the House of Orange. Returning to Holland late in life, Coornhert died in Gouda in 1590.[4]

In his many religious writings Coornhert showed himself a champion of nonconfessional spiritualism and religious toleration. For Coornhert, true religion was always inward and spiritual, a direct experience of the soul. He thus had little interest in ecclesiastical tradition, and he believed all external forms of religion to be of value only as stages of preparation for the true, inner religion. He criticized the major Protestant reformers of the sixteenth century for putting too much stress on externals and he declared that a true reformation of religion would concentrate on developing the invisible, spiritual church.[5]

Coornhert's spiritualism led him to criticize the visible churches of his day, which he believed had erred by putting outer forms of religion above the true, spiritual love of God. For this reason Coornhert saw all of the visible congregations as corrupt, and he encouraged truly pious Christians to withdraw from these churches and to live their lives apart from institutional religion. He urged true believers patiently to await the coming of new, divinely inspired apostles who would be sent by God into the world to reform the decayed visible churches and to reunite all of the many Christian sects into one universal church of Christ. During this period of waiting, which could be lengthy, Coornhert advised Christians to develop a kind of interim organization or community apart from the established churches within which they could carry on a simple, collective religious life. He saw this interim organization as a purely human and secular institution having no preachers, doctrines, or ceremonies and not claiming to be the one, holy church. All members of this community would enjoy the right of free speech in religious meetings for the purpose of mutual Christian education, and Scripture would be the sole foundation for religious belief.[6] In these ideas the influence of Schwenkfeld was clearly evident, and here, too, in embryo, was the outline for the future Collegiant movement. It could well have been these ideas that inspired Gijsbert van der Kodde in his founding of the Rijnsburg college, and it was certainly these ideas that made Coornhert's view of the church so attractive to Adam Boreel and the other leaders of the Amsterdam college.

Coornhert developed his spiritualistic theories in the midst of the bitter passions of the late Reformation era and the stormy religious conflicts of the Dutch revolt. This was a time of great turmoil within the Christian community of Europe, and it must indeed have seemed to many people that all of the visible churches had gone astray. In view of the great con-

---

[4] Jones, pp. 106–107; *EB*, vol. 8, p. 92.

[5] Jones, pp. 109–112.

[6] Ibid., pp. 112–113.

fusion, distrust, and divisiveness produced by the Reformation, Coornhert concluded that no established church with state protection and doctrinal authority could foster true belief.[7] His ideas struck a receptive
chord in Adam Boreel, who further developed the theory of church decay
and introduced it into Collegiant thought.

Boreel was born in 1602 in the city of Middelburg, in Zeeland, the son
of Jacob Boreel van Duynbeke and Maria Gremmink. His family had a
strong Protestant background beginning with his grandfather Pieter, who
had been forced to flee to England to escape the advance of Alva's armies.
Adam grew up in a household that was both fervently Calvinistic and
decidedly humanistic in atmosphere. Adam's brother Johaan was a close
friend of Hugo Grotius, greatest of seventeenth-century Dutch humanists,
while another brother, Willem, moved in very cosmopolitan circles as a
result of his position as an ambassador of the States General to several
European countries. All three Boreel brothers had strong interests in science and literature, and these interests led Adam to enroll in Leiden University during the fall of 1628.

During his five years at Leiden, Boreel devoted most of his effort to the
study of theology, and through these studies he came into contact with
the conservative professor of theology Andreas Rivetus (1572–1651). In
a series of discussions with Rivetus in 1632, Boreel began to develop his
own theological ideas. While he was a student at the university Boreel
might also have attended meetings of the Collegiants in nearby Rijnsburg,
as this was a common practice for Leiden theology students during the
1620s and 1630s, but no solid evidence of such visits exists. In any case,
Boreel ended his studies at Leiden late in 1632 and immediately made a
trip to England, where his tolerant manner and developing religious ideas
brought him into contact with a group of religious radicals. His associations with these radicals, whom the government considered dangerous,
caused Boreel to be imprisoned in England for a few months. After being
released thanks to the mediation of English friends, Boreel returned home
to Middelburg, shaken by his experience. In Middelburg he began to
study theology again. At first his primary interest was in the study of the
Old Testament and the Mishnach, because of his concern with the conversion of the Jews to Christianity, but his interests soon turned to other
areas. In 1644 Boreel withdrew to the isolation of a small hut outside of
Middelburg to concentrate on the writing of his first and greatest original
theological work, *Ad legem et ad testimonium*.[8]

In *Ad legem* Boreel maintained that every true ecclesiastical institution
on earth had to be founded on the direct authority of Christ. Christ had

---

[7] Roldanus, *Zeventiende eeuwse qeestesbloei*, pp. 14–15; Williams, pp. 774–775.
[8] Schneider, pp. 32–44.

given this divine authority to the first Christian church both in the form
of his Holy Spirit and in the form of the Holy Scripture. For Boreel, the
Holy Scripture was an infallible guide to salvation and the sole true foundation of belief for the church, while the Holy Spirit was given to believers to enable them to correctly interpret and proclaim the divine word.
Jesus and the apostles had been inspired by the Holy Spirit to proclaim
the word of God to the world, and the leaders of the second generation
of the church had been similarly inspired to continue the work of the
apostles. After the second generation, however, the truly inspired preachers of the word vanished from the church, Boreel declared. As the early
church became involved in worldly politics it broke its spiritual covenant
with Christ, and as a result it lost the inspiration of the Holy Spirit. Rapid
decline followed. Without divine guidance in the preaching of the word
many people went about teaching false doctrines, and as a result schisms
arose in the church. For Boreel, as for the spiritualist Sebastian Franck,
the spiritual decline of the Christian church began during its early period
and continued up to his own day.[9]

Boreel saw the growing confessionalism of the Christian churches of
the seventeenth century as clear evidence of their spiritual corruption. Before its fall the first true Christian church had never permitted any fallible
human teachings or doctrines to be considered of equal value with the
Holy Scripture, Boreel maintained. The apostolic church never adopted
confessions or catechisms containing anything that was not clearly stated
in Scripture. Such nonbiblical confessions could only have been admitted
into the church if God directly commanded it, Boreel argued, but no such
divine charge was ever made. For this reason, when humanly constructed
creeds and confessions began to make their appearance in the church during the third generation it was a certain sign of the church's spiritual decay. Similarly, no special divine command had been given to the Christian
churches of the seventeenth century to allow them to adopt as authoritative nonbiblical creeds and confessions composed by men, Boreel argued,
and thus all such confessions were clear evidence of the spiritual decadence of these churches. Boreel demanded that all humanly developed
doctrines and confessions be immediately removed from church life in
order to leave the Bible as the sole foundation of the Christian religion.
All churches built upon the foundation of human doctrine he considered
to be disloyal to God and lacking in the divine sanction that was necessary for them to conduct their services in God's name.[10]

Boreel believed the Christian churches of his day to be corrupt and
decadent despite the efforts at religious renewal made by the Protestant

[9] Ibid., pp. 44–47.
[10] Ibid., pp. 49, 59.

reformers of the preceding century. Boreel considered the efforts of the
reformers illegitimate because God had not given them a direct command
to establish a new and inspired visible church of Christ. But even though
God had not ordered the rebuilding of the true visible church, he would
permit the construction of a temporary congregation or interim church in
which true believers could carry on a pious religious life. Following
Coornhert, Boreel saw this interim church, or "church of toleration" as
he called it, as a purely human and secular institution without divine authority. Because the established Christian churches had in effect cut themselves off from God by rejecting the Bible as their sole religious foundation, Boreel urged all true Christians to leave these churches. Once they
had severed their links with these corrupt churches, true Christians could
carry on a pious religious life through private prayer and Bible reading
until such time as an interim "church of toleration" could be set up to
provide a new basis for Christian fellowship and collective worship. Boreel believed the colleges that he established across the Low Countries to
be the beginnings of this "church of toleration."[11]

Boreel modeled his conception of the interim "church of toleration" on
Coornhert's ideas. Boreel's temporary church would be based entirely on
biblical principles but would make no pretense of having divine authority. Because the church would not possess the divine inspiration necessary
infallibly to proclaim God's word, it would appoint no preachers and its
services would consist simply of Bible reading followed by a discussion of
Scripture in which all members present would have the right of free
speech.[12] Boreel's ideas also perfectly mirrored the practices of the college
meeting in Rijnsburg. It is not surprising that Boreel joined with the Collegiant Daniel De Breen to establish the Amsterdam college in 1646.

All of the elements of the spiritualist critique of the visible churches, as
it had been modified and passed on by Coornhert, were present in *Ad
legem*. Boreel stressed the corrupt condition of all established churches as
well as the need for true Christians to leave these churches and establish
temporary religious gatherings in which the pious could worship individually and freely. Boreel's work was a harsh indictment of the growing
confessionalism and doctrinal rigidity of the established churches. In
place of the external forms and human formulas of the institutional
churches, Boreel favored a religion of individual Bible reading and free
discussion. In his view, the interim church that he proposed, as well as all
of the established churches of his day, were humanly constructed religious institutions lacking the authority, sanction, and inspiration of God.
The idea of the separation of all human religious institutions from God

---

[11] Ibid., pp. 51–52.
[12] Goeters, p. 50; Lindenboom, *Stiefkinderen van het Christendom*, pp. 342–343.

acted as a powerful weapon with which to attack the authority of the ecclesiastical institutions of the seventeenth century, and it also brought Boreel an important step closer to a worldview that denied divine intervention in the secular world. If God did not inspire his own church, how could he be expected to intervene in other aspects of secular life? While Boreel himself did not draw such radical conclusions from his ideas, some of his followers among the Rijnsburgers did, especially after they combined Boreel's theories with the pessimistic millenarian conception of the temporal world introduced into the colleges by De Breen and others.

Boreel completed work on *Ad legem* in 1645 and immediately set out to put his theories into practice. In his native city of Middelburg he founded a small congregation that had no ties to any of the established churches. This was the first of the so-called "Boreelist colleges," others of which Boreel soon established in the cities of Rotterdam, Vlaardingen, Kampen, and Zwolle. In these independent congregations Boreel spread his own religious views. He considered this network of colleges to be the beginning of the interim "church of toleration," the last refuge of sincere Christians in a world in which the established churches had become too corrupt to retain the loyalty of pious people.

In 1646 Boreel arrived in Amsterdam and joined with Daniel De Breen in founding a college there. While the other Boreelist colleges lasted only a very short time, the Amsterdam college developed important links to the Rijnsburger movement through the participation of De Breen. Shortly after its establishment, the Amsterdam college became a vital member of the larger Collegiant brotherhood. In this way Boreel became a Rijnsburger and the Collegiants first came into contact with his ideas. In 1650 the young Mennonite preacher Galenus Abrahamsz. joined the Amsterdam college, where he immediately came under Boreel's influence. Thanks mainly to Boreel's guidance, Galenus was converted to the doctrine of church decay. By 1651 he was discussing Boreel's idea of the "church of toleration" in the Rijnsburger college, and before the year was out he founded a separate college among his own Mennonite followers where Boreel's ideas also were discussed. The college among the Mennonites quickly developed links to Boreel's own group, and after 1651 the two merged into one Rijnsburger college in which Galenus came to play a leading role. Because Boreel's thought included much that was already dear to the Collegiants—such as the rejection of clergy in favor of free speech—his ideas were easily incorporated into the Rijnsburger worldview. It was Galenus's eloquent advocacy of the theory of church decay that insured a prominent place for this idea within the mainstream of Collegiant thought. Boreel himself, like De Breen, tended to move more and more into the background of Collegiant affairs as Galenus asserted his strong leadership over the Amsterdam college beginning in the early

1650s. In 1654 Boreel again traveled to England, not returning to Amsterdam until 1660. He died in 1665.[13]

Galenus Abrahamsz. was Boreel's intellectual heir. Through his influential writings and his magnetic personality he spread and popularized Boreel's ideas within the Collegiant movement and beyond. Galenus presented these ideas to the Collegiants not in Boreel's scholarly Latin but in a Dutch version that even today radiates Galenus's own personal spiritual warmth and intellectual vitality. Although in 1650 Latin was still the common currency of universities and humanists, writing in the vernacular assured an author of a much wider audience among the intellectually active urban middle classes, whose interest in religious reform led them to swell Collegiant ranks. With these people Galenus communicated on an almost intuitive level. Even more important than the fact that he wrote in Dutch was the way in which Galenus and his disciple Serrarius fit Boreel's ideas into the Collegiant conceptual framework by integrating them into the chiliastic worldview so popular in the colleges. In this way Galenus produced a thoroughly Collegiant conception of the condition of the Christian churches of the seventeenth century that won rapid approval among the Rijnsburgers. Into accepted ideas of a decayed premillennial world the idea of a decayed church fit like a piece in a puzzle.

Galenus Abrahamsz., nicknamed "*de Haan*" (the cock), was born in Zierikzee, a small town in Zeeland not far from Boreel's native Middelburg, on 8 October 1622. His parents were Abraham Geleynsz. and Katrijntje Gillis, both pious Mennonites. After completing Latin school in Zierikzee, Galenus enrolled at Leiden University in 1642 to study medicine. Following his graduation in 1645 he moved to Amsterdam, where he set up practice.[14] Shortly after settling down Galenus joined Amsterdam's United Mennonite congregation, which met in an old brewery on the Singel that the congregation had renamed "*Het Lam*" (the lamb). In 1646 he married the daughter of Abraham Bierens, one of the leaders of the Lamb congregation, and when his father-in-law died in 1648 Galenus was chosen to replace him as lay preacher. Thus began, almost by accident, Galenus's long and distinguished career as one of the most influential and respected religious leaders in seventeenth-century Amsterdam. A man of uncommon personal appeal, extraordinary eloquence, and unusual power as a writer, Galenus made a lasting impression on the Dutch Mennonite movement and became the most influential single force in Collegiantism after 1650. With the grace of his personality and the

[13] Schneider, pp. 52–70.
[14] *ME*, vol. 3, pp. 431–435.

strength of his mind he forcefully wrote his name into Dutch religious history.

Upon his assumption of the office of Mennonite preacher Galenus was required, like all such appointees, to make a confession of his personal belief. His confession stressed an active spiritual life over precision of doctrine, but it made no specific mention of the orthodox teachings on the Trinity and the divinity of Christ. These omissions led some conservative members of the congregation to suspect Galenus of heterodox opinions on these points. Thus began what was to become a long history of mutual suspicion and rivalry between Galenus and the old guard in the Lamb congregation.

Shortly after Galenus assumed his office in the Lamb congregation an episode took place that had an immediate bearing on the new pastor's religious development. The Amsterdam Waterlander Mennonite congregation, a rival of Galenus's church, offered to open discussions with the Lamb congregation concerning the possibility of a union of the two congregations. The Waterlanders were much more liberal than Galenus's congregation, chiefly because they rejected the use of confessions and catechisms much as did the Collegiants. For this reason the offer of union stirred up opposition among conservatives in the Lamb congregation. The conservatives favored the use of confessions because they believed that obedience to such doctrinal formulas was an essential guarantee of the spiritual purity of their congregation, which they considered to be the one and only truly inspired church of Christ on earth. Galenus favored the Waterlander union as a first step toward an eventual reunification of the entire Christian church, but in 1649 the Lamb congregation voted to turn down the offer. This disappointing vote came only after much bitter squabbling within the congregation, which initiated Galenus into the often impassioned differences of opinion that existed among the Mennonites over the nature of church authority and the legitimacy of the claim of any congregation to exclusive possession of divine inspiration.[15] These debates were of a profound nature in a century in which it was common for every church to claim that it was the only true Christian church on earth. Galenus's experiences during the Waterlander union debate helped to form his later views on ecclesiastical authority and the condition of the established churches of his day.

The year 1650 was eventful for Galenus. At a synod of the United Mennonite church held in Haarlem and attended by the leaders of the Lamb congregation as well as by representatives from congregations in Haarlem and several other cities, the church officially adopted a confession of faith

[15] H. W. Meihuizen, *Galenus Abrahamsz. 1622–1706. Strijder voor een onbeperkte verdraagzaamheid en verdediger van het Doperse Spiritualisme* (Haarlem, 1954), pp. 32–39.

for its members. In addition, the synod forbade members of United Mennonite congregations from listening to any preacher who opposed the
confession's articles. Galenus was extremely disturbed by these events.
He placed little importance on doctrines and confessions and he felt that
by concentrating on these matters the church was turning away from its
true purpose—the fostering of inward religion and love of God. Galenus
also resented the authority that the synod gave to Mennonite preachers
as protectors and enforcers of the new confession. It was at this critical
juncture in his intellectual and spiritual development that Galenus met
Adam Boreel, and in his state of religious reflection he was very receptive
to Boreel's nonconfessional ideas. Brought by Boreel into contact with the
Amsterdam college, Galenus soon began to consider Boreel's theory of
church decay as well as other Rijnsburger ideas. Before the year was out
Galenus had joined the college and had taken up Boreel's ideas with the
zeal of a new convert.

Galenus's association with the Collegiants, who were widely suspected
of Socinianism, immediately brought him renewed criticism from the
Mennonite conservatives. While the majority of the Lamb congregation
remained loyal to Galenus because of his sincere piety, his enemies continued their efforts to discredit him. In these efforts they were aided by a
crisis that developed in 1655 when the Collegiants requested permission
to move their meetings into the Mennonite chapel. Galenus supported the
request but the conservatives objected strongly. They accused Galenus of
trying to turn the Lamb congregation into a Rijnsburger college and they
demanded that he stop attending college meetings. The Collegiant request
was refused and the entire episode succeeded only in releasing the bitterness and pent-up hostility of Galenus's critics, who called him a Socinian
and accused him of trying to smuggle heretical doctrines into the congregation. In order to counter these accusations and to clarify for his fellow
Mennonites his true beliefs concerning religion and the Christian church,
Galenus held a number of discussions with conservative leaders during
1657 in which he outlined his opinions. Galenus was dissatisfied with the
outcome of these talks because he believed that his opponents still mis-
understood his views, and for this reason he produced a written explanation of his position on the nature and condition of the church, the *Bedenckingen over den Toestant der Sichtbare Kercke Christi op Aerden,
Kortelijck in XIX Artikelen Voor-Ghestelt* . . . (Considerations regarding
the state of the visible church of Christ on Earth, briefly proposed in nineteen articles . . . [1657]).[16] This work was to become one of the most

---

[16] Ibid., pp. 40–57. David Spruyt coauthored the *XIX Artikelen* with Galenus. Spruyt
was the chief supporter of Galenus and his ideas within the Mennonite congregation, but as
Spruyt wrote nothing of his own it is difficult to determine the extent to which he influenced
the content of the *XIX Artikelen*.

important documents in the history of both the Collegiant movement and Dutch Mennonitism. It was a powerful statement of the Collegiant conception of the state of the Christian churches and it contained views that became a major foundation for the secularized worldview that developed in the colleges.

The central theme of the *XIX Artikelen* was the great contrast that Galenus perceived between the first, apostolic Christian church and the congregations of the seventeenth century. In reaction to the conservative Mennonites' claim of exclusive divine authority for their church, Galenus set out to show that such claims were illegitimate in the seventeenth century. For Galenus, the one and only true Christian church had been the church of the New Testament. Christ himself appointed the apostles, prophets, evangelists, pastors, and teachers of that church and it was their task to build up the new church, carry on its services, and spread the Gospel. In order for these divinely appointed officers to complete their tasks properly, Christ provided them with the necessary "gifts of the Holy Spirit," special abilities resulting from divine inspiration. These abilities included wisdom and the knowledge of all truths and secrets of religion, the ability to proclaim infallibly the divine truth of the Gospel to all peoples, the ability to distinguish divine from satanic spirits, the strength to punish God's enemies, the ability to make other people teachers of divine wisdom by imparting to them the necessary gifts of the Holy Spirit, and, finally, the ability to perform miracles. Because Christ gave the servants of the first church the divine ability to proclaim infallibly God's truth, everyone who heard these first Christian teachers announce the Gospel could be fully certain of its truth and could follow these teachings without any doubt or hesitation. The first leaders of the church were therefore truly inspired ambassadors of Christ who spoke directly for the Lord himself, Galenus declared. In fact, every single member of the apostolic church was gifted with the Holy Spirit in the exact measure of his belief. Both shepherds and flock were baptized through one spirit into one body: the church of Christ.[17]

In stark contrast to the first true church, Galenus saw the Christian churches of the seventeenth century as having fallen into total spiritual decay. Over the centuries following the death of the apostles the church had gradually declined into corruption through a careless neglect of its gifts. The Protestant Reformation had been unable to remedy this situation because mere humans could neither build nor rebuild the divine church without God's instruction and inspiration. For this reason, anyone

[17] Galenus Abrahamsz. and David Spruyt, *Bedenckingen over den Toestant der Sichtbare Kercke Christi op Aerden, Kortelijck in XIX Artikelen Voor-Ghestelt: en aen onse mededienaren, op den 11 Januarij 1657, Schriftelijck over-ghelevert* (Amsterdam, 1657), pp. 2–5, 20.

who hoped to reform the corrupt church would need a direct command from God to do so in order to succeed. The builders of the first church had received such a divine command and Christ had given them the gifts of the Holy Spirit required for their task. But nowhere in the New Testament was there any command or example instructing people to rebuild or restore the true church, and thus the Protestant reformers of the sixteenth century had neither the divine command nor the gifts of the Holy Spirit required to rebuild the church. For this reason, no church erected by these reformers could be the true, inspired church of Christ, according to Galenus. The Protestant churches of the seventeenth century, having been established without divine authority, did not resemble the true apostolic church in either institution or nature, Galenus declared, and this was a criticism that he did not hesitate to apply to his own congregation:

> These [humanly erected] churches, and among them our own, both with respect to their institution and with respect to their present state, wholly fail to conform to the institution and state of the first and only true church, which alone, and no other, is given by the New Testament the name church of God.

> (Dat mede dese soo op gerechte en ingestelde kerken, en onder dese ook die Gemeente, daer wij tegenwoordigh nu noch onder sorteren/[so ten opsichte van haer op-rechtinge/en instellinge/als ten aensien van haer tegenwoordigen stant/en staet:] heel niet conform zijn, de op-rechtinge/instellinge/en standt/ van die eerste en eenige kerk: wien alleen/en geen ander/de naem van een Gemeente Gods . . . in de schriften des Nieuwen Testements ghegeven wordt.)[18]

For Galenus, the many divisions within what should have been one universal church of Christ provided clear evidence of the corrupt condition of seventeenth-century Christianity. Despite the many different parts into which the church was divided, each and every sect, no matter how small, continued to consider itself the one and only true church of Christ. Even though none of these churches could produce anything resembling gifts of the Holy Spirit or miracles as signs of their divine institution and authority, they nevertheless refused to recognize that they had no such authority, Galenus argued. In his view, the churches of his day were a product of the efforts of pious but uninspired people, and they were thus constructed according to imperfect human knowledge and ability. The officers of these churches had none of the spiritual gifts or divine authority possessed by their predecessors in the apostolic church. The churches of the seventeenth century had been erected by well-meaning people who hoped that their efforts would be pleasing to God, Galenus continued, but God had as yet given no sign of his pleasure. Galenus therefore called

---

[18] Ibid., pp. 5–6.

upon all Christians to recognize that their churches were human institutions without divine authority, and he appealed to them to carry on their religious life with humility and toleration and without binding confessions.[19]

Galenus described in graphic terms the difference between the first Christian church and the churches of his own day. The first church was in direct contact with God through the inspiration of the Holy Spirit, but the corrupt churches of the seventeenth century were cut off from such divine inspiration. Between the apostolic church and the churches of his own day Galenus saw a wide gulf separating two radically different worlds: the one holy and inspired by God, the other unholy and spiritually corrupt; the one sacred and spiritual, the other secular and unspiritual. The idea of a church and world unholy, separated from God's influence, was a revolutionary notion posing a direct threat to the existence of the traditional providential worldview.

These unconventional ideas unleashed a storm of controversy within the Mennonite congregation at the same time that they were being eagerly discussed in the college. Galenus had declared to his conservative critics that their church was not the one true church of God. What was worse, he had maintained that the true church was nowhere to be found on earth. In response to the *XIX Artikelen* Galenus's critics produced a refutation of his ideas that contained so many misrepresentations that Galenus felt obliged to publish a reply further explaining his ideas. The *Nadere verklaringe van de XIX Artikelen* (Further explanation of the nineteen articles [1659]) was an extremely important work because it established a connection between the spiritualistic theory of church decay and Collegiant millenarian ideas. The work also contained what was to become the standard Collegiant criticism of the Protestant Reformation.

In the *Nadere verklaringe* Galenus combined his idea of the corruption of the churches with the chiliastic vision of a decadent premillennial world, but he held out hope for the reformation of both church and world in the millennium. In the introduction to the *Nadere verklaringe* Galenus wrote that he intended his book to serve as an introduction to the "times to come," times that would be a period "of the re-erecting of all things." According to Galenus, God had spoken of the coming days through the mouths of his prophets throughout the ages, and he had promised that in that period "the decayed church will again be erected to its previous splendor and restored in the strength of Jesus Christ." Galenus therefore called upon all pious Christians to recognize the utter decay of the churches of the seventeenth century and to wait for the Lord to come again in the millennium to restore the true church of Christ: "People must

[19] Ibid., pp. 7–8, 10.

rightfully learn to recognize the present condition of the Christian church, but at the same time, during the time of this decay, they should patiently wait until the Lord shall come" ("[Men moet] de tegenwoordige gheleghentheydt der kercke Christi rechtmatigh te leeren onderkennen . . . maer teghelijck oock, gedurende den tijdt deses vervals, sorghvuldighlijck te waken, tegens dat de Herre komen sal").[20]

Galenus urged that Christians should not themselves attempt to reform the corrupt church, but rather they should wait for Christ to do so in the millennuim. A true reformation of the church would require direct divine authority as well as the appropriate gifts of the Holy Spirit, Galenus explained, and any person claiming to have received such divine authority and gifts and to be an ambassador of Christ sent to rebuild the church would have to offer some proof of this divine inspiration—perhaps by performing a miracle. Galenus saw no such proof forthcoming from either the church leaders or their congregations in his own day, nor did he detect any signs of true inspiration among the great Protestant reformers of the sixteenth century.[21] For this reason Galenus declared that none of the congregations of his day could be considered the true church of Christ.

Galenus believed that the Protestant Reformation had been a failure because the Protestant reformers had neither divine authority nor inspiration to reform the church. He did not doubt the sincere motives of the reformers, but he insisted that their confessions, creeds, doctrines, and bans were merely human inventions. Galenus felt that it was crucial for all Christians to distinguish clearly between the true and holy church of Christ, built by the apostles but soon thereafter vanished from the earth, and the churches produced by the Reformation, which were divided, confused, and devoid of all divine inspiration. If believers did not make this vital distinction and continued stubbornly to insist that their own decayed churches were the true church of Christ, the Lord's return to earth to restore the true church might be delayed, Galenus warned. He also pointed to the abuse of supposed divine authority by clerics as another evil result of failing to make this important distinction between holy and unholy churches.[22]

Even though Galenus saw no chance for a true reform of the church before the millennium, he did believe that pious Christians could work for an improvement of their own religious lives in the temporal world.

---

[20] Galenus Abrahamsz. and David Spruyt, *Nadere verklaringe van de XIX Artikelen, Voor desen Door G. Abrahamsz. ende D. Spruyt aen hare Mede-dienaren over-ghegeven: Dienende tot Wederlegging van 't geschrift, genaemt: Antwoorde by forme van aenmerckingen, vragen, ende redenen, etc.* (Amsterdam, 1659), pp. viii–ix.

[21] Ibid., p. x.

[22] Ibid., pp. xi–xxi.

Following the conception of the interim church outlined in the writings of Coornhert and Boreel, Galenus put forward the model of the Rijnsburger college as an alternative form of religious organization in a world in which the established churches were hopelessly corrupt. According to Galenus, pious believers could carry on a religious life without pretense of divine authority by coming together to read the Bible and to educate, admonish, and comfort one another. Collective prayer, spiritual song, and other activities carried on humbly and in the hope of pleasing God could contribute to the improvement of religious life in the pre-millennial world. Galenus called on all Christians to practice toleration and to depend on the Bible as the sole foundation for belief and life.[23] Later Collegiants would adopt these ideas and use them as the basis for more elaborate programs of religious reform.

In his critique of the visible churches Galenus followed the spiritualist tradition handed down to him from Franck and Schwenkfeld, Coornhert and Boreel. Under the influence of these ideas Galenus considered the cessation of divine inspiration in the established churches, indeed in all institutional religious life, an accomplished fact. As a spiritualist, however, Galenus also found it necessary to preserve the possibility of divine inspiration of the individual soul even in the absence of general inspiration in the church. He addressed this difficult issue in another work, *Wederlegging van 't geschrift, genaemt: Antwoorde by forme van aenmerckingen, vragen ende redenen aen Laurens Hendricksz . . . overghegeven* (Refutation of the writing entitled: Answer by means of remarks, questions and reasons, given to Laurens Hendricksz. [1659]). By preserving the possibility for a certain kind of individual inspiration even in a world unholy, Galenus preserved the possibility of individual salvation in a decadent world and he also kept alive the tradition of spiritualism in the colleges. In the hands of Galenus's disciples Pieter Balling and Jarig Jelles, this spiritualism eventually would evolve into a form of intuitive rationalism.

Like Franck and Schwenkfeld, Galenus held that the church of Christ could be divided into the visible and the invisible. The true visible church, the external organization of people confessing Christ and provided with the gifts of the Holy Spirit, no longer existed on the earth. But even in the absence of a true visible church there were still some truly believing members of Christ's spiritual community on earth, he maintained. These few true believers were scattered among the corrupt churches, and they continued to be inspired by Christ's spirit in the midst of the general decay. Along with the saints in heaven, these pious survivors made up the invisible church of Christ.[24]

[23] Ibid., pp. x–xi.
[24] Galenus Abrahamsz., *Wederlegging van 't geschrift, genaemt: Antwoorde by forme van aenmerckingen, vragen ende redenen, etc.* (Amsterdam, 1659), pp. 6–8, 10–11.

But how could there be any spiritual souls left on earth if God's inspiration no longer reached the churches and religious institutions? This was a very difficult and yet a very important question, because without divine inspiration no one could be saved, since God's grace was generally considered to be a function of the Holy Spirit. Galenus answered these perplexing questions by maintaining that despite the general cessation of inspiration in the church, pious Christians could still receive some gifts of the Holy Spirit on a purely individual basis. This was possible because of a distinction he made between two basic kinds of these gifts.

According to Galenus, the gifts of the Holy Spirit given to the first church were general, miraculous, and extraordinary. He called these the *Heerlijkmaking* gifts: gifts that made the servants of the first church true ambassadors of Christ and inspired teachers capable of infallibly proclaiming and spreading the Holy Gospel. Galenus wrote that these gifts did not cease with the death of the apostles but were passed on to the second generation of the church, and the church remained divinely inspired all during the persecutions of the early years. When the emperor Constantine brought the secular state and the Christian church into alliance, however, the church was corrupted by secular influence. As a result, spiritual zeal slackened in the hearts of Christians, love for God was replaced by love for the world, and human superstition produced a pall of darkness and ignorance that descended over the church. An angry God responded by taking away the gifts of the Holy Spirit from the church, and thus it began its irreversible decline.[25] God continued, however, to provide some people in the church with gifts of the Holy Spirit on an individual basis in order to make personal salvation possible. These individual gifts were not considered by Galenus to be of the same kind as the extraordinary and general gifts of the first church. Galenus called these individual gifts the *Heiligmaking* (salvational) gifts, and he considered them to be of a lesser order than the *Heerlijkmaking* gifts. The *Heiligmaking* gifts enlightened the individual understanding, purified the heart and allowed the growth of love and virtue in the soul so that individual salvation would be possible. These gifts did not, however, provide the individual with inspired and infallible teaching abilities or prophetic powers to convert others.[26] These were not gifts of leadership or communication but purely personal gifts designed only to permit individual salvation. In this way Galenus kept open the avenue of personal salvation and preserved the possibility for a religion of individual spiritual illumination, but these personal gifts did not enable the inspired few to lead or

---

[25] Ibid., pp. 16–27; Galenus Abrahamsz., *Verdediging der Christenen die Doopsgezinden genaamd worden* (Amsterdam, 1699), pp. 18–24.

[26] Galenus Abrahamsz., *Korte grondstellingen van de Christelyke leere* (Amsterdam, 1677), pp. 65–67; Galenus Abrahamsz., *Wederlegging*, pp. 28–29.

teach others, to stem the tide of corruption in the world, or to rebuild the true, visible church. Galenus did not see humankind as entirely cut off from God, but because divine inspiration could only be individual and personal in nature all further possibility of true religion could be based only on the individual conscience. This radical separation of individual from institutional religion had characterized the spiritualist doctrine of the invisible church since the sixteenth century. This separation was also a point of extreme importance for the Collegiants, who, after accepting the hopeless decay of the established churches, founded their plans for religious reform on toleration and an individual understanding of religious truth.

Galenus's criticism of the church was an unqualified rejection of the sixteenth-century Reformation as well as a blanket condemnation of the corrupt state of seventeenth-century Christianity. He criticized the disunity, confessional rigidity and worldliness of the Protestant churches of his day and he offered an embryonic plan for a new reform, not of the visible church but of individual religious life. Galenus's ideas were essential in the formation of the secularizing trend in Collegiant thought because of their emphasis on the separation of man's religious institutions from God's inspiration. This sense of separation had several important consequences. It tended to put new emphasis on the human element in religion as it accentuated the human origins of existing churches. Because of its rejection of the teaching authority of the churches it established the primacy of the individual conscience as man's chief means of religious enlightenment. Among the Rijnsburgers this rejection of ecclesiastical authority eventually led to a dependence on individual human reason. For Galenus the fruits of chiliastic and Boreelist pessimism, mitigated by the spiritualist's hope for personal illumination, became a religion of individual spiritual enlightenment in a world unholy. For other Collegiants it was to become a religion of reason.

The *XIX Artikelen* and Galenus's subsequent writings on the nature of the church had a tremendous impact both on the Collegiant movement and on Galenus's own Mennonite congregation. Among the Rijnsburgers his ideas found broad acceptance, but in the Mennonite congregation they caused bitter debate and finally schism.

In the congregation of Het Lam the *XIX Artikelen* aroused a storm of indignation among conservatives. To these conventional men, Galenus's ideas seemed to attack the very heart of the church: its teaching authority and sacraments. The conservatives believed that God could only address his people through the inspired institution of the church, and they also believed that their own Mennonite congregation was a direct and undefiled descendant of the apostolic church and thus the one and only true

Christian church on earth. Such claims to the exclusive possession of divine authority were common to sixteenth- and seventeenth-century churches, and it was precisely for this reason that Galenus's ideas were such a bold departure from accepted views and at the same time such a serious threat to the traditional structure of religion. These radical ideas, when combined with Galenus's own great personal popularity among the Amsterdam Mennonites, were seen by the conservative party as extremely dangerous. The conservatives therefore took quick action to combat Galenus's ideas and to reduce his influence over other Mennonites.

A general meeting of conservative leaders of the United Mennonite congregations hastily and secretly gathered in the university town of Leiden in 1660, and there the frightened old guard agreed to make every effort to remove Galenus from his pastoral office. A special deputation was sent from the meeting to confront Galenus in Amsterdam and to demand his resignation. He refused. A substantial majority of Galenus's own congregation supported him in this decision, but several conservative leaders within the congregation continued to make things difficult for him. This internal conflict produced great bitterness on both sides as well as a flood of pamphlets directed against Galenus by his conservative opponents, the preachers Tobias Govertsz. and Samuel Apostool. The battle flared openly from the pulpit of Het Lam as the opposing preachers attacked each other in their sermons. To the populace of Amsterdam this conflict became known as the *Lammerenkrijg* (war of the lambs), after one of the pamphlets directed against Galenus. Non-Mennonites from all over the city flocked to sermons in Het Lam to witness the fireworks. In 1662 the opposing parties agreed to a temporary truce, but hostilities resumed later that same year when Pieter Locren, a supporter of Galenus, was chosen as one of the congregation's leaders.[27] During 1663 Galenus and Apostool exchanged a series of vituperative personal attacks from the pulpit and the Mennonite services were soon filled with such rancor that the municipal authorities intervened in the interests of public peace. Nevertheless, malicious pamphlets continued to pour from the presses and the conservatives tried unsuccessfully to exclude Galenus from communion. Galenus's opponents did manage to have him called before the Court of Holland in The Hague on charges of Socinianism, but the justices cleared him of those accusations. This act of extreme ill will only served to stoke the fires of hatred still higher. The final act in this bitter drama took place in 1664 when a dispute developed between the two parties over control of the congregational treasury. When the party of Galenus successfully asserted its control over the common funds, the conservative party broke away from the main congregation and formed its own assembly. The con-

[27] Meihuizen, pp. 58–83.

servatives set up their new church in an abandoned warehouse called "*De Zon*" (the sun) and thus became known as the "Zonnists."

Even with this secession the battle was not over. The Zonnists and Lammists continued to oppose each other at every possible opportunity, and each party sought to line up the support of other Mennonite congregations behind its own cause. In this way the Amsterdam dispute spread over the rest of the Netherlands and eventually tore apart the entire Dutch Mennonite movement. The Zonnists won many of the United Mennonite congregations to their side, but in 1668 the Lammists countered by finally making a union with the Waterlander Mennonites. The dispute continued to fester long after Galenus's death in 1706, and the divisions were not finally healed until 1801.[28]

The reception that Galenus's ideas found among the Collegiants was quite different. In the colleges the theory of church decay found a home, and the popularity of chiliastic ideas among the Rijnsburgers was instrumental in their acceptance of the idea of a church unholy. Not only was it easier to accept the notion of a decayed church where there was already such emphasis on the corrupt state of the premillennial world, but also the Rijnsburgers' belief in the coming of the millennium made it psychologically more bearable for them to view the world and church before that time as separated from divine inspiration.

In an age in which the traditional providential Christian worldview was still dominant, it would have been extremely difficult for most thoughtful people to make the transition all at once from belief in a world infused with the Holy Spirit to a view of the world in which the guiding hand of divine authority was largely absent. The chiliastic view of history made this transition possible for the Collegiants because it provided a middle ground that could be occupied by thinkers who were coming to see the world more and more in secular terms but who were not yet able to consider the world's separation from divine inspiration as final. During the crucial decade of the 1660s, when the millennium repeatedly failed to appear on the dates assigned for its arrival, what was initially an idea of temporary premillennial corruption began to take on an air of greater permanence for many Collegiants. The hope for the coming of the millennium helped to make the idea of church decay acceptable to the Collegiants and thus promoted the rise of secularism in the colleges, especially as that hope waned. In the case of the Rijnsburgers, traditional millenarianism functioned as a link between radical religion and the age of reason.

Among the many Collegiants who became proponents of Galenus's view of the church, the Amsterdam millenarian Pieter Serrarius best illus-

---

[28] Ibid., pp. 83–118; N. van der Zijpp, *Geschiedenis der Doopsgezinden in Nederland* (Arnhem, 1952), pp. 103–106.

trated the important Rijnsburger linkage between chiliasm and the theory of church decay in his important writing *De vertredinge des heyligen Stadts* . . . (The trampling of the Holy City [1659]). Serrarius was both a Rijnsburger and a member of the Lamb congregation, and it was in defense of Galenus against the attacks of his conservative Mennonite opponents that Serrarius wrote this work. Serrarius disagreed with those Mennonites who insisted on the right of their church to determine which people stood outside of salvation because, like Galenus, he considered the Mennonite church to be no more holy than any other church in the corrupt, premillennial world.[29]

According to Serrarius, the visible churches of the seventeenth century were worldly and decayed institutions that were not guided by the Holy Spirit. Even though these congregations invoked the name of Christ they did not have the special spiritual gifts of the first, true church. In reply to the many objections made against these ideas by Galenus's conservative critics, Serrarius declared that the very obvious decay of the visible churches should be bemoaned, not argued over, by all good Christians. After all, if any church in the world had the gifts of the Holy Spirit it would be clear to everyone, Serrarius maintained. The first Christians had such gifts and they thus "shone like shining stars in the darkness of the world, clearly showing that Christ was among them" ("als blinckende sterren in de duysternisse deses werelts uytluchtende ende oogen schijnlick betuygende, dat Christus onder haer was"). None of the churches of his own day could give such clear and indisputable evidence of divine guidance, Serrarius argued. All of the existing churches were structures built by men who had not been divinely authorized or gifted with God's spirit.[30]

Serrarius believed that the decay of the churches of his day had been foretold in biblical prophecy. In 2 Thess. 2, Paul predicted that there would be an age of terrible corruption in the church before Christ's return to earth, and Serrarius believed that this prophecy of premillennial decay had come true. He also cited Matt. 24–25, in which Christ predicted that before his second coming there would be a terrible period of persecution and division among Christians, and false Christs would arise to tempt the faithful. Serrarius interpreted this prophecy to mean that before the millennium arrived there would be a time in which the apostolic congregations would decay and vanish. Because Serrarius had no doubt that the arrival of the millennium was imminent, he believed himself to be living in the predicted period of church decay. For Serrarius and other Colle-

---

[29] Serrarius, *De vertredinge des heyligen stadts;* Hylkema, vol. 1, pp. 131–132; Meihuizen, pp. 63–64.

[30] Serrarius, *De vertredinge des heyligen stadts*, pp. i–v.

giant chiliasts, the biblical prophecies of premillennial decay were proof of the corruption of all seventeenth-century churches. Serrarius argued that all good Christians who expected the coming of the millennium had also to accept the idea of the corruption of all existing churches, because to deny this corruption would be tantamount to rejecting the millennium and thus denying Scripture. In a bizarre twist of logic, Serrarius considered it a denial of Scripture to consider the church on earth as holy: "If one considers the present churches, constructed as previously described, to be the community of the holy, how can he expect the coming of the true community of the holy, which will accompany Christ's return?" ("Wie, segge ick/dat wesen der tegenwordige Gemeenten soo gestelt/als voorseght/voor een Gemeynschap der Heyligen aensiet, hoe sal die de rechte Gemeynschap der Heiligen, die ter naeste komste Christi gespeurt sal worden . . . konnen verwachten?").[31]

Serrarius believed that the general corruption of the church had only been worsened by the Protestant Reformation. The Reformation had been a failure because God did not intend for any human to restore the true church before Christ himself did so in the millennium. If God had wanted mere men to reform the church, Serrarius argued, he would have provided specific instructions for that task in Scripture. But God had not done so, and when the Protestant reformers tried to restore the church without divine authority the result was disastrous. Serrarius pointed to what he considered to be the sorry plight of the Lutherans, Calvinists, and Mennonites of his own day as proof of the Reformation's failure. The only true reform of the church would come in the millennium, Serrarius declared, when Christ would gather his elect, erect his kingdom on earth, and initiate the new Jerusalem.[32]

Even though he believed that the true church of Christ could not be restored before the millennium, Serrarius did not give up hope for a pious religious life on earth for the few true believers. In Luke 17:22–23 Christ had foretold that in the last days many people would look for the true church but none would find it. For Serrarius, this prophecy was further proof that the last days had indeed arrived, because in the seventeenth century there was such a bewildering variety of religious opinion that everyone was totally confused. Many people searched for the true church of Christ on earth, but it was nowhere to be found. Serrarius argued, however, that even in such times of despair individual believers could still find Christ, not in any visible church but rather inside themselves—in their own heart and soul. For Serrarius, as for Galenus, the only true religion in a world unholy was an individual, inner religion. Also like Ga-

[31] Ibid., pp. 7–8, 20.
[32] Ibid., pp. 7–8, 10–15, 18.

lenus, Serrarius believed that in such times of corruption individual believers could gather together to read and discuss Scripture as well as to
comfort and admonish one another while they awaited the arrival of the
millennium. These temporary and informal gatherings were important
during the last days, Serrarius argued, in order to protect true Christians
from the many false prophets that would arise.[33] Serrarius thus used chiliastic arguments not only to explain the decay of the Christian churches
of the seventeenth century but also to present the college as an alternative
form of religious organization to the decayed visible churches.

The men who developed the Collegiant theory of church decay lived in
the tumultuous period of religious strife produced by the Protestant Reformation and the confessional conflicts that followed it. Against the
background of a century and a half of religious turmoil, the Collegiants
developed their theory of church decay in part as a response to what they
perceived to be the failure of the sixteenth-century Reformation. Galenus
and Serrarius saw in the religious chaos of the post-Reformation era
proof both of the Reformation's bankruptcy and of the corruption of the
established Protestant churches. For both men, personal experience of
Protestant religious life in the years after the Reformation crystalized and
reinforced their pessimistic vision of seventeenth-century Christianity. As
Mennonites they reflected with sadness upon the tumultuous course of
Anabaptist history since the sixteenth century, and their disappointment
became the catalyst for a scathing critique of the Reformation that provided an essential foundation for the Collegiant theory of church decay.

Galenus Abrahamsz. belonged to a generation uniquely situated to survey the spiritual wreckage of over a hundred years of religious conflict.
Like other members of his generation Galenus was deeply saddened by
the schisms, quarreling, and violence that had followed in the wake of the
Protestant Reformation. For Galenus, however, the failings of the Reformation were sharply focused and magnified in the experience of his own
Mennonite church, which was by the seventeenth century splintered into
over a dozen small sects, each of which considered itself to be the one and
only true church of God.

From its very beginnings, the Dutch Anabaptist/Mennonite movement
was riven by factional disputes. Church historian Wilhelm Goeters even
concluded that the movement was structurally inclined to disunity because of the nature of its theology and confessions.[34] But the chief causes
of Anabaptist disunity in the Low Countries were the claims of each congregation to the exclusive possession of divine authority and the practice

[33] Ibid., pp. 1–5.
[34] Goeters, p. 46.

of the ban, which was used to keep the "true church" spiritually pure. It was precisely these ideas that Galenus found most disagreeable.

Soon after the chiliastic preacher Melchior Hoffman first brought Anabaptism to the northern Netherlands in the early sixteenth century, the process of factional splintering began. By 1530 there were Anabaptist congregations in Amsterdam, Leeuwarden, and other Dutch cities, but the disaster of Münster in 1535 led to deep divisions within the Dutch movement. A moderate wing of Dutch Anabaptists led by Menno Simons rejected the example of Münster and decried violence as a tool for realizing Christ's kingdom on earth, but a group of radicals under Jan van Batenburg continued to preach the violent overthrow of the sinful world. Within these two major divisions the Dutch Anabaptist movement continued to splinter into even smaller factions as groups of believers gathered around individual charismatic leaders to form such sects as the Obbists, Davidjorists, Batenburgers, and Mennonites.[35]

Each individual Anabaptist sect considered itself to be the community of the holy—the one and only true church of God on earth—and each made use of the practice of banning to exclude from its body any member that it deemed morally or doctrinally impure. The only thread holding the Anabaptist movement as a whole together was a kind of compromise concerning the degree of severity with which the ban would be applied to fellow Anabaptists. This compromise fell apart at a synod of Dutch Anabaptists held in Harlingen in 1557 when a conservative majority led by Menno's disciple Dirk Phillips declared itself in favor of a more rigorous application of the ban. In response to this action a minority favoring greater toleration and a relaxation of the ban broke away from the main body of Dutch Anabaptism to form the Waterlander movement.

During the mid-1560s disunity within the Dutch Anabaptist movement increased still further when a large number of Flemish Anabaptists, driven from their homeland in the southern provinces by the Inquisition, came to settle in the northern Netherlands. In the north the newcomers clashed with more conservative Friesian Anabaptists, and the two groups banned each other in 1568. In 1587 a dispute over the application of the ban split the Flemish Anabaptists into conservative and moderate wings, the so-called "old" and "young" Flemish. Several years later the Friesians split along similar lines. Continuing schisms within the Anabaptist movement soon produced such sects as the Pieterjeltjesvolk, the Janjacobsgesinden, the Vermeulensvolk, the Groningen Old Flemish, the Danzig Old Flemish, and others. The more conservative of these groups came to call

---

[35] S. Voolstra, "De Roerige jaren dertig" in S. Groenveld, J. P. Jacobszoon and S. L. Verheus, eds., *Wederdoopers, Menisten, Doopsgezinden in Nederland, 1530–1980* (Zutphen, 1981), pp. 18–22; I. B. Horst, "De Strijd om het fundament des geloofs," ibid., pp. 25–45.

themselves Mennonites, in memory of Menno Simons, while the Water-landers and other moderate groups opposed to the strict ban adopted the label *Doopsgezinden* (baptists). By the 1650s there were more than four-teen Anabaptist sects in the United Provinces alone. During the seven-teenth century there were some efforts at reunion among various groups of Anabaptists in the Netherlands. The major fruit of these efforts was the 1639 joining of the Young Flemish, Young Friesians, and a German sect to form the United Mennonite church, the Amsterdam congregation of which was led by Galenus Abrahamsz. Even this limited union was destroyed, however, when the Lammerenkrijg ripped apart the United Mennonite church after 1664.[36]

This history of sectarian intolerance and spiritual fission had a substan-tial impact upon Galenus and helped to form his ideas concerning the condition of the Christian churches of the post-Reformation era. His own personal involvement in the Waterlander union proposal of 1649 and later in the Lammerenkrijg gave him firsthand experience of the disas-trous effects of church disunity. The impact of these experiences upon Galenus's thought became clear when he reflected upon the history of the Anabaptist movement in his work *Wederlegging van 't geschrift, ge-naemt: Antwoorde*. For Galenus, the turbulent and divisive history of An-abaptism provided a perfect example of the sad outcome of a religious reform movement that had not been directed by God. The founders of Anabaptism had based their reformation of religious life not on divine authority but rather on their own fallible reading and interpretation of Scripture, and the result was error and confusion. In Galenus's view, re-form of the church was properly the work of God alone. From this point of view Galenus easily expanded his critique of Anabaptist history into a condemnation of the Protestant Reformation as a whole. The Protestant Reformation, Galenus boldly declared, had not been the will of God. The sad state of the Protestant churches of his own day proved to Galenus the failure of the first Protestants truly to reform the church, and the failure of the Reformation guaranteed the continuing decay of the church in the premillennial world.[37]

The theory of church decay developed by Boreel, Galenus, and Serrarius found many other active proponents among the Rijnsburgers. The chiliast Daniel De Breen maintained in several of his works that the worldly, vis-ible churches of his day did not belong to the kingdom of Christ. De Breen believed that there was a true, invisible church of pious Christians who

---

[36] J. A. Oosterbaan, "Vlekken en rimpels," Ibid., pp. 62–69, 70–73, 74–78; van der Zijpp, pp. 78–86.

[37] Galenus Abrahamsz., *Wederlegging*, pp. 44–61.

held themselves apart from the world while waiting to join Christ in his millennial kingdom on earth. Pieter Smout, one of the leading Collegiants of Leiden, wrote in his book *Het helder licht der vryheyt* . . . (The bright light of freedom) that the Christianity of his day had become "so filled with the thistles and thorns of human invention" that it could be reformed only by God's direct intervention. Pieter Balling, a member of the Amsterdam college and of the United Mennonite congregation and a close friend of both Galenus and Spinoza, wrote two substantial works during 1663–1664 in defense of Galenus's ideas. In these works Balling took a purely secular and uncharismatic view of the Mennonite church. In his opinion, any religious association in the corrupt world of his day could be nothing more than a gathering of like-minded people freely confessing their similar beliefs. He emphatically rejected the idea that his own congregation or any other could rightfully claim to be the one and only true church of Christ on earth.[38] Many other examples could easily be taken from Collegiant writings to demonstrate that the idea of church decay became both a widespread and a deeply-rooted element of Rijnsburger thought after 1660.

The Collegiants' belief in the corruption of the premillennial world and its churches was not simply a negative or destructive principle in Rijnsburger thought. The idea of the world and church unholy formed an essential foundation for the development within the colleges of a body of positive thought dealing with man's religious life on earth. Like the spiritualists of the Radical Reformation, the Collegiants rejected the visible churches as corrupt while embracing the idea of an invisible church of true believers. The Collegiants believed that even in the corrupt premillennial world there were a few truly pious Christians who could maintain and perhaps even improve their own religious life by meeting together apart from the established churches in small conventicles or colleges. The Rijnsburgers believed that their colleges were not divinely ordained churches but rather humanly constructed secular institutions that permitted each believer the freedom to worship and express his ideas according to his own individual conscience. In this worship the practice of free prophecy was central.

[38] Kolakowski, pp. 199–205, 213–216. Pieter Smout, *Het helder licht der vryheyt, behoudster der Waerheyd, vyandinne van alle meesterschap en dooling: over het godlijke vrijpropheteren in de gemeynte Jesu Christi* (Rotterdam, 1679), p. 149: Pieter Balling, *Verdediging van de regering der Doopsgezinde gemeente, die men de Vereenigde Vlamingen, Vriezen, en Hoogduytsche noemt, binnen Amsterdam, zijnde een wederlegging van het zoo genoemde Nootwendig Bericht, etc.* (Amsterdam, 1663), and *Nader verdediging van de regering der Doopsgezinde gemeente, die men de Vereenigde Hoogduytsche, Vriezen, en Vlamingen noemt, binnen Amsterdam, zijnde een wederlegging van d'Antwoort op de verdediging, etc.* (Amsterdam, 1664), p. 28.

Despite the fact that the Collegiants did not believe that any true reform of the corrupt visible churches was possible before the millennium, the Rijnsburgers did offer a positive vision of individual religious life by placing it within a secularized institutional context and by stressing toleration and a personal approach to religious truth. These ideas produced elaborate plans for the reorganization and regeneration of religious life on the college model that carried the Rijnsburgers beyond simple despair over worldly corruption to visions of a reconstituted universal Christianity. Because they were based in part on Galenus's ideas concerning the separation of the premillennial world and its churches from divine inspiration, these Collegiant reform visions differed in significant ways from other Second Reformation plans for church reform. Taking Galenus's ideas as their starting point, the Collegiants developed a religion of reason and toleration that provided an important foundation for their developing rationalistic worldview.

Chapter Five

THE IDEAL OF THE UNIVERSAL CHURCH:
A RELIGION OF REASON AND TOLERATION

The world was from olden days with cathechisms filled,
After the choleric brain of the theologians swelled,
With vain knowledge.

(De wereld was van ouds van kathechismen vol,
Na dat het driftig brein der godgeleerden zwol,
Van yd'le wetenschap.)
—Joachim Oudaan

THE INFLUENTIAL ideas of Galenus Abrahamsz. concerning the corrupt state of the Christian churches of the seventeenth century dominated Collegiant thought after 1660. Galenus's critique of the visible churches as cut off from divine inspiration stressed the human and secular nature of religion and provided the essential intellectual background for Rijnsburger religious thought during the second half of the seventeenth century. Against this background the Collegiants created a vision of universal religious reform. Beginning with a rejection of the spiritual authority of all institutional churches, the Rijnsburger ideal of religious reform was built upon the principle of individual conscience that Luther had enunciated at Worms in 1521. When this principle was combined with the idea of the separation of the premillennial world from divine inspiration, however, the result was that a religion of individual conscience soon evolved into a religion of reason and toleration.

The Collegiant movement formed a part of the great second wave of reforming zeal that swept through the Protestant communities of northern Europe during the seventeenth century. This movement, which has been called the Second Reformation of the seventeenth century, was composed of many diverse elements and was truly international in scope, including English Puritanism and Quakerism, German Pietism, and a Dutch branch that was itself composed of several distinct parts. Despite the great internal diversity of the movement, however, its various parts were tied together by common roots and common goals.

4. Joost van Geel

The various groups making up the Second Reformation were unified by a dissatisfaction with the outcome of the original Reformation and by the desire to effect a more thoroughgoing reform of Christian life along moral and spiritual lines. While the more moderate of the new reformers proposed to work within the established Protestant churches to carry out a further reformation of these churches that would build upon and extend the work of the first reformers, the radical new reformers rejected the work of the original Reformation as a failure and called for a reconstitution of Christian religious life on earth that went far beyond the reform of individual congregations or churches to encompass a complete reorganization of universal Christianity and of Christian society as well.[1]

The Dutch branch of the Second Reformation included both moderate and radical groups. The moderate wing of the Dutch Second Reformation has been called the *Nadere Reformatie* (Further Reformation) and was led by a group of ministers within the official Dutch Reformed church. Influenced by English Puritanism, these men sought a moral and spiritual regeneration of individual religious life within the framework of the established church. They saw themselves not merely as *Gereformeerde* (Reformed) believers, but as *Reformeerende* (Reforming) believers, because they insisted on a continually ongoing and ever-deepening process of reform in religious life. Despite their zeal for a spiritualistic reform of church life, however, these moderate reformers accepted the vital truth of the major Reformed doctrines that had been adopted during the sixteenth century and afterward refined at the Synod of Dordrecht, and they upheld the divinely inspired nature of the Reformed church as well as the spiritual legitimacy of the Reformation that had given birth to it.[2]

The radical wing of the Dutch Second Reformation did not call merely for a regeneration of the established church. The radicals completely rejected the original Protestant Reformation and proposed a complete reform and reconstitution of the entire life and structure of universal Christianity that aimed at restoring to Christian society the pristine spiritual purity of the apostolic church.[3]

Among the radicals there were mystics and prophets, unworldly ascetics, penitential preachers, university-trained theologians, and self-educated popular preachers. There were as many different reform programs as there were reformers among these radicals, but they were bound to-

---

[1] For the Second Reformation of the seventeenth century, see Kolakowski, pp. 9–10.

[2] T. Brienen et al., pp. 5–6. As mentioned in chapter 1, I include the *Nadere Reformatie* in my conception of the Second Reformation even though Kolakowski did not, preferring to see Voetius, Teellinck, and their followers as part of a "Calvinist Counter Reformation." In my view, the motives and goals of the *Nadere Reformatie* justify inclusion of this movement in the Second Reformation.

[3] Evenhuis, vol. 3, pp. 309–312.

gether by their call for a reform of Christian life along moral and spiritual lines, their devaluation of ecclesiastical doctrine and their rejection of the spiritual legitimacy of the institutional churches. They were united as well by their desire to effect a renewal of religious life through a return to a spiritually pure and doctrinally tolerant universal (*algemene*) Christianity above confessional divisions.[4]

The Collegiants were an important part of the radical wing of the Second Reformation in the Netherlands. In their ideal of the universal church (*algemene kerk*) the Rijnsburgers presented plans for a general Christian renewal that contained many of the characteristic ideas of Collegiantism. Rijnsburger plans for religious reform were very much a part of the Second Reformation, but at the same time they diverged in significant ways from the reform visions held by other individuals and groups within the Second Reformation. This divergence can be explained in large part by the influence of the ideas of Galenus Abrahamsz. within the colleges. As the Rijnsburgers reflected upon Galenus's ideas they gradually developed a secularized conception of church and world, and as a result they came to rely primarily on toleration and the operation of natural human reason for the improvement of earthly religious life. The Collegiant ideal of the universal church was therefore an important stage in the development of a rational and secular worldview in the colleges.

The Collegiant vision of religious reform was characterized by an emphasis on the universality of true Christianity and on the essentially individual nature of religion. The Collegiants were convinced of the need to eliminate confessional divisions within Christianity because they saw such factionalism and quarreling as signs of the spiritual corruption of the Christian church. Rijnsburger reformers believed that by restoring the Christian church to its pristine apostolic spirituality they could likewise restore its original unity and ecumenicity. With this Christian universalism the Rijnsburgers resembled tolerant spiritualists like Schwenkfeld as well as Erasmian reformers who saw in the invisible church of all true believers the earthly embodiment of the true Christian faith.[5] Like the Erasmians, the Collegiants believed that the universal Christian community should be united by its adherence to a few fundamental articles of faith taken directly from Scripture. Beyond these few biblical principles, however, the Rijnsburgers insisted on doctrinal toleration and rejected the right of theologians to compose confessions, creeds, and doctrines belief in which would separate true from false Christians. The Collegiants

---

[4] Ibid. The best sources on the radical reformers are Lindeboom, *Stiefkinderen van het Christendom*; Hylkema; Kolakowski; Roldanus, *Zeventiende eeuwse geestesbloei*; and Zilverberg. On the moderate reformers the classic source is Goeters, while Brienen et al. is a good recent study of the principle Dutch reformers.

[5] Roldanus, *Coenraad van Beuningen*, p. 156.

believed that in a premillennial world and church unholy, no theologian or church official had the divine authority to compose such binding articles of faith.

The Collegiants put their tolerant Christian universalism into practice in their own organization and activities. The Rijnsburgers did not claim that their community was the visible embodiment of God's kingdom on earth nor did they claim to be a church possessing divine authority. Although they were fully aware of the secular nature of the colleges, the Rijnsburgers did believe that their meetings provided truly pious Christians with an opportunity to continue a sincere religious life in the world unholy. Because the Collegiants did not consider themselves a church they adopted no ceremonies or confessions, elected no preachers, upheld the right of individual free prophecy, and emphasized the need for toleration in religious life. College membership was open to anyone who believed in Christ as savior. Baptism as practiced by the Rijnsburgers was not considered a sign of entry into any specific church or sect but rather a sign of membership in the *algemene Christelijke kerk*, the universal Christian church. The Collegiants did not consider themselves to be primarily Remonstrants, Socinians, Mennonites, or even Rijnsburgers, but simply Christians.[6]

For the Collegiants, the only confession required of anyone wishing to be considered a Christian was belief in Jesus Christ as the source of human salvation and belief in the Holy Bible as the true word of God. All other doctrinal points were considered adiaphorous, matters of indifference. Because the Rijnsburgers considered Christ to be the only true lawgiver and teacher for Christians they believed that all human formulations of religious doctrine were necessarily lacking in divine inspiration and authority and thus productive only of further religious schism. In place of religious doctrine the colleges adopted extreme toleration toward many varied theological viewpoints and promoted free discussion of diverse opinions. Critics of the Collegiants pointed to such toleration as evidence of religious indifference, but Rijnsburger toleration sprang from very different sources. Frustrated over the extremely imperfect way in which divine truth was reflected in ecclesiastical institutions and convinced that this failure was a result of the separation of the premillennial world from divine inspiration, the Collegiants came to believe that religious truth could only be approached on an individual basis. No person had the right to judge another in matters of belief because no one in the seventeenth century was gifted with the Holy Spirit in the way in which the servants of the first church had been.[7] This insistence on toleration

[6] Van Slee, *De Rijnsburger Collegianten*, pp. 6–12, 268–272.
[7] Roldanus, *Zeventiende eeuwse geestesbloei*, p. 101; Meihuizen, in Groenveld, ed., p. 85; Van Slee, *De Rijnsburger Collegianten*, pp. 272–287; Price, pp. 170–177.

and the individual nature of religious truth complemented and supported the Rijnsburger belief in Christian universalism. In a series of important writings on religious reform the Collegiants used these ideas to create a series of blueprints for Christian renewal that can collectively be called the ideal of the universal church. In these plans tolerant Christian universalism and the idea of an individual, inward religion were combined to produce a program for the secular reformation of Christian life in the world unholy.

The Collegiant idea of an individual and inward religion flowed directly from the spiritualistic critique of the visible churches popularized by Galenus and Serrarius, and thus it became a central principle of Collegiant religious reform. Because God no longer gave his inspiration or authority to temporal religious institutions, and because he no longer gave the *heerlijkmaking* gifts of the Holy Spirit to individuals to enable them infallibly to proclaim, teach, or communicate divine truth, institutional religion was bankrupt in Collegiant eyes. But because God did continue to give the lesser, or *heiligmaking*, gifts of the Holy Spirit to individuals in order to give them faith and assure their salvation, there was a true invisible church of Christ on earth consisting of those people who were able to believe and live individually as true Christians. These believers could meet in small informal groups to practice a religious life based on common prayer, fellowship, and freedom of religious belief. These ideas became the foundation for Collegiant plans for the reform of universal Christianity that rejected the authority of ecclesiastical institutions and based religious life instead on the individual believer and his inner ability to know religious truth.

The concept of the individual's inner ability to know religious truth was crucial to Collegiant thought for several reasons. Not only was this inner ability the avenue for individual salvation and the believer's sole source for knowledge of religious truth, it was also the foundation for Collegiant free prophecy and for the entire structure of Rijnsburger worship. Furthermore, the idea of individual inner knowledge became the crucial point of transition for the Collegiants between spiritualism and rationalism. The principle of inner knowledge was open to either a spiritualistic or a rationalistic interpretation, and it received both in Collegiant thought. In the variety of terms used by the Collegiants to refer to inner knowledge the transition from spiritualism to rationalism was clearly evident. As Collegiant thought evolved the Rijnsburgers referred to their inner knowledge variously as individual conscience, the inner light (*innerlijke licht*), the Spirit (*Geest*), the inner word (*innerlijke woord*), the inner truth (*innerlijke waarheyd*), individual understanding (*verstand*), and reason (*rede*). For purposes of clarity and consistency, the

Collegiant principle of individual inner knowledge will henceforth be referred to as the principle of individual conscience. Just as Luther rejected the doctrinal authority of popes and councils in favor of the convictions of his own conscience at Worms in 1521, the Collegiants rejected the authority of all institutional religion in favor of their own individual inner knowledge of truth. It is one of the chief objectives of this study to show how this central Rijnsburger epistemological idea was transformed from a concept of the divine inspiration of the individual soul to an idea of the operation of natural human reason. The beginnings of this important transition can be seen in the Collegiant ideal of the universal church.

The Rijnsburger conception of the individual conscience grew out of the tradition of radical spiritualism. The spiritualists Franck and Schwenkfeld located the true center of religion in the individual conscience—the inner light of divine inspiration—and for them this inner light had to be entirely free from the institutional authority of the established churches. When these ideas were passed through Coornhert and Boreel to Galenus Abrahamsz., the idea of the individual conscience became the center point for a new vision of religious reform.

Galenus and Serrarius combined the spiritualistic idea of church decay with the tradition of Collegiant millenarianism to place great stress on the separation of the premillennial world and its churches from divine inspiration, but they retained a spiritualistic conception of the individual conscience by making a distinction between the *heerlijkmaking* and *heiligmaking* gifts of the Spirit. When other Collegiant thinkers adopted the idea of church corruption and made it the starting point for a new program of religious reform, their primary focus was on the separation of the premillennial world from God's inspiration, because this idea provided a powerful weapon for use against the spiritual authority of the established churches. These thinkers often failed to make the distinction that Galenus had made between the two kinds of gifts of the Holy Spirit. As these Rijnsburgers described a premillennial world devoid of all gifts of the Holy Spirit, a secularized conception of the individual conscience began to emerge.

As many Collegiants came to see the external world as cut off from God's influence, they also gradually came to see the internal world of the individual conscience as equally separated from divine inspiration. The result was an increasing tendency in Collegiant thought after 1660 to see a person's inner ability to know truth as a result of the operation of natural human reason. In this way, Galenus's criticism of the visible churches tended to have a powerful secularizing effect not only on the Collegiant view of the premillennial world but also on the Rijnsburger conception of the individual conscience. The introduction of the idea of natural reason into the Rijnsburger conception of the individual conscience began in

Collegiant plans for religious reform. In a world cut off from divine inspiration, the Collegiants proposed to regenerate religious life by using the principles of reason and toleration.

One of the most important Collegiant writers on religious reform was the Rotterdam poet and classical scholar Joachim Oudaan. In many ways a typical Rijnsburger, Oudaan combined in his thinking a firm attachment to the doctrine of the millennium, an acceptance of Galenus's ideas concerning the corruption of the premillennial world and its churches, and a reliance on the power of human reason. For Oudaan, reason became the chief guide to religious truth in a world devoid of divine inspiration.

Oudaan was among the most important figures in Rijnsburger intellectual history because he reflected so clearly the main trends in Collegiant thought. In his religious thinking he was what might be termed a biblical rationalist. His faith was based firmly on the divine revelation contained in Scripture, but his understanding of Scripture relied to a considerable extent on rational interpretation. Faithful to the Collegiant principle of individual conscience, Oudaan condemned religious confessionalism and dogmatism as leading only to decay in the church. He also rejected the special spiritual authority of the clergy, in part because he wanted each individual to accept God's word according to his own personal experience of it, not as a result of the authority of others.[8] Oudaan's religious ideas were best expressed in his chief work on the universal church, *Overweginge eeniger grond-stellingen door J.V.G. in des zelfs redenering over de algemeene kerk ter neder gestelt: en der zelver onrechtmatigheid aangewezen* (Considerations of some principles put down by J.[oost] V.[an] G.[eel] in his argument regarding the universal church: and the incorrectness of the same shown [1689]).

Like Galenus, Oudaan believed that the true Christian church did not exist in any visible form on earth in the seventeenth century. The true universal church had been established on earth by Christ and the apostles, he argued, but the emperor Constantine's alliance of church and state had robbed the church of its spiritual purity and precipitated its decline into worldly corruption. Secular influence led to schism, hatred, and intolerance that destroyed the true universal church, Oudaan maintained, and even though the visible church that remained bore the name "Catholic," it had lost all claim to true Christian universalism. It excluded from its communion anyone who deviated the slightest bit from church doctrine, no matter how pious a person he or she might be. This "Catholic" church was not the true universal Christian church but rather a church of schism,

---

[8] Melles, pp. 82–183.

Oudaan claimed, built by human hands and lacking divine authority. For him, schism and intolerance were marks of spiritual degeneration.[9]

In Oudaan's view, the various Christian churches of the seventeenth century were the corrupt descendants of the decadent Catholic church of the Middle Ages, and consequently these churches were just as intolerant and riven by schism as the medieval church had been. As a consequence of the spiritual corruption of all visible churches, Oudaan argued, there were no preachers or religious leaders present in the world of the seventeenth century on whom pious Christians could rely for religious guidance. There were, of course, many religious leaders who claimed to have sole possession of divine truth, but none of them could show any proof of divine inspiration. Christ had proven his divine authority to the disciples by performing miracles, Oudaan declared, but God no longer gave people on earth the gifts of the Holy Spirit enabling them to work miracles. Because Oudaan believed that God no longer granted people the gifts of the Holy Spirit, he maintained that no one in the world of the seventeenth century had the divine power and authority infallibly to preach God's truth. He lamented the absence of such divine prophets, whom he referred to as "speaking Judges" (*sprekenden Rechter*), but he insisted that the clergy of the seventeenth century possessed no special divine abilities or authority placing them above ordinary believers. For this reason, if Christians relied on clerical guidance in religious matters they would be like the blind led by the blind.[10] In the absence of divinely inspired religious leaders Oudaan argued that man was left with but one option in his search for religious truth—he had to turn to his own individual reason: "Since we have no speaking Judge here on earth, and especially none who can show his character with miracles, we have only our understanding, however great or small, . . . or our reason, however weak or powerful, and the dictates of our conscience, that can be our guide in these matters" ("Want dewijl wij op aarde geen sprekenden Rechter en hebben, en inzonderheyd geenen zoodanigen die met zegels van wonderheden zijn karakter kan toonen, zo hebben wij niet anders dan ons verstand, 't zij hoe groot of hoe kleyn, of . . . ons vernuft, 't zij hoe zwak of hoe magtig, en het dictamen van ons geweten . . . dat ons in dezen de richtdraad en wegwijzer om het op te volgen, strekken kan").[11]

[9] Joachim Oudaan, *Overwegginge eeniger grond-stellingen door J.V.G. in des zelfs redenering over de algemeene kerk ter neder gestelt: en der zelver onrechtmatigheid aangewezen* (Amsterdam, 1689), pp. 3–5.

[10] Ibid., pp. 10, 13, 21. The idea of the "speaking Judge" (*sprekenden Rechter*) can be traced back to the Remonstrant tradition, as Wiep van Bunge points out. Van Bunge is writing a thesis on the Rotterdam Collegiants at Erasmus University in Rotterdam. He suggests that the idea of the "speaking Judge" may go back as far as Erasmus or Castellio.

[11] Ibid., p. 21.

Oudaan believed that Christians could find religious truth in the world unholy by following their own reason and by refusing to submit themselves to false external authorities. If people subjected their reason to the authority of others, he argued, they would put themselves in the position of becoming like animals easily controlled by their masters. It was because of such blind obedience that the Roman church was able to impose its corrupt rule on unthinking people for so many centuries, Oudaan added. The knowledge obtained through natural reason was therefore the key to religious truth and freedom.[12]

Oudaan defined human reason as "the ability of man's understanding to rightly judge all things." The accuracy of reason was assured, in Oudaan's view, by the fact that it was a gift from God. Like most seventeenth-century Christians, Oudaan upheld the divine authority of the Bible as a source of religious truth and believed that salvation depended upon following God's commands as they were laid out in Scripture. For Oudaan, however, it was human reason rather than clerical or ecclesiastical authority that enabled people to interpret Scripture.[13]

Along with human reason Oudaan considered religious toleration to be the second essential characteristic of the true Christian. The universal church established by Christ and his apostles had but one clear and simple confession, Oudaan wrote. All who confessed that Jesus Christ was the son of God and the savior of the world were true Christians, and the apostolic church excluded no one on any other basis. Such tolerant Christian universalism had been a key element of the spiritual purity of the first church, Oudaan continued, but this true visible church had long ago vanished from the earth. The intolerance of the churches of the seventeenth century proved that they were spiritually decadent, he declared. Like Galenus, however, Oudaan believed that a true invisible church did exist on earth, composed of pious believers scattered among the various corrupt congregations. Christ alone knew who these true believers were, but one way that people gave a clear indication that they did not belong to the true invisible church was through doctrinal intolerance. For Oudaan, religious toleration was a vital component of the spiritual purity of Christianity.[14]

The idea of toleration played an important role in the religion of individual conscience adopted by the Collegiants and in the religious reform plans that they proposed. The belief that religious knowledge could be obtained only on an individual basis necessitated a doctrine of toleration that would preserve the autonomy of each individual conscience. The

[12] Ibid., pp. 19–20, 14–18.
[13] Ibid., pp. 18–19.
[14] Ibid., pp. 6–8.

Collegiant doctrine of toleration found perhaps its best expression in the thought of Johannes (Jan) Bredenburg (d. 1691), another Rijnsburger heavily influenced by the ideas of Galenus Abrahamsz.

Although Bredenburg was one of the leading intellectual figures in the Rotterdam college during the last quarter of the seventeenth century, surprisingly little is known about his life. He was born in Rotterdam, presumably sometime in the early 1640s, and he was for most of his life a wine merchant in that great trading city. He befriended Joachim Oudaan when Oudaan arrived in Rotterdam and he married Oudaan's sister Katarina in 1666. With Oudaan, Joan Hartigveldt, Jan Dionysius Verburg, and his own brother Paulus, Bredenburg became an important member of the Rijnsburger college in Rotterdam after 1668. Throughout his merchant years Bredenburg read and studied philosophy in his spare time. When the French invasion of the United Provinces disrupted business activity and forced his wine shop to close in 1672, Bredenburg took advantage of this opportunity to devote himself full time to philosophy. The ideas that he developed during this period of intense intellectual activity stirred much debate within the colleges and greatly enriched the tradition of Rijnsburger thought. After writing two early works on religious reform and toleration, Bredenburg turned to the problem of the role of reason in religion. In his thinking on this question Bredenburg was heavily influenced by the ideas of Benedict Spinoza, and during the 1670s and 1680s he produced a number of highly controversial writings arguing for the supremacy of natural reason as man's primary source of religious truth. These works created a sensation throughout the entire Rijnsburger movement and contributed greatly to the formation of the Collegiant rational worldview.[15] While Bredenburg's rationalism will be the subject of the ninth chapter of this study, his early works on religious reform are of interest here for their typically Collegiant emphasis on universal toleration.

In 1671 Bredenburg published *Een praetje over tafel* . . . (A table talk) extolling Rijnsburger religious toleration and arguing that even the Remonstrants and Mennonites were inferior to the colleges in this respect. Like Oudaan, Bredenburg maintained that a church's lack of toleration was a direct measure of its spiritual corruption. Since the Rijnsburgers practiced full toleration, the college was, according to Bredenburg, the last remaining vestige of the true Christian church. In conclusion, Bredenburg declared that a reform of the religious life of the temporal world could be achieved only through the adoption of universal toleration in all questions not vital to salvation. Bredenburg accepted as Christians all

---

[15] *NNBW*, vol. 4, pp. 292–293. For some of my information regarding Bredenburg's early life, I would like to thank Mr. van Bunge, who kindly provided me with a copy of the first chapter of his thesis.

people who recognized Jesus as savior, and he considered all other doctrines matters of indifference. He envisioned universal religious reform as a return to the spiritual purity of the first church through the adoption of toleration by all Christians.[16]

In Bredenburg's second major work on religious reform the Collegiant desire to rebuild universal Christianity on the basis of unity and toleration was even more clearly expressed. The *Heylzame raad tot Christelijke vrede of te aanwijzing van het rechte middel tot Christelijke vereeniging* (Salutary advice for Christian peace or to show the right means to Christian unity [1672?]) was, like the *Praetje over tafel*, written on the occasion of discussions held between Bredenburg's Mennonite congregation and the Rotterdam Remonstrants for the purpose of considering a union between the two congregations.[17] Although this union never took place, Bredenburg presented in the *Heylzame raad* a plan to unify the Mennonites, Remonstrants, and the Collegiants into one church on the basis of mutual toleration. While the *Heylzame raad* was written in part with this concrete objective in mind, Bredenburg also saw in his plan the possibility for a reunification of the universal Christian church along Collegiant lines.

In the *Heylzame raad* Bredenburg followed Galenus in proclaiming that there was no true visible church of Christ on earth. As evidence he pointed to the widespread intolerance practiced by the established churches, an intolerance that he equated with spiritual corruption. From the time of Constantine, he argued, intolerance and schism had destroyed the unity and spiritual purity of the universal church, and the many councils and synods held since apostolic times had done nothing to restore peace and unity to the church. For Bredenburg, this long history of schism was ample proof of the church's steady decline into spiritual corruption.[18]

Among the churches of the seventeenth century, Bredenburg spoke favorably of both the Remonstrants and the Mennonites because they called for greater religious toleration in an effort to restore peace to universal Christianity. Unfortunately, he added, they rarely practiced what they preached. Even his own Collegiants did not practice full toleration, Bredenburg lamented, qualifying his earlier praise for the Rijnsburgers,

[16] Kolakowski, pp. 283–284.

[17] Authorship of this work has mistakenly been attributed to Laurens Klinkhamer, since Bredenburg's name does not appear on the title page. Bredenburg's authorship of this work is evident, however, from the fact that the author mentions Bredenburg's *Praetje over tafel* as another of his works. Furthermore, the issues addressed in the work concerned Rotterdam affairs that would not have interested Klinkhamer, who lived in Leiden.

[18] Johannes Bredenburg, *Heylzame raad tot Christelijke vrede of te aanwijzing van het rechte middel tot Christelijke vereeniging* (Rotterdam, n.d.), pp. iii–iv. The publication date, determined from the book's content, was most likely 1672.

because they condemned pastoral sermons in favor of free prophecy. But he declared that a renewal and reunification of universal Christianity was urgently needed to return the Christian religion to its original spiritual purity, and he believed that this renewal should be based on Collegiant principles of toleration and individual conscience.[19]

Bredenburg saw the many doctrinal disputes that divided the various Christian churches as pointless because there was no divinely inspired and infallible prophet of God on earth who could judge which doctrines accorded most closely with God's wishes. Although he admitted that the world of his day desperately needed such a divine prophet to guide people to religious truth, he nevertheless argued that all sincere Christians would have to concede that such an ambassador of Christ was sadly lacking in the world of the seventeenth century. Because there was no such divine spokesperson on earth, Bredenburg continued, all Christians were in a state of "collaterality" (*collateraliteit*) or "equality" (*evengelijkheid*). In this state each individual believer could rightfully claim that his religious opinion was correct because, in the absence of a divinely inspired prophet who could proclaim God's truth, the opinions of all individuals were equally valid. Thus, Bredenburg made the case for a religion of individual conscience and toleration. In his view, toleration represented the only path to Christian unity in a world cut off from divine inspiration.[20]

In the final sections of the *Heylzame raad* Bredenburg presented a plan for the reunification and renewal of Christianity based on the practice of toleration and a restructuring of the universal Christian church following the Collegiant model. The new universal church would be organized as a federation of autonomous congregations with the Collegiant communion meeting in Rijnsburg serving as the central unifying body. The various congregations of Mennonites, Remonstrants, Collegiants, and others would continue to meet separately for their regular services, but periodically they would all come together in Rijnsburg to celebrate communion as a symbol of universal Christian brotherhood. These periodic general meetings would be the heart of the reborn universal church, and they would take place in a spirit of toleration and equality. Despite the fact that the universal church would be composed of many different ideas and practices, mutual toleration would unite its members and make it the true church of Christ.[21]

The universal church would be erected throughout the Christian world by the efforts of the Collegiants, whom Bredenburg appointed as the missionaries and organizers of reborn Christianity. While the first elements

[19] Ibid., pp. iv–vi, 1.
[20] Ibid., pp. 3–4.
[21] Ibid., pp. 12–15, 5–6.

of the new church organized themselves around the Rijnsburg communion meeting, Collegiant missionaries would go forth into the world to set up additional communion gatherings modeled on the one at Rijnsburg. These new gatherings would then act as the unifying points for congregations of tolerant Christians all over the world. Thus, the restored universal church would consist of a network of individual congregations united by a number of Rijnsburger-style common meetings practicing toleration and individual religion.[22] In this way Bredenburg planned to reconstruct universal Christianity in the image of the Collegiant system.

Slightly different plans for the reformation of universal Christianity were offered by two other Collegiant writers, Joost van Geel and Daniel Zwicker. While both men saw the Christian churches of the seventeenth century as badly decayed and in need of thorough reform, their plans for Christian renewal differed somewhat from the ideas of Oudaan and Bredenburg. Nevertheless, both writers retained the characteristic Collegiant stress on a religion of toleration and individual conscience, and Zwicker zealously campaigned for the guiding light of reason.

Joost van Geel (1631–1698) was born in Rotterdam, the son of Jan van Geel, a wealthy brandy distiller, and Ingetje van Leeuwen. He was educated for commerce and he made his living as a Rotterdam merchant, but he also spent much time in other pursuits. Indeed, it was not as a businessman that van Geel made his reputation in Rotterdam, but rather as a poet, painter, theologian, and Collegiant. In his youth van Geel made numerous trips to France, Germany, and England to study painting, while at home in Holland he studied with the renowned Dutch artist Gabriel Metsu (1629–1667). Van Geel lacked great talent as a painter, however, and the common judgment on his work has been that it was the product of a gifted dilettante with little power of imagination. Van Geel's painterly style was quite similar to that of his teacher Metsu, naturally enough, but his work was also considered by contemporaries to resemble that of another well-known Rotterdam painter of the time, Jacob Ochtervelt (1634–1683).

In 1666 van Geel married Maritge van Wetterman, a granddaughter of the van der Koddes. The couple had five children, two of whom died young. As he grew older, van Geel's weak physical constitution subjected him to repeated bouts of illness, but he nevertheless continued his intellectual and poetic activities. In his poems van Geel expressed Collegiant sentiments, criticizing the religious intolerance of Rome, Geneva, and Wittenburg while praising the "bright light of Rijnsburg." Toleration, peace, and love were his common themes. Very few of van Geel's poems were published in his own lifetime. One was included with poems by Bredenburg and other Rijnsburgers in a book of poetry entitled *Lusthof der Zielen* (Pleasure-garden of souls, 1681) collected by the Hoorn Collegiant Claas Stapel, and another was later published with some of Oudaan's poems in a book dedicated to the memory of the Remonstrant historian Geerart Brandt. Van Geel's collected poetry was finally published by one of his disciples twenty-five years after the poet's death. In the introduction to that collection the editor, Cornelisz. van Arkel, described van Geel as "a Christian in both name and deed, a confessor of a simple evangelical religion, an enemy of all sectarianism and a friend of general toleration."[23] Van Geel showed himself to be all of these things in his two major works on religious reform, *Redenering over de algemeene kerk ofte het rijk der heiligen* (Argument concerning the universal church or the kingdom of the saints [1687]) and *Nader verklaringe eeniger zaken in zijn redenering over de algemeene kerk, tegen de overweging van J. Oudaan Fransz.* (Further explanation of some issues in his argument concerning the universal church, against the considerations of J. Oudaan Fransz. [1689]).

Like Galenus, Oudaan, and Bredenburg, van Geel believed that there was no one in the world of his day who could speak with the direct authority and inspiration of God to proclaim divine truth infallibly and then perform miracles as proof of his divine mission. In view of this fact, van Geel proposed a religion of reason, toleration, and individual conscience. Since there were no inspired ambassadors of God on earth, he argued, Christians could rely only on the direction of their own understanding (*verstand*) in religion. For this reason, Christians should never subject their conscience to the religious opinions of other persons, and they should also never attempt to force their own ideas on other people by insisting that their ideas are the only true ones. For any religious doctrine to compel the assent of all Christians, that doctrine would have to be clearly infallible, van Geel asserted, but human opinions lacking divine authority could make no such claim.[24]

Because human opinion lacked divine authority, van Geel argued that it was not permissible for Christians to break away from the universal church of Christ in order to build new congregations based on their own ideas. He thus condemned not only the Protestant Reformation but all church schisms caused by disputes over doctrine. According to van Geel, the Holy Scripture nowhere instructed or permitted the construction of any church according to fallible human ideas, and it was because this had

[23] *NNBW*, vol. 7, pp. 482–485. One can see Joost van Geel's genre painting *Courtship* in the Detroit Institute of Arts, 67.114. His self-portrait is in the Rijksmuseum, Amsterdam.

[24] Joost van Geel, *Redenering over de algemeen kerk ofte het rijk der heiligen* (Rotterdam, 1687), pp. 10–12.

repeatedly occurred that the true universal church had been corrupted
and destroyed.[25]

Even though van Geel considered the visible churches of the seventeenth century to be corrupt, he believed that each church retained at its
innermost core a single vestige of the original universal church: the confession of Christ as savior. The apostolic church had adopted this simple
confession as its one rule of faith and the apostles had used this confession
to baptize thousands of believers. When the pretentious wisdom of later
theologians combined with the evil desires of politicians to expand this
simple confession into complex and abstract doctrinal formulas, schism
and spiritual corruption destroyed the universal church. Human doctrines and theology continued to breed schism within Christianity up to
the seventeenth century, van Geel added, and the prevalence of such doctrines within the established churches was a direct measure of their spiritual corruption. But even amid this great confusion of doctrines, these
corrupt churches nevertheless retained the simple confession of Christ
that van Geel and the other Collegiants considered the only true criterion
for membership in the universal church. For van Geel, therefore, the key
to the renewal and reunification of the universal Christian church was the
elimination of all of the competing theological doctrines upheld by the
various congregations and the unification of these churches into one spiritual body based on the simple confession of Christ.[26]

Van Geel believed that the first step in the reformation of the universal
church was the replacement of religious doctrines with love and toleration. In his view, unity was an essential aspect of the spiritual purity of
the true universal church, and he was convinced that such unity could
never be achieved through agreement on doctrine. Mutual love and toleration held the only key to Christian unity because the true end of all
religious knowledge was love.[27] If reform along these lines proved impossible for the corrupt visible churches, van Geel continued, each individual
believer could make himself a member of the true invisible church of
Christ by adopting love and toleration in his own life. Van Geel saw the
true universal church as a great spiritual body of tolerant Christians that
would exist whether or not the visible churches were reformed.

While van Geel stressed love and toleration as the chief means for the
reform of universal Christianity, a somewhat different view of reform
was presented by the Amsterdam Collegiant Daniel Zwicker (1621–
1678). Zwicker described his plan for the reunification of all Christian
congregations into one universal church in his work *Vredeschrift der vre-*

[25] Ibid., pp. 1–2.
[26] Ibid., pp. 3–6.
[27] Ibid., pp. 6–8.

deschriften (Irenicum Irenicorum). Published in the year of Zwicker's death, the *Vredeschrift* combined Galenus's conception of church corruption with a strong emphasis on the use of reason in religion.

Daniel Zwicker was a very interesting figure whose career was somewhat different from that of most Collegiants. Born in Danzig in 1621, Zwicker became a Socinian early in life. Little is known about his education or early experiences before 1648, but in that year an event occurred that was to decide the course of his later career: a meeting in Danzig with several missionaries of the Slovak Hutterite (Anabaptist) church. Zwicker was so impressed with Hutterite efforts to imitate what they believed to be the primitive Christian form of communal life that he entered into a long correspondence with the Slovak bishop, Andreas Ehrenpreis. In 1654 Zwicker visited the Hutterite community at Sobotisk, where he joined the Hutterite church despite the fact that as an antitrinitarian he had reservations about the more orthodox theology of the Slovaks. In 1655 Zwicker returned to Danzig advocating a union between the Socinians and the Hutterites. His plan met with stiff opposition from most of the Socinians, and in 1656 he was expelled from their congregation. Following this defeat Zwicker left Danzig, and after some wanderings he arrived in Amsterdam in 1657. There he was to spend the remainder of his life.

Immediately after his arrival in Amsterdam, Zwicker joined the Collegiants and became a frequent speaker at their meetings. He criticized the Mennonites and other congregations for spiritual decay and he advocated the views of the sixteenth-century spiritualist Christian Entfelder, who had maintained that it was best for Christians not to join any visible church.[28] Zwicker was active in Collegiant circles during the 1660s and 1670s, finding both supporters and opponents. He was one of very few Rijnsburgers to criticize openly the practice of free prophecy, for which he won the enmity of Galenus and others.[29] With his opposition to the central Collegiant principle of free prophecy Zwicker demonstrated the degree of toleration that existed in the colleges, for even though some Collegiants held his ideas in low esteem, Zwicker was never prevented from voicing his opinions or from taking full part in college discussions.

Zwicker was especially interested in Rijnsburger projects for church reform, and he held lengthy discussions on this topic with fellow Collegiant Jan Amos Comenius (1592–1670). This exiled Moravian ecumenicist and educator, who had also arrived in Amsterdam in 1657, favored a union of all Protestant churches as the first step toward universal peace

[28] *ME*, vol. 4, p. 105. Serrarius translated a work by Entfelder.

[29] Hylkema, p. 43. See Zwicker's works *Openhertige vertooninge dat de Algemeene vryheyt van spreken in de Gemeynte . . . behoort Afgeschaft te worden* (n.p., 1660), and *De verdwynende On-Apostolische vryspreecker* (n.p., 1669).

and brotherhood. Out of these discussions with Comenius came the *Vredeschrift*. Despite Zwicker's initially friendly relations with Comenius, the *Vredeschrift* contained so many Socinian ideas repugnant to the Moravian pedagogue that Zwicker and Comenius later became involved in a long and bitter dispute.[30]

Zwicker considered himself above all else a religious reformer. In works such as his *Vredeschrift* the Collegiant ideal of the universal church took the form of concrete reform proposals. Zwicker believed that a new reformation of all visible churches was needed because all of the established Christian congregations had been weakened and corrupted by the decadent times in which they existed. Following standard Collegiant ideas, Zwicker held that none of the existing congregations could claim to be the one and only true church because all of the visible churches had deviated from the pure doctrines and practices of the apostolic church. Zwicker considered the many doctrinal differences separating the various Christian congregations as unimportant, and like van Geel he called for reform and reunification of these congregations based on the simple confession of Christ as savior.[31]

Zwicker believed that the various corrupt Christian congregations could be reunited into one spiritually pure universal church because each had something good to offer. He praised the Hussites and Lutherans for beginning the Reformation and thus for instigating Christian freedom, and he congratulated the Calvinists for being the first to use reason in religion. The Remonstrants had brought progress in freedom of conscience, while the Socinians demonstrated capable judgment and the Mennonites best portrayed the life of Christ. Finally, Zwicker claimed that the Greek church had the remnants of apostolic truth in its church fathers, and he applauded the Catholics as well for reminding Christians of the need for good works. If all of these sects adopted mutual toleration in doctrinal matters, Zwicker believed, they could be reunited in one universal church based on their underlying similarities.[32] The first step would be to unite the Lutherans and Calvinists, a union that was in fact the object of a life of tireless effort by the ecumenicist John Dury (1596–1680), who was often in Amsterdam during the years in which Zwicker lived there. Dury knew Comenius, Serrarius, and other Collegiants.[33] Once the Lutheran-Calvinist union was achieved, Zwicker continued, the

---

[30] Wilbur, pp. 574–575; Zilverberg, pp. 64–67; Henry Kamen, *The Rise of Toleration* (New York, 1972), pp. 107–110, 126–17; Rood, pp. 184–195.

[31] Daniel Zwicker, *Vredeschrift der vredeschriften of drie dubbelde regelmaet des vereenigers der hedendaghse Christenen, de gesonde reden van alle menschen, de H. Schriftuere, en de overleveringen* (n.p., 1678), pp. iv–v, 69–76.

[32] Ibid., pp. 69–70.

[33] See Turnbull.

Calvinists would be able to bring their former colleagues the Remonstrants into the fold. The Remonstrants would then bring along the Socinians, because both of these groups were already united by their advocacy of freedom of conscience. Finally, the Greeks and Catholics, divided since the eleventh century, would heal their differences and join the other churches for the sake of Christian unity. With the universal church thus restored and all believers once again united in the body of Christ, a return to pure Christian life and a restoration of the spiritual perfection of the apostolic church would follow.[34]

In his zealous pursuit of church reform Zwicker saw human reason as the most effective tool for achieving the changes needed in religious life. Because he believed that reason was the chief guide for the understanding of Scripture, Zwicker held that the use of reason could help restore to the church the apostolic truth lost during the long period of medieval decay. In the final section of the *Vredeschrift* Zwicker attempted to demontrate by way of example how reason could restore true doctrine to the church. He undertook a rational investigation of the doctrine of the dual nature of Christ, and in this discussion his Socinian leanings became evident. Christ could not have had both a human nature and a divine nature, Zwicker argued, because nobody could have two different natures at one and the same time. As proof Zwicker cited what he called the "rule of distinction": It is impossible to predicate two contrary things of one subject at the same time. Zwicker explicitly rejected the argument of some orthodox theologians who maintained that the doctrine of the dual nature of Christ, like other religious doctrines, was a divine mystery that could not be grasped by reason. This could not be the case, Zwicker proclaimed, because any doctrine that contradicted reason was "impossible and false."[35]

Zwicker placed such great faith in reason as the chief guide to religious truth that he was convinced that without reason, heresy would overwhelm the church. If reason were not the guide in religious matters, Zwicker argued, it would be impossible for believers to prove that absurd and erroneous religious doctrines were false. Since heretics often tried to seduce the faithful with absurd doctrines, without reason people would be helpless against heresy. Thus, Zwicker believed it was the duty of every true Christian to use reason to understand and to follow the truth in religion.[36]

Zwicker's conception of reason was of a practical, nonspeculative, and empirically based ability to judge accurately, without resort to the use of

[34] Zwicker, *Vredeschrift*, pp. 76–79.
[35] Ibid., p. 4.
[36] Ibid.

intellectual subtlety. His was a kind of commonsense rationalism that was typical of many Socinians. Thus, reason ruled out the popularly accepted idea that God, a spiritual being, had hands and feet. In Zwicker's view, one and the same being could not be pure spirit and also have bodily parts at the same time. Zwicker also used rational analysis of various scriptural passages to make his case for the Socinian idea that Christ had no divine nature.[37] This Socinian argument most upset Comenius.

Zwicker's belief in reason was in part a product of his Socinian background, for Socinianism had a long tradition of humanist rationalism behind its criticism of orthodox doctrine. Among the other Collegiant writers on religious reform, Oudaan too was influenced by Socinian ideas on reason. Zwicker's concern with religious reform, however, as well as the central place in his thought occupied by the ideal of the universal church, demonstrated that by 1678 he was thoroughly Collegiant in many of his views.

The rationalism of Zwicker, Oudaan, and other Rijnsburger writers on religious reform was part of a developing trend toward a secular view of the individual conscience that began to emerge in Collegiant thought as Galenus's ideas spread. This rationalist tendency, encouraged by the influence of Socinianism within the colleges after 1660, was a result of the inclination of pious and educated people to fall back on their own reasoning abilities in an attempt to find religious truth in a world that they perceived as being cut off from divine inspiration. Without divinely inspired prophets or divinely ordained religious institutions capable of infallibly showing the way to God, many Collegiants turned to the Bible and their own rational ability to interpret it in order to carry on religious life as best they could. Universal adherence to a simple confession of Christ, combined with toleration on other doctrinal points and a reliance on human reason for individual religious enlightenment, seemed to these Collegiants to be the only avenue open for people who hoped to restore some measure of spiritual integrity and unity to Christian life in a world unholy. The embryonic rationalism contained in these reform plans provided an all-important first foundation upon which a more elaborate rational religion, and finally a true philosophical rationalism, could be built in the colleges. Among the most important influences on the developing Collegiant religion of reason and toleration was the evangelical rationalist creed known as Socinianism.

[37] Ibid., pp. 1–12.

PART TWO

Secularization of the Individual Conscience:
The Development of Collegiant Rationalism

Chapter Six

THE ARTICULATION OF RATIONAL RELIGION: COLLEGIANT SOCINIANISM

Neither old delusion nor own wisdom,
Neither church nor priest, habit nor custom,
Hold fast to nothing but God's reason.

(Oude waen, noch eygen wijsheijd,
Kerk noch priester, wenst noch seden,
-Nergens vast dan aen Godt's reden.)
—Camphuysen

THE DEVELOPMENT of a fully articulated and systematic Collegiant rational religion was in large part the work of Socinian-influenced Rijnsburgers such as Frans Kuyper and Daniel Zwicker. Building upon foundations already present in Collegiant thought on religious reform, these Collegiant Socinians joined the rationalistic inclination present in Rijnsburger plans for universal Christian renewal with the evangelical rationalism of Socinian thought to produce a fully developed rational religion. For this reason, the exiled Polish Socinians who came to the United Provinces during the mid-seventeenth century brought with them ideas that had an important influence on the Collegiants and their developing rationalistic worldview.

When Socinian refugees first appeared in the United Provinces during the early 1660s, Dutch political and religious authorities reacted with horror. Because the Socinians held many extremely heterodox views, such as antitrinitarianism, rejection of the divinity of Christ, and rejection of the doctrine of Christ's satisfaction, Socinianism was regarded as unchristian by all of the established churches in the Netherlands. Even the normally tolerant civil authorities of Holland viewed the Socinians as a threat to public morality. As a result of these attitudes Socinian meetings, books, and even the public discussion of Socinian ideas were outlawed everywhere in the United Provinces. With public worship out of the question, Socinians in the Netherlands were forced to resort to secrecy in the practice of an underground religion, meeting in private homes, issuing their books illegally, and living under public anathema for their ideas. Because of their position on the radical fringes of Dutch religious life, a number

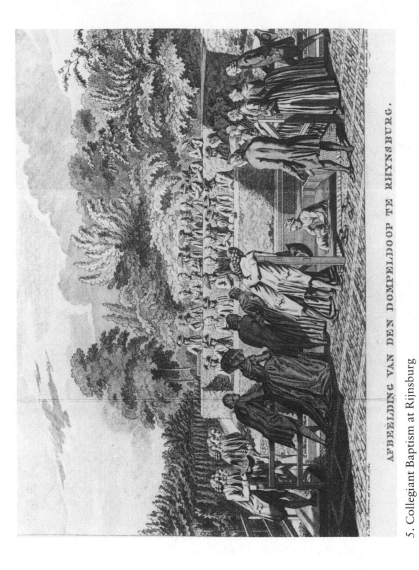

AFBEELDING VAN DEN DOMPELDOOP TE RHYNSBURG.

5. Collegiant Baptism at Rijnsburg

of Socinians gravitated naturally toward the Collegiant movement, where their influence on some Rijnsburgers was profound.

Despite their public image as a sect of iniquitous and dangerous heretics, the Socinians were in fact a religious movement with a distinguished heritage. Socinianism's religious and intellectual roots can be traced back to the very beginnings of the Radical Reformation of the sixteenth century, and the Socinian exiles in Holland were the last survivors of the once important and powerful Polish antitrinitarian church. The Socinian religious program called for a rational and moral religion based on Scripture and influenced in part by Italian humanism. Socinianism can thus be characterized as a biblically based creed with a pronounced rationalistic inclination, and it was the rationalistic character of Socinianism that had the greatest impact on the Collegiants.[1]

The Socinian movement derived its name from Laelius and Faustus Socinus, radical Italian Protestants whose influence was felt most significantly in the flowering of Polish antitrinitarianism during the late sixteenth century. Laelius Socinus (1525–1562) was born in Siena and studied law at Padua, but his main interest was in theology. After learning some Hebrew and Greek he undertook an intensive study of the Bible, a study that eventually led him to reject Catholicism. Forced by the growing menace of the Inquisition to leave Italy in 1547, Socinus traveled widely around Europe, and in the course of these travels his originally moderate evangelical views grew more radical.

At Chiavenna, Socinus came under the influence of the mystical reformer Camillo Renato (1500–1572) and he adopted Renato's view of the merely symbolic significance of the sacraments. During 1550–1551 he was a guest of Philip Melanchthon in Wittenberg, and he also became acquainted with the Swiss reformers Bullinger and Calvin. It was the execution of the antitrinitarian Michael Servetus in Geneva in the fall of 1553, however, that made the greatest impression on Socinus. By the end of his life Socinus had rejected orthodox Protestant views on the Trinity, predestination, the resurrection of the body, the nature of repentance, and the sacraments. Although he tended to keep his religious views to himself, Socinus passed on many of his most radical ideas to his admiring nephew Faustus. When Laelius died in Zurich in 1562, Faustus took possession of his library and papers.[2]

Faustus Socinus (1539–1604) also was born in Siena. He studied law and logic for a time but was unwilling to persevere in these studies, and

---

[1] Roldanus, *Zeventiende eeuwse qeestesbloei*, p. 102; Roldanus, *Coenraad van Beuningen*, p. 157.

[2] Williams, pp. 565–571, 630–633; *EB*, vol. 25, pp. 320–321.

he spent most of his early life dabbling in poetry and reading humanistic literature under the influence of his uncle Celso, founder of a short-lived academy in Siena. Even during his youth, however, Faustus's attention was attracted by the unorthodox religious opinions of his uncle Laelius. As early as 1563 Faustus expressed unorthodox views of his own in a letter to a friend, but he continued to conform outwardly to the Catholic church in order to maintain his position at the court of Isabella de Medici, daughter of Grand Duke Cosimo of Tuscany.

After serving Isabella de Medici for what he later called twelve useless years, Faustus left Italy for Basel in 1574 to study theology. He never returned to his native land. In 1578 Socinus published his first major theological treatise, *De Jesu Christo Servatore*, an extremely radical work in which he denied the divinity of Christ, the Trinity, and divine providence. This work soon attracted the attention of leaders of the antitrinitarian movement in Transylvania, and they invited Socinus to their country for a series of religious debates. After a short stay in Transylvania Socinus moved on to Poland, the site of another already well-established antitrinitarian movement called the Minor Reformed church. Within a few years Socinus placed himself at the head of the Polish antitrinitarian movement, and from 1580 to 1604 his influence over the doctrine and practice of the Minor church became so great that the entire Polish antitrinitarian movement came to be called Socinianism.[3]

The movement that Socinus came to lead in Poland had its beginnings some fifteen years before Socinus himself appeared on the scene. The pioneer of antitrinitarianism in Poland was Peter Giezek (Gonesius, 1530–1571), a theologian who believed that Christ and the Holy Spirit were not of one substance with God. Giezek planted the seeds of antitrinitarianism within the developing Reformed church in Poland and these seeds germinated at the Reformed academy in Pínczów, where the zealous French Protestant Peter Statorius (Stoinius) was rector. Statorius, a follower of Servetus, did much to spread the antitrinitarian message within the Polish Reformed church. His antitrinitarian party gained the support of many moderate Polish Calvinists, in part as a result of the rigidly doctrinaire position adopted by the orthodox opposition. Many moderates feared that tolerance and freedom of expression would be exterminated if the trinitarians prevailed. The Krakow pastor Gregory Paulus followed Statorius as leader of the antitrinitarians, and he was aided by the arrival in Poland in 1562 of Paolo Alciati and Valento Gentile, both followers of Servetus and former associates of Laelius Socinus.[4]

---

[3] Williams, pp. 749–763; Robert Mandrou, *From Humanism to Science, 1480–1700* (London, 1978), p. 142; *EB*, vol. 25, pp. 321–322.

[4] Wilbur, pp. 285–314.

The rapid growth of antitrinitarianism within the Polish Reformed church led to heated controversy and finally, in 1565, to schism. The antitrinitarians broke away from the orthodox Calvinist majority, formed the Minor Reformed church, and quickly developed a new doctrinal system stressing practical Christianity, freedom of conscience, toleration, and the use of reason in religion. The Minor church gradually came to oppose infant baptism, favoring instead baptism of adults by immersion in the Anabaptist style. This new church immediately drew opposition from both the orthodox Reformed church and the Catholics, but this opposition did not prevent the Minor church from growing and prospering, especially in its two major centers of Krakow and Lublin.[5]

Such was the state of Polish antitrinitarianism when Faustus Socinus arrived in Krakow in 1579. Just at the point when the first leaders of the movement were beginning to die out, Socinus appeared on the scene to fill the leadership vacuum. His fame as an antitrinitarian had preceded him by way of his work *De Jesu Christo Servatore*, which had been printed in Poland through the efforts of a friendly antitrinitarian noble. Socinus gave the Minor church a unity of spirit and a sense of purpose that made it a powerful religious force in Poland. In debates, correspondence, and published works Socinius spread his religious ideas throughout the Minor church and defended the church from the attacks of its critics. He became the authoritative interpreter of church doctrine as well as the official spokesman for the church. The Racovian Catechism, the official statement of Polish antitrinitarian belief published in 1605, reflected Socinus's ideas. The catechism remained unchanged as the official doctrine of Socinianism for over fifty years, becoming well known far beyond the borders of Poland.[6]

The flowering of Polish antitrinitarianism under Socinus's leadership tended to mask the fact that the members of the Minor church made up only a very small minority of the population in a predominantly Catholic country. To make matters worse, the Socinians could not even count on the support of other, more orthodox Polish Protestants. When the fervor of the Catholic Counter–Reformation reached Poland during the last quarter of the sixteenth century, the position of the Socinians quickly became embattled. As early as 1587, at the beginning of the reign of King Sigismund II, Jesuit influence within the Polish government was growing steadily. Sporadic persecution of Socinians by the Catholic populace made it clear to Socinian leaders that some kind of union with other like-minded Christians was essential in order for Socinianism to gain the support it needed to survive in such a hostile environment. The Minor church

[5] Ibid., pp. 326–338.
[6] Ibid., pp. 384–407.

made efforts to gain the friendship of Anabaptist groups in both Poland and Prussia, although without much success. Overtures were made to the Mennonites of Amsterdam, but these efforts backfired when the Mennonites not only refused Socinian offers of union but also wrote letters to their brethren in Poland warning them against antitrinitarian influence.[7]

During the early seventeenth century persecution of the Socinians by Polish Catholics increased dramatically. Acts of harassment began to take on a systematic character and were largely supported by the courts. As early as the 1620s, many Polish Socinians began to flee persecution by leaving their native land, some finding refuge in Holland. In 1635 the important Socinian church at Lublin was closed by court order, and in 1638 the courts decreed the destruction of the Socinian church, printing press, and academy at Rakow. The government also decreed that all Socinian inhabitants had to leave Rakow, the town that had long functioned as the capital of Polish antitrinitarianism. The loss of the centers of Lublin and Rakow was a major blow to the Polish Socinian movement, and the coup de grace soon followed. In 1648 a war between the Polish crown and a rebellious army of Cossacks and Tartars resulted in the destruction of nearly all Socinian churches in the Polish Ukraine. Then, in 1655 a Swedish invasion ravaged Socinian settlements in western Poland. Finally, in 1658 King Jan Casimir, a former Jesuit priest and cardinal, issued a decree banning Socinianism from his realm. All Socinian inhabitants were ordered, on pain of death, to either recant their beliefs or leave the country. The history of Polish Socinianism had come to a bitter end.[8]

Soon after the decree of 1658 the Socinians departed Poland for exile in Transylvania, Silesia, East Prussia, Brandenburg, and Mannheim. When war and plague made conditions unbearable for the Socinian colony in Mannheim, these exiles moved down the Rhine to Holland. Another group of Socinians who had settled at Friedrichstadt in Schleswig-Holstein also moved to Holland after encountering difficulties with local inhabitants. Apart from the colonies in Transylvania and East Prussia, which became permanent, almost all of the Socinian exiles eventually found their way to the Dutch republic. The United Provinces seemed to be a natural point of refuge for the exiles for several reasons. By 1660 the republic was the most tolerant nation in Europe, and the Socinians had reason to assume—wrongly as it turned out—that Dutch toleration would be extended even to antitrinitarians. As a result of the busy sea link between Amsterdam and Danzig, many Polish Socinians had already visited Holland, and a few had settled there prior to the exile. In addition, Socinian scholars had long maintained contacts with liberal Mennonite

[7] Kühler, pp. 197–203.
[8] Wilbur, pp. 443–475.

and Remonstrant theologians in Amsterdam, and this gave the Socinians reason to hope that these churches would welcome them when they were forced to leave Poland.[9]

The reception that the Socinians received in Holland was not what they had hoped for. The combination of fear and hostility with which most Dutch Christians—lay and clerical alike—met the Socinians took the exiles by surprise. The Socinians might have expected such a reception, however, in view of the reaction of Dutch authorities to the first visit of Socinians to Holland. In 1598 the zealous antitrinitarians Christoph Ostorodt and Johannes Wiodowski had disembarked from a ship in Amsterdam with a cargo of Socinian books for inspection by the theology faculty at Leiden. The Socinians hoped to win friends at Leiden, but the outcome of their journey was quite the opposite. The travelers were jailed by authorities in Amsterdam and their books were confiscated. After some deliberation city officials sent the Socinian books to Leiden for judgment after all, but at Leiden the conservative theologian Gomarus declared the books to be not only heretical but heathen. The books then were sent to the States of Holland in The Hague where they were burned. The States ordered Ostorodt and Wiodowski to leave the country, which they did only after discussing their ideas with interested church members in Amsterdam and Haarlem.[10]

Once the influx of Socinian exiles into Holland began in earnest after 1660, Dutch government officials repeatedly expressed their desire to put an end to the unwanted immigration. In practice, however, the authorities could do little to prevent the entry of Socinians into the country. Once they were settled some Socinians tried to hold organized worship services, but the government would not tolerate public meetings of antitrinitarians, and in this case it was able to enforce its will. The authorities could not, however, effectively prevent the printing of Socinian books on the many presses of Amsterdam. As a result, these books were turned out in great numbers, spreading Socinian ideas all over Holland. Socinian books had been printed in Amsterdam even before the exile. In 1642, for example, 450 copies of one Socinian tract had been seized and burned by the sheriff. After 1660, however, the volume of Socinian books in circulation in Holland increased greatly despite official injunctions against them. Works of all the major Socinian authors in Polish, Latin, Italian, German, and Dutch translations were available to the reading public. The flow of Socinian books was hindered only by very limited and infrequent

[9] Ibid., pp 481–535. On the Socinians in Holland, see also J. C. van Slee, *De geschiedenis van het Socinianisme in de Nederlanden* (Haarlem, 1914).

[10] Kühler, pp. 51–57.

efforts on the part of the government to crack down on Amsterdam print-ers.[11]

Although the Socinians were not permitted to organize formal, public worship services or to create any church structure in Holland, religious life went on for the exiles in their new home. Small groups of Polish So-cinians and their Dutch converts gathered in private homes in Amsterdam and other major cities to pray, sing, and read Scripture.[12] Because of the atmosphere of relative toleration that prevailed in urban Holland, the So-cinians were not forced to hold their meetings in absolute secrecy, but they did try to keep their activities out of the public eye. Nevertheless, reports and rumors of Socinian meetings tended to spread quickly among the orthodox population. Such reports were of great concern to the Re-formed church, which was constantly vigilant in defense of such ortho-dox doctrines as the Trinity and the divinity of Christ. Most of the prin-cipal Reformed theologians of the second half of the seventeenth century wrote at least one tract against the Socinians, and almost any report of Socinian activity was enough to cause considerable agitation in the Re-formed church councils of the major Dutch cities.[13]

The Reformed church did not remain inactive in the face of the Socin-ian threat. Calvinist preachers warned their flocks from the pulpits about the dangers of Socinianism, and the clergy placed constant pressure on local and national government authorities to eradicate the Socinian men-ace. As early as 1628 the Reformed church had warned the States of Hol-land against the emerging Socinian threat and had petitioned that Socin-ianism be officially outlawed, but the States had taken no action. As growing persecution in Poland brought an increasing stream of Socinian refugees into the Dutch republic, the Reformed church synods of north and south Holland, along with the Leiden University theology faculty, directed a strong remonstrance to the States of Holland in 1651 warning against the dangers of Socinianism. This time the States issued a decree forbidding Socinian meetings and books. In 1653 the States General of the United Provinces issued a similar decree in response to clerical pres-sure, and in 1656 the States General was again moved to action by ortho-dox complaints, resulting in a resolution directing local government au-thorities to crack down on Socinian meetings. This resolution was repeated in 1659. In the years between 1650 and 1657 most of the prov-inces of the Dutch republic passed their own anti-Socinian laws, and in 1674 the Court of Holland, that province's highest judicial body, banned by name the most important Socinian book, the *Bibliotheca Fratrum Po-*

[11] Ibid., pp. 135–138; Zilverberg, p. 39.
[12] Wilbur, pp. 554–555.
[13] Kühler, pp. 222–226.

lonarum. Enforcement of these governmental decrees was extremely lax, however, because civil authorities were not at all eager to stir up any avoidable trouble in the absence of a direct threat to the ruling powers. The frequent repetition of ordinances against the Socinians itself testifies to the limited effectiveness of such laws.[14]

Dutch religious and political authorities had reason to fear Socinian ideas. The centerpiece of Socinian doctrine was a rejection of the doctrine of the Trinity based on arguments from both Scripture and reason. The Socinians believed Christ to be God's messenger and the divinely chosen head of the church, but they did not believe that he had a divine nature. For the Socinians, Christ was merely a man without sin. Socinianism also denied the orthodox doctrine of satisfaction—the belief that Christ, by his suffering and death on the cross, had satisfied God's desire to punish sinful humanity. The Socinians' main objection to this doctrine was that it left no need for individual conversion. The Calvinist docrine of predestination was rejected for similar reasons; according to the Socinians, it eliminated moral choice and made God the author of sin. In place of church dogma the Socinians stressed a practical, ethical religious life based on human reason and free will. With their criticisms of orthodox doctrine the Socinians struck at the very heart of Reformation theology. Unlike those Protestants who believed grace to be a free and undeserved gift of God to sinful humanity, the Socinians believed that salvation would come only to the person who fulfilled God's commands.[15] In the view of the Dutch Reformed church, a sect that rejected so many key Protestant doctrines and actually denied the divinity of Christ was involved in the most iniquitous possible heresy.

By and large, the other Protestant churches in the United Provinces agreed with the Calvinists in condemning Socinianism. The Remonstrants, who already stood under considerable public suspicion for their differences with orthodox Calvinist doctrine, could ill afford to be associated with a radical creed that was widely viewed not only as anti-Christian but even as atheistic. During the early seventeenth century when the persecution of Socinianism in Poland was accelerating, the Remonstrants had some contacts with Polish Socinians seeking allies in the Low Countries. During the period of the Remonstrant exile in Antwerp following the Synod of Dordrecht, however, Simon Episcopius turned down offers of aid and alliance from Socinian leader Johannes Schlichting. A Similar offer from the Socinian theologian Martinus Ruarus was refused by the

---

[14] Ibid., pp. 141–143; Wilbur, p. 555.

[15] W. J. Kühler, "Remonstranten en Socinianen," Heering, ed., pp. 138–139; Kühler, pp. 57, 64–65.

Remonstrants in 1632. After the arrival of the Socinian exiles in Holland a few Remonstrants were influenced by Socinian ideas, but Remonstrant leaders condemned this influence and Socinian sympathizers were excluded from the brotherhood. Only later in the century could the liberal Remonstrant theologians Etienne de Courcelles and Philip van Limborch show some sympathy for Socinian ideas in their writings.[16]

Among the other Dutch Protestant churches the Mennonites were the only group at all open to Socinian influence. Several points of similarity existed between Socinian and Mennonite religious views, perhaps in part because of the common roots of both movements in the Radical Reformation. Both the Socinians and the Mennonites tried to cultivate Christian life in its primitive simplicity, relied on Scripture in place of tradition, stressed Christian conduct and character above doctrinal orthodoxy, practiced pacifism, and refused government service.[17] Many of the more liberal Mennonites were open to the influence of other Socinian ideas as well, but such influence was usually confined to a rejection of the doctrine of satisfaction. When Jacques Outerman (1547–1639), a leader of the Flemish Mennonite congregation in Haarlem, became an advocate of Socinian antitrinitarianism, a great conflict arose within the Mennonite movement and Outerman and his followers were heavily criticized. No less than the Remonstrants, the Mennonites feared the brand of Socinianism.[18]

Socinianism thus found no great toleration even in tolerant Holland. Its adherents were treated as religious pariahs by the established churches and often branded as atheists. Under such circumstances it is not surprising that the Socinians drifted into contact with the Collegiants, the most radical and most tolerant group in seventeenth-century Dutch religious life. The colleges closed their doors to no one, and Socinian exiles as well as Dutchmen influenced by Socinianism were found at college meetings from the mid-1650s. Socinian religious doctrine was not generally accepted by the Rijnsburgers but Socinian rationalism strongly influenced the formation of the Collegiant rational religion. While antitrinitarianism held little appeal for most Rijnsburgers, who were in any case generally indifferent to doctrinal matters, the central place given to reason in Socinian theology attracted Collegiants whose inner religion was already becoming inclined to rationalism. A number of Collegiants were deeply influenced by Socinian ideas, and it was through the personal appeal and the writings of these men that the Socinian conception of the role of reason in religion became part of Collegiant thought.[19]

[16] Kühler, pp. 77–79, 204–216; Kühler, in Heering, ed., pp. 141–145.
[17] Wilbur, pp. 561–562.
[18] Kühler, pp. 92–97.
[19] Kühler, in Heering, ed., pp. 146–147.

The leading Collegiant Socinians were not Polish refugees but Dutchmen influenced by personal contact with Socinian exiles or by the reading of Socinian books. Even before the great influx of Polish exiles into Holland, several important Collegiants had been influenced by Socinian ideas. One such person was Johannes Geesteranus (1576–1622). Geesteranus came from a family with contacts among the Polish Brethren, and during his years of service as a Remonstrant pastor in Alkmaar he was inclined to Socinian opinions. After being deposed from his post in Alkmaar by the Synod of Dordrecht in 1619, Geesteranus went to Warmond, where he became the first person baptized by immersion among the Collegiants. Van Slee suggested that it was Geesteranus who first introduced the Collegiants to baptism by immersion, a practice that was common among the Polish Socinians. In any case, Geesteranus settled in Warmond in 1620 and made his living as a weaver while attending college meetings. In 1622 the Socinian theologian Martinus Ruarus invited Geesteranus to become rector of the theological school at Rakow, but he declined the offer for personal reasons. Geesteranus died of plague in Norden later that same year.[20]

In Norden, Geesteranus became acquainted with another thinker inclined toward Socinian ideas, the poet Dirk Camphuysen. Camphuysen was especially influenced by the Socinian rejection of the doctrines of predestination, hereditary sin, and satisfaction. He saw Christ as an ambassador of God and as a lawgiver, but not as divine. Along with his rejection of the divinity of Christ, Camphuysen further claimed that the Holy Spirit was only a power of God and thus not identical in essence with God. Following both Socinian and Collegiant principles, Camphuysen maintained that Christians could depend for their salvation only on the knowledge that they drew from Holy Scripture, and he held that Scripture could only be interpreted by reason. In 1623 Camphuysen translated Faustus Socinus's important work *De Auctoritate Sacrae Scripturae* into Dutch. Camphuysen probably learned of the Collegiants from Geesteranus in Norden in 1622, and during a trip to Delft in 1625 he visited Rijnsburg and became an advocate of Collegiant ideas. That same year Camphuysen was offered a professorship at the Rakow school, but he too declined the offer.[21]

In the period after the Polish exile, when Socinian influence was increasing rapidly within the Collegiant movement, several men influenced by Socinianism rose to positions of prominence in the colleges. Johannes Becius (1626–1690) was born in Middelburg and studied theology at Utrecht. Following his graduation he became a proponent (candidate for

[20] Van Slee, *De Rijnsburger Collegianten*, p. 378; *BLNP*, vol. 2, pp. 210–211.
[21] Kühler, pp. 138–147.

the ministry) in the Reformed classis of Walcheren, and he later served for a time as preceptor of the Latin school in his native Middelburg. In 1652 Becius became a Reformed pastor in Antwerp, and in 1660 he moved on to a similar post at Franeker. When he returned home to Middelburg in 1664 the Reformed church there began an investigation into his religious views, which were rumored to be antitrinitarian. As a result of this investigation Becius left the Reformed church in 1666. His religious views did indeed involve a rejection of the Trinity and the divinity of Christ, and he defended these ideas in his *Apologia modesta et Christiana*, published in 1668. Soon after this publication both Becius and his book were banished from Middelburg. Becius then settled in Amsterdam in 1671, where he published a further defense of his views in the *Defensio apologia modesta et Christiana*. Soon after his arrival in Amsterdam Becius became an active Collegiant.

In the college Becius debated various points of antitrinitarian doctrine with the Socinian theologian Martinus Ruarus and his followers Daniel Backer and Jacob Jansen Voogt. Becius also became a staunch advocate of Collegiant principles. In his book *Wederlegging van het tractaet welckers titul is: reden waerom de Ed. Act. Magistraet den Mennisten tot Deventer niet mach toelaten conventicelen te houden* (Refutation of the tract entitled: Reasons why the honorable magistrates may not allow the Deventer Mennonites to hold conventicals, 1671) Becius praised Rijnsburger toleration. In 1678, the same year in which he published his theological magnum opus, the *Institutio Christiana*, Becius moved to Rotterdam, where he remained an active Collegiant. In 1681 he published a long work defending Socinianism and free thought, and in the years that followed he carried on a protracted pamphlet debate with critics of the Socinians and Collegiants. In his book *Twijfelingen en Swarigheden* (Doubts and difficulties, 1686) he combined a defense of Socinian ideas with a ringing declaration of loyalty to the Collegiant principles of toleration and freedom of conscience. Becius died in Amsterdam.[22]

Another Socinian-influenced Collegiant in Amsterdam in these years was Jan Knol (d. 1672). A regular member of the college, Knol sometimes visited Socinian meetings as well, and under the influence of Socinianism he rejected the doctrine of the Trinity as contrary to reason. Knol held philosophical discussion meetings in his home that were attended by some of the most radical freethinkers in Amsterdam, including Adrian Koerbagh, one of the few people jailed for their religious beliefs in seventeenth-century Amsterdam.[23] The Reformed church council of Amsterdam complained repeatedly to municipal authorities about Knol's activities, but the government took no action. In 1659 Knol published the first Dutch translation of the *Racovian Catechism*, but most Socinians rejected this translation because Knol made numerous changes in the sections concerning baptism and communion. Knol was also a firm opponent of all ecclesiastical institutions and he rejected church offices as useless. In his work *Samenspraeck Tusschen een Rustsoeckende Ziel en Christ* (Conversation between a rest-seeking soul and Christ), which survives today only in manuscript, Knol strongly ciriticized the pope, Luther, and Calvin while giving Menno and Arminius only slightly more sympathy, but he praised Socinus as the only true theologian and antitrinitarianism as the only true Christianity. Knol was a friend and defender of Galenus Abrahamsz. during the Lammerenkrijg and he was also a main source for Socinian ideas in the Amsterdam college.[24]

Galenus Abrahamsz. himself was influenced by certain aspects of Socinian thought. During the *Lammerenkrijg*, Galenus's conservative Mennonite opponents repeatedly charged him with Socinianism, and they even caused him to be summoned before the Court of Holland to answer these accusations. The court cleared Galenus of the charges, and certainly he was not a Socinian in the sense of being a convinced adherent of antitrinitarianism. Galenus was, however, influenced by some aspects of Socinian belief, including the rejection of the doctrine of Christ's satisfaction. Galenus held that Christ had died for humankind's good—to reconcile humanity with God—but not to change or transform human nature. Galenus believed that because Christ did not die in humanity's place, automatically uniting humankind with God, all people still had to fulfill the evangelical commands necessary to obtain their own salvation. Samuel Apostool, leader of the Zonnists, claimed that Galenus took these ideas directly from Socinus. While Galenus was no doubt influenced to some extent by Socinian ideas and by his friendship with Collegiant Socinians, his own personal preference was for a religion centered on a practical, moral Christian life.[25]

By the last quarter of the seventeenth century the influence of Socinianism within the Collegiant movement reached a high point. In 1694 the Amsterdam Collegiant Reynier Rooleeuw produced a new "Rijnsburger

[23] On Adrian Koerbagh, see Hubert Vandenbossche, *Spinozisme en Kritiek bij Koerbagh* (Brussels, n.d.); Zilverberg, pp. 79–85; Evenhuis, vol. 3, pp. 350–360; and P. H. van Moerkerken, *Adriaan Koerbagh, een strijder voor het vrije denken* (Amsterdam, 1948).

[24] *BLNP*, vol. 1, p. 99; Zilverberg, p. 43. A. de Groot does not believe that Knol was a Socinian, see A. de Groot, "De Amsterdamse Collegiant Jan Cornelis Knol," *Doopsgezinde Bijdragen*, n.s. 10, no. 12 (1984), pp. 77–88.

[25] Kühler, pp. 158–160.

translation" of the Bible that was influenced by Socinian ideas. In place of the orthodox reading of John 1:1, "And the word was God," the Rooleeuw translation read, "And the word was a god." Other passages relating to such doctrinal points as hereditary sin, the divinity of Christ, Christ's preexistence and the Trinity also showed Socinian influence. While the Rijnsburgers often were accused of Socinianism by their critics, in fact the colleges included both proponents and opponents of Socinian ideas. Most Collegiants were eclectic, adopting certain Socinian ideas that attracted them without becoming Socinians in any true sense. With respect to their ideas on such controversial issues as the working of grace, most Rijnsburgers were closer to the Remonstrants than to the Socinians, and only a very few Collegiants rejected the Trinity. The Collegiants were, however, greatly influenced by the Socinian call for a rational religion.[26] The most important impact of Socinianism upon Collegiant thought was in giving both form and content to a Collegiant rational religion that was present only in embryonic form in the Rijnsburger ideal of the universal church.

Socinian thought was built upon the twin foundations of the Bible and human reason, and it was for this reason that George Huntston Williams called Socinianism a kind of evangelical rationalism. Like their humanistic predecessors the Italian Valdesian evangelicals of the sixteenth century, the Socinians stressed both a rational approach to Christianity and a sober biblicism. Socinianism was a complex intellectual system that combined elements of humanist rationalism, Florentine Platonism, and Paduan Aristotelianism along with Anabaptist and Calvinistic components.[27] In addition to antitrinitarianism, a rejection of the deity of Christ and of Christ's satisfaction, pacifism, and a belief in the separation of church and state, the Socinians stressed human free will and rationality as well as the central importance of the individual's natural knowledge of God. These ideas led the Socinians to adopt a very rationalistic interpretation of Scripture.

   The Socinians accepted the Bible as the literally true, inspired, and authoritative revelation of God, and they based their own religious doctrines exclusively on Scripture. At the same time, the Socinians believed that human reason was the primary guide in interpreting the Bible, and they therefore drew their arguments against orthodox doctrines from both Scripture and reason.[28] While the precise relationship between Scripture and reason could vary from one Socinian thinker to the next (as did

[26] Ibid., pp. 190–192, 185, van Slee, *De Rijnsburger Collegianten*, pp. 384–385.
[27] Williams, pp. 762, 856; *EP*, vol. 7, pp. 474–475.
[28] *ME*, vol. 4, pp. 565–566.

the interpretation of other Socinian doctrines), in its broad outlines Socinian thought regarding scriptural interpretation followed the ideas presented by Faustus Socinus in his work *De Auctoritate Sacrae Scripturae* (1588). In this work Socinus held the Bible to be the sacred revelation of God, and he also declared that it did not contain doctrines contrary to reason.[29] Socinus believed that people could only know God by accepting as true the revelations contained in the Bible and by using human reason rather than church tradition or clerical authority to interpret Scripture. Many Socinians accepted scriptural accounts of miracles as literally true and constructed elaborate (and tortured) rational explanations for how such miracles had occurred.[30] While some later Socinian thinkers were less rationalistic in their biblical interpretation than Faustus, others (such as Samuel Crellius and Andreas Wizowaty) were even more rationalistic. The Socinians refused to accept traditional doctrines simply because they were traditional, calling instead for a religion suited to each individual's own insight and experience. This approach appealed to many people who were already rationally inclined in their religious thought, and many of these people were Collegiants.[31]

The influence of Socinian ideas upon the developing Collegiant rational religion produced what can best be described as a biblically based commonsense rationalism in the colleges. In this Socinian-influenced Rijnsburger rational religion, reason was primarily a tool for interpreting the truths contained in Scripture. Reason in this system was instrumental, nonspeculative, nonmetaphysical, empirically based, and practical, and thus it differed significantly from the speculative and a priori rationalism of Cartesian and Spinozistic philosophy. Socinian rationalism was based on biblical premises and on observation, not on intuitive first principles. In Collegiant rational religion, reason was tied closely to its function of Bible interpretation and wholly subservient to the revealed content of truth. While in the later development of Collegiant rationalism reason would lose this subservience to scriptural revelation and would itself become a source of true ideas, at this early stage the role of reason was limited strictly to interpretation.[32]

An excellent example of Socinian-influenced Collegiant rational religion was provided by the work of Frans Kuyper (1629–1692), one of the most active Rijnsburgers during the 1670s and 1680s. Little is known of

[29] Williams, p. 750.

[30] Kühler, pp. 230–233; Roldanus, *Zeventiende eeuwse geestesbloei*, p. 104; Hylkema, vol. 2, p. 290.

[31] Roldanus, *Zeventiende eeuwse geestesbloei*, p. 105; Kühler, p. 91.

[32] To compare this approach to Calvin's use of reason in religion, see William J. Bouwsma, *John Calvin: A Sixteenth Century Portrait* (Oxford, 1988), chap. 6, "Rational Religion."

Kuyper's early life, but in 1650 he was a proponent studying at the Remonstrant Seminary in Amsterdam, and in 1652 he became a Remonstrant preacher in Vlaardingen. At the Seminary it is likely that Kuyper came into contact with some of the Polish Socinian students who were often sent by their church to the Remonstrant school for theological instruction, a practice that became more common after the closing of the Rakow academy in 1638. In any event, Kuyper held radical views from the very earliest stage of his career. In 1653 he resigned his post in Vlaardingen because of his opposition to child baptism, and soon thereafter he left Zeeland for Amsterdam, where he became a printer and a Collegiant. The tenor of Kuyper's religious opinion at this time was demonstrated by the fact that one of the first works to come from his press was a new edition of the *Bibliotheca Fratrum Polonorum*, the collected writings of the fathers of Polish Socinianism. As a Rijnsburger Kuyper was very active in religious discussions in the Amsterdam college, and he continued his activity when he later moved to Rotterdam and became deeply involved in the debates surrounding the ideas of Jan Bredenburg. Kuyper was also an amateur chemist, and while searching for herbs to make his so-called *Kuyperbalsem* he was struck and killed by a windmill blade in 1692.[33]

Like other Socinian-influenced Collegiants, Kuyper was most interested in the ideas of Socinus regarding the uses of reason in religion. Kuyper respected rational thinking and strove to explain the Bible with rational argumentation. His deep belief in the authority and veracity of the scriptural text, even in its accounts of miracles, anchored his respect for reason in the firm foundation of faith.[34] In the tradition of Socinus himself, Kuyper made reason a tool of religion, and this tool was always subservient to the revealed source of religious truth in Scripture. His Socinian-influenced rational religion was given clear expression in three works known collectively as "The Philosophizing Peasant," written by Kuyper with the cooperation of his Rotterdam friend and collaborator Barend Joosten Stol during the years 1676–1677. In these works Kuyper and Stol used the character of a "simple" peasant to defend the idea of a biblically based rational religion against the objections of a Cartesian philosopher and a Quaker. The peasant's two opponents represented the extremes of speculative philosophical rationalism and mystical irrationalism that Collegiant rational religion rejected and defined itself against. To the Cartesian philosopher the Collegiant peasant proclaimed the merits of a sober, biblical religion. Against the spiritualistic Quaker the peasant stressed the need for a reasoned religion that comprehended the truths of faith clearly.

---

[33] *NNBW*, vol. 4, pp. 868–869; Evenhuis, pp. 322–324.
[34] Hylkema, vol. 2, p. 350; Kühler, pp. 243–247.

With these criticisms of spiritualism and speculative rationalism Kuyper and Stol pointed out both the rational and the biblical sides of Rijnsburger rational religion and thereby sketched the outlines of a very important stage of Collegiant intellectual evolution as the Rijnsburgers moved away from spiritualism in the direction of rationalism.

The first work in the series, *Den Philosopherenden Boer, eerste deel: Handelende van de dwalingen der hedendsdaagse Christenen, Philosophen, Cartesianen en Quakers* . . . (The philosophizing peasant, part one: Dealing with the errors of present day Christians, philosophers, cartesians, and Quakers [1676]), was written by Stol, but it contained so many of Kuyper's ideas that we must assume that the two men cooperated closely in the work's composition. Barend Joosten Stol was a watchmaker from Schiedam who became an important member of the Rotterdam college. A Mennonite influenced by Socinian ideas, Stol was a close friend and supporter of Kuyper in the latter's disputes with the Quaker Benjamin Furly and with the Collegiant Jan Bredenburg.[35] In *Den Philosopherenden Boer* Stol followed Kuyper in rejecting both Quaker spiritualism and the brand of speculative philosophical rationalism proposed by the Cartesians and Spinoza and later adopted by Bredenburg. Stol specifically rejected the Cartesian contention that humans had an innate rational knowledge of God, emphasizing instead the need for a religion based on the Bible and common sense.

Den Philosopherenden Boer was constructed in the form of a dialogue between a peasant and a philosopher, who perhaps represented ideas that Bredenburg was already discussing in the Rotterdam college. After taking a long walk in the countryside the two friends retired to the peasant's cottage for rest and refreshment. As the two men entered the cottage the philosopher noticed that the "simple" peasant owned quite a few books, and he asked the peasant if he was studying to become a doctor, lawyer, or theologian. The peasant replied that his books were theological works that he read and studied in his spare time. When the philosopher remarked that such a pastime was a bit unusual for a peasant, the peasant replied that his simple understanding was quite capable of discovering which among the various teachings most agreed with Scripture. In this passage Stol used the peasant to express a central tenet of Collegiant rational religion: the idea that even ordinary people without formal education could use their natural reason to understand religious questions in the light of scriptural evidence, because religion was itself rational and

[35] On Stol, see Melles, p. 154. For Stol's authorship and Kuyper's contribution to *Den Philosopherenden Boer*, see Hylkema, vol. 2, p. 313, n. 541; and the anonymous pamphlet *Eenige Aanmerkingen voor den Philosopherenden Boer, met eenige vragen aan den zelven voorgestelt door die gene, diemen spots-gewijse noemt Quakers* (Rotterdam, 1676). See also Evenhuis, vol. 3, p. 324; and van Slee, *De Rijnsburger Collegianten*, pp. 348–349.

open to the investigations of common sense. To emphasize the fact that the peasant had no formal education, Stol had him tell the Cartesian that all of his books were written in the vernacular (in *Duyts* [German], the seventeenth-century term for what today is called Dutch) because he could not read Latin.[36]

After admiring the peasant's library the philosopher expressed his esteem for his friend's life of study and suggested that they discuss the principles of religion. When the peasant asked the philosopher what he meant by the principles of religion, the latter replied, in true Cartesian (or Spinozistic) fashion, that he was referring to the first principles or axioms of religious truth upon which all religion was based. The peasant then insisted that he had never heard of such axioms, and he asked the philosopher to explain them further. Stol thus used the peasant to point out the opposition between the empirical and commonsense conception of reason contained in Collegiant rational religion and speculative philosophical rationalism that made use of a priori principles.

In order to demonstrate such principles at work and thus to convince the peasant of their validity, the philosopher proposed what he called a "mathematical proof from natural reason" for the existence of God. Following a confused version of part of the argument for God's existence presented in Descartes's Third Meditation, the philosopher maintained that since humankind was created or caused, and since a cause always had to be greater than its effect, there thus existed a God who had created humankind. The philosopher followed this argument with another semi-Cartesian (or perhaps Scholastic) proof in which he claimed to demonstrate God's existence from the existence of human thought itself. The philosopher declared that he had discovered by introspection that he had the power of thinking and that he in fact did think. He also knew, he said, that he had received this ability not from himself but from another. The philosopher then concluded that his reasoning powers had to have been given to him by God, who thus necessarily existed. This barrage of speculative reasoning based loosely on Cartesian foundations proved too much for the peasant. In exasperation he responded to the philosopher's first argument by declaring that his "peasant understanding" could comprehend only that humans were caused or created by other people—their parents. In reply to the philosopher's claim that a cause always had to be greater than its effect, the peasant argued that common sense dictated that like always produced like and therefore causes and effects were equal. The peasant maintained furthermore that his reason did not lead

---

[36] Barend Joosten Stol, *Den Philosopherenden Boer, eerste deel: Handelende van de dwalingen der hedendaagse Christenen, Philosophen, Cartesianen en Quakers, In Verscheyden Onvermeynde Zaaken* (Rotterdam, 1676), pp. 2–3.

him to postulate a first cause of the world, as the philosopher claimed, but rather his reason led him to conclude that the world was eternal. Divine revelation alone assured him that God existed and was the cause and creator of the world.[37] The peasant thus rejected speculative philosophical rationalism in favor of biblical revelation and common sense.

Undeterred by the peasant's objections, the philosopher argued that another proof for God's existence was the individual's immortal soul, which was given by God. The peasant replied that Gen. 1:28 proved that human begat human, complete with body and soul, and he added that Scripture nowhere taught the immortality of the soul. The philosopher next resorted to the argument from design, a proof for God's existence that was popular during the seventeenth and eighteenth centuries. When we see the marvelous workings of a clock we assume that it was made by an intelligent creator, the philosopher argued. It is the same when we observe the wonderful working of the world: we must conclude that it was made by an all-wise God. The philosopher called this argument "a mathematically sure proof" of the existence of God, but the peasant disagreed. If a person simply looked at the world without first having any knowledge of God from Scripture, the peasant argued, he would have to doubt that any intelligent cause was behind a world in which humans and beasts harmed each other, where the mighty ruled by violence, and where pious people were murdered. "Could such a world be the work of a wise creator?" the peasant asked.[38]

The philosopher was not ready to concede the argument to his friend so easily. He continued to argue his case for a natural rational knowledge of religion by maintaining that moral commands such as the prohibition of murder, theft, and adultery as well as the Golden Rule ("do unto others as you would have them do unto you") were innate in all people. Since the principles of morality were thus natural, he argued, people did not need to learn them from the Bible. In reply, the peasant maintained that natural abilities such as sight and hearing were in fact innate in people, but moral commands were learned in the same way that speaking, writing, and handicrafts were learned. Moral commands had to be learned, the peasant explained, because unlike sight and hearing they were contrary to human nature and thus they conflicted with people's natural desires. For this reason moral commands could not be founded on natural inclinations but had to be based instead on the promise of great supernatural reward. The peasant argued that human nature and reason taught people to seek only their own good, not the good of others, while Scrip-

---

[37] Ibid., pp. 3–5. The peasant's claim that reason taught that humans were caused by their parents was an objection dismissed by Descartes in the Third Meditation.

[38] Ibid., pp. 5–10.

ture alone taught altruistic virtue and morality. For this reason, all that
people needed to know to lead a moral life was clearly revealed in the
Bible. The peasant added that everything that God revealed of himself in
Scripture he revealed in such a way that even a simple peasant could understand it without abstract speculation.[39] Stol's peasant thus rejected
natural religion in favor of a commonsense approach to scriptural interpretation.

While standing firm on the basis of Scripture as the chief source for
Christian truth, Collegiant rational religion also emphasized the importance of human reason as the primary tool for interpreting Scripture. This
rational side of Collegiant biblical rationalism was illustrated in Frans
Kuyper's work *Tweede Deel of Vervolg van de Philosopherende Boer: In
Welk de geheyme gevoelens der Quakers, uyt haar eygen Schriften . . .
ontdekt worden* (Second part or continuation of the philosophizing peasant. In which the secret opinions of the Quakers are revealed from their
own writings [1676]).

In the *Tweede Deel* Kuyper argued against the extreme spiritualism of
the English Quakers. The Quakers had come to Holland in 1653 seeking
converts among the Mennonites and Collegiants, and they were received
initially as kindred spirits by Galenus Abrahamsz. and the Amsterdam
Collegiants. To the Collegiants, the Quaker religion of the inner light
seemed at first to have much in common with their own religion of individual conscience. During the 1660s, however, several lengthy discussions were held between the Quakers and the Collegiants during the
course of which the Rijnsburgers came to realize the full extent of the
Quaker rejection of reason. As a result of these discussions the Quakers
and Collegiants parted ways, but not without considerable bitterness on
both sides, as was evidenced by the vituperative pamphlet war that raged
between the two groups after 1660. In this struggle, about which more
will be said in subsequent chapters, the Quakers attacked Galenus and his
ideas concerning the church, while Galenus's fellow Collegiants Pieter
Serrarius and Pieter Balling defended the Rijnsburger cause. In 1673 Kuyper also clashed with the Rotterdam Quaker leader Benjamin Furly, and
it was partly as a result of this conflict that Kuyper wrote the *Tweed Deel*.
This work should therefore be viewed in part as a defense of Collegiant
rational religion against the extreme spiritualism of the Quakers.[40]

[39] Ibid., pp. 11–17.
[40] Roldanus, *Zeventiende eeuwse geestesbloei*, pp. 110–114; W. I. Hull, *The Rise of
Quakerism in Amsterdam, 1655–1665* (Swarthmore, Penn., 1938), pp. 233–266. For Kuyper's clash with Furly and the relationship of this episode to *Den Philosopherenden Boer*,
see *Eenige Aanmerkingen voor den Philosopherenden Boer, met eenige vragen aan den zelven voorgestelt door die gene, diemen spost-gewijse noemt Quakers* (Rotterdam, 1676);
and Hull, *Benjamin Furly and Quakerism in Rotterdam* (Swarthmore, Penn., 1941).

In *Tweede Deel* Kuyper's Collegiant peasant undertook a religious discussion with a Quaker. Throughout this discussion the peasant repeatedly asked that the Quaker explain his religious beliefs in clear language, but the Quaker refused and insisted on discussing his ideas in vague, mystical terms. When the peasant asked the Quaker his opinion concerning the millennium, the Quaker rejected the idea of the future coming of Christ's visible kingdom on earth and declared that Christ's kingdom came to earth whenever the Holy Spirit lived in humanity. The peasant next asked the Quaker his opinion about the immortality of the soul, and in reply the Quaker argued that the souls of true believers were all parts of one divine essence and were reunited with God after the death of the body. But the Collegiant peasant was most annoyed by the Quaker's claim that belief in God resulted from a direct inworking of the Holy Spirit in humanity and not from the consent of rational understanding to ideas encountered in the Bible. By depicting Christian faith as a spiritual rather than a rational process, the Quaker rejected the principal foundation of Collegiant rational religion.[41]

The Quaker also attacked the Collegiants' idea of morality by maintaining that the doing of good works did not please God unless Christ worked these things through people, because otherwise the good works were simply idolatrous. For the Quaker, human reason and free will played no significant role in religion. He insisted that the only source for religious knowledge was the inner light, the direct inflowing of the Holy Spirit into the soul of each believer, and he furthermore maintained that in order for a person to obtain this inflowing of the divine spirit he or she deliberately had to forsake human reason. In order to stress this point the Quaker declared that "as long as reason lives, Christ is dead." The Quakers were God's chosen people, he continued, because the Holy Spirit revealed truths to them that were not recorded in the Bible. As for the Collegiants, the Quaker said that they understood neither the Bible nor the ideas of the Quakers because they depended on human reason instead of divine inspiration.[42]

The Collegiant peasant responded to this declaration of extreme spiritualism by asserting that the Quakers had been deceived by Satan. Because they rejected their own natural reason and refused to accept the Bible as the source of religious truth, the Quakers could no longer distinguish good from bad or true from false, the peasant argued. He further maintained that the Quaker belief that natural reason was a hindrance to religious knowledge was seriously mistaken because reason had been cre-

[41] Frans Kuyper, *Tweede Deel of Vervolg van de Philosopher ende Boer: In Welk de geheyme gevoelens der Quaakers, uyt haar eygen schriften, en met haar eygen woorden, ontdekt worden* . . . (Rotterdam, 1676), pp. 1–8.

[42] Ibid., pp. 8–18.

ated by God and was thus both necessary and good. The devil had deceived the Quakers into rejecting reason because only reason could expose the devil for what he was by comparing his words to the truth of Scripture. While it was true, the peasant continued, that people should not make natural reason the only judge of truth, reason was nevertheless essential for understanding the spiritual doctrines revealed in the Bible. To conclude his argument, Kuyper's peasant used Galenus's ideas to dismiss Quaker claims regarding divine inspiration. The notion that people got religious knowledge from a direct inflowing of the Holy Spirit was mistaken, he maintained, because the gifts of the Holy Spirit had not been given to people on earth since apostolic times. The Quakers' claim that they were God's inspired ambassadors on earth was also obviously false, the peasant concluded, because they could perform no miracles as proof of their special divine authority.[43] In Kuyper's rejection of Quaker spiritualism two radically different approaches to Second Reformation religious reform were evident. Both Quakers and Collegiants favored a religion of individual conscience, but the Collegiants had moved beyond the Quakers' spiritualistic approach to a rational and secular conception of religious knowledge.

In the third and last work of the peasant series, *De Diepten des Satans, of Geheymenissen der Atheisterij ontdekt en Vernielt* (The depths of Satan, or secrets of atheism uncovered and destroyed [1677]), Kuyper further outlined Collegiant rational religion by contrasting it with an extreme brand of philosophical rationalism that he attributed to Spinoza (and perhaps also to Bredenburg). Kuyper distinguished between two kinds of reason that according to him were often employed by thinkers in dealing with religious and philosophical questions. The first kind he called "healthy reason," which he defined as "man's natural ability to reason and understand."[44] It was this ability that the Collegiants used to interpret Scripture, Kuyper explained. "Healthy reason" was also employed to interpret the evidence presented by the outer senses, Kuyper continued, and nothing in Scripture or religion could be accepted as true if it was judged by "healthy reason" to be contrary to the testimony of the senses. With his idea of "healthy reason" Kuyper described the empirical, commonsense rationalism that formed the basis for Collegiant rational religion.

The second kind of reason that Kuyper discussed was what he called "natural reason." He rejected this kind of reason as consisting primarily of judgments drawn from "innate passions" (*ingeschaape hartstochten*).

---

[43] Ibid., pp. 21–26.

[44] Frans Kuyper, *De Diepten des Satans, of Geheymenissen der Atheisterij ontdekt en Vernielt . . .* (Rotterdam, 1677), pp. i–iii.

Some philosophers who used "natural reason" called these innate passions "first principles," Kuyper said, obviously referring to the intuitive rationalism of the Cartesians and Spinozists. Such a priori principles were, however, based on nothing more than people's inner prejudices, he argued, and these principles also contradicted the evidence of the senses. Reasoning based on these principles could never be the proper guide to religious truth because such reasoning ignored biblical revelation.[45]

Kuyper believed that deductive and nonempirical rationalism based on intuitive first principles was not in fact reason at all. For Kuyper, reason was a mental power or method, not a stock of intuitive, a priori truths. He saw reason as the ability to interpret Scripture along empirical and commonsense lines in order to obtain religious truth. For all of its emphasis on reason, Collegiant rational religion could not yet do without the Bible as the source for true ideas. "It is useful to investigate from the ground up whether the truth of the Bible and the existence of God stand on good grounds," Kuyper wrote, "but without seriously doubting the truth of these things."[46]

Kuyper opposed deductive rationalism with its a priori principles perhaps because he feared that if human reason were considered to be a source of true religious principles independent of Scripture, a separation of rational philosophy from scriptural revelation would take place that would have the effect of damaging the religious authority of Scripture as it elevated that of reason. If reason alone could supply religious truth, what would be the role of revelation? In natural religion Kuyper saw a deadly threat to scriptural revelation: If natural reason was made a source of true religious ideas independent of revelation, the possibility of competing and perhaps even contradictory religious truths would destroy the authority of Scripture in the same way that the competing churches produced by the Reformation had destroyed the authority of institutional religion. Kuyper clearly recognized this threat in Spinoza's *Theologico-Political Treatise* (1670), and he later saw the same danger in the rationalism of Jan Bredenburg. He attempted to avoid the damaging separation of reason from revelation by declaring that biblical truth never contradicted reason or nature. Kuyper therefore argued that to maintain that an idea could be rationally false even though the Bible proved it true (or vice versa) was "to forsake God." Even though he was a firm advocate of constructing rational proofs for scriptural doctrines, Kuyper nevertheless insisted that no religious truth was possible without biblical revelation.[47]

[45] Ibid.
[46] Ibid., p. iii.
[47] Ibid., pp. iv, 1.

For him, the authority of Scripture depended on its monopoly on the truth content of religion.

De Diepten des Satans based its conception of rational religion not just on Socinian-inspired ideas concerning the role of reason in religion but also, and perhaps more importantly, on the ideas of Galenus Abrahamsz. Kuyper argued that in the days of Christ and the apostles there were men in the world gifted with the Holy Spirit and ordained by God to teach people religious truth. These early ambassadors of God used their divine inspiration in order to interpret religious truth for the masses, and in this way the word of God was proclaimed infallibly. In the corrupt world of the seventeenth century, however, people no longer received such divine inspiration, Kuyper lamented. For this reason he declared that the believers of his day could rely only on the Bible for religious knowledge, and everyone had to interpret the Bible individually and act as his or her own judge in matters of religion.[48] Clearly, the ideas of Galenus Abrahamsz. formed an essential foundation for the development of Collegiant rational religion.

An excellent example of the way in which Kuyper used reason in biblical interpretation was provided by another of his works, *Bewijs dat noch de schepping van natuur noch de mirakelen, die de H. Schrift verhaalt op eenigerhande wijze teegen de natuurlijke reeden strijdig zijn* (Proof that neither the creation of nature nor the miracles of which Holy Scripture tells are in any way contrary to natural reason [1685]). In this work Kuyper set out to show that all biblical miracles could be explained rationally. He began by disagreeing with those who maintained that the miracles of the Bible were contrary to reason. Kuyper argued that he recognized something as contrary to reason only if it was prevented from happening by the order of nature itself. For example, he held that it was contrary to reason to claim that something could both exist and not exist at the same time. Because being was the eternal opposite of nonbeing, he argued, these two states could never exist together. From this it followed that if the being of a thing existed in nature, its nonbeing was automatically excluded from nature. Thus, Kuyper maintained that the order of nature made it impossible for something both to exist and not exist at the same time, and he argued that to reject this conclusion was equivalent to rejecting reason itself.[49]

Following this line of argument, Kuyper declared that in order to prove that the miracles of the Bible were contrary to reason it would be necessary to prove that they were contrary to the laws of nature. He firmly

[48] Ibid., pp. 176–179.

[49] Frans Kuyper, *Bewijs dat noch de schepping van natuur noch de mirakelen, die H. Schrift verhaalt, op eenigerhande wijze teegen de naturlijke reeden strijdig zijn* (Amsterdam, 1685), p. 3.

believed that such proof was impossible, and to show this he used the example of the scriptural account of Christ's feeding of the multitude. In Matt. 14:13–21 the Bible told how Christ fed the multitude with five loaves of bread and two fish and still had more food left over than he had started with. Some people claimed that this miracle was contrary to both reason and the laws of nature, Kuyper explained, because it violated the natural principle that stated that to give out portions of a quantity without taking any in would necessarily result in the diminishing of the overall quantity. But even though the Bible stated that Christ had more food left over than he had started with, Kuyper argued that this miracle did not contradict the laws of nature or reason. It was quite possible, he maintained, that angels commanded by God had added material to the bread and fish without being seen, and in so doing had increased the food supply sufficiently to feed the multitude and even to have something left over. Furthermore, Kuyper argued, since the additional material did not come from nothing, the miracle did not violate the rational principle that something cannot come from nothing.[50]

Kuyper also disagreed with those skeptics who maintained that the miracle of Christ walking on the water (Matt. 14:22–33) violated the natural principle that a large, heavy body could not be supported by a thin, light body. Kuyper explained this miracle by suggesting that God had used his infinite power to stop the wind from blowing and to hold the water rigid so that Jesus could walk on it. Even though Kuyper agreed with Galenus that there was no longer any divine intervention in the world of the seventeenth century, his literal understanding of Scripture led him to view the world of biblical times as one in which the laws of nature regularly were manipulated by supernatural forces. Kuyper, however, saw divine intervention in nature not as an impossible abrogation of immutable laws but as part of a larger and entirely rational system of universal operation that had since apostolic times ceased to function.

Despite his belief in biblical miracles, however, when Kuyper discussed the biblical creation story he used rational arguments to reject the commonly accepted principle of *creatio ex nihilo*. God could not have created the world from nothing, he argued, because all created things must have both a beginning principle and a final form. All things that were created had to be brought forth from something and they had to become something. If God had made the world from nothing, Kuyper argued, its beginning principle would have been nothing. But since nothing does not exist, there would in fact have been no beginning principle, and that would have been contrary to reason and nature. Therefore, *creatio ex*

---

[50] Ibid., p. 4.

nihilo was impossible and the Bible could not be interpreted in that way, Kuyper concluded.[51]

A somewhat different example of the Socinian-influenced Collegiant rational religion was provided by Adrian Swartepaert in his work *Openbaringe van het ware algemeen geloof* . . . (Revelation of the true universal belief [1678]). Nothing is known of Swartepaert's life beyond his involvement in Collegiant circles in Amsterdam during the late seventeenth century and his close association with Daniel Zwicker. Zwicker's ideas, as discussed earlier, were themselves illustrative of the development of Collegiant rational religion under Socinian influence. Swartepaert wrote prefaces for many of Zwicker's works and showed the influence of Zwicker's ideas in his *Openbaringe*.

Unlike many Collegiants who were influenced by Socinianism, Swartepaert subscribed not only to Socinian rationalism but also to many of the substantive points of Socinian theology. In the *Openbaringe* he proclaimed Socinian antitrinitarianism to be the most certain doctrine in Christianity because it was a doctrine whose truth was demonstrated by the fact that it could not be refuted rationally. The reason that antitrinitarianism could not be refuted rationally, Swartepaert argued, was that it was based upon true rules of scriptural interpretation. Foremost among these rules was the principle that no interpretation of Scripture that contradicted reason could be permitted. Swartepaert declared this principle to be central to all biblical interpretation because "whatever contradicts right reason contradicts God himself." Reason's dictates were true because they came from God, Swartepaert declared, and Socinian doctrine was true because it was in complete agreement with reason. Swartepaert further argued that the doctrine of the Trinity was false because it was based on what he considered to be a logical contradiction. He condemned orthodox Trinitarians for deviating from the rules of rational biblical interpretation in their efforts to protect and promote their mistaken ideas. Swartepaert boldly and finally declared that all illogical doctrines and interpretations were necessarily false.[52]

Swartepaert concluded the *Openbaringe* by presenting his own "twenty-one ground rules for the interpretation of Scripture." In true Socinian fashion, these rules featured a combination of rational and biblical guidelines. Rule 1, for example, stated: "It is impossible that one and the same thing can, at the same time, both be and not be. Therefore, two contradictory ideas cannot both be true at the same time." Rule 6 adopted a

[51] Ibid., pp. 4–6.
[52] Adrian Swartepaert, *Openbaringe van het ware algemeen geloof* . . . (n.p., 1678), pp. 54–59.

different tone: "That which the Scripture says of damnation and salvation ought not to be disagreed with." Here, in microcosm, was the Collegiant rational religion, resting on the twin foundations of Scripture and reason.[53]

The writings of Stol, Kuyper, and Swartepaert demonstrated the important role played in Rijnsburger thought by Socinian ideas concerning the use of reason in religion. Socinian rationalism did not alone create the Rijnsburger rational religion, but it was extremely important in reinforcing and elaborating tendencies already present in Collegiant thought. Millenarianism and Galenus's ideas about the separation of the temporal world from divine inspiration led the Collegiants to an embryonic religion of reason and toleration in their writings concerning the reform of the universal Christian church. Because they were already inclined toward a rational interpretation of religious life, many Rijnsburgers readily absorbed the ideas of Faustus Socinus and his followers regarding the use of reason in religion when these ideas entered the colleges after 1660. The resulting Collegiant rational religion formed a major stage in the development of Rijnsburger rationalism. Although this rational religion limited the role of human reason to that of being a tool for interpreting the revealed truths of Scripture, it was nevertheless the first systematically organized and theoretically elaborated presentation of the rationalistic conclusions that flowed naturally from the main assumptions of Collegiant religious thought. Socinianism gave order to the rationalistic impulses that emerged within Collegiantism after 1655.

The Collegiants were not Socinians. Very few of the Rijnsburgers adopted the fundamental points of Socinian theology. Socinianism itself was not a monolithic set of doctrines as much as it was a general approach to religion following in the tradition of sixteenth-century evangelical rationalism, but with many individual and local variations. One particular aspect of Socinian thought—the ideas of Faustus Socinus regarding the role of reason in scriptural interpretation—had the greatest impact upon the Collegiants when they encountered these ideas among the intellectual heirs of Socinus in seventeenth-century Holland. In its later stages Collegiant rationalism moved beyond the instrumental conception of reason contained in Rijnsburger rational religion, but the initial focus on the powers and uses of reason in religion provided by Kuyper, Swartepaert, Stol, and other Socinian-influenced Collegiants was an important first step along the path to a more thoroughly secular rationalism.

[53] Ibid., pp. 82–90.

Chapter Seven

PROPHECY AND REASON: COLLEGIANT FREE PROPHECY AND THE SECULARIZATION OF THE INDIVIDUAL CONSCIENCE

> But he that prophesieth speaketh unto men to
> edification, and exhortation, and comfort.
> —1 Cor. 14:3

THE COLLEGIANT practice of free prophecy provides an important key for understanding the gradual process of secularization that transformed the Rijnsburger conception of the individual conscience from a belief in individual spiritual enlightenment to a belief in the operation of natural human reason. The transformation of the Rijnsburger idea of inner knowledge can be traced clearly in changing Collegiant attitudes toward free prophecy, a practice that the Collegiants believed to be the outward manifestation of the believer's inner religious knowledge. Between the years 1620 and 1680 the Collegiants gradually moved away from their original belief that the practice of free prophecy was made possible by divine inspiration and came instead to believe that it resulted from the operation of individual human reason.

The secularization of the Collegiant conception of inner knowledge and the change in the Rijnsburger view of free prophecy that accompanied it came about chiefly as a result of the influence within the colleges of the ideas of Galenus Abrahamsz. In the early years of the movement the Collegiants saw the practice of free prophecy as resulting from direct divine inspiration of the individual conscience in the form of the "gift of prophecy," an outstanding (*heerlijkmaking*) gift of the Holy Spirit bestowed by God. After 1657, however, Galenus Abrahamsz.'s ideas concerning the disappearance of all such outstanding gifts of the Spirit from the earth brought about a major reevaluation of the idea of free prophecy in the colleges. The Rijnsburgers gradually came to see free prophecy as resulting not from the gift of prophecy but from the operation of human reason.

Nothing was more fundamental to both the theory and the practice of Collegiant religious life than free prophecy. This free witnessing or evidencing by individuals in the college meeting was the primary vehicle by

6. Meeting of the Collegiants at Amsterdam in Their Meeting Hall in the Orphanage De Oranje-Appel

which the Rijnsburgers explained and interpreted the scriptural texts that were studied at these meetings. Although Collegiant free prophecy traced its origins to sixteenth-century Protestant spiritualism, the Collegiants did not follow the most radical of the earlier spiritualists in rejecting Scripture in favor of direct and personal divine illumination. For the Rijnsburgers, free prophecy was the exercise of an inner spiritual gift to interpret, not to replace, the written word of God. In Rijnsburger meetings the reading and interpretation of biblical texts occupied the central place held by pastoral sermons in conventional Protestant services, and for this reason free prophecy was the chief means of religious education in the colleges. Every person present at a college meeting had the freedom to "prophesy," or speak in order to interpret the subject text according to his or her own individual understanding of it. The Collegiants felt that Bible reading and individual interpretation provided the only means by which believers could further their knowledge of religion and gain the insight they needed to live a good Christian life.[1] The practice of free prophecy was thus the central element of Collegiant religious life.

As the chief vehicle for the expression of individual religious insight, free prophecy was theoretically grounded directly in the Rijnsburger conception of the individual conscience. Because free prophecy was therefore the concrete and practical embodiment of the Collegiant religion of individual conscience, any change in the Collegiant attitude toward free prophecy can be considered a reflection of a more fundamental change in the Rijnsburger conception of a person's inner ability to know truth. In the years after 1660 a number of factors, including the ideas of Galenus, the failure of the millennium to arrive on schedule, and the influence of Socinianism, combined to turn the Collegiant religion of individual conscience into a rational religion.

From the beginnings of the Collegiant movement in the 1620s to the period of its greatest intellectual activity in the 1670s and 1680s, the Rijnsburgers wrote a great deal about free prophecy. Most of the works devoted to free prophecy were intended either to explain the practice to other religious groups or to defend free prophecy against the attacks of its critics. Because of these didactic and polemical purposes, Collegiant writings on free prophecy clearly outlined the Rijnsburgers' own understanding of this central religious practice. From these writings it is apparent that the Collegiant view of free prophecy underwent a significant transformation between 1620 and 1680.

During the early years of the Collegiant movement the Rijnsburgers believed free prophecy to be the result of direct divine inspiration of the

---

[1] Meihuizen, in Groenveld, ed., p. 85.

individual conscience. This belief in inspired prophecy placed the Collegiants squarely in the tradition of the sixteenth-century Protestant Reformation. According to Christopher Hill, the Reformation stimulated belief in prophecy because the reformers' abolition of mediators between humans and God and their stress on the individual conscience of the believer convinced many Protestants that God spoke directly to his people through divine inspiration. The reformer John Knox, for example, believed that he had the gift of prophecy and that God spoke directly to him. Luther and other moderate reformers accepted the Bible as the source of religious truth and believed that divine inspiration was necessary for the correct interpretation of Scripture, while radical spiritualists like Thomas Müntzer claimed to have direct divine inspiration that transcended the written word of the Bible.[2] Free prophecy as practiced by the Rijnsburgers was tied closely to the biblical text and was the chief expression of an individualism and anticlericalism that had roots in the Protestant Reformation.

The Collegiants inherited their idea of free prophecy, like their critique of the visible churches, from the spiritualists of the Radical Reformation. Kaspar Schwenkfeld and his followers in southern Germany held conventicles for Bible study, prayer, and prophecy during the 1540s. In these conventicles the worshippers undertook, according to Schwenkfeld, "the correct understanding and interpretation of Scripture after the Spirit, as much as we are able through prayer and the revelation of His Spirit."[3] These Bible study conventicles were never led by a minister—Schwenkfeld himself was a layman—and everyone present had the right to prophesy freely.[4] The influence of these spiritualist conventicles can be seen clearly in the interim church gatherings proposed by Schwenkfeld's Dutch disciples Coornhert and Boreel, gatherings in which free prophecy was given a central role. It was this idea of the interim church found in the writings of Coornhert and Boreel that provided the model upon which the colleges themselves were constructed.

The use of informal meetings featuring free discussion for the purpose of understanding biblical texts was not limited to the spiritualists and Rijnsburgers. Among the institutional Protestant churches of the Reformation era several favored such meetings as a means for educating laypersons and future ministers in Scripture, but these meetings were not intended to take the place of the standard worship service directed by a preacher. In Zurich these discussion groups developed into exegetical col-

---

[2] Hill, *The World Turned Upside Down*, pp. 91–95; Peter Klassen, *Europe in the Reformation* (Englewood Cliffs, N.J., 1974), pp. 53–58; Paul Althaus, *The Theology of Martin Luther* (Philadelphia, 1966), pp. 76–78.

[3] Williams, pp. 466–467.

[4] McLaughlin, pp. 140–143.

leges and the term "prophesying" came to be attached to the spontaneous explanation of biblical texts. In 1568 the national synod of the Dutch Reformed church recommended the establishment of colleges for the purpose of lay Bible education. These meetings were to be led by a "prophet" who would interpret Scripture, and everyone present would have the freedom to speak in order to elaborate upon the prophet's explanation. The synod specifically forbade these discussions from taking place in the form of questions and answers, however, in order to prevent the colleges from becoming debating societies. According to the synod's recommendation, any member of a Reformed congregation who wanted to put his "gift of prophecy" to use in the education of his fellow believers could become a prophet and leader of such a college simply by giving proof of his ability and by promising never to distort the meaning of Scripture. These lay prophets were expected to sit on the church council when it discussed matters concerning the education of the congregation. Despite the synod's recommendations, however, very few such colleges were ever set up. The turmoil of the Eighty Years War against Spain (1568–1648) initially prevented much lay interest in the groups, and after the founding of Leiden University in 1575 the Reformed church no longer needed to rely on informal colleges for the training of its ministers. Nevertheless, colleges of laymen intended primarily as religious discussion groups did grow up outside of the structure and sanction of the official church in the years after 1600. In these meetings, which were popular especially in Amsterdam and other large cities, people gathered to express themselves freely on matters of Scripture and religion and to learn from the ideas of their neighbors.[5]

During the early and mid-seventeenth century Gisbertus Voetius, leader of the *Nadere Reformatie* within the Dutch Reformed church, also favored the establishment of lay conventicles in which Scripture was interpreted and applied to practical situations. Voetius insisted on the right of individual believers to interpret Scripture, a process that he called "prophesying," and he defended this practice with examples from the apostolic church as well as from English Puritanism. Voetius believed that prophesying helped in the growth of spiritual knowledge, was useful for the prevention of error and in defense of orthodoxy, and encouraged individual renewal of faith, hope, and charity. But Voetius placed strict limits on the freedom of prophesying. He favored placing a minister in charge of the prophecy meeting and he did not extend freedom of prophesying to questions the discussion of which he felt would harm the unity of the church. He granted full freedom of prophesying in the application of basic truths of faith to specific situations, but he did not allow the

---

[5] Van Slee, *De Rijnsburger Collegianten*, pp. 30–34.

questioning of these basic truths or any attempt to find new meaning in Scripture. Voetius explicitly rejected the idea that free prophecy justified the use of the inner light independently of Scripture or dogma, and he also rejected the idea that reason possessed rights of interpretation of Scripture independent of the goals of faith.[6]

The practice of free prophecy also evolved from the custom in some Protestant groups of allowing free discussion of the sermon topic to take place within the structure of traditional worship services. One of the earliest examples of this development took place in the Dutch Reformed congregation in London during the years 1550–1553. This group met in the former Augustinian church in London under the leadership of the Polish exile Johannes á Lasco (1499–1566). Among these Protestants it was the custom to discuss the content of the formal Sunday sermon at "sessions of prophecy" (*profetie* or *Schrift-collatie*) immediately following the service. Preselected prophets led the group's consideration of scriptural and sermon topics for the purpose of bringing those present to a better understanding of the Bible.[7]

It was common practice among many sectarian groups in England during the sixteenth and seventeenth centuries for a general religious discussion to be held following the sermon. For many religious radicals, worship required the active participation of the entire congregation, and for this reason they were not content with listening passively to the word preached by a minister. In the English Baptist churches such discussion was institutionalized and the preacher often called for objections after his sermon was over. English radicals even took this practice abroad with them. In 1634 John Cotton arranged for worship services in the church of Boston to include prophesying by members of the congregation and free discussion of questions addressed to the minister. In the Netherlands the Pilgrim Fathers encouraged members of their Leiden congregation to speak freely for the edification of the group when the public ministry was over. Such prophesying was considered a protection against errors made by the preacher and it clearly reduced the importance and authority of the pastoral sermon as a means of religious education.

In 1609 an English Brownist congregation settled in the Netherlands just outside Warmond. The Brownists believed that each member of their congregation had the right freely to prophesy in order to proclaim God's word. After the regular sermon, any person present who felt moved by the Holy Spirit was allowed to interpret or expand upon the preacher's words, and afterward both the sermon and the prophetic interpretation

[6] McGahagan, pp. 78–82.

[7] Otto J. De Jong, *Nederlandse Kerkgeschiedenis* (Nijkerk, 1978), pp. 104–105; Goeters, p. 51.

were discussed by the entire congregation. Later in the century the English Quakers similarly encouraged their members to prophesy freely in meetings, and they even disrupted the worship services of other congregations in England and the Netherlands by interrupting pastoral sermons with questions and demands for free discussion. The authority and importance of the pastoral sermon declined in direct proportion to the increase of prophesying and free discussion within the worship service. Van Slee considered it possible that the first Collegiants were influenced in their own adoption of free prophecy by the practices of their English Brownist neighbors, but it seems more likely that the college adopted the idea of free prophecy from the writings of Coornhert.[8]

It was above all the Rijnsburgers who gave free prophecy a prominent place within seventeenth-century Protestantism. In the colleges the pastoral sermon was completely replaced by free prophecy, which was the founding principle of the Warmond college and the central element of Rijnsburger religious practice. The college in Warmond first adopted free prophecy as a matter of practical necessity when the Synod of Dordrecht left the congregation without its Remonstrant preacher. Under the forceful leadership of Gijsbert van der Kodde the college soon elevated free prophecy into the guiding principle of a new religious movement.

When the Remonstrant Brotherhood, operating from exile in Antwerp, dispatched a secret preacher to minister to the Warmond flock, Van der Kodde became the leader of a party within the congregation that favored retaining free prophecy as the organizing principle for its meetings. He held a series of discussions with the various pastors successively delegated to Warmond by the Remonstrants, and in these debates Gijsbert showed that his devotion to the practice of free prophecy was more than a result of practical necessity. Basing his arguments on Coornhert's ideas and on scriptural passages such as 1 Cor. 14, Gijsbert maintained that free prophecy was the means by which the apostolic church educated believers in the faith, and for this reason he declared that free prophecy was preferable to pastoral sermons on the basis of antiquity. He furthermore declared that the office of preacher was contrary to both Scripture and apostolic practice and was therefore injurious to the spiritual welfare of the Christian congregation. He even claimed that the office of preacher had been invented during the postapostolic period by people who sought to create a clerical profession where none was needed in order to provide employment for men who would not learn a trade.[9]

---

[8] Van Slee, De Rijnsburger Collegianten, pp. 374–376; Hill, The World Turned Upside Down, pp. 104–106.

[9] See Paschier de Fijne, Kort, waerachtigh en getrouw verhael van het eerste begin en opkomen van de nieuwe seckte der propheten often Rijnsburgers in het dorp Warmont anno 1619 en 1620 ("Waerstadt," 1671).

After considerable bickering over these and other issues within the Warmond congregation, Gijsbert's faction broke away from those members of the congregation who favored the direction of a preacher and established the first Rijnsburger free prophecy college. College meetings were held once a month on a Sunday. They began with a prayer, followed by the reading of a scriptural text and the interpretation of the text by free prophecy. Meetings closed with a final song and a prayer. This remained the basic pattern for all Collegiant meetings in Warmond and Rijnsburg as well as in the many other colleges that soon arose throughout the United Provinces. Most college meetings featured a succession of four, five, or more lengthy prophecies that often caused meetings to last far into the night. Variations in this order were slight from locale to locale. The only significant procedural innovation during the later seventeenth century was the practice that arose in the Amsterdam college during the late 1650s of designating several persons as prophets to speak in each meeting in the event that no one else felt moved to do so.[10] The fact that the need for such preselected prophets was felt is perhaps indicative of some lessening of spiritual zeal in the practice of free prophecy. It is interesting to note that the practice of designating speakers arose just as Galenus's ideas concerning the absence of the gifts of the Spirit were starting to spread in the colleges.

Free prophecy was both the outward symbol and the functional principle of the Rijnsburger religion of individual conscience, and as such it represented the epistemological and educational foundation of Collegiantism. The purpose of Collegiant meetings was individual religious education that would enable each believer to understand better and follow God's will. The essential starting point for obtaining such knowledge was a reading of God's word in Scripture, but the vitally important second step in the educational process was the interpretation of the scriptural passage using free prophecy. For the important function of interpretation the Collegiants rejected clerical and ecclesiastical authority, formal theology, and tradition because of their belief that each person's primary source of guidance in religion was his own individual conscience, a direct inner knowledge of truth unmediated by external authority. The Rijnsburgers despised traditional theological argument as "devil's vanity" and they valued free prophecy so highly that at times they seemed to give it an authority nearly equal to that of Scripture itself.[11] As Wilhelm Goeters noted, the Rijnsburgers "held free prophecy so high that it was more than once placed on the same level as the Bible." Concerning the Collegiants

---

[10] Van Slee, *De Rijnsburger Collegianten*, pp. 61, 276, 308–9, 373; De Fijne, pp. 20, 23–24.

[11] Van Slee, *De Rijnsburger Collegianten*, pp. 47–50; Roldanus, *Zeventiende eeuwse geestesbloei*, p. 100.

Goeters concluded: "in their regard for prophecy we can see an outward sign of their growing subjectivism."[12]

From the beginning of their movement the Collegiants based their idea of free prophecy on scriptural foundations. In 1 Cor. 14, the apostle Paul spoke at length of the extraordinary gifts of the Holy Spirit given by God to the members of the early Christian congregation. The first among these gifts, according to Paul, was the gift of prophecy. Using this gift the Corinthians understood, interpreted, and proclaimed God's will with an infallibility that flowed directly from divine inspiration. The Collegiants initially saw their own free prophecy as a result of this prophetic gift of the Holy Spirit. The early Rijnsburgers believed that each individual who interpreted the Bible by prophecy was following his or her own personal guidance of the Holy Spirit. Since the right to speak in the college meeting depended upon the inflowing of the Holy Spirit into the speaker, any believer who felt moved by the Spirit had the freedom to speak for the edification of the gathering.[13] In such circumstances, clerical authority had no meaning.

According to traditional Christian belief, the gifts of the Holy Spirit were special abilities or qualities given by God through the inspiration of the Holy Spirit. As Galenus noted in several of his writings, these gifts were generally considered to be of two kinds. The salvational (heiligmaking) gifts were intended for the personal sanctification of the individual to whom they were given. These gifts were considered by theologians to be supernatural spiritual entities infused into the souls of people in order to render them receptive to the inworking of the Holy Spirit bringing grace and individual salvation. These gifts, as listed in Isa. 11:2–3, included piety, fortitude, wisdom, fear of God, knowledge, and understanding.[14] According to Galenus, God continued to give these gifts to individuals in the corrupt premillennial world, but they only effected the condition of the individual soul and did not in any way effect the individual's ability to teach or communicate divine truth.

The second kind of gifts of the Holy Spirit were those that Galenus called the extraordinary (heerlijkmaking) gifts, more generally known as the outstanding gifts or the charismata. These gifts gave individuals an infallible ability to know and to communicate divine truth, and thus they allowed believers to serve God by spreading his word. According to Paul in his first letter to the Corinthians, these gifts were given abundantly to the members of the first church for the purpose of spreading the faith and

[12] Goeters, pp. 50, 52.

[13] Van Slee, De Rijnsburger Collegianten, p. 273; Lindeboom, Stiefkinderen van het Christendom, p. 5; Hylkema, vol. 2, p. 13.

[14] CE, vol. 7, pp. 413–414.

building the church. In 1 Cor. 12:7, the apostle called these gifts "manifestations of the Spirit," and he included among them the gift of speaking with wisdom, the gift of speaking with knowledge, the gift of speaking in tongues, the gift of discerning spirits, the gift of healing, the gift of miracles, and the gift of prophecy.[15]

In 1 Cor. 13:2, Paul explained that the gift of prophecy allowed the believer to "understand all mysteries and all knowledge." The Catholic Church taught that the revelation of Christ contained in Scripture was the definitive message of God to man, and the church also maintained that along with Scripture God had given his church the infallible assistance of the Holy Spirit, in part by way of the gift of prophecy, so that the church could help believers to understand the meaning of Christ's revelation more clearly.[16] The early Rijnsburgers based their concept of free prophecy on the biblical idea of the gift of prophecy as an inspired ability to understand and to proclaim God's truth. For the early Collegiants, however, the gift of prophecy was given not to the church as an institution but to individuals alone, and thus the teaching authority of the church was transferred to individual believers.

The Rijnsburgers built their concept of free prophecy upon firm biblical foundations. In his defense of free prophecy against the Remonstrant preachers, Gijsbert van der Kodde repeatedly cited passages from First Corinthians. This is clear from the only eyewitness account of the founding and early development of the college in Warmond and Rijnsburg, the *Kort, waerachtigh en getrouw verhael van het eerste begin en opkomen van de nieuwe sekte der propheten often Rijnsburgers in het dorp Warmont anno 1619 en 1620* (Short, true, and trustworthy story of the first beginnings and growth of the new sect of prophets or Rijnsburgers in the village of Warmond in the years 1619 and 1620). This account was written by Paschier de Fijne, one of the preachers dispatched by the Remonstrants to Warmond in 1620. It gives eloquent testimony concerning the spiritualistic conception of free prophecy upon which the first college was built.

Although de Fijne was an opponent of the Collegiants, his account of their early years is a detailed recording of events that has been accepted as accurate by later writers. De Fijne was a moderate and compromising man who had many dealings with the van der Koddes and who wrote admiringly of their pious life and great biblical knowledge. His *Kort . . . verhael* is critical of the Collegiants but it is not bitter or polemical in tone, as so many such works tended to be in the seventeenth century. De Fijne clearly and calmly outlined the points on which he and the Colle-

---

[15] *CE*, vol. 7, p. 414.
[16] *CE*, vol. 12, pp. 479–481.

giants disagreed, and he had no obvious reason to misrepresent the way in which the first Rijnsburgers viewed the practice of free prophecy. De Fijne's testimony on this subject is particularly valuable because he had firsthand knowledge of the actual Rijnsburger practice of free prophecy. He personally attended Collegiant meetings on several occasions after Gijsbert and his followers broke away from the main Warmond congregation, and he more than once took advantage of the practice of free prophecy to make his own views known in those meetings.[17]

In the *Kort . . . verhael* de Fijne reported that college gatherings usually opened with a prayer, followed by a reading from Scripture. According to de Fijne, when the reading was completed someone would speak the following words: "Is there anyone in this gathering who has some prophecy or spiritual gifts for the education of the group? Has anyone any teachings or comforting words or admonishments? If so, please speak" ("Isser yemant onder dese vergadering die eenighe Prophetie ofte Geestelijcke gaven heeft tot stichtinge der Gemeynte? . . . ofte heeft yemant eenighe leeringe, vertroostinge ofte vermaninghe? Die gelieve het voort te brengen").[18] Often the speaker would add the words of 1 Cor. 14:26: "What then brethren? When you come together, each one has a hymn, a lesson, a revelation, a tongue or an interpretation. Let all things be done for edification." After the invitation to speak, de Fijne reported, there would follow a series of prophecies. From de Fijne's account it is clear that the first Collegiants believed their practice of free prophecy to be based on the spiritual gift of prophecy spoken of by the apostle Paul. The Rijnsburgers took the words of 1 Cor. 14:3 literally: "he that prophesieth speaketh unto men to edification, exhortation and comfort."

The early Collegiant conception of free prophecy was further illustrated by de Fijne's account of the opinions of Gijsbert's younger brother Jan. According to Van Slee, young Jan once claimed to possess the indwelling of the Holy Spirit as strongly as had the apostles.[19] In 1620 de Fijne held a series of discussions with young Jan during which the Remonstrant pastor tried to work out a compromise with the van de Koddes in order to prevent a permanent schism in the Warmond congregation. De Fijne hoped to convince the van der Koddes and their followers to give up free prophecy, either entirely or in part, and to permit him to preach to the congregation. All of de Fijne's efforts were in vain, however, because young Jan declared that free prophecy was absolutely necessary in all Christian meetings. According to Jan, free prophecy allowed the believer "to express what the Spirit puts in him at the very moment that it

[17] De Fijne, p. 24.
[18] Ibid.
[19] Van Slee, *De Rijnsburger Collegianten*, p. 387.

is put in him." On one occasion when de Fijne was speaking at a college meeting, young Jan interrupted him in the middle of his prophecy by claiming that he had just had a revelation and wanted to share it immediately. As justification for his interruption young Jan cited 1 Cor. 14:30: "If anything be revealed to another that sitteth by (during a prophecy) let the first hold his peace."[20] From evidence such as this it is clear that the first Collegiants firmly believed that their practice of free prophecy was based on direct revelation from God.

The conception of divinely inspired free prophecy exercised great influence in the colleges during the first thirty years of their existence. In the years around midcentury one of the most ardent defenders of free prophecy in the Amsterdam college was the former mayor and convinced chiliast Coenraad van Beuningen, whose support for the practice was based on his belief that God could reveal himself to anyone at any time.[21] Even when rationalistic tendencies began to appear in Collegiant thought after 1660, some Rijnsburgers continued to insist that individual inspiration was the only way to obtain religious truth. In 1667 the millenarian Pieter Serrarius attacked the ideas of the Amsterdam physician Ludovicus Meyer, who believed that human reason was the best interpreter of Scripture. In a work entitled *Responsio ad exercitationem*, Serrarius followed the mystics Tauler, Ruysbroeck, and Suso by maintaining that the correct interpretation of the Bible was a matter of internal revelation and a work of divine grace.[22] Already by midcentury, however, new ideas were afoot in the colleges. As early as 1650 Galenus began to elaborate on and to spread Boreel's ideas concerning church decay. In 1655 he held a series of open discussions with conservative Mennonite leaders during which he outlined his conception of the decayed premillennial world, and in 1657–1659 his major writings on this topic were printed and circulated.

Galenus's ideas furnished a powerful justification for the practice of free prophecy. Since the churches of his day lacked the divine inspiration and authority of the first church, Galenus declared that their clergy could have no authority over ordinary believers. Since there were no preachers in the world with the extraordinary gifts of the Holy Spirit to proclaim infallibly the Gospel, all believers had to be given the freedom to speak in Christian meetings to proclaim God's truth as they understood it. The consciences (*geweten*) of individual believers stood under the supervision of God alone, Galenus declared, and no one had the right to attempt to control the conscience of other persons nor to deprive them of their right to proclaim God's truth.[23]

[20] De Fijne, pp. 20, 24.
[21] Roldanus, *Coenraad van Beuningen*, p. 173.
[22] Van den Berg, in Knox, ed., p. 193. On Meyer, see Meinsma, pp. 147–150.
[23] Galenus Abrahamsz., *Wederlegging*, pp. 82–93.

At the same time that Galenus's ideas promoted and justified the practice of free prophecy, his theories also fundamentally changed the Rijnsburger conception of the practice. The gift of prophecy was one of the gifts of the Holy Spirit that Galenus declared lost from a corrupt premillennial world. For this reason the feeling began to spread in the colleges that even though the members of the first church had had the gift of the Holy Spirit to prophesy with the inspiration of God, Christians of the seventeenth century lived in a world that was profoundly different. Many Collegiants concluded that in a world of spiritual decay and schism in which no vestige of the true church was left as a link to God's spirit, believers could continue to prophesy and interpret God's word only by using their own natural reason. Galenus's ideas thus upheld the Collegiant principle of individual religious knowledge while at the same time robbing the principle of its spiritual foundation, leaving a rationalistic interpretation of free prophecy as the only means by which the Rijnsburgers could maintain their religion of individual conscience.

In the works of such Collegiants as Barend Joosten Stol, Laurens Klinkhamer, Pieter Langedult, and Pieter Smout we can see the secular interpretation of free prophecy developing. As this interpretation gained influence in the colleges some Rijnsburgers even began to see the free prophecy practiced in the apostolic church as a product of reason. As influential as Galenus's ideas were within the colleges, however, the secularization of free prophecy advanced only slowly, and it met with considerable resistance along the way. A good example of the changing Collegiant attitude toward free prophecy can be found in the work of Barend Joosten Stol, friend and associate of Franz Kuyper.

One of the most revealing Collegiant discussions of free prophecy is found in *Den Philospherenden Boer, eerste deel*, written by Stol in 1676. In this work Stol's Collegiant peasant informed the Cartesian philosopher that he had been convinced by his reading of 1 Cor. 14 that free prophecy was the method of religious education employed in the apostolic church. For this reason the peasant maintained that free prophecy was the only suitable means of religious education for the Christians of his own day. The peasant declared that all of the churches of his day were devoid of the gifts of the Holy Spirit, and for this reason they had no right to choose preachers and to give them a special authority to proclaim the Gospel that was denied to ordinary believers. Preaching and church order were human inventions that lacked spiritual authority because they were established without God's direct command, the peasant insisted.[24]

[24] Stol, pp. 28, 29.

The peasant proudly told the philosopher that because of his belief in free prophecy he did not attend church services where preachers presided. Instead he went to the Rijnsburger college whenever he was in Amsterdam or Rotterdam. At the college the members investigated Holy Scripture to discover its true meaning, the peasant noted in approving terms, but he also seemed to be somewhat unhappy with certain aspects of the Collegiant practice. He commented to the philosopher: "I wish that God would give them [the Collegiants] more gifts of the spirit, and that with their exercise of the understanding and heart they might use more simplicity, and avoid all Latin words" ("Maar did wensch ik/dat dien God aller genaden/dit volk noch eens met meerder gaven des geestes wil aandoen/en datze neffens die oeffeninge des verstands en gemoeds/noch meer eenvoudigheyt mochten gebruyken/en alle Latijnse woorden . . . mochten vermijden").[25]

Stol's peasant sensed a changing attitude toward free prophecy in the colleges, and he disapproved. He linked a decrease in the simplicity and spontaneity of the prophecies, which the Rijnsburgers sometimes referred to as *oeffeninge* (exercises), to a lessening of the gifts of the Holy Spirit. The practice of appointing prophets, which began in Amsterdam in the late 1650s, was perhaps another result of this decline of spontaneity. Stol still believed free prophecy to be based on the gift of prophecy and he viewed with misgivings the changing attitude toward the practice that he noticed among his fellow Rijnsburgers. What Stol perceived as a decline of inspiration in the practice of free prophecy was no doubt a result of the increasingly secularized conception of the practice that resulted from Galenus's ideas. Stol himself was influenced by those aspects of Galenus's thought that legitimized and supported free prophecy, but he did not take Galenus's ideas as far as other Collegiants who believed them to imply a secularized free prophecy. As many Collegiants came to see free prophecy as based not on inspiration but on natural ability, their esteem for the learnedness of interpretations, of which the use of Latin words was a sign, increased. Stol's peasant lamented these changes by recalling earlier times when passion and inspiration, not reason and learning, ruled the colleges: "It seems to me that several years ago, when the colleges had not long been in fashion, I noticed more simplicity and humility there, and they used to be more serious and fiery of heart in their prayers and thanksgivings" ("Mij dunkt dat ik over ettelijke Jaren, toen die Collegien niet langen hadden in zwang geweest, meerder eenvoudigheyt en nederigheyt bespeurde, als mede datze in haar gebeden en dankseggingen veel ernstiger en vieriger van herten plachten te zijn").[26]

[25] Ibid., p. 30.
[26] Ibid.

The method of prayer in the colleges was linked closely to free prophecy because prayer was offered just as freely as prophecy in college meetings. Clearly unhappy with the secularization that prayer and prophecy were undergoing by the 1670s, the peasant declared that "to pray takes more than merely a natural ability—it also takes the spirit of prayer." The peasant went on to say that he favored the shedding of tears during prayer because the tears were caused by the moving of God's spirit within a person, and he added that he preferred prayer with tears to long, learned prayers "no matter how reasoned they might be." In prayer, as in free prophecy, Stol considered divine inspiration essential and frowned on attempts to rationalize the process. True prayer had to be "inflamed with God's grace" the peasant declared. If someone wanted to speak, pray, or sing in the college he or she had to feel moved by the spirit to do so.[27] If someone felt that he or she was not inspired but that another person in the meeting was, the inspired person should be given the first opportunity to speak. Only if no one else in the meeting spoke would it be permissible for a person to speak without divine inspiration, and then only to prevent the meeting from breaking up, the peasant maintained. This might have been a reference to the use of appointed prophets.

The peasant also insisted that great subtleties should never be used in the explanation of biblical texts because that was only an effort by educated people to show off their secular learning. But even worse than such pretended wisdom, in the peasant's view, was the fact that some people really did not understand how the inspiration of the Holy Spirit operated in people, and for this reason they sometimes tried to feign great inspiration in their prophecies. This practice had to be avoided, the peasant insisted, because if a person could not speak or pray with true inspiration he or she was obliged to be silent. In response to the peasant's ideas the philosopher could only object: "I prefer a reasoned prayer to all of this soft-hearted crying. I do not believe God is served with all of this emotion." This comment brought a brief but incisive reply from Stol's peasant: "The apostles taught trust and belief, not philosophy."[28]

Stol's work revealed a transitional phase in the Rijnsburger conception of free prophecy. While Stol himself still viewed the practice as a product of divine inspiration, he detected a changing attitude toward free prophecy among other Rijnsburgers. Further evidence of this shift from spiritual to rational free prophecy was offered in two other Collegiant writings: Laurens Klinkhamer's *Vrijheijt van spreecken inde gemeynte der geloovigen, bewesen met geboden, exempelen, redenen, weerlegging van tegenwerpingen* (Freedom of speaking in the congregation of believers, proven

[27] Ibid., pp. 31, 32, 34, 37–38.
[28] Ibid., pp. 39–41.

with Commands, examples, reasons, and refutation of objections [1655])
and Pieter Langedult's *De apostolice outheyt van de vrijheijt van
spreecken in de vergaderingen der Christenen* (The apostolic antiquity of
the freedom of speaking in the Christian gathering [1672]). These were
also transitional works that saw free prophecy as based both on divine
inspiration in the form of a "lesser gift" of the Holy Spirit and on one's
natural ability to know and communicate truth. While Klinkhamer's
book put greater stress on the "lesser gift" and Langedult emphasized
natural ability, elements of both the spiritualistic and the rationalistic interpretations of free prophecy were present in both works, creating an
ambiguity characteristic of transitional thought.

Dr. Laurens Klinkhamer (1626–1687) was the son of a Mennonite
family in Leiden, where he attended the university to study medicine.
When he became a doctor of medicine at the age of twenty-five, Klinkhamer set up his practice in Leiden. As the years went by he spent much
of his spare time studying the Bible and attending Collegiant meetings. A
man of fiercely independent judgment, Klinkhamer rejected all theological doctrines and confessional formulas that did not agree with the Bible.
He was a strong proponent of individual conscience and free prophecy—
the two interlocking foundations of Collegiant religion—and he quickly
became a pillar of the college in Leiden. Like Stol's peasant, Klinkhamer
believed that Rijnsburgers should never attend religious services where
preachers presided. He published several books in defense of free prophecy and engaged in written disputes on the issue with the Remonstrant
preachers Isaac Pontanus and Paschier de Fijne, as well as with fellow
Collegiant Daniel Zwicker.

Klinkhamer's writings were very influential within the Collegiant
movement because his emphasis on practical piety appealed to the Rijnsburgers' desire for a moral regeneration of Christianity. He was a good
friend of the Haarlem Collegiant Pieter Langedult, and in 1684 he published a posthumous edition of Langedult's *Ethics*, providing his own
notes and commentary. During the Bredenburg dispute Klinkhamer acted
as a mediator, trying to heal the damaging divisions that had opened up
within the Collegiant movement and stressing the harmful effects of
schism in his work *Losse en quaade gronden van de scheurkerk* (Loose
and bad grounds of the schismatic church, 1686). He was a strong leader
of the Leiden college who showed great toleration for other peoples'
points of view and who exhibited a personal warmth and devout piety
much like that of another Mennonite physician, Galenus Abrahamsz. It
was Klinkhamer's habit to care for needy patients at his own expense,
and when he died on 11 November 1687, all Leiden must have experienced a tremendous sense of loss.[29]

[29] *BWPG*, vol. 5, pp. 21–25; Goeters, pp. 50–51.

Klinkhamer wrote his *Vrijheijt van spreecken* in 1655, just as Galenus's ideas were becoming known within the Collegiant movement. Not surprisingly, therefore, his defense of free prophecy and individual conscience showed the influence of Galenus's ideas. Klinkhamer believed free prophecy to be based on a gift of the Holy Spirit, but not on an extraordinary (*heerlijkmaking*) gift. Rather, he saw a free prophecy as based on what he called a "lesser gift of the Spirit," a gift that he identified with human reason. Thus, even while Klinkhamer was coming to see free prophecy as based on human reason, he sought nonetheless to preserve the original inspirational basis of the practice by emphasizing that reason itself was a gift of God. It is in an idea such as this that the ambiguity of transitional forms of thought shows itself most clearly.

Like many other Collegiants, Klinkhamer believed that Christians of his day did not receive the kind of divine inspiration that the apostles had, and thus they had to rely on their own reason to interpret religious truth. But Klinkhamer did not view human reason as a completely natural ability. For him, reason was a gift of God by which divine truths could be indirectly revealed to humankind. The secularization of the individual conscience had thus reached a crucial transitional stage in Klinkhamer's thought. Even though reason and not direct divine inspiration provided religious truth, this reason bore the mark of God and could thus be trusted not to deceive people. The psychological advantage of such a transitional concept is obvious. As reason came to replace the gifts of the Holy Spirit as the guide to religious truth, the believer could feel confident in the exercise of his natural ability by believing it to be divinely directed. Other Collegiants such as Joachim Oudaan and Frans Kuyper seem at times to have shared this transitional idea of reason, as did many other thinkers of the late seventeenth century, including the deist John Toland and the Cambridge Platonists in England.[30]

Like most Collegiant writers who dealt with free prophecy, Klinkhamer built his discussion around the key biblical texts in 1 Cor. 14. Using these texts to discuss the practice of free prophecy in the early church, Klinkhamer argued that in the first church free prophecy was practiced by believers who had a "special ability" to interpret correctly God's will. The apostle Paul, however, did not always identify this special ability with an extraordinary gift of the Holy Spirit that enabled believers to proclaim infallibly divine truth. In fact, Paul maintained that individual prophecies were open to the examination of other believers so that the congregation could determine to what extent the speaker had been inspired by the Holy Spirit. While some of the prophecies might indeed be infallible revelations of God's spirit, others were the product of another

---

[30] See John Toland, *Christianity Not Mysterious* (London, 1695).

kind of special ability possessed by the members of the early church, an ability that allowed them to understand God's will with unusual clarity.[31]

Klinkhamer's conception of the nature of this special ability became clearer when he discussed the practice of free prophecy in the colleges of his own day. Like Galenus, Klinkhamer stressed that the Christians of his day did not have the outstanding spiritual gifts possessed by some members of the first church. But this did not mean, he asserted, that the believers of his day were totally without the gifts of the Spirit. In place of the extraordinary gifts of the Holy Spirit, God had given people of the seventeenth century the Holy Bible and rational minds with which to interpret it. Thus, while the early Christians had to await special divine revelation to know God's truth, the believers of his time could hear God speak daily by using the Bible and their own reason. Even though the Christians of his own day had smaller gifts of the Spirit than some members of the first church, he continued, God nevertheless permitted even believers with these "lesser gifts" to prophesy freely in Christian meetings. Following 1 Cor. 12:4–11, Klinkhamer declared that even though the gifts possessed by believers of his day differed from the gifts of the first Christians, the Spirit working in both was the same. The revelation of the Holy Spirit was given to all believers, he continued, to some in the form of one kind of gift, to others in the form of another kind of gift.[32] By viewing human reason as a lesser gift of the Spirit, Klinkhamer was able to preserve part of the original spiritualistic basis of free prophecy while at the same time recognizing that the practice was essentially a rational one.

The primary purpose of Klinkhamer's book was not, however, to explain free prophecy. *Vrijheijt van spreecken* was written chiefly to defend free prophecy against critics who denied that it was the proper method of education for Christian meetings. Klinkhamer argued that in the days of the apostles, when some believers did indeed receive the direct inspiration of the Holy Spirit in the form of the outstanding gifts, free prophecy was judged the best method of religious education for the Christian congregation. Free prophecy was needed even more in his own day, he declared, specifically because the extraordinary gifts of the Holy Spirit were no longer given to believers. Free prophecy would prevent decay and schism in the church by assuring free discussion of Scripture and thus preventing the erroneous interpretations of preachers from going unchallenged. According to Klinkhamer, free prophecy would increase Christian toleration

---

[31] Laurens Klinkhamer, *Vrijheijt van spreecken inde gemeynte der geloovigen, bewesen met geboden, exampelen, redenen, weerlegging van tegenwerpingen* (Leiden, 1655), pp. 66–71.

[32] Ibid., pp. 91, 92.

and Christian unity and thus help to give rise to a universal Christian church united by one heart and one soul.[33]

Klinkhamer considered the practice of religion to be the responsibility of every individual, and he believed every person equally capable of directing his or her own religious life. For this reason he maintained that no believer should ever entrust his or her soul to the religious guidance of a preacher, because preachers had no more authority in spiritual matters than the ordinary believer. Furthermore, he saw it as the obligation of all believers to educate and admonish one another in matters of religion. Like Galenus Abrahamsz., Klinkhamer insisted that no individual be granted power or authority over the consciences of other people in matters of belief. He concluded by advising his readers to pay no heed to old customs, theological opinions, confessions, or synodal decisions. Instead, he encouraged them to "read, understand, examine, and judge" for themselves all questions of religion.[34]

Another important Collegiant work on free prophecy was Pieter Langedult's *Apostolice outheyt*. Langedult (1640–1677) was born in Haarlem to Mennonite parents and graduated from Leiden University with a degree in medicine in 1663. After returning to Haarlem, Langedult did not actually practice medicine. Instead, he spent his time in study, wrote often on theological questions, and became a leader in the Flemish Mennonite congregation as well as a devoted member of the Rijnsburger college. When another Haarlem Mennonite leader, Antonius van Dale (1638–1708), wrote a work against Collegiant free prophecy entitled *Het outheyt van alleen spreecken* (The antiquity of speaking alone, 1670) Langedult wrote his *Apostolice outheyt* in reply. The great knowledge of Jewish antiquity and of the Christian church fathers that Langedult displayed in this work was highly esteemed even among the independent-minded Rijnsburgers. When Langedult died at age thirty-seven, Klinkhamer saw to the posthumous publication of his last major work, the *Ethics*. The volume was embellished by poems in Langedult's honor written by Joachim Oudaan.[35]

In *Apostolice outheyt* Langedult moved toward an interpretation of free prophecy that saw the practice a result of natural human intellectual ability. He agreed with Klinkhamer that in the apostolic church some believers had the outstanding gifts of the Holy Spirit to proclaim infallibly God's truth, but not all members of the first church had such gifts. Nevertheless, free prophecy was practiced by the entire congregation because the right of free prophecy in the first church was not given to believers

[33] Ibid., pp. 99–100, 237.
[34] Ibid., pp. ix–xxxvii.
[35] *BWPG*, vol. 5, pp. 537–539; *NNBW*, vol. 3, pp. 309–310.

because they possessed special spiritual gifts. Each believer in the early church had the ability to educate others, and as a result of this ability each believer possessed the right to speak "as a general right of nature."[36]

In the church of his own day Langedult found no outstanding gifts of the Holy Spirit, but he maintained nevertheless that free prophecy could be practiced by all believers who had the "gift or ability for it." In Langedult's view this ability came from God, and only the individual could know whether or not he or she possessed it. Langedult thus believed free prophecy to be the natural right of anyone who felt capable of it.[37] He saw free prophecy as based not on extraordinary divine revelation but rather on an "ability" given by God in much the same way that Klinkhamer's "lesser gift" of reason was bestowed by God. Free prophecy could continue to function in a world devoid of the extraordinary gifts of the Holy Spirit, but the ability to interpret divine truth was not yet seen in a purely secular light.

The ambiguity present in transitional works on free prophecy disappeared in later Collegiant writings that saw the practice as based entirely on natural human reason. Such a work was Pieter Smout's *Het helder licht der vryheyt, behoudster der waerheyd, vyandinne van alle meesterschap en dooling: over het Godlijke vrij-propheteren in de gemeynte Jesu Christi* (The bright light of freedom: Protector of truth, enemy of all mastery and error: Concerning Godly free prophecy in the congregation of Jesus Christ [1679]). Little is known about Smout's life beyond the fact that he was active in the colleges of Rotterdam, Leiden, and Amsterdam during the 1670s and 1680s. He was familiar with the ideas of both Langedult and van Dale, as appears from a letter written by Smout to van Dale from Rotterdam on 10 December 1668.[38] Smout's views on free prophecy illustrated the ideas that were becoming common in the colleges during the late 1670s and early 1680s.

Smout's view of free prophecy was quite clear in *Het helder licht*, where he declared: "Among the things that are useful for Christians, and necessary because of man's weakness, nothing is more useful nor more necessary than the use of the right rational and wholly Godly freedom of speaking in the religious meeting." Smout maintained that the principle of free prophecy was in accord with "the nature of right reason and the grounds of true religion" because it was based on the assumption that all people were united in Christ and that each person had an equal right to

[36] Pieter Langedult, *De apostolice outheyt van de vrijheijt van spreecken in de vergaderingen der Christenen, tegens Dr. A. van Dalens alleen-spreecken* (Haarlem, 1672), p. 15.

[37] Ibid., pp. 13, 16.

[38] Antonius van Dale, *De Oudheid van 't Alleen spreken in de Gemeente verdedigd* (Amsterdam, 1670), pp. 111–112.

interpret and explain God's laws: "This freedom holds, according to the nature of right reason and the grounds of the true Christian religion, that we all are equally brothers in Christ who must have equal right and freedom to interpret, explain, and confess the laws of God as each comprehends and understands them" ("Dese vrijheijt leert en stelt na den aert en natuer van de rechte reden en gronden van de waer Christelijke Godsdienst, dat wij alle even hoog en tot broeders in Christo ghestelt zijn, die alle even veel recht en vrijheijt moeten hebben, om de wetten Godts uyt te leggen, verklaren, en beleven, so als een yder die kan bevatten en verstaen").[39]

Smout argued that it was clear from both Scripture and reason that free prophecy was the method of education that should be followed in Christian meetings. From Scripture it was clear that free prophecy had been practiced in the first church, and reason required that everyone have an equal right to express his or her ideas. Smout believed that nature itself gave all people an equal right to speak in religious meetings because no person was born with exclusive authority to interpret God's truth, and he furthermore believed that Scripture nowhere denied this "natural right."[40] For Smout, therefore, free prophecy was a natural right dictated by reason and confirmed by Scripture.

In Smout's discussion of 1 Cor. 14 his rational interpretation of free prophecy became clearer. He agreed with Langedult that some Christians in the first church had received the extraordinary gifts of the Holy Spirit, but these spiritual gifts were not necessary for free prophecy even in that early time. The first Christians used their "natural gifts" to educate each other in the true religion, Smout declared, because "God had erected a wholly rational religion and a wholly new covenant contrary to the first one." This new religion was bound not to Old Testament laws but to reason. In Smout's view the Corinthians were a perfect example of this new religion. They had no links to the old laws and therefore they could know God directly, through the use of their reason, without needing to be taught by people of authority.[41]

Smout believed that the example of the Corinthians was important for the churches of his own time. The Christians of his day lived in a world that no longer possessed the gifts of the Holy Spirit, he wrote, and thus believers had only "common and natural gifts" for knowing God's will. For this reason Smout argued that free prophecy was the best means of religious education for Christians in the seventeenth century. Anyone who wanted to come to a knowledge of the truth in order to serve God

---

[39] Pieter Smout, *Het helder licht der vryheyt*, p. vii.
[40] Ibid., pp. xvi, 158, 20.
[41] Ibid., pp. 89, 90.

needed no help from preachers, teachers, or authoritative books, he insisted. Believers could obtain this knowledge by using only the Holy Scripture and their own reason. In Smout's view, free prophecy was a process of individual rational interpretation of biblical revelation. In order to assure his readers that the true religion was indeed based on reason, and that by following their own reason believers would not transgress any of God's commands, Smout declared that "God gives no command that contradicts reason," and he added, "all that people have done, if it agrees with reason, is Godly."[42]

A final example of the Rijnsburgers' rationalistic approach to free prophecy can be found in a work by an anonymous Collegiant author entitled simply *Copye enes brief van sekere voor-stander der vrijheijt van spreecken in de gemeynte* (Copy of a letter from a certain proponent of freedom of speech in the congregation), a short piece included in a collection of Collegiant works published in 1672. In this work the author began with Galenus's theory of church decay and quickly arrived at a completely rationalistic interpretation of free prophecy.

The anonymous Collegiant opened his argument by stating the familiar Rijnsburger view that in the days of the apostles the leaders of the first church had been given special divine authority to interpret religious truth, but in the seventeenth century such was no longer the case. All people possessing special divine inspiration had long since disappeared from the earth as a result of the decay of Christianity and the consequent loss of the gifts of the Holy Spirit, he added, and for this reason all Christians of his day possessed equal authority to interpret God's will. He compared this situation to that of a prince who, seeing his chosen servants die, gave equal authority to each of his remaining subjects rather than appoint new servants. So it was with religious life in the seventeenth century: In the absence of divine inspiration all of the various religious opinions came not from God but from "the understanding and free will implanted in man from birth." For this reason the "law of nature" demanded absolute freedom of speech for all Christians so that each believer would be free to interpret divine truth as he or she saw fit. The Collegiants derived their practice of free prophecy from reason, the law of nature, and the principle of equality in religious life, the anonymous Rijnsburger wrote, and he added: "This free prophecy agrees with the rational nature of our religion, which wants each man to investigate for himself and not come to know God from another."[43] The Rijnsburgers had come a long way from

[42] Ibid., pp. 97, 52, 111.
[43] *Copye enes brief van sekere voor-stander der vrijheijt van spreecken in de gemeynte,* (n.p., ca. 1672), pp. 95–96, 103.

the belief in inspired free prophecy that had been present in the early college.

Because free prophecy was the most fundamental practical and theoretical expression of the Collegiant religion of individual conscience, its transformation can be considered symptomatic of a general trend in the colleges toward a rational and secular conception of the individual's inner ability to know truth. This trend began with the spread of Galenus's ideas after 1655 and was strengthened by Socinian rationalism, which was present in the colleges from the early 1660s. By the 1670s a fully rationalistic interpretation of free prophecy had emerged in the colleges. The last Rijnsburger writing to mention the spiritualistic interpretation of free prophecy was Stol's *Den Philosopherenden Boer* (1677), and from this work it was clear that the spiritualistic conception of the practice was quickly being displaced by another, more secular view. During the 1680s the climactic stage of Collegiant rationalism was reached with the writings of Jan Bredenburg. The evolution of the Rijnsburger view of free prophecy charted the progress of the secularization of the Collegiant conception of the individual conscience during the second half of the seventeenth century. The influence of Galenus's ideas on the transformation of free prophecy presents a microcosmic picture of the impact of his thought on the wider worldview of Collegiantism.

Chapter Eight

THE RATIONAL INNER LIGHT:
THE TRANSFORMATION OF SPIRITUALISM INTO
RATIONALISM

whatsoever doth make manifest is light.
—Ephesians 5:13

FROM BIBLICAL times the Christian tradition used the metaphor of light
to stand for Christ and the inspiration of the Holy Spirit in humanity, an
inspiration revealing divine truth and leading to individual salvation. In
the intellectual tradition of the Middle Ages light was a standard metaphor for truth and continued to be associated with the inworking of the
Holy Spirit. Throughout the Renaissance and the Reformation the metaphor of light retained its central position in European religious and philosophical thought, and thinkers of the seventeenth century were no less
interested in the idea of light. As Rosalie Colie has observed: "The eighteenth century is traditionally the age of enlightenment, but the seventeenth century was no less preoccupied with light, in search of light, dedicated to human recovery of divine light and truth."[1] In the late
seventeenth century, however, the metaphor of light began to acquire a
new, more secular usage. Cornelia Roldanus described that period as one
in which spiritualism and rationalism flowed together to create a divine
reason of individual enlightenment. When a new and secular worldview
based primarily on human reason emerged during the eighteenth century,
it was called the Enlightenment.[2]

Nothing more clearly illustrates the role of Collegiant thought in the
monumental seventeenth-century intellectual transition from faith to reason than the changing conception of the inner light found in Collegiant
writings. Among the Collegiants, spiritualism and rationalism flowed together through the traditional metaphor of light to produce the idea of a
human reason divine in its infallibility but secular and temporal in its
operation. Rijnsburger thought combined the tradition of inner-light spiritualism inherited from Franck and Schwenkfeld with the secularizing

[1] Colie, p. x.
[2] Roldanus, *Coenraad van Beuningen*, pp. 152–155.

7. The Great House with Baptism Service at Rijnsburg

tendencies present in Galenus's writings to develop an idea of human reason as the inner light of truth. In this conception reason was no longer a mere interpretive tool subservient to the revealed content of religious truth, but rather it became a source of religious truth in its own right. As Johannes Lindenboom has noted, "at first the Collegiant discussion of intellectual problems occurred mostly in the light of faith, but the light gradually became secularized into a worldy and rational science."[3]

Inner-light spiritualism came to the Collegiant movement along two interrelated paths—from spiritualistic tendencies within the Mennonite movement and from the thought of Sebastian Franck and Kaspar Schwenkfeld, reformers whom George H. Williams called radical spiritualists. The spiritualists believed that the inner light was an inspiration from God, an indwelling of the Holy Spirit in the soul of the individual believer providing him with a knowledge of God far surpassing that provided by the unaided human intellect. The inner light was a spark of the divine in the human soul that acted as a source of divine truth and as a vehicle for individual salvation.[4]

The radical spiritualists of the sixteenth century developed their idea of the inner light partly in reaction to the doctrines and authority of the institutional churches produced by the Protestant Reformation. The radicals objected to the Lutheran and Calvinist alliance of church and state and they also believed that the magisterial reformers had enclosed the essentially individualistic message of Protestantism within the confines of ecclesiastical institutions and codified doctrines that, in effect, altered the meaning of the original Protestant message. For these reasons the radicals condemned the institutional churches and rejected most doctrinal and ceremonial aspects of religion, turning instead to an individualistic inner religion that they felt was more in accord with the basic principles of Protestantism as well as with the tenets of true Christianity itself. The spiritualists stressed an inward, direct, and personal experience of the divine and they focused on the individual soul as the center of true religion.

The great German chronicler Sebastian Franck (1499–1543) was perhaps the most influential of all of the sixteenth-century spiritualists. Franck believed that the inward enlightenment of each individual soul by the Holy Spirit was superior to the doctrines of the visible churches both as a means for religious education and as the avenue to personal salvation. He believed that each person possessed the native capacity to hear

---

[3] Johannas Lindeboom, *Geschiedenis van het vrijzinnig Protestantisme* (Huis ter Hede, 1929–1935), vol. 1, p. 102.

[4] Jones, p. xxx; Hyklema, vol. 2, pp. 390–391; H. W. Meihuizen, "Spiritualistic Tendencies and Movements among the Dutch Mennonites of the Sixteenth and Seventeenth Centuries," *Mennonite Quarterly Review* 27 (October 1953), p. 259. See also Williams.

the inward word of God, and he therefore called on all believers to "notice what God says in us and to pay attention to the witness of our own hearts." In Franck's view, there was a divine element in each individual soul that was the starting point for all spiritual progress and the source of all religious truth. He called this divine element the word of God, the Spirit, the mind of Christ, and the inner light of truth. This light illuminated all people and formed an essence common to both God and humanity, allowing people to find God in themselves and themselves in God.[5]

Franck considered the inner light vital for the correct interpretation of Scripture. The dead letter of Scripture could not be interpreted literally, he believed, because in this way biblical texts could be made to support many divergent viewpoints. For this reason Franck declared: "Let nobody confound himself with Scripture but let everyone weigh and test Scripture to see how it fits his own heart. If it is against his conscience and the word within his soul, then he can be certain that he has not reached the right meaning according to the mind of the spirit, for the Scripture must give witness to the Spirit, never against it."[6]

Like other spiritualists, Franck considered human reason to be a good guide in earthly affairs but not in matters of religion. He saw natural human reason as blind to God, but he believed that when a person received the inner illumination of the Holy Spirit his or her reason also became illuminated and was capable of higher, religious knowledge because it then cooperated with the will of God.[7] The spiritualists thus maintained a distinct separation between natural human reason and the inner light, and they considered reason incapable of knowing divine truth without the aid of divine inspiration. A crucial step in the process by means of which later Collegiant thought evolved from spiritualism to rationalism was the closing of this gap between the inner light and human reason, resulting in a fusion of these two key concepts.

Kaspar Schwenkfeld was another of the leaders of sixteenth-century spiritualism whose ideas influenced the Collegiants. Schwenkfeld described the inner light as "a precious gift of the Holy Spirit" that flowed from God into the heart of the individual believer. He considered this gift of the Spirit to be a sign of membership in the true invisible church of Christ. The inner light was also the key for understanding the true sense of Scripture. Schwenkfeld believed that only through this inner, spiritual word could the outer word of the Bible be properly interpreted. This idea was central to the original Collegiant conception of free prophecy.[8]

[5] Ibid., pp. 50, 53–54.
[6] Ibid., p. 50.
[7] Ibid., pp. 55–57.
[8] Ibid., pp. 72–80.

After the deaths of Franck and Schwenkfeld their ideas moved north into the Low Countries. Translations of Franck's works began to appear in the Netherlands as early as 1564, and disciples like D. V. Coornhert and Aggaeus van Albada spread Schwenkfeld's doctrines. The humanist Coornhert passed spiritualistic ideas on to his Dutch readers, including the Collegiant Adam Boreel, who in turn gave these ideas to his disciple Galenus Abrahamsz. The doctrine of the inner light was readily adopted by the Collegiants, whose Second Reformation critique of the established Protestant churches of the seventeenth century was similar in many respects to the reform program of the earlier radical spiritualists. Without a doubt, Franck and Schwenkfeld were the most important sources for Collegiant spiritualism. Their ideas became so popular in the colleges during the early seventeenth century that George H. Williams described the Collegiants as "seventeenth-century spiritualists similar to Schwenkfeldians."[9]

Another avenue by which spiritualistic ideas reached the colleges was through the Anabaptist-Mennonite movement. Spiritualism was popular in the seventeenth century among certain groups of Dutch Mennonites, who inherited these ideas from their Anabaptist forebears. The roots of Anabaptist spiritualism went back at least as far as the early German Anabaptist leader Hans Denck (1495–1527), who adopted certain spiritualistic ideas from the radical reformer Thomas Müntzer during the first quarter of the sixteenth century. Following the medieval mystic Johannes Tauler, Müntzer maintained that there was a divine inner word that God spoke in the depths of the human heart. He believed that God bestowed on the elect the sevenfold gifts of the Spirit, one of which was the ability to receive direct instruction from the Holy Spirit in the form of vision, dream, ecstatic utterance, or inspired exegesis. Similarly, Denck held that the outer word of God in Scripture could be understood only by believers in possession of the inner spiritual word, the inward revelation of the divine spirit witnessing to God in the souls of all believers. Denck further believed that while Christ was known outwardly as a historical personage, he was known inwardly by believers as the divine light. No external ceremonies could bring a person to God if that person lacked this inner light, Denck maintained, but those in possession of this divine spark were united to God. Among those converted to Anabaptism by Denck's preaching was Johannes Bunderlin (1499–1533), who carried on the tradition of Anabaptist spiritualism with his belief that the inner light was an eternal image of God implanted in human nature to draw believers toward God. Christian Entfelder, another disciple of Denck, believed that true religion was based on a direct relationship between the divine spirit

[9] Williams, p. 788.

and the human soul. For Entfelder, the inner light was the voice of the Holy Spirit speaking within the individual believer.[10] Entfelder's ideas were later translated into Dutch by the Collegiant spiritualist Pieter Serrarius.

Anabaptist spiritualism came into the Low Countries with Melchior Hoffman (1495–1543) and Michael Sattler (d. 1527), both of whom stressed the importance of the personal guidance of the Holy Spirit in religious life. It was David Joris (1501–1556), however, who introduced an extreme brand of spiritualism among the Dutch Anabaptists. Under the influence of Schwenkfeld, Joris and his followers believed that all true religion was internal, and they therefore rejected the external sacraments of baptism and communion. In reaction to this extreme spiritualism some Anabaptist leaders in the Low Countries, including Menno Simons (1496–1561) and his disciple Dirk Philips (1504–1568), favored biblical literalism and a strict application of the ban in order to preserve the external aspects of their religion. One result of the efforts of Simons and Philips was an institutionalization of the Anabaptist movement in the Low Countries and a corresponding decline in spiritualistic fervor. The strict application of the ban soon became a divisive issue within the Dutch Anabaptist movement, however, and the resulting quarrels led to the formation of the Waterlander movement in 1555. It was especially among the Waterlanders that Anabaptist spiritualism lived on into the seventeenth century, fed in part by the increasing circulation of Dutch translations of the writings of Franck.[11] While not himself a Waterlander, Amsterdam Mennonite leader Galenus Abrahamsz. was sympathetic to many of the ideas of the movement, as he demonstrated during the 1649 Waterlander union discussions.

Galenus Abrahamsz. stood at the intersection of two important streams of spiritualistic thought feeding into Dutch religious life during the seventeenth century. An heir to the spiritualism of his Anabaptist ancestors, Galenus was also influenced by the ideas of Franck and Schwenkfeld through his contact with Adam Boreel. Galenus's own thought had a spiritualistic character, in part because of the distinction that he made between the two kinds of gifts of the Spirit, and he shared his ideas with his closest associates in the United Mennonite congregation and the Amsterdam college: Pieter Serrarius, Jarig Jelles, and Pieter Balling. These men supported Galenus in his struggle with the conservative Mennonites during the *Lammerenkrijg,* and in the process they placed great emphasis on the value of personal inspiration in religious life. According to the

---

[10] Jones, pp. 19–27, 36, 41; Williams, p. 49.

[11] Williams, pp. 484–501; Meihuizen, "Spiritualistic Tendencies and Movements among the Dutch Mennonites of the Sixteenth and Seventeenth Centuries," pp. 264–282, 286–304.

Mennonite historian N. van der Zijpp, Galenus and his supporters during the *Lammerenkrijg* put so much stress on the working of the Holy Spirit that they sometimes seemed to neglect the important role of Scripture in religious life. Van der Zijpp also noted that throughout his entire life Galenus "remained above all a spiritualist."[12]

Galenus put forward his moderate spiritualism in a work entitled *Korte verhandeling van de redelyk-bevindelyke godsdienst* (Short treatment of the rational-experiential religion), first published in Amsterdam in 1674 but probably written earlier. This work presented the picture of a religion in which contact with the divine was exclusively personal and individual. Despite its curious title, Leszek Kolakowski has described the *Korte verhandeling* as a work reminiscent of the spiritualistic roots of Anabaptism.[13] Galenus believed that the human spirit came from the essence of God and would by its very nature always strive to return to its divine origin. While the spirit was in the human body, however, it was subjected to temptations of bodily and sensual pleasures that it could not resist. For this reason Galenus believed that humanity needed a spiritual rebirth in order to be united with God. In Galenus's view, this rebirth could be achieved only by the inflowing of God's Spirit into the human soul.[14]

Galenus's conception of the operation of divine grace was similar to ideas found in Franck and Schwenkfeld. He defined grace as a supernatural communication from God through the Holy Spirit, a communication that came directly from God, using no natural agents. As divine grace flowed into the soul it acted upon the human understanding in the same way that Franck's inner light did in order to give "more and clearer intelligence and enlightenment." Following the apostle Paul, Galenus described this process as the obtaining of "enlightened eyes of the understanding" through "the Spirit of wisdom and revelation." The Holy Spirit "purified, brightened, and enlarged" understanding, thus making it capable of knowing all of the secrets of religion. According to Galenus, this process of enlightenment changed the way in which people understood Scripture. Before enlightenment people could understand the Bible only in a literal and dark way, but after the inflowing of the Holy Spirit one could understand Scripture in a truer, more spiritual sense. Galenus believed that people received the illumination of the Holy Spirit partly in order to understand God and the divine plan for humankind, and he upheld the traditional spiritualistic separation between the divine inner light and natural human reason. Galenus concluded his work with a vivid description of the mystic rapture that people experienced when God's Spirit

---

[12] Van der Zijpp, pp. 99–101.

[13] Kolakowski, pp. 195–197.

[14] Galenus Abrahamsz., *Korte verhandeling van de redelyk-bevindelyke godsdienst* (Amsterdam, 1674), pp. 2–4.

filled their souls. Even though Galenus never used the term inner light, the *Korte verhandeling* was very much in the tradition of spiritualism.[15]

Many of Galenus's Collegiant followers did not remain as spiritualistic as he did. Just as the secularizing tendencies within Collegiant thought that resulted from Galenus's rejection of the extraordinary gifts of the Spirit gradually transformed the Rijnsburger conception of free prophecy, so too did these ideas bring about a change in Collegiant spiritualism. As the Rijnsburgers' conception of the individual conscience was gradually secularized, their doctrine of the inner light was transformed from a belief in direct divine inspiration of the individual soul to an embryonic idea of the natural light of reason. In the writings of Galenus's followers Pieter Balling and Jarig Jelles the distinction so carefully maintained by spiritualists like Franck between the inner light of the Spirit and natural human reason was erased. The resulting fusion of the ideas of the inner light and reason produced a concept of the natural light of reason. In this concept reason retained some of the epistemological characteristics of the spiritual inner light. Most importantly, reason came to be seen as an infallible source of true ideas in its own right. The transformation of Collegiant spiritualism into rationalism thus represented a very important step in the development of Collegiant thought. Reason was no longer seen as a mere tool for interpreting the revealed truth of Scripture, but instead came to be seen as a source of true ideas that provided the content of truth as well as its interpretation. With this new view of reason the Collegiants took a decisive step in the direction of both natural religion and philosophical rationalism.

The writings of Balling and Jelles were important transitional works between the thought of Rijnsburger spiritualists like Galenus and the philosophical rationalism of Jan Bredenburg. While the thought of Balling and Jelles was clearly moving in the direction of a rationalism that came to maturity in the colleges with the work of Bredenburg, their writings did not represent a complete secularization of the individual conscience. In their thought the transformation undergone by the idea of the inner light resulted in a conception of a divine reason not unlike ideas held at the same time by the Cambridge Platonists. Because reason was identified so closely with the spiritual inner light, reason was spiritualized almost as much as spirit was rationalized. In the process, however, the power and authority gained by human reason seen as a divine light created the epistemological foundation in Collegiant thought for a powerful new rationalist system. The transitional thought of Balling and Jelles might be called, for lack of a better term, rational spiritualism.

[15] Ibid., pp. 11, 13; Vekeman, pp. 29–34.

The transformation of spiritualism into rationalism evident in the writings of Balling and Jelles was the result primarily of ideas that developed within the Collegiant movement after 1660. The secularization of the Rijnsburger conception of the individual conscience that resulted from Galenus's theory of church decay (first discussed in 1655 and first published in 1657–1659) had an important impact on the thought of Galenus's friends Balling and Jelles. As members of Galenus's Mennonite congregation and of the Amsterdam college that Galenus led, both men backed Galenus during the *Lammerenkrijg* as well as during a dispute between Galenus and a group of English Quaker missionaries led by William Ames. The controversy with the Quakers, which began in 1657 but became intense during the years 1660–1661, was an event of great importance for the development of Collegiant rationalism. Galenus, Balling, Jelles, and Pieter Serrarius argued against the radical brand of inner-light spiritualism practiced by the Quakers, and a result of this controversy both Balling and Jelles moved further in the direction of a rationalistic conception of the inner light. Balling's major work, *Het Licht op den Kandelaar*, was a product of this controversy. The decade of the 1660s was also one that saw several popular dates for the arrival of the millennium pass uneventfully, and it was during the years after 1660 that most Polish Socinian exiles arrived in Amsterdam. The influence of Socinian ideas within the college could only have encouraged the developing rationalism of Balling and Jelles.

These and other developments within Collegiant thought after 1660 created in Balling and Jelles an active interest in the new rationalistic philosophy of René Descartes. Descartes's ideas spread rapidly in the United Provinces after the philosopher took up residence there in 1628, and the subsequent publication of his *Discourse on Method* in Leiden in 1637 only increased this interest. Balling and Jelles were encouraged in their interest in Cartesianism by their friend Benedict Spinoza (1632–1677), who joined the Collegiants after being expelled from the Amsterdam Jewish community in 1656. Spinoza maintained close contact with Collegiant circles in Amsterdam during the years 1657–1664. Balling translated Spinoza's first book, *The Principles of Descartes' Philosophy*, into Dutch and corresponded with him when he left Amsterdam to live in Rijnsburg. Jelles wrote an introduction to the posthumous edition of Spinoza's works published in 1677, and dedicated his own major work, the *Belijdenisse des Algemeenen en Christelyken geloofs* . . . , to Spinoza. Balling and Jelles learned much about Cartesianism from Spinoza and his influence was evident in their writings, but their inclination toward rationalism arose out of their involvement in Collegiantism. Balling and Jelles were not Cartesians, much less were they Spinozists. They were Mennonites and Collegiants. Their thought represented the evolution of Collegiant spiritualism in a rationalistic direction, impelled by a changing Rijnsburger conception of the individual conscience. They used Cartesian ideas to express rationalistic convictions that evolved organically from the secularization of Collegiant thought after 1660.

One of the most important events for the secularization of Collegiant thought after 1660 was the Rijnsburgers' contact with the English Quakers. The spiritualistic inclination among the early Rijnsburgers was so pronounced that C. B. Hylkema later wrote that the Collegiants' kinship to Quakers was stronger than to rationalist philosophers.[16] The history of the Collegiants' relationship with the Quakers, however, does not bear out Hylkema's claim. Toward the middle of the seventeenth century a group of English Quakers did indeed recognize what they believed to be a kindred spirit among the Collegiants, and for this reason they made the Rijnsburgers prime targets for conversion when the first Quaker missionaries arrived in the United Provinces in 1653. When the Quakers arrived in Amsterdam, however, a profound change was already under way within the colleges. Professor Van den Berg has noted that as late as 1660 there were still many Collegiants who agreed with Serrarius in holding a spiritualistic belief in the direct inworking of the Holy Spirit, but Van den Berg also pointed out that there were many other Collegiants who were by that time moving in a rationalistic direction.[17] The Quaker missionaries were surprised to encounter this secularizing trend in Collegiant thought when they arrived in Amsterdam, and the result was a bitter quarrel between the two groups that had the effect of pushing some Rijnsburgers still farther down the path to rationalism.

The first English Quaker missionaries to Holland, William Caton and John Stubbs, began preaching in Middleburg and Vlissingen in 1653. They were soon followed by William Ames, who arrived in Amsterdam in the spring of 1656 and quickly became the recognized leader of the Dutch Quakers. Ames made the Mennonites and Collegiants prime targets of his conversion efforts because he believed that similarities existed between the Quakers and these groups that would make progress possible. Ames did indeed make some headway among the Mennonites. Not long after his arrival in Amsterdam he was able to establish a small Quaker congregation made up primarily of former Mennonites like William Sewel and Judith Zinspenning, parents of the famous Quaker historian William Sewel.[18]

At first Ames hoped to convert the Collegiants to Quakerism by pointing out the similarities between the two groups: both practiced free

[16] Hylkema, vol. 2, p. 15.
[17] Van den Berg, pp. 181–193.
[18] ME, vol. 4, p. 501.

speech in religious meetings, both criticized institutional religion, and both held meetings primarily for religious education.[19] Galenus, Pieter Serrarius, and Pieter Balling were among the Collegiants initially attracted by Quaker preaching, but serious differences arose between Ames and Serrarius as early as 1657. Almost from the first, the extreme brand of inner-light spiritualism practiced by the Quakers was rejected by the Rijnsburgers, whose own spiritualism was being gradually moderated and transformed by Galenus's ideas. When the first open quarrel between the two groups erupted in 1657, Ames and Serrarius agreed on the need for divine inspiration to interpret Scripture correctly, but Serrarius objected to the Quaker claim that the inner light of the Spirit was superior even to the Bible itself as the supreme authority in religion. Ames, on the other hand, repeatedly and vigorously insisted on the absolute primacy of the inner light. In a work published in Amsterdam in 1657 and entitled *Een wederlegging van een boeck genaemt antwoort op 23 vragen* (A refutation of a book entitled Answer to twenty-three questions) Ames rejected Serrarius's moderate spiritualism.[20]

The essence of the Quaker religious position was belief in an extreme form of inner-light spiritualism that led the Quakers to call for a radical cleansing of all of the established Christian churches of the seventeenth century. In this demand the Quakers, like the Collegiants, were very much a part of the Second Reformation. They called for a thorough reform of the ecclesiastical system of the day and for an immediate restoration of true Christianity, which they believed to be the dedicated following of Christ by way of the inner light. The Quakers favored simplicity and brotherhood in all things; a strict code of moral conduct; and worship without sacraments, ordinances, clergy, or liturgy. They repudiated violence, refused oaths, and had a strong missionary purpose.[21]

The Quakers saw themselves as a chosen people following the will of God, a people who could not be prevented from carrying God's word into the world.[22] The Quakers' belief that they were divine ambassadors chosen by God to bring spiritual truth to humankind brought them into conflict with Collegiants like Galenus, Serrarius, and Balling who had come to believe that no one in the temporal world could claim such extraordinary divine inspiration or authority. In addition, the extremely ardent and aggressive way in which the Quakers sought to spread their ideas, combined with the peculiar demeanor that they adopted as a result of their convictions, repelled the Collegiants as it did many other people. The Rijnsburgers considered the Quakers' great zeal and sense of election

[19] Van den Berg, in Knox, ed., p. 184; Hull, *The Rise of Quakerism*, p. 145.
[20] Van den Berg, in Knox, ed., p. 193.
[21] *ME*, vol. 4, p. 501.
[22] Hylkema, vol. 1, p. 84.

to be spiritual arrogance, and they were disturbed as well by the Quaker habit of interrupting the services of other religious groups in order to argue with the preacher. The Collegiants were also repulsed by the Quakers' often animated public preaching as well as by their refusal to bare their heads as a sign of public greeting. What the Rijnsburgers perceived as the arrogant and overzealous behavior of many Quakers no doubt helped to discredit spiritualism in the eyes of the more moderate Collegiants. On 24 August 1660 a meeting between Quakers and Collegiants was held in the Amsterdam home of Serrarius. At this meeting great bitterness arose when Collegiant Adam Boreel and Quaker John Higgins became involved in a heated argument, and the resulting dispute led to the final break between the Quakers and the Collegiants.[23] A protracted pamphlet war between the two groups followed during 1660–1661, both the principle arguments and the vitriolic nature of which demonstrated the deep and fundamental differences that existed between the Quakers and Collegiants. While the Quakers remained firmly attached to inner-light spiritualism and the idea of divine providence, the Rijnsburgers had begun to move away from these positions.

The pamphlet war began with the publication in Amsterdam of Williams Ames' *Het Licht dat in de duisternis schijnt beweesen den weg tot God te zijn* (The light that shines in the darkness proven to be the way to God). In this work Ames attacked article 16 of Galenus's important treatise *XIX Artikelen*, first published in 1657. Galenus had argued that his own Mennonite congregation lacked any special divine authority or inspiration, and he used this claim to support his general argument that all established churches were separated from divine inspiration and were therefore merely the creations of fallible humans.[24] In *Het Licht* Ames reacted angrily to this argument. To set up a church without the direction of God's Spirit could only produce an illegitimate congregation, Ames declared, and he furthermore maintained that to worship God in a form that was not directly commanded by God was "heathen." Ames bitterly proclaimed that Christ had left Galenus without any certainty of the divine will because Galenus did not believe in the inner light and was therefore not one of God's chosen people. If the Holy Spirit truly lived in Galenus, Ames asserted, then he would have the divine authority and instruction that he freely admitted both he and his followers lacked.[25]

Ames also rejected Galenus's claim that all established churches lacked divine inspiration. "Are all men then outside of the church of Christ?" Ames asked. "Has Christ no body separate from the world, and are no

---

[23] Van den Berg, pp. 188–189.

[24] Galenus Abrahamsz. and David Spruyt, *XIX Artikelen*, p. 8.

[25] William Ames, *Het Lict dat in de duisternis schijnt beweesen den weg tot God te zijn* (Amsterdam, 1660), pp. 9–10.

people guided by God?" In Ames's opinion the Holy Spirit was in all places, and it therefore had to be in the temporal world as well. He further declared that God had collected the Quakers as his chosen people, to walk in his light and to have full certainty of his will. Galenus was simply too blind to see that the day had come in which God would appear in many thousands of his saints to reprimand false dreamers like the Collegiants.[26]

Galenus replied to Ames's arguments in 1660 with a pamphlet entitled *Drie vragen* (Three questions), and Ames followed with a new attack on the Rijnsburgers in his *De verborgenheden van het Rijcke Gods* (The hidden things of God's kingdom [1661]). There then followed a series of pamphlets from the Collegiant side by Galenus's followers Pieter Serrarius and Pieter Balling. Serrarius published three works in 1661: *De ware weg tot God* (The true way to God), *23 vragen aen William Ames en John Higgins* (Twenty-three questions to William Ames and John Higgins), and *Een antwoordt op eenige aenmerckingen door John Higgins* (An answer to some remarks by John Higgins). Balling published his important work *Het Licht op den Kandelaar* in 1662. On the Quaker side, Higgins wrote *Eenige waerdige ende gewichtige aenmerckingen voor Galenus Abrahamsz. ende Adam Boreel* (Some worthy and weighty remarks for Galenus Abrahamsz. and Adam Boreel) in 1660 and Ames published *Het waere licht beschermt* . . . (The true light defended) in 1661. In his attacks on the Collegiants, Ames repeatedly stressed the importance of the spiritual inner light as the single avenue to enter heaven. Ames firmly believed that the Holy Spirit was in every believer in the form of the inner light, and he unconditionally rejected any role for reason in religious life. The things of God could only be known through the Spirit of God, Ames wrote in *Het Licht*, and therefore to reject the inner light was to reject the wisdom, strength, and majesty of God. People who were without the light could not truly worship God because no one could follow any of God's commands if they did not first follow the light.[27]

The Quakers repeatedly and explicitly rejected the Collegiants' use of reason in religion. In *Het Licht* Ames put the question plainly when he asked whether the light in the human conscience was by nature human or from God, leaving no doubt that he believed the light to be supernatural.[28] John Higgins declared that one could never know God through human wisdom nor hope to understand religious truth by natural learning or science. Anyone who tried to know God through natural knowledge was blind, Higgins declared, and he scolded Galenus: "Your college's dis-

---

[26] Ibid., pp. 6, 7–11.
[27] Hull, pp. 233–236; Van den Berg, p. 185; Ames, pp. 13–14.
[28] Ibid., p. 20

puting about and explaining Scripture is not the way that the saints of old or of today come to the knowledge of God's secrets. They come to know them by the light." Another Quaker, James Park, accused the Collegiants of knowing no other worship of God than through their reason, which Park called: "a dark and fleshly reason that you call the light."[29]

In the face of these spiritualistic attacks the Collegiants reacted in various ways. Moderate spiritualists like Galenus and Serrarius were severely tested in their beliefs by the seemingly fanatical use to which the Quakers put the doctrine of the inner light. While they did not reject the principles of spiritualism itself, Galenus and Serrarius rejected Quaker claims to be the chosen people of God and the divinely inspired rebuilders of the true church. In Galenus's opinion, the Quakers considered their own religious experience to be something so great that they were under the delusion that they were sent by God and spoke under the influence of the Holy Spirit.[30] Serrarius accused the Quakers of claiming the status of divine revelation for their own personal opinions. He added that, because the true church no longer existed on earth, human opinions were fallible and no one could rightfully claim divine authority for their own beliefs. "The light of the saints was blessed, but ours is unblessed," Serrarius declared. As for the Quakers, he concluded that they had "never heard the voice of God nor seen his form nor had his word living inside them."[31]

Moderates like Galenus and Serrarius did not totally reject Quaker spiritualism but they did criticize the most extreme uses of that doctrine by the Quakers. In reply to the Quakers' claim that people could find God only in the spiritual inner light, Galenus recommended the use of Scripture and common sense. "Where does the Bible say that the apostles and prophets taught believers to turn inward to the light to learn everything about God?" Galenus asked. "Did not the apostles give the people laws, doctrines, and commands to instruct them in the will of God?" And would it not therefore be proper, Galenus asked, "to refer people to the Bible, laws, and teaching of Jesus and the apostles so that they can be educated and then closely follow the light of their own consciences?"[32]

Galenus's attitude toward Quaker spiritualism was perhaps best exemplified by a story told by H. W. Meihuizen in his biography of the

---

[29] John Higgins, *Einige waerdige ende gewichtige aenmerckingen voor Galenus Abrahamsz. ende Adam Boreel ende haare aenhangers* (Amsterdam, 1660), pp. 2–3; James Park, *Christus Jesus verhooght/En een getuygenis gedragen tot sijn Waere Licht/Welck een yegelijck mensch verlicht die in de werelt komt . . .* (Amsterdam, 1670), p. 16.

[30] Meihuizen, "Spiritualistic Tendencies and Movements among the Dutch Mennonites of the Sixteenth and Seventeenth Centuries," p. 159.

[31] William Ames, *Het Waere Licht beschermt ende de innooselheydt van de eenvoudige bevrijt van de onwaerheden ende valsche beschuldingen door Petrus Serrarius op haar geleyt . . .* (Amsterdam, 1661), pp. 26–28.

[32] Ames, *Het Ligt dat in de duisternis schijnt*, pp. 11–13.

Collegiant leader. According to Meihuizen, late in 1656 a Quaker named Isaac Furnier felt himself moved by the Spirit to take a knife and scratch away the title of "Dr." that Galenus had painted before his name on the doorpost of his Amsterdam home. Furnier no doubt believed the title to be a sign of Galenus's sinful desire for worldly honors. As Furnier was scratching away at the doorpost Galenus came outside to ask why the Quaker was disfiguring his house. When Furnier replied that he did so because the Spirit had moved him, Galenus asked whether he would also follow the moving of the Spirit if it told him to run Galenus through with the knife. When Furnier replied that he would, Galenus recoiled in shock and horror.[33]

Other Collegiants reacted to Quaker spiritualistic zeal by modifying traditional Collegiant spiritualism in a rationalistic direction. By developing a secular interpretation of the inner light these Rijnsburgers perhaps hoped to undercut the legitimacy of Quaker claims based on the inworking of the Holy Spirit. At the same time the Collegiants attempted to move away from what they considered to be the bad example provided by the Quakers by shifting Collegiant truth claims to an epistemological foundation not discredited by Quaker spiritualistic excess. Such a work was Pieter Balling's *Het Licht op den Kandelaar, Dienende tot opmerck inge van de voornaamste dingen in het boeckje genaamt De verborgentheden van het Rijke Ghodts tegens Galenus Abrahamsz. en zijn toestemmers verhandelt en beschreven door William Ames* (The light on the candlestick, serving to remark on the foremost things in the book called The hidden things of God's kingdom, against Galenus Abrahamsz. and his supporters by William Ames [1662]), intended as a reply to a work by Ames.[34]

Balling was born in Amsterdam and received a classical education, probably at Leiden. He worked for a time as a merchant in Amsterdam and as an agent in Spain for several Amsterdam and Haarlem trading

---

[33] Meihuizen, p. 59.

[34] This work has been attributed by Van den Berg, Van der Wall, and others to William Ames, in part because the edition of 1662 lacked the author's name. In 1683 a copy of the work was mistakenly included in a collection of the writings of Adam Boreel, leading some later scholars to believe it to be one of Boreel's works. In the 1684 edition of *Het Licht*, however, the name Pieter Balling did appear on the title page. Since this edition was printed by Jan Rieuwertsz., a friend of Balling and the long-time printer for Collegiant works in Amsterdam, his attribution of the work to Balling must be considered authoritative. In the edition of 1684, *Het Licht* was bound with a very similar Collegiant writing, Jarig Jelles's *Belijdenisse*. This edition is held by the University of Amsterdam Library in its church history collection and it bears the stamp of the library of the Amsterdam United Mennonite congregation, the congregation of Balling, Jelles, and Galenus Abrahamsz. On this point, see also S.B.J. Zilverberg, "De plaats von het collegiantisme in de zeventiende-eeuwse kerkgeschiedenis," *De Zeventiende Eeuw* 5, no. 1 (1989), p. 117.

companies. In his capacity as a businessman Balling first met Benedict Spinoza, who was active in his own family's business.[35] Balling was a member of Galenus's Mennonite congregation and an advocate of many of Galenus's religious ideas. During the *Lammerenkrijg* Balling wrote two lengthy works in defense of Galenus in which he presented a non-charismatic picture of the Christian church on earth (see chapter 3). Like Galenus and Serrarius, Balling saw the established churches as merely human institutions. Because he considered the churches to be devoid of all gifts of the Spirit he criticized the dogma and confessions of conservative Mennonites, calling them the uninspired work of fallible humans. Balling condemned clerical authority and called instead for toleration and freedom in religious life.[36] He was a dedicated friend of Spinoza and a member of a small group of thinkers who regularly discussed philosophy with him. Balling was sufficiently close to Spinoza both personally and intellectually that he corresponded with Spinoza after the philospher left Amsterdam. In Spinoza's correspondence a letter is preserved from the philosopher to Balling, dated 29 July 1664, in which Spinoza offered Balling consolation on the death of a child.[37] At about this same time Balling translated Spinoza's book on Cartesian philosophy (*The Principles of Descartes' Philosophy*), but toward the end of 1664 Balling died of plague in Amsterdam.

Het Licht op den Kandelaar was a work solidly anchored in the Collegiant religion of individual conscience as well as in the tradition of inner-light spiritualism, but it also contained unmistakable rationalistic elements. Balling's embryonic rationalism developed organically out of the doctrine of the inner light under the influence of Galenus's ideas, the Collegiant-Quaker controversy and Cartesianism. Because of its mixture of spiritualistic and rationalistic elements, Balling's work has long been considered puzzling by historians. Even though *Het Licht* was in the spiritualistic tradition, Balling only once employed the term "spirit" (*geest*) in the work. Furthermore, while Balling often referred to the inner light in unmistakably Cartesian terms, he never used the term "reason." Balling's primary stress throughout *Het Licht* was on the individual, inner nature of human knowledge. Perhaps this stress indicated that the Collegiants considered the principle of inner knowledge itself to be more important than the gradually changing nature of that principle.

Balling began *Het Licht* in true Collegiant fashion with a condemnation of the many divisions within seventeenth-century Christianity. In his

---

[35] Roldanus, *Zeventiende eeuwse geestesbloei*, pp. 130–131; Theun de Vries, *Spinoza: Beelden-Stormer en Wereldbouwer* (Amsterdam, 1983), pp. 57–58, 127–128.

[36] Kolakowski, pp. 214–216.

[37] See *Benedict de Spinoza: On the Improvement of the Understanding, the Ethics, Correspondence*, R.H.M. Elwes, trans. and ed. (New York, 1955), p. 321 (letter 30).

view these divisions were caused by mistrust and intolerance among Christians and by the prevalence of subtle but ultimately superficial arguments among the various sects. Balling assured his readers, however, that "true religion is not this at all." The purpose of his work, Balling wrote, was not to convert his readers from one sect to another but rather to direct them to religious truth so that they could obtain the means for their own salvation. To find this truth, Balling advised his readers: "We direct you then to look within yourself, that is, that you ought to turn into, to mind, and have a regard unto that which is within you—the light of truth, the true light which enlightenth every man that comes into the world . . . Here you shall find a principle certain and infallible" ("Wij wijzen U dan tot U zelven/dat is dat gij moet inkeren/acht geven/ende opmerken 't gene dat in U is/namelijk op het licht der waarheit, het waarachtige licht, 't welcke verlicht een yder mensche komende in de werelt . . . heir zult gij vinden een beginzel dat zeker is en onfeilbaar").[38]

The image of the light of truth was taken by Balling from the spiritualist tradition, and the phrase "the truth light which enlighteneth every man that comes into the world" came from the scriptural passage John 1:9, where the light referred to was Christ. The phrase "here you shall find a principle certain and infallible," however, was taken from Descartes. In the Second Meditation, Descartes sought a single principle of certainty upon which to rebuild all human knowledge: "Archimedes, to move the earth from its orbit and place it in a new position, demanded nothing more than a fixed and immovable fulcrum; in a similar manner I shall have the right to entertain high hopes if I am fortunate enough to find a single truth which is certain and indubitable."[39] Balling saw the inner light of truth as just the kind of "truth which is certain and indubitable" that Descartes sought. Balling defined the light of truth in clearly Cartesian terms: "The light . . . is a clear and distinct knowledge of truth in the understanding of every man, by which he is so convinced of the being and quality of things, that he cannot possibly doubt thereof" ("Het Licht . . . is een klare en onderscheidene kennisse van waarheit in het verstant van een ygelijck mensch, door welk hij zoodanich overtuight is, van het zijn en hoedanich zijn der zaken, dat het voor hem onmogelijk is, daar aan te kunnen twijfelen").[40] Balling thus identified the light of truth with that fundamental and indubitable rational knowledge upon which Des-

[38] Pieter Balling, *Het Licht op den Kandelaar* (Amsterdam, 1662), pp. 2–3. The English translations are taken from a contemporary English version of the work appended to William Sewel, *The History of the Rise, Increase, and Progress of the Christian People called Quakers* (London, 1725).

[39] René Descartes, *Meditations on First Philosophy*, in Norman Kemp Smith, ed., *Descartes: Philsophical Writings* (New York, 1958), p. 182.

[40] Balling, *Het Licht op den Kandelaar*, p. 4.

cartes built his new philosophy. Descartes believed the truths of reason to be clear and distinct and thus so self-evidently true to the rational mind that they could not possibly be doubted. He thus made rational clarity his primary criterion for truth in the *Discourse on Method:* "The first rule was to accept nothing as true which I did not evidently know to be such, that is to say, scrupulously to avoid precipitance and prejudice, and in the judgements I passed to include nothing additional to what had presented itself to my mind so clearly and so distinctly that I could have no occasion for doubting it."[41]

By calling the inner light of truth a "clear and distinct knowledge" Balling associated it with the Cartesian conception of reason. In other places in *Het Licht,* however, he maintained a more traditional spiritualistic interpretation of the inner light: "We say then, that we exhort everyone to turn unto the light that is in him. (We give it rather the name of light, than anything else, otherwise it is all the same to us whether you call it Christ, the Spirit, the Word, etc., since these all denote one and the same thing)" ("Wy zeggen dan/dat wij een ygelijk mensche aanmanen in te keren tot het licht dat in hem is/[Wij noemen het liever met de benaming van licht, als met enige andere/anders is 't ons om 't even/of men het noeme Christus, den Geest, het Woort enz. dewijle alle deze op een en zelve zake uitlopen]").[42]

In much of the rest of *Het Licht* Balling referred to the inner light in terms that would permit either a rationalistic or a spiritualistic interpretation. He was never ambiguous, however, in his insistence that the inner light was an independent source of true ideas superior in authority to all other sources, including Scripture. Balling called the light a "preaching to every creature under heaven to lead them to the truth and into the way of God even if they have never read or heard of Scripture." The light gave people a knowledge of truth and falsehood and of good and evil without which they would wander forever in darkness, uncertainty, and sin, Balling declared. For this reason the light had "preeminence before any writing, Scripture, doctrine, or any thing else that we meet with from without . . . since this [the light] is infallible." He continued: "the light is also the first principle of religion, because there can be no true religion without knowledge of God, and no knowledge of God without this light" ("het licht is ook het eerste beginzel van de Ghodtsdienst: want dewijl qeen ware Ghodtsdienst kan zijn/zonder kennisse Ghodts, en qeen kennisse Ghodts zonder dit licht"). Balling then turned again to Cartesian imagery when he wrote that the knowledge obtained through the light was a "firm foundation" upon which people could "build all firm and lasting things."

[41] René Descartes, *A Discourse on Method*, in Smith, ed., pp. 107–108.
[42] Balling, *Het Licht op den Kandelaar*, p. 4.

Most importantly, Balling declared, this knowledge would enable the individual to obtain his salvation, which consisted of union with God.[43]

If Balling had conceived of the inner light of truth in purely spiritualistic terms, his elevation of the light above Scripture would have been clearly in the Quaker tradition. As his usage of Cartesian phraseology suggests, however, Balling thought of the light of truth also in terms of human reason. This move toward rationalism can be seen in part as a reaction to that extreme Quaker spiritualism that in Collegiant eyes led to fanaticism and intolerance. Seen in this perspective, Balling's elevation of the inner light above Scripture takes on a meaning that sets *Het Licht* dramatically apart from the spiritualistic tradition. Balling's work represented the beginnings in Collegiant thought of a conception of human reason as an infallible source of true religious ideas that was independent of church authority and the revelation of Scripture.

Balling again revealed his rationalistic leanings when he discussed the origin of sin and error. "Now if it so happens," he wrote, "that a man chooses the worst before the best, it is for want of knowledge . . . and so he errs, not being led by the light . . . for people knowing better, would do better." For Balling, the light was the cause of all good deeds:

> "Without this light man has no power or ability to do good. It must first awaken him out of the death of sin and make him living. Darkness is only driven away by the light, ignorance only by knowledge. It is folly to want something where there is nothing. There is no effect without cause. If man does anything, something causes him to do it. And this cause must contain all that the effect contains. If there is the effect of the light, the light alone must be the cause."

> ("Zonder dit licht is in de mensche geen macht, of vermogen om ijet ghoedt is te konnen doen. Dit moet hem aldereest opwekken/en levendich maken uit den doot der zonden. De duisterniss wort niet verdreven als door licht; het onverstant niet als door kennisse. 't Is dwaarsheit iets te willen daar niet is/ zonder oorzaak is geen werkinge/daar moet dan iet zijn/dat den mensche veroorzaakt te doen; zoo hij iet zal doen. En deze oorzaak moet in zich hebben alles wat zoodanigen uit werkinge/alzer gewrocht wort/in zich heeft: zoo er uitwerkingen van 't Licht veroorzaakt zullen werden; het Licht moet het doen/en niet anders").[44]

The idea that human error resulted from a lack of knowledge and not from a corrupt will was an integral component of philosophical rationalism, as was the doctrine of causal determinism ("There is no effect without cause"). A version of the idea that "the cause must contain all that

---

[43] Ibid., pp. 4, 5, 7.
[44] Ibid., pp. 5, 6.

the effect contains" was used by Descartes in the Third Meditation to prove the existence of God from the idea of God: "it is obvious, according to the light of nature, that there must be at least as much reality in the total efficient cause as in its effect, for whence can the effect derive its reality, if not from its cause?"[45]

Despite his inclination toward rationalism, however, Balling often returned to a traditional spiritualistic interpretation of the inner light, calling it "the truth and the word of God," "a living word that translates man from death to life," and that which "lifts man out of the depths of sin." *Het Licht* concluded on a final interesting philosophical note. Balling declared that the light was the means by which people came to know God, and he added that this inner knowledge necessarily preceded the knowledge of any external sign of God. If God said "I am God," people would not understand the signification of the word "God" unless they already had the inward and immediate knowledge of God from the light, Balling argued. This argument again reflected Balling's Cartesianism because Descartes used similar arguments in discussing the innate idea of God.[46]

Het Licht has attracted more scholarly attention than any other Collegiant work. Interpretations of Balling's book have varied widely because most have been undertaken without placing the work in its proper context within the overall framework of evolving Collegiant thought. Leszek Kolakowski, for example, placed Balling in the mystical tradition because of his insistence on direct contact with the divine, his belief that the inner light was inside all people, and his conviction that God revealed himself only through internal experience. J. Van den Berg considered Balling's work so spiritualistic that he attributed the 1662 edition to the Quaker William Ames. Heine Siebrand, in an article on Spinoza's influence in Holland, described *Het Licht* as strongly influenced by spiritualism because of its emphasis on the absolute evidence of the inner light.[47] Finally, Stanislas van Dunin Borkowski, in his important study of Spinoza's early years, called Balling "mystisch angehauchtes." On the other side of the ledger, Johannes Lindeboom saw Balling as a rationalist who had stripped the inner light of all connection to God's revealed word and made the light into an inner reason. Lindeboom described the contents of

---

[45] Descartes, *Meditations*, in Smith, ed., p. 199.

[46] Balling, *Het Licht op den Kandelaar*, pp. 6, 8; Jones, pp. 125–132.

[47] Kolakowski, p. 212; Van den Berg, in Knox, ed., p. 181; Heine Siebrand, "The Early Reception of Spinoza's *Tractatus Theologico Politicus* in the Context of Cartesianism," a paper delivered at the Amsterdam International Conference on Spinoza in November 1982. Mr. Siebrand kindly provided me with a copy. See also Heine Siebrand, *Spinoza and the Netherlanders: An Inquiry into the Early Reception of His Philosophy of Religion* (Assen and Maastricht, the Netherlands, 1988).

Het Licht as "rationalism with a soft tempering of pious agnosticism." Theun de Vries referred to Balling's idea of the inner light as "reason, the first principle of all certainty." Rufus Jones also considered Balling to be a Cartesian, and Cornelia W. Roldanus interpreted Balling's light as the light of reason.[48] Finally, Lewis Feuer compared Balling's idea of the light to Spinoza's intellectual love of God.[49]

The division of scholarly opinion concerning Balling's thought is eloquent testimony to the fact that *Het Licht* represented a truly transitional form between spiritualism and rationalism. Viewed in its proper intellectual and historical context, within a tradition of Collegiant thought evolving from spiritualism to rationalism, *Het Licht* can be recognized as an intermediate work of great importance. As a writing representing the Rijnsburger religion of individual conscience in the midst of a process of secularization, Balling's work gives the reader a rare glance into the anatomy of intellectual transition.

In 1684, at the height of an internal Collegiant debate over the rationalism of Jan Bredenburg, a second edition of *Het Licht* was printed by Jan Rieuwertsz. in Amsterdam. Rieuwertsz. was the chief printer for Rijnsburger works in Amsterdam, a friend and supporter of Galenus Abrahamsz., and an active Collegiant himself. Bound in the same volume with Balling's work was another Collegiant writing entitled *Belijdenisse des Algemeenen en Christelyken geloofs; vervattet in een brief aan N.N.* (Confession of universal Christian belief contained in a letter to N.N.), written some years earlier by Jarig Jelles. In his foreword to the volume, Rieuwertsz. noted that he published the two works together because of their similar contents. Indeed, Jelles's book was another very interesting example of the evolution of Collegiant thought from spiritualism to rationalism. In Jelles's work, however, rationalism was much more clearly expressed than in *Het Licht*. Under the influence of both Cartesianism and Spinozism, Jelles repeatedly used the term reason (*reden*) to refer to the inner light of truth.

Jarig Jelles (d. 1683) was born in Harlingen, a port town in Friesland, probably sometime in the 1620s. During the 1640s he operated a successful grocery business in Amsterdam and came to know Spinoza through

---

[48] Stanislas von Dunin Borkowski, *Der junge Spinoza* (Münster, 1910), p. 467; Lindeboom, *Stiefkinderen van het Christendom*, p. 350; de Vries, p. 127; Roldanus, *Zeventiende eeuwse geestesbloei*, p. 132.

[49] Lewis Feuer, *Spinoza and the Rise of Liberalism* (New York, 1958), p. 230. For a more balanced assessment of Balling's work, see Hubertus Hubbeling, "Zur frühen Spinozarezeption in den Niederlanden" in Gründer and Schmidt-Biggemann, eds., pp. 155–158; and W.N.A. Klever, "De Spinozistische prediking von Pieter Balling," *Doopsgezinde Bijdragen*, n.s. 14 (1988), pp. 55–85.

business contacts. Jelles was a member of Galenus's Mennonite congregation in Het Lam, rising to the rank of deacon in 1653. Sometime around 1650 Jelles was stricken with doubt over the value of his worldly calling, and shortly thereafter he came to believe that the search for truth was each person's primary obligation in life. As a consequence of this intellectual conversion Jelles retired from his business and spent the last thirty years of his life studying religion and philosophy, attending the Amsterdam college, and keeping company with Spinoza and his circle of friends. Jelles's *Belijdenisse des Algemeenen Christelyken geloofs* was the product of these years of study. Originally composed as a long letter to Spinoza, the *Belijdenisse* was influenced by the ideas of Galenus Abrahamsz. and other Collegiants as well as by the thought of Descartes and Spinoza. Jelles worked with Rieuwertsz. in the publication of Spinoza's *Opera posthuma* in Amsterdam in 1677, and he wrote a foreword for the edition that became an important source for his own ideas. Jelles died in Amsterdam in 1683, probably of consumption.[50]

Jelles intended the *Belijdenisse* to be his personal confession of faith and thus he divided it into separate articles, a common organizational scheme for confessions at the time. In the first article, "Concerning God and His Qualities," Jelles confessed his belief in an eternal, almighty, and all-knowing God who was the source of all good, the creator of heaven and earth, and the supremely perfect being. In article 2 "Of God's Son and the Holy Spirit," Jelles's own special blend of spiritualism and rationalism began to emerge. Christ was a true man in his fleshly body, Jelles wrote, but he was divine in respect of the sanctifying Holy Spirit that lived in him. Because Christ had this Spirit he was sent to earth by God to be prophet and king, to testify to the divine truth, and to show the way to salvation. In short, Jelles declared, Christ came to earth to proclaim "the light of truth and reason" in which God's will was known, and he taught all believers "to follow the light." Jelles clearly identified the inner light of truth with reason. In fact, he seemed to make no essential distinction in the *Belijdenisse* among Christ, the Holy Spirit, the gospel of truth, and reason. God's son was God's reason, Jelles argued, and as proof he referred to John 1:1: "In the beginning was the Word, and the Word was with God, and the Word was God." Jelles maintained that the Greek term *logos* (word) in this verse referred to the Holy Spirit incarnate in Christ and was more properly translated as "reason." God's reason was not something apart from God, Jelles argued, because in the beginning it was God.[51] By indentifying Christ and the Holy Spirit with God's reason,

---

[50] *ME*, vol. 3, p. 105; *BWPG*, vol. 4, pp. 335–336; Hubbeling, in Gründer and Schmidt-Biggemann, eds., p. 158.

[51] Jarig Jelles, *Belijdenisse des Algemeenen en Christelyken geloofs; vervattet in een brief aan N.N.* (Amsterdam, 1684), pp. 1–17, 23.

Jelles implied that God's sending of the messiah was a divine bestowal of reason upon humanity.

Jelles believed that it was through reason that people obtained the divine knowledge that was the necessary principle of all human salvation. "All things pertaining to man's salvation are done through God's reason or through God's understanding, and the hearts of men are radiated with a wonderful light as they are made to participate in divine understanding and knowledge" ("Alle dingen, ten minsten die de zaligheit der menschen aangaan, door God's reden of door God's verstant gemakt zijn, en . . . het gemoed der menschen door 't deelagtig worden van 't Godlijk verstant, of van de Goddelijke kennis, met een wonderlijk ligt bestraalt word"). As people were irradiated with the "wonderful light" of divine reason they obtained the knowledge and understanding necessary for their salvation, Jelles argued. In his view, human salvation lay in the use of reason because knowledge was a primary vehicle of divine grace. People inherited the kingdom of grace by following God's commands, and the first among those commands was to love God and one's neighbor. Jelles saw love as a power by which people overcame their evil desires when they were "led by the light of reason, the spirit, and the truth." Thus, when a person followed the light of reason he or she fulfilled God's command of love and obtained salvation.[52] The love of God came from the knowledge of God, Jelles maintained, and failure to love God came only from a failure to know him. By following the light of reason people obtained a "pure intellectual knowledge of God." Like Balling, Jelles adopted a moral rationalism that made knowledge the principle of all right action by assuming that the rational intellect informed and controlled the will.

Along with these rationalistic ideas, the influence of Galenus's thought was also present in the *Belijdenisse*. Jelles declared that people were born empty of the "pure intellectual knowledge" needed for salvation and thus they had to be "reborn through the spirit" to achieve mastery over their passions.[53] Following Galenus's idea of rebirth, Jelles maintained that the essence of salvation was union with God through Christ. He added that God's son, the Holy Spirit, and reason had to dwell in a person like an "inner light" for that person to be saved.

Jelles believed that the sanctifying inner light of truth was the light of reason, and like Balling he placed this light above even Scripture as the supreme source for religious knowledge. Referring to James 1:21 ("Having put aside all foulness and overflowing evil, receive with humility the word that is planted in you and which can bring your soul salvation"), Jelles declared that the implanted word was not the written or spoken

---

[52] Ibid., pp. 21–23, 34, 36.
[53] Ibid., pp. 42–43.

word of Christ but rather "the reason that in the beginning was God, the truth." Reason was no simple analytical tool dependent on Scripture for the content of truth. He saw reason as an independent and infallible source of truth in its own right, and throughout his manuscript he referred to reason as the "light of truth" and "divine knowledge." Paraphrasing John 1:9, Jelles argued that the light of reason was the truth and the Holy Spirit that enlightened every person who came into the world.[54] As reason came to be identified with the inner light of the Spirit rather than being separated from it as it was in traditional spiritualism, reason itself became a kind of divine revelation.

Jelles conluded his confession by anchoring the truth of his ideas firmly in Descartes's rationalistic criterion for truth: "I say that it must be true, because who can deny that that which is clearly understood is true, or is as it is comprehended to be" ("Ik zeg ook/dat het moet waar wezen, want wie kan loochenen/dat het geen/'t welk klaarlijk verstaan werd/waar is; of zodanig is als het bevat werd"). Jelles specifically applied the criterion of rational clarity to the process of scriptural interpretation. The truth of Scripture was not to be found in its words but in its sense, he argued. In order to come to an infallible knowledge of the true sense of Scripture one had only to investigate how far the sense could be "understood clearly and distinctly." As far as the sense of Scripture could be so understood it was indeed the true sense, but if the sense could not be clearly understood, due to internal contradictions, absurdities, or impossibilities, it was not the true sense. Jelles believed that the truth of a clearly understood passage of Scripture was self-evident because "the truth is always known only throught itself, never through others." With this idea Jelles followed Spinoza, who wrote in a letter of 1675 to Albert Burgh: "I don't claim that I have found the best philosophy, but I do know that I understand the true one. If you ask how I know this, I answer 'just as you know that the three angles of a triangle equal two right angles . . . the truth is after all evident through itself.' "[55]

Having put forward his Cartesian idea of scriptural interpretation, Jelles backed it up with a biblical example. When Paul and the apostles revealed the truths of salvation to the people, the people immediately assented to these truths and recognized the apostles as proclaimers of true doctrine. This was because, Jelles argued, the people understood the truth of these doctrines "in their hearts" and were therefore fully certain of their validity. In the same way, the true sense of a passage of Scripture would be understood by the individual in his or her heart.[56]

Jelles concluded his discussion of scriptural interpretation on a very

[54] Ibid., pp. 68–83, 21–25.
[55] Ibid., pp. 92–96; Spinoza to Albert Burgh, in *Benedict de Spinoza*, p. 410.
[56] Jelles, *Belijdenisse*, pp. 92–96.

spiritualistic note. The message of the Bible was divided into two distinct parts, he argued: the historical facts and the teaching of the Holy Spirit. The historical facts of the Bible could be understood by "natural men" who did not have "the gift of prophecy or any spiritual revelation." But it was the teaching of the Holy Spirit that was the true and important sense of Scripture, Jelles maintained, and this sense could only be understood by the spiritual person who had "the strength of the Holy Spirit to show and explain the truth."[57]

In his discussion of biblical interpretation Jelles thus combined the idea of individual spiritual understanding of religious truth with the Cartesian idea of the self-evidence of truth to the rational mind. For the spiritualist, truth could be perceived directly because the soul was linked to the divine nature of truth through the indwelling and illumination of the Holy Spirit. For the rationalist, one could perceive truth directly because the truth was considered to be by nature rational and thus inherently linked to the rational mind by a community of structure. Because of the rational structure of the mind, rational truth was self-evident to it. In both spiritualist and rationalist epistemologies, therefore, the human mind was linked directly to the nature of truth itself by sharing in the very structure of truth. No external referent or criterion of truth was necessary. Because of these basic structural similarities between the two epistemological systems, the transition from spiritualism to rationalism was made more easily by Jelles and others.

Like Balling's *Het Licht*, Jelles's *Belijdenisse* has attracted considerable scholarly attention. Cornelia W. Roldanus described Jelles's thought as an "intellectual mysticism" close to Quaker spiritualism in its stress on the inner testimony of the spirit but close also to Spinozism in its designation of Christ and the wisdom of God as reason.[58] Borkowski noted the transitional nature of Jelles's thought in particularly graphic terms:

> As soon as one reads Jarig Jelles's introduction to Spinoza's *Opera posthuma* one meets ideas from the writings of the men of the inner word that have been well known for centuries and have already become commonplaces. All the scriptural texts that Jelles uses to prove that the outer word of the Scripture is insufficient are drawn from the old bedchamber of those spriitualists. Jelles simply sets the words "reason" or "knowledge" in place of the "inner word" or "inner light." This same observation comes to the fore when one pages through his other writing, *Confession of the Universal Chrisitan Belief*.
>
> Liest man die Einleitung Jarig Jelles zu Spinozas *Opera posthuma* so stösst man alsbald auf die aus dem Schriftem der Männer des inneren Wortes seit

---

[57] Ibid., pp. 97, 98.
[58] Roldanus, *Zeventiende eeuwse geestesbloei*, p. 132.

einem Jahrhundert wohlbekannten und bereits zu Gemeinplätzen versteiner-
ten Anschauungen. Alle Schrifttexte, die Jelles anführt um zu beweisen, dass
das äussere Wort der Schrift nicht ausreicht, sind aus der alten Rüstkamer
jener Spriitualen geholt; Jelles setzt einfact "vernunft" oder "Erkenntnis" ein
an die Stelle des inneren Wortes, des "inneren Lichtes." Dieselbe Beobach-
tung drängt sich auf beim Durchblättern seiner anderen Schrift, *Belijdenisse
des Algemeene Christelijcken Geloofs*.[59]

A process of secularization was clearly evident in Jelles's conception of
the inner light and the individual conscience. This was demonstrated
again in the preface that he wrote for the Dutch edition of Spinoza's
*Opera posthuma: De Nagelate Schriften van B.D.S. als Zedekunst, Staat-
kunde, Verbetering van 't verstand, Brieven en Antwoorden uit Verscheide Talen in de Nederlandsche Gebracht* (Posthumus works: The
posthumus writings of B.D.S. such as the ethics, politics, and improvement of the understanding, letters, and answers translated from various
languages into Dutch), published in Amsterdam in 1677 by the Collegiant
bookseller Jan Rieuwertsz. In this preface Jelles took issue with critics
who claimed that Spinoza proposed a code of truth and morality that
contradicted the teachings of Christ and the apostles. In Jelles's opinion,
Spinoza's doctrine did not differ at all from the teachings of Christ. All
that Spinoza recommended was what reason prescribed for living well
and for obtaining the highest good, Jelles argued. If one compared Spinoza's doctrines to the teachings of Christ one would see a very great
agreement between the two. In fact, Jelles argued, there could be no conflict between the commands of reason and the teachings of Christ because
"in the prescriptions of reason the moral teachings of the Christian religion are included."[60] Jelles proposed an essentially natural religion by
maintaining that reason was a sufficient source for religious knowledge
because the truths revealed by Christ could be discovered through the use
of reason alone.

Jelles further suggested that this rational knowledge of religion could
make the inspiration of the Holy Spirit unnecessary. Scripture taught that
the ability to perform miracles was a gift of the Holy Spirit used by Christ
and the apostles to confirm the divine authority of their teachings, Jelles
wrote, and he added that in his own day the divine authority of a religious
doctrine could be guaranteed by the occurrence of a miracle. But why did
Christians need miracles to assure them of the truth of religion when they

[59] Borkowski, p. 406. See also Hubbeling, in Gründer and Schmidt-Biggemann, eds., pp.
158–162.

[60] Jarig Jelles, "Voorrede," in *De Nagelate schriften van B.D.S. als Zedekunst, Staatkunde, Verbetering van 't Verstant, Brieven en Antwoorden uit Verscheide Talen in de
Nederlandsche Gebragt* (Amsterdam, 1677), pp. viii–xiii.

could understand and be certain of the truth of Christian doctrine simply by using their own reason? Reason provided people with a "pure intellectual knowledge" of Christian doctrine that was certain and infallible, Jelles argued, and for this reason a true Christian could find more certainty inside himself than in all miracles.[61]

The writings of Balling and Jelles were accepted in the Amsterdam college as the works of pious men seeking religious truth. It is perhaps significant that their writings were printed (or reprinted, in the case of Balling) by Rieuwertsz. in 1684, at the height of the Rijnsburger controversy over the rationalism of Jan Bredenburg. It is possible that Rieuwertsz., himself a friend of Spinoza, was attempting to point out to his fellow Collegiants that Bredenburg's rationalism was a natural development out of the earlier ideas of Rijnsburgers like Balling and Jelles. As the Rijnsburger idea of the individual conscience became more and more secularized, the conception of reason as an independent source of religious truth, present in embryo in the thought of Balling and Jelles, assumed ever greater importance in Collegiant thought. Pieter Smout wrote in *Het helder licht der vryheyt* (1679) that one could use reason to judge the truth of sacred writings because "the things that are true are such that they teach us from themselves that they are true."[62] In 1670 another Collegiant, Jan Knol, argued against the Quaker idea of the spiritual inner light by appealing instead to reason: "I shall show you what kind of light is in you and in every man; in a word it is reason, which separates man from the beasts" ("Ik sal U toonen, wat voor een Licht in U, en in een yder Mensche is; met een woort, het is de Reden, door welcke den Mensch van de beesten onderscheyden wort"). Knol's Quaker opponent, James Park, responded by accusing Knol and the Collegiants of "knowing no other worship of God than through your reason."[63]

The angry quarrel between the Collegiants and the Quakers was a revealing episode in the controversy-marred history of Dutch religious thought during the seventeenth century. The innovative nature of Collegiant thought can be directly measured by the bitterness of the attacks directed against it by the Quakers. Despite surface similarities, these two Second Reformation sects were divided by a fundamental difference of outlook. The Quakers believed themselves to be inspired by the Holy Spirit to reform the church according to the direct command of God. The Rijnsburgers, on the other hand, largely abandoned the idea of divine inspiration in the secular world and fell back instead on a religion of rea-

[61] Ibid., pp. xxvii–xxviii.
[62] Pieter Smout, *Het helder licht der vryhyt*, p. 39.
[63] Park, pp. 15, 16.

son and toleration. The Collegiants and the Quakers stood on opposite sides of an ever-widening fissure separating the traditional, providential Christian worldview from the emerging secular and rationalistic worldview of the Enlightenment. The Quaker-Collegiant dispute allows the intellectual topographer to map this historic chasm at close range. Powerful forces were at work in the late seventeenth century transforming the European intellectual landscape in fundamental ways, and Collegiant thought was a reflection of the operation of these forces.

The conflict between the Collegiants and the Quakers to a certain extent mirrored the struggle between Puritans and latitudinarians in England during the late seventeenth century. The increasingly rationalistic nature of Collegiant thought paralleled similar developments within the Church of England during the years 1660–1700 as moderate Anglicans reacted against Puritan enthusiasm by moving toward a more rational and tolerant religion. In its early stages Rijnsburger rationalism resembled the commonsense rationalism of latitudinarians like Burnet and Glanville, the conception of divine reason held by the Cambridge Platonists, and even the Lockean reliance on reason found in early deists like John Toland. In his *Christianity Not Mysterious* (1695), Toland wrote that reason was "the candle, the guide, the judge that he [God] has lodged within every man that cometh into the world."[64] Toland's reference to John 1:9 certainly would not have been lost on the Collegiants.

Just as Collegiant rationalism had parallels in English religious thought of the late seventeenth century, the process of intellectual evolution that transformed the spiritual inner light into the natural light of reason was not unique to the Rijnsburgers. In his book on radical thought during the English Revolution, Christopher Hill discussed the evolution of Quaker spiritualism during the later seventeenth century. According to Hill, one factor that enabled Quaker thought to evolve freely was its doctrine of the inner light, which was able to change with a changing intellectual climate. The Quaker practice of placing the guidance of the inner light above that of the Bible led to some very interesting consequences when the Puritan Revolution was over and religious passions began to cool. As the intellectual climate in England began to change, "the appeal to the light within became difficult to differentiate from an appeal to simple human reason."[65]

Just such a process of intellectual transformation was taking place within the Collegiant movement during the 1660s and 1670s, a time when strong forces of rationalism and secularism were beginning to influence Collegiant thought. As the ideas of Galenus and the Socinians spread

---

[64] As quoted in Cragg, p. 146.
[65] Hill, *The World Turned Upside Down*, pp. 256, 268.

through the colleges during the early 1660s, and as millennial expectations peaked and then were disappointed, the Rijnsburgers' experiences with the Quakers further discredited extreme spiritualism in the colleges. These various secularizing forces had the effect of pushing the spiritualism of Balling and Jelles in a rationalistic direction and of opening the two men to the influence of Cartesianism, which they encountered primarily through their association with Spinoza.

While Spinoza's Cartesianism had an important influence on the developing rationalism of Balling and Jelles, it would be a mistake to see the lines of intellectual influence operating in only one direction in this relationship. Spinoza met the two men before his excommunication from the Amsterdam Jewish community in 1656, and in the years immediately following this traumatic event Balling, Jelles, Rieuwertsz., and other Collegiants were Spinoza's closest friends. This small circle of Rijnsburger friends played an important role in Spinoza's life at just the time that he was undergoing a difficult transition from the Jewish community to the wider world of Dutch social and intellectual life. The group often met in Rieuwertsz.'s book shop to discuss religion and philosophy. Just as Spinoza had an influence on the ideas of his friends during these meetings, so too their ideas must have had an impact on him. When circumstances forced Spinoza to leave Amsterdam to seek a new home in which he could work in peace and toleration, he selected the tiny village of Rijnsburg, the cradle of Collegiantism. In the rear gable of Spinoza's house in Rijnsburg (which still stands) a verse from "May Morning" by the Collegiant poet D. R. Camphuysen is inscribed:

> Alas, if all men were but wise
> and would be good as well,
> The earth would be a paradise,
> where now 'tis mostly hell.

During his Rijnsburg years Spinoza corresponded frequently with the circle of Collegiant friends that he had left behind in Amsterdam. For their instruction he wrote his first book, *The Principles of Descartes' Philosophy*, which was translated by Balling in 1664.[66] As Spinoza's thought matured it moved away from its Cartesian foundations to develop its own unique character. While Spinoza's philosophical Monism was rationalistic in its conception of a nature governed by the laws of reason, it showed the influence of spiritualism as well in its conception of a God transcending all description, in its idea of the intellectual love of God, and in its emphasis on union with God.[67] These spiritualistic elements in Spinoza's

[66] Meinsma, pp. 195–197. See also de Vries.
[67] Feuer, p. 199; Roldanus, *Zeventiende eeuwse geestesbloei*, p. 134.

thought have most often been attributed to the influence of either Jewish mysticism or the Neoplatonism of Giordano Bruno, but the possibility of Collegiant influence should not be overlooked.[68] In the thought of his close friends Balling and Jelles, Spinoza would have found important elements of a spiritualistic tradition that was still alive in the colleges. While Spinoza influenced the Rijnsburgers in the direction of rationalism, the great philosopher might well have preserved part of the older tradition of Collegiant spiritualism in his own revolutionary philosophy. This possibility will be discussed further in the next chapter.

In the thought of Balling and Jelles the tradition of Rijnsburger spiritualism was combined with the secularizing trend in Collegiant thought and the influence of Cartesianism to produce an important new stage of Collegiant rationalism. As reason came to be equated with the spiritualistic idea of the inner light it became a source of true ideas independent of the Bible. The implications of reason's new independence were enormous. In the thought of Balling and Jelles (as in the thought of Descartes himself) the truths of reason always agreed with those of revealed religion. Nevertheless, reason's epistemological independence created the possibility that it could establish truths contrary to (and even superior to) the truths of biblical revelation. In the thought of Jan Bredenburg this possibility became a reality, and the result was a genuine philosophical rationalism around which swirled the most heated internal controversy in the history of Collegiantism.

[68] See, for example, Harry A. Wolfson, *The Philosophy of Spinoza* (Cambridge, Mass., 1934); and Abraham Wolfson, *Spinoza: A Life of Reason* (New York, 1934).

Chapter Nine

JAN BREDENBURG: THE LIMITS OF REASON

Reason and belief are
both realms of truth,
each in its own way.

(De reden en het geloof zijn
dan beyde rijken der waarheid,
doch ieder op zijn wijs.)
—Jan Bredenburg

THE DEVELOPMENT of Collegiant rationalism reached its peak in the writings of the Rotterdam merchant Jan Bredenburg. Like his fellow Rijnsburgers Pieter Balling and Jarig Jelles, Bredenberg believed reason to be an independent source of true ideas that, alongside the truths of divine revelation, provided religious knowledge. But unlike Balling and Jelles, who resembled the Cambridge Platonists and other English latitudinarians in their belief that reason and revealed truth were essentially in agreement, Bredenburg came to the conclusion that the truths of reason and those of revelation could often be contradictory. Despite these contradictions, Bredenburg maintained both reason and revelation as independent, valid, and autonomous sources of religious truth. With this partial separation of reason from revelation Bredenburg brought the Collegiant development of a secular and rationalistic conception of human knowledge to its climax, and he also approached the more complete separation of philosophy from theology accomplished by Spinoza in his controversial *Theologico-Political Treatise*.[1]

Bredenburg developed his thought in two distinct phases. In his early writings, composed during a time in which he was very much under the influence of Spinoza's thought, Bredenburg took an extremely rationalistic approach to religious knowledge. In this stage of his intellectual development he saw reason as the primary source for the knowledge of God and religion, while he considered biblical revelation to be merely a supplemental source of such vital truth. These ideas stirred opposition from

[1] For a discussion of the position of the Cambridge Platonists on the relationship between reason and revelation, and for their interpretation of Spinoza's philosophy, see Colie, p. 78; and Cragg, p. 42.

Collegiants who still saw reason as only a tool for interpreting the true ideas received through revelation. Bredenburg's critics were especially upset by the fact that some of his rational arguments seemed to contradict revealed truth. A heated dispute ensued within the Collegiant movement between supporters and opponents of Bredenburg, and this quarrel forced Bredenburg to modify his views.

In response to his critics Bredenburg admitted that from time to time the truths supplied by reason could be found to contradict those of revelation, but he insisted that this conflict did not mean that either source of truth had to be rejected as false. He argued that in such cases reason and revelation could be accepted as two coexisting, autonomous, and valid sources of truth, the one rational and the other nonrational. When the two sources of truth were in open conflict, believers had to give precedence to the truths of revelation because they represented knowledge of a higher, more perfect order. This choice did not, however, imply the falsity of rational truth. It merely signified reason's obligation to yield to a higher order of knowledge. In such cases, Bredenburg argued, a person might believe something to be true based on revelation while at the same time he rationally understood it to be false.

In Bredenburg's writings reason as a source of true ideas gained more independence and power than ever before in Collegiant thought. By insisting that reason was an autonomous source of truth while at the same time maintaining that the conflicting truths of revelation were not rational, Bredenburg created two orders of truth and introduced a separation between these two kinds of knowledge that had the effect of freeing the truths of reason from the influence of revelation. Reason could be superceded by revelation, but this did not mean that the truths of reason were false. Furthermore, even though the truths of revelation were of a higher order than those of reason, they were nonrational and thus they could only be accepted as true, not rationally understood as such. Bredenburg's separation of reason from revelation removed the rational operations of the individual conscience from the direct influence of supernatural revelation and thus produced a highly secularized and rationalistic conception of human knowledge.

Jan Bredenburg was one of the leading figures in the Rotterdam college after 1668. During 1671–1672 he wrote two works on religious toleration that showed the influence of the ideas of Galenus Abrahamsz. (see chapter 4). Bredenburg was also interested in speculative philosophy, and when his merchant office in Rotterdam was forced to close during the French invasion of 1672, he devoted himself full-time to philosophical studies, often discussing philosophical topics with a circle of Collegiant friends. During this period Bredenburg became acquainted with Cartesian ideas and probably read Spinoza's *Theologico-Political Treatise*, which had been published anonymously in Amsterdam in 1670. Although Bredenburg's understanding of the ideas of Descartes and Spinoza was extremely limited, he was clearly inspired by their rationalistic spirit. In 1673 Bredenburg shared with his Collegiant friends in Rotterdam the manuscript of a work that he had written during his year of philosophical study, the *Verhandling van de oorsprong van de kennisse Gods en van desselfs dienst, alleen uyt natuurlijke reden afgeleyd, buyten alle openbaringen of mirakelen* (A treatment of the origin of the knowledge of God and of his service, taken only from natural reason without any revelations or miracles [1684]). The *Verhandling* contained a very rationalistic approach to religious knowledge that showed traces of Cartesian influence as well as the influence of Spinoza's *Theologico-Political Treatise*.[2]

In the *Verhandling* Bredenburg attempted to explain how people arrived at their knowledge of God. He first briefly discussed the three basic opinions concerning God and religion that he claimed were current in his day. The atheists believed that there was no God, Bredenburg explained, either because they could see no evidence for God's existence or because they believed that the evidence that they did see proved that God did not exist. Another group of people, who Bredenburg called the "simple believers," held that God existed but that his existence could not be proved rationally. These believers therefore argued that God could be known only through revelation. The third opinion held that there was a God and that his existence could be proved by reason alone, while revelation served only to supplement and reinforce this natural knowledge of God. Bredenburg set out to argue for this third position in the *Verhandling*.[3]

Since the positions of the atheists and the simple believers both rested on their rejection of the possibility for rational proofs of God's existence, Bredenburg attacked those two points of view by arguing that there were "irrefutable proofs from nature and reason that God exists." The first proof that Bredenburg offered was what he called the "argument from the ascent of beings" (*opklimminge der wesens*). Nature consisted of a graded hierarchy of beings ascending from the lowest existing thing through humans to the most perfect being and cause of all. Because this hierarchy could not continue to infinity it had to come to rest upon a first cause, and this first cause was God, he argued. For this proof Bredenburg dipped into Scholastic rationalism to combine two of the *Quinque viae*

[2] Hylkema, vol. 2, pp. 243–254; Kolakowski, pp. 251–254.

[3] Johannes Bredenburg, *Verhandling van de oorsprong van de kennisse Gods en van desselfs dienst. Alleen uyt natuurlijke reden afgeleyd, buyten alle openbaringen of mirakelen* (Amsterdam, 1684), pp. 1, 2.

proofs that Thomas Aquinas had developed on Aristotelian foundations in *Summa theologiae* 1:2:3:C.[4]

Bredenburg's second major proof for the existence of God was a version of Descartes' main argument in the Third Meditation. There could be no representation without a subject from which the representation was formed, and that subject necessarily had to contain all of the qualities that its representation contained. People had an idea of God as the supremely perfect being, and that idea could have been caused only by God himself since the idea of a being supremely perfect could be created only by a being containing such perfection. Bredenburg called this proof the "argument from the idea." He concluded the first section of the *Verhandling* by presenting two minor proofs for God's existence. The first he called the "argument from the spirit of man": since the human spirit was an ethereal and heavenly entity, it could only have been given by God. The second minor proof he called the "argument from the desire of man's spirit for God." This argument maintained that the human spirit had a natural desire to be reunited with God, who created it, and since the spirit possessed this yearning to return to its divine origin, God, who was the object of this desire, had to exist.[5] While the first of these minor proofs was probably of ancient origin, the second could likely be traced to the mystical Neoplatonism of the Middle Ages or even to Galenus's conception of the soul in the *Korte Verhandeling*.

Bredenburg believed that all of these rational proofs were founded ultimately on the one basic principle that a created thing had to have a creator. For Bredenburg, this principle was so clear and certain that it could not be rationally refuted. In order to reject this principle one would have to prove either that creatures were produced without any cause outside of their own natures or that they existed eternally, but Bredenburg insisted that reason could prove neither of these things. Human reason could not even conceive of how something could be created by itself, he argued, because humankind had never experienced anything created without an external cause. Nor could reason conceive of something existing eternally, because the human mind was finite and could not understand the infinite. Bredenburg's discussion of these matters was based loosely on Descartes's argument for the existence of God in the Third Meditation. He concluded his argument by briefly mentioning an idea that he would develop more fully in later writings. According to Bredenburg, Christians believed that God was eternal but they did not rationally understand how.[6]

---

[4] Ibid., p. 3; *EP*, vol. 8, pp. 110–111.
[5] Bredenburg, *Verhandling*, p. 3.
[6] Ibid., p. 4.

Having shown reason to be an infallible source for the knowledge of God's existence, Bredenburg next considered the role of revelation. Possibly under the influence of Spinoza's discussion of miracles in chapter 6 of the *Theologico-Political Treatise*, Bredenburg declared that neither revelation nor miracles could provide a certain knowledge of God. Any divine revelation or any miracle performed by God to convince people of the divine origin and truth of revelation would have to be perceived through one's outer senses, Bredenburg argued. But for anything to be perceived by the senses, which are natural organs, the thing perceived would itself have to be natural. Because Bredenburg considered both revelation and miracles to be supernatural in origin and essence, he concluded that neither could occur in nature. For this reason, revelation and miracles could not be perceived by humans and could not provide people with any knowledge of God.[7]

Even though miracles and revelation could not be perceived by humans in nature, Bredenburg continued, it might still be argued that they could prove God's existence by appearing outside of nature. But in Bredenburg's view there could be no knowledge of miracles or revelation outside of nature either, because outside of nature there was no medium in which revelation and miracles could exist and no means by which they could appear. Everything that humans perceived had to exist within the context of nature, Bredenburg argued, because outside of nature there was only void.[8] Bredenburg thus presented a thoroughly secularized idea of human perception and knowledge. His rejection of divine revelation and miracles as sources for the knowledge of God might have been influenced by his understanding of Cartesian dualism or by his reading of Spinoza's arguments concerning miracles in the *Theologico-Political Treatise*. Spinoza had argued that supernatural miracles could provide no knowledge of God because they would be beyond natural understanding, and thus they could not give the clear and distinct ideas upon which all human understanding was based. Spinoza went on to deny in effect the existence of supernatural miracles by claiming that what people called miracles were not acts of God abrogating natural laws but rather unusual natural events that, although they could not be explained as ordinary natural occurrences, nevertheless took place within the regular laws of nature.[9] While Bredenburg never explicitly rejected the existence of supernatural miracles or revelation, his argument was perhaps influenced in part by his imperfect understanding of Spinoza's position.

The influence of Spinoza was again evident when Bredenburg argued

[7] Ibid., p. 6.

[8] Ibid., p. 8.

[9] Benedict Spinoza, *A Theologico-Political Treatise and A Political Treatise*, trans. R.H.M. Elwes (New York, 1951), pp. 82–87.

that it was the rational knowledge of God, not revelation, that made salvation possible. According to Bredenburg, it was God's will that people follow the guidance of reason because in so doing they would follow the natural law. The first principle of the natural law was that one must do everything necessary for one's own well-being, and it was a natural right to use all one's abilities to this end. Bredenburg held that the most important of these abilities was the rational capacity to judge what had to be done to obtain well-being. In contrast to Hobbes and Grotius, however, Bredenburg argued that one's well-being did not consist merely in the preservation of the life of the body. Human beings were made up of both a material body and an immaterial spirit, he argued, and while the body desired the goods of the earthly life the spirit contained intellectual desires for a spiritual, heavenly life. Bredenburg thus saw human well-being as dual: well-being for the body consisted of worldly pleasures, but spiritual well-being resulted from the possession of eternal spiritual life through salvation.[10]

The well-being of the spirit always had priority over that of the body, Bredenburg argued, but humans were incapable of obtaining the good of the spirit because God alone was the source of salvation. It was God's will that man "follow the leading of his spirit or understanding," Bredenburg continued, and for this reason the second principle of the natural law was that one must follow the guidance of reason in order to please God and obtain the eternal well-being of salvation. By following the guidance of reason one could obtain the rational knowledge that their well-being depended on God and God would provide the opportunity to obtain salvation. Bredenburg believed that this rational knowledge would lead the individual to have faith in God. He thus adopted the rationalistic position that intellectual knowledge determined the emotional commitment of faith, a position similar to the one adopted by Spinoza in chapter 14 of the *Theologico-Political Treatise*.[11]

By showing reason to be the certain and infallible source for the knowledge of God, and by teaching people to depend on reason for their own salvation, Bredenburg appeared to leave no place in religion for revelation or Scripture. Nevertheless, Bredenburg did in fact retain a place for revelation as a source of religious truth. He argued that God's commands given through revelation in Scripture made up a source of "positive law" founded only in God's will, not in nature or reason. Just as people followed the rational natural law they also had to follow God's positive law, Bredenburg maintained. While positive law could not alter the natural law in any way, it could "explain and expound upon" the natural law in

---

[10] Ibid., pp. 29–34, 43.
[11] Ibid., pp. 34–39; Spinoza, *A Theologico-Political Treatise*, pp. 184–186.

cases in which human reason alone could not fully comprehend it. Bredenburg thus made revelation a secondary source of religious truth whose function was to supplement reason in certain cases and thus to bring religion "closer and clearer before man's understanding."[12]

Bredenburg's treatment of scriptural revelation was probably influenced by Spinoza. In the *Theologico-Political Treatise* Spinoza called human reason the "natural light" and assigned to it the chief responsibility for supplying the knowledge of God and religion. By the light of reason people were able to understand the goodness and divinity of God and to deduce therefrom their obligations toward God. In Spinoza's view, a person could be completely ignorant of Scripture and yet know by natural reason the few basic and necessary truths about God. While the primary object of reason therefore was to supply the knowledge of God, this was not the purpose of Scripture. Biblical revelation was not intended to impart rational knowledge but rather to move people to obedience to God by means of divine commands. Spinoza argued that Scripture defined the doctrines of the faith only insofar as this was necessary to impress devotion and obedience to divine commands upon the minds of ordinary people. It was therefore necessary for human reason to define further the precise meaning of these doctrines, Spinoza continued, and a person of strong rational powers could know almost all important religious truths from reason alone. Yet Spinoza did believe that the revelation of Scripture was necessary for people to have a full and complete knowledge of religion. This was because the most basic doctrine in all of religion—the idea that "man was saved by obedience alone"—could not be proved by reason. This doctrine, which Spinoza considered vital for individual salvation, could be taught only by the special grace of God through revelation.[13] It was perhaps from these ideas that Bredenburg developed his theory of revelation as a supplementary source of religious knowledge.

Despite his reliance on certain of Spinoza's ideas, Bredenburg was not a Spinozist. His attitude toward Spinoza's thought was complex and he differed with the great philosopher on many points, as he made clear in later writings. Bredenburg was first and foremost a Collegiant, and from their very inception the Collegiants placed great emphasis on the Bible as the primary source of religious knowledge. As the Rijnsburgers gradually moved from a spiritualistic to a rationalistic conception of scriptural interpretation, the Bible remained their chief source for the content of religious knowledge. Even when reason became an independent source of religious truth for some Collegiants, this new source of truth was still assumed to agree with biblical revelation. It would have been extremely

---

[12] Bredenburg, *Verhandling*, pp. 47–48, 8.
[13] Spinoza, *A Theologico-Political Treatise*, pp. 67–78, 178–198.

difficult for Bredenburg to drop revelation completely as a source for religious truth without rejecting the entire Collegiant religious tradition,
and this he was not prepared to do. By describing revelation as merely a
supplemental source of religious truth, however, Bredenburg set off a
storm of controversy within Collegiantism. His reaction to this controversy was to modify his views in order to increase the role of revelation
in religious knowledge, but he was careful not to reduce the role of reason
correspondingly. Even though Bredenburg moved closer to the development of a true philosophical rationalism than any other Collegiant with
the exception of Spinoza himself, he was too integral a part of an evolving
religious tradition to break cleanly with the past.

Despite all of its claims for reason, the *Verhandling* was not the most
rationalistic of Bredenburg's early works. In *Wiskunstige demonstratie
dat alle verstandelijke werking noodzaakelijk is* . . . (Mathematical demonstration that all intelligible action is necessary) Bredenburg developed
an extremely rationalistic view of nature and also attempted for the first
time to deal with the apparent contradictions between his rationalistic
conclusions and the truths of revelation. Written sometime in the early
1670s, although not published until 1684, the *Wiskunstige demonstratie*
drew directly upon the geometric method and causal determinism of Spinoza's *Ethics*, which Bredenburg must have known in manuscript. Bredenburg realized that the doctrine of determinism conflicted with the revealed truths of religion by putting God under the rule of causal necessity,
and because he supported determinism some Collegiants suspected that
Bredenburg did not believe in the God of revelation. But Bredenburg
showed himself deeply concerned with this conflict between reason and
revelation in the introduction to the *Wiskunstige demonstratie*, where he
sought to explain his motives for writing the book.[14]

Bredenburg declared that his two major reasons for writing the *Wiskunstige demonstratie* were his "insatiable desire for knowledge of truth"
and his "love of the Christian religion, which from my youth to this very
hour has entirely ruled my heart." His love for the Christian religion led
him to hope that the outcome of his work would be an accord between
the truths of reason and those of religion, Bredenburg wrote, adding that
the chief goal of his book was thus "a saving enlightenment in my understanding regarding the accord that reason and the Christian religion
might have." Bredenburg's desire to come to a knowledge of truth did not
permit him to allow religion to be founded on prejudice or bias, he wrote,
but he also realized that his love of religion had to hold his desire for truth
in check so that this desire would not needlessly draw him away from
religion. Bredenburg was deeply troubled by reason's apparent conflicts

---

[14] Kolakowski, pp. 258–262.

with revelation, and for this reason he stressed the need for a reconciliation between the two sources of truth. Also for this reason he concluded his introduction by announcing his intention to "embrace faith even if the accord between faith and reason is not found, so as to find salvation in Christ."[15] With these words Bredenburg hinted at the curious doctrine of double truth that he would later develop as a solution to the conflict between faith and reason.

A compromise between the truths of reason and those of revelation was clearly Bredenburg's ideal, but it was his high regard for the power of human reason that determined the argument of the *Wiskunstige demonstratie*. In his introduction he referred to reason in these terms: "Reason, which takes its origin from the eternal being, offers man eternal truth and is the light in men's eyes and the guiding star of all human endeavor" ("Reden, die van 't eeuwige wezen haar oorspronk neemt, die de eeuwige waarheden aan des menschen verstant offereert, die 't licht is in aller menschen oogen, ende leidster van alle menschelijke betrachtingen").[16]

The core of the *Wiskunstige demonstratie* was taken up by Bredenburg's rationalistic argument in favor of the doctrine of causal determinism, the doctrine that held that everything that happened in nature was determined by necessity to happen just as it happened. In order to prove this doctrine Bredenburg first attempted to prove the necessary existence of God. In this way he could then argue that, because God was the final cause of all actions in nature, these actions were equally necessary.

Following his understanding of the geometric method pioneered by Spinoza in the *Ethics*, Bredenburg prefaced his main argument with a set of definitions and axioms upon which his deduction was based. His first definition was modeled on the first definition in book 1 of the *Ethics*: "by a necessary being is meant a being whose reality is part of its essence: a being necessarily real." This idea had a long history as part of the ontological argument for the existence of God, found first in Anselm of Bec and later in Descartes's Fifth Meditation. Bredenburg's second definition was adapted from the fourth definition in book 1 of the *Ethics*: "properties are qualities that make up the essence or nature of a thing of which they are the properties in such a way that they are indistinguishable from the thing whose essence they compose." Bredenburg's final definition was perhaps based loosely on definitions three and five in book 1 of Spinoza's *Ethics*: "action is a modification, or thus or so to act." Bredenburg also proposed three axioms (*gemeene kennissen*): (1) "From nothing comes nothing"; (2) "Something never becomes nothing, because something and

[15] Johannes Bredenburg, *Wiskunstige demonstratie dat alle verstandelijke werking noodzaakelijk is, met de weerlegging van F.K. van de wiskunstige demonstratie, uytgegeven door Abraham Lemmerman* (Amsterdam, 1684), pp. 3–5.

[16] Ibid., p. 4.

nothing are total opposites and to propose one necessitates the denial of its opposite"; and (3) "Effects are the same in nature as their cause."[17] The third axiom was probably taken from Descartes.

Having prepared his argument, Bredenburg next set forth his central thesis in terms of four propositions, each one "proved" in Spinozistic fashion. In his first proposition Bredenburg maintained that "there exists an essentially necessary being," and he identified this being with God, as Descartes had done. To prove this proposition Bredenburg argued that "it is obvious beyond contradiction that something real does exist." By then following his second axiom Bredenburg concluded that that which existed, existed necessarily, since something could not become nothing. In this way Bredenburg believed that he had rationally proved God's existence.[18]

Bredenburg's second proposition asserted that all properties of the necessary being were also necessarily real. In his proof for this proposition Bredenburg argued that the necessary being was by definition necessarily real, and from definition 2 it was clear that the properties of a thing shared in the essence of the thing. Proposition 3 stated that action was a property of the necessary being. By way of proof Bredenburg argued that "it is obvious that there is action," and by referring again to axiom 2 he asserted that if action existed, it had to exist necessarily. Since action existed necessarily, Bredenburg concluded, it had to be a property of the necessarily real being. In proposition 4 Bredenburg completed his argument by maintaining that "actions, creations, and effects of the necessary being become or are such as they are through eternal necessity" because, as properties of the necessary being, they too are necessary. With these four propositions, which were at least in part inspired by Spinoza's deterministic argument in propositions 19 through 33 of book 1 of the *Ethics*, Bredenburg believed that he had rationally proven the necessity of all natural occurrences by showing them to be actions or properties of a necessarily existing God. Bredenburg ended his argument in true rationalist fashion by maintaining that his conclusions were "so clear to me that I cannot believe that any man of understanding could deny them."[19]

The many weaknesses, flaws, and obscurities in Bredenburg's argument need not detain us here. As an amateur philosopher Bredenburg had absorbed a great deal of Spinoza's rationalistic spirit and a limited understanding of the geometric method, but he had only a very imperfect grasp of Spinoza's arguments for causal necessity. This lack of understanding

[17] Ibid., pp. 5, 6.

[18] Ibid., pp. 7–8. The fact that his first proposition also seemed to "prove" the necessary existence of all existing things simply pointed out how close Bredenburg was to Spinoza's conception of God and nature.

[19] Ibid., p. 8.

did not set Bredenburg apart from his contemporaries, however, because few seventeenth-century readers of the *Ethics* had both the philosophical training and the rational acuity required for a proper understanding of Spinoza's complex and technical arguments. The importance of Bredenburg's argument in the *Wiskunstige demonstratie* was that he himself believed that he had proved God's existence and the necessity of natural events from reason alone. Despite his expressed desire to find a reconciliation between faith and reason, Bredenburg made no reference to revealed truth anywhere in his argument. From this fact it is not necessary to conclude that he was not sincerely troubled by the apparent conflict between the truths of reason and those of revelation on just such points as causal determinism, but in his *Wiskunstige demonstratie* Bredenburg made reason alone the arbiter of truth.[20]

The extreme rationalism of the *Verhandling* and the *Wiskunstige demonstratie*, and especially Bredenburg's treatment of revelation as a mere supplemental source of truth, was a position that was too radical even for many Collegiants. Just as Spinoza's thought met with opposition from more conservative proponents of rational religion such as the Cambridge Platonist Henry More and the Dutch Arminian Philip van Limborch, Bredenburg's works stirred up a storm of protest among moderate rationalists in the colleges. The reaction that developed against Bredenburg's thought within the Collegiant movement clearly showed the limits placed upon the process of secularization during the late seventeenth century even within a group that represented many of the most tolerant and liberal elements in Dutch society.

Many Rijnsburgers who respected the power of human reason for interpreting revealed truth and even for providing some religious truth nevertheless strongly objected to Bredenburg's position that reason could produce true ideas that contradicted revelation. In the *Wiskunstige demonstratie* these people saw an attempt by Bredenburg to supplant revelation with reason as the sole source of religious truth. They feared that Bredenburg's failure to reconcile the truths of reason with those of revelation would inevitably lead to the rejection of revealed truth, and for this reason they declared war on the idea of reason as a source of religious truth. Bredenburg's opponents presented the contradictions between his rational arguments and the doctrines of revealed religion openly and plainly and they called on him to choose between the two rival sources of

---

[20] Even though the *Wiskunstige demonstratie* was published in 1684 by Bredenburg's opponent Abraham Lemmerman, I have no reason to believe that Lemmerman altered Bredenburg's original text.

truth. The result was an intellectual controversy that divided the entire Collegiant movement.

The roots of what later became known as the "Bredenburg controversy" can be traced as far back as 1672, the year in which Bredenburg first began to discuss his ideas at the Rotterdam college with fellow Rijnsburgers Adrian Paets, Barend Joosten Stol, Joan Hartigveldt, and Frans Kuyper. It was Kuyper who became Bredenburg's earliest critic. After extended discussions between the two men Bredenburg gave Kuyper a manuscript of the *Wiskunstige demonstratie* for further study. Kuyper proposed numerous objections to Bredenburg's ideas in a work of his own entitled *Weerlegging van de verdediging van J.B. tegen de aanmerkingen van F.K.* (Rejection of the defense of J.[an] B.[redenburg] against the remarks of F.[rans] K.[uyper]), which was circulated in manuscript among the Collegiants and later published in Amsterdam in 1684.[21] In this work Kuyper charged that Bredenburg was a Spinozist and that his argument for causal determinism in the *Wiskunstige demonstratie* was a denial of God. Kuyper believed causal determinism to be incompatible with Christian belief, and thus he attempted to refute Bredenburg's argument for determinism by overturning several of its key points. He rejected Bredenburg's second definition, which held that properties composed the essence of a thing, by arguing that if properties did compose the essence of a thing they would not be properties but the thing itself. Kuyper also rejected Bredenburg's assertion in proposition three that action was a property of God. For something to be a property of anything it first had to have an essence, Kuyper argued, but action had no essence and thus could not be a property of anything. Kuyper furthermore maintained that since actions had no essence they could easily end without violating the axiom that something could not become nothing. For this reason Kuyper argued that actions that existed did not have to exist necessarily, as Bredenburg asserted.[22]

Kuyper's charges of atheism deeply offended Bredenburg, who considered himself a pious Christian. Bredenburg also clearly recognized the danger of being associated too closely with Spinoza, whose *Theologico-Political Treatise* had gained him the reputation of being an atheist as early as the mid-1670s. Bredenburg had no wish to disassociate himself from the doctrines of traditional religion as Spinoza had done, and for this reason he wrote a work entitled *Enervatio tractatus theologico-politicus* (1675), in which he undertook to turn back charges of Spinozism by pointing out his disagreements with Spinoza's philosophy. In the *Ener-*

---

[21] Van Slee, *De Rijnsburger Collegianten*, pp. 239–244; Meihuizen, in Groenveld, ed., p. 95.

[22] Frans Kuyper, *Weerlegging van de verdediging van J.B. tegen de aanmerkingen van F.K.* (Amsterdam, 1684), pp. 10–14.

vatio Bredenburg denied one of the chief theses of the *Theologico-Political Treatise* by rejecting Spinoza's idea that revelation was primarily a source of commands requiring obedience and not a source of truth requiring understanding. Bredenburg insisted that he considered revelation to be a source of religious truth as he had outlined in the *Verhandling*. In this way Bredenburg hoped to divert charges of Spinozism and atheism by stressing the points on which his thought differed from that of Spinoza, especially with regard to the importance of revelation. Both Siebrand and van Bunge believe that the *Enervatio* represented a major shift of Bredenburg's position away from rationalism, but the work can better be seen as indicating a moderation and adjustment of his views.[23]

Despite the initial disagreements between Bredenburg and Kuyper, their dispute was kept under control during the mid-1670s by the mediation of a mutual friend, Joan (Johan) Hartigveldt (1616–1678). One of the founders of the Rotterdam college, this remarkable man typified the Collegiant spirit of irenicism and toleration that came under increasing strain as a result of the Bredenburg controversy. Born in Rotterdam in 1616, he was the son of Cornelis Hartigveldt, mayor of the city and a director of the East India Company. After obtaining a degree in law from Leiden University in 1637 Hartigveldt traveled to the courts of Europe, accompanying the future stadtholder William II to England in 1641 and afterward visiting Paris. While Hartigveldt was in Paris in 1645 he received news of his father's death. Grief stricken he returned home, but upon his arrival he forsook the important roles in political and social life to which he was heir as a patrician's son and retired to an isolated farm near Brill. Even after he left Brill and returned to Rotterdam, Hartigveldt refused all offices and dignities, wore simple clothing, gave his father's fortune to the poor, and led a pious, introverted life. For a time he was a member of the Remonstrant church in Rotterdam, but in 1654 he joined the Rijnsburger college. Hartigveldt soon became an important figure in the college and a champion of free prophecy, millenarianism, and pacifism. He encouraged his fellow Rijnsburgers to refuse to hold government office and never to attend any religious service where a preacher presided.[24] As an advocate of simple piety and broad religious toleration, Hartigveldt was deeply disturbed by the divisiveness of the Bredenburg controversy. For this reason he sought to act as mediator in a calm exchange of opinions in order to preserve the unity of the Rotterdam college. After his death in 1678, however, the controversy entered a new and bitter stage.

[23] Kolakowski, pp. 255–257; Wiep van Bunge, "Johannes Bredenburg and the Korte Verhandeling," pp. 321–328; Siebrand, *Spinoza and the Netherlanders*, pp. 154–156.

[24] *BWPG*, vol. 3, pp. 531–533.

Kuyper was determined to line up supporters behind his opposition to Bredenburg's ideas, and in so doing he spread the controversy beyond the Rotterdam college when he recruited to his side Abraham Lemmerman (d. 1694), an influential member of the Amsterdam college. Lemmerman was a substantial merchant, resident in the Warmoesstraat, who had married Huibertina van Overveldt in 1671. After lengthy discussions with Kuyper, Lemmerman became convinced of his point of view and agreed to speak out against Bredenburg in the Amsterdam college. At a college meeting in early 1681 Lemmerman accused Bredenburg of atheism, but he failed to convince his colleagues to demand Bredenburg's exclusion from the Collegiants' general communion meeting at Rijnsburg.[25] The majority of the members of the Amsterdam college were sympathetic to Bredenburg, either because they agreed with his point of view or because they favored toleration for all religious opinions. The college listened to Lemmerman's accusations as well as to arguments from Bredenburg's supporters, including Galenus Abrahamsz. himself, who believed Lemmerman's charges of atheism unjustified. After hearing the arguments of both sides, the Amsterdam college voted to revoke Lemmerman's right to speak in college meetings. The Rotterdam college took similar action later that same year when it voted in favor of Bredenburg and withdrew Kuyper's right to speak in college meetings.[26]

The unprecedented censures of Lemmerman and Kuyper developed out of a complex set of conditions. These actions certainly reflected the influence of Galenus both in the Amsterdam college and within the Rijnsburger movement as a whole. In addition, the censures indicated both the level of passion aroused by the dispute and the belief on the part of many Collegiants that the charges of atheism made against Bredenburg were unjustified. The votes against Kuyper and Lemmerman furthermore showed that Bredenburg's ideas had attained a significant level of support, or at least acceptability, among the Collegiants. A true atheist would certainly not have been tolerated even in the colleges.

The censure votes in Amsterdam and Rotterdam did not put an end to the Bredenburg controversy. Deprived of the right to speak against Bredenburg in college meetings, Lemmerman put his objections in print in a work entitled *Eenige bewijzen dat Johannes Bredenburg staande zijn stellingen geenszins kan gelooven dat 'er zulk een God is als de H. Schrift leert* . . . (Several proofs that Johannes Bredenburg, in view of his positions, can in no sense believe that there is such a God as the Holy Scripture teaches, [1684]). In this work Lemmerman renewed his charge of

[25] *BWPG*, vol. 5, pp. 736–739.
[26] See Pieter Smout, *Copye van een brief door Pieter Smout aan Galenus Abrahamsz. geschreven in welk zijn onbehoorlijken handel tegen A.L. en F.K.* . . . (n.p., 1685).

atheism against Bredenburg and insisted that the *Wiskunstige demonstratie* argued that all actions in the world took place as a result of the necessary and eternal linkage of natural causes. Such a conclusion was, according to Lemmerman, completely contrary to the teachings of revealed religion because it denied the omnipotence of God. What was even worse, by making natural necessity the only lord over nature Bredenburg denied the very existence of God and branded religion a fraud.

In Lemmerman's view, Bredenburg could not possibly embrace the Christian religion because he believed that reason contained all truth and reason taught him that religion was false. Bredenburg himself had admitted that reason conflicted with revelation, Lemmerman argued, and since he held reason to be the sole source of truth he could only reject revealed truth as false. Lemmerman dismissed as impossible and absurd Bredenburg's claim in the introduction to the *Wiskunstige demonstratie* that he could still believe in the biblical God even if his rational arguments led him to a different conclusion. Lemmerman compared this claim to Bredenburg saying that he would sincerely believe two times three equals five to be a true statement even though rationally he knew it to be false. In Lemmerman's view, no one could believe something to be true that he rationally understood to be false. If Bredenburg rationally understood his arguments in the *Wiskunstige demonstratie* to be true, then he could not possibly also believe in the God of revelation.[27] With this argument he hoped to present Bredenburg with the choice of rejecting either his rational arguments or the Christian religion, of either renouncing reason as an independent source of truth or being branded an atheist. Bredenburg was not prepared to make this choice.

During 1685 the controversy grew still more rancorous as increasingly bitter arguments on both sides changed few minds but produced a wealth of hard feelings. In Amsterdam the quarrel became so unruly that the regents of the Orangje-Appel, the orphanage in which the college held its meetings, barred both supporters and opponents of Bredenburg from the building. The Bredenburgers promptly rented their own meeting house on the Prinsengracht, while Lemmerman and his followers leased a building on the Keizersgracht. The Amsterdam college thus experienced the first and only schism in its history as the rival groups met separately starting in 1686. The Rotterdam college also split into two separate gatherings, and personal enmities soon mixed with religious and philosophical differences to spread the dispute throughout the entire Collegiant move-

---

[27] Abraham Lemmerman, *Eenige bewijzen dat Johannes Bredenburg staande zijn stellingen, geenzins kan gelooven dat 'er zulk een God is als de H. Schrift leert. Beweezen uyt zijn eygen schriften, hier acter aangevoegt, en uyt zijn mondelinge duydelijke bekentenis* (Amsterdam, 1684), pp. 3–9.

ment. From 1686 the rival parties even met separately at the twice-yearly communion gatherings at Rijnsburg.

During the later 1680s many bitter polemical writings issued forth from both sides in the dispute. In support of Bredenburg some of the most respected Collegiant leaders of the day took up their pens, including Jan Dionysius Verburg of Rotterdam, whose eloquent style earned him the sobriquet "the Christian Cato." Kuyper and Lemmerman found few other Collegiants who were willing to lend their names to anti-Bredenburg pamphlets, but several such works did appear under the curious pseudonyms "Latinus Serbaltus Sartensius" and "J.N.G.V.S." There are no figures or estimates available regarding the number of Collegiants who belonged to each side in this dispute, but in view of the earlier college votes in favor of Bredenburg it seems reasonable to assume that a majority of Collegiants remained in his camp.[28]

Religious ideas exerted a powerful influence on the life and thought of educated people in seventeenth-century Holland. There can be no doubt that the central issue of the Bredenburg dispute was the role of reason in religion, and there can likewise be no doubt that it was this intellectual issue that played the primary role in a drama that ripped apart the tolerant and stable religious movement of Collegiantism. In addition to this dominant issue, however, other factors also helped to make the Bredenburg controversy an extremely acrimonious dispute. One such factor was a reservoir of personal animosity left over from an earlier disagreement within the Rijnsburger movement. During the late 1660s Kuyper and a few of his friends urged the Collegiants to exclude from their fellowship and communion all persons who held government office. Kuyper argued for this exclusion by pointing out that most Rijnsburgers were pacifists who disapproved of the exercise of coercive authority. At a general Collegiant gathering in Rijnsburg, Bredenburg spoke against Kuyper's proposal and led a majority of members in voting it down. Bredenburg argued that the Collegiant commitment to toleration made such an exclusion unjustified. It seems likely that Kuyper and some of his friends transferred their resentment over this defeat to their later quarrel with Bredenburg.

There is no indication that either social status or occupational factors played a significant role in the formation of the rival factions in the Bredenburg dispute, but there was division along geographical lines. Most of the colleges in the province of Holland saw a majority of their members side with Bredenburg, while the colleges in Friesland and the north tended

---

[28] Van Slee, *De Rijnsburger Collegianten*, pp. 244–255, 167–171; Meihuizen, in Groenveld, ed., pp. 95–96. Pierre Bayle identified Latinus Serbaltus Sartensius as Aubert de Versé, see *Dictionnaire Historique et Critique* (Paris, 1820), vol. 13, p. 437, n. 84. See also Kolakowski, p. 266.

to favor his opponents. This division can perhaps be explained by the fact that there was a greater resistance to new ideas in the smaller and more provincial Friesian colleges than in the colleges located in the large and cosmopolitan urban areas of Holland. Two notable exceptions to this rule were the important colleges in Haarlem and Leiden, both of which remained neutral in the dispute. Pieter Smout, a leader of the Leiden college and a thinker who was strongly influenced by Collegiant rationalism, tried to act as a mediator in the quarrel. Another leader of the Leiden college, Dr. Laurens Klinkhamer, wrote a long work deploring the schism entitled *Losse en quaade gronden van de scheur-kerk* (1686). Despite these efforts at peacemaking, however, the fires of conflict only began to die down as the major figures in the dispute one by one passed from the scene: Bredenburg died in 1691, Kuyper in 1692, and Lemmerman in 1694. By 1699 the Amsterdam college was reunited and in 1700 the general meetings in Rijnsburg were once again unified.

The Collegiant movement continued as a force in Dutch religious life throughout the eighteenth century, but after the Bredenburg dispute it was never again the same. The great battle over the place of reason in religion seemed to drain the intellectual energy of the movement, and after 1700 the Rijnsburgers never again produced writings dealing with controversial religious or philosophical topics. In the eighteenth century Collegiants continued to write devotional works, poetry and works of history, but little of philosophical or theological interest. Bredenburg's rationalism and the debate that it engendered represented both the climax and the conclusion of the golden age of Collegiant intellectual activity. For the Rijnsburgers the eighteenth century was a period of decline and dissolution. In 1775 the Amsterdam college was dissolved and in 1787 the last general meeting was held in Rijnsburg. During a century of increasing toleration within the various Protestant churches in the Netherlands, the need for the colleges as places for the free expression of ideas faded. Most Collegiants simply became members of other churches. As the Collegiant principles of freedom of conscience, reason, and toleration became more and more generally accepted in society at large, the once lonely light of Collegiantism dissolved into the bright dawn of the Enlightenment.[29]

The limits of Collegiant rationalism during the seventeenth century were revealed clearly by the controversy surrounding Bredenburg's thought as

---

[29] Van Slee, *De Rijnsburger Collegianten*, pp. 255–264; Marieke Quak, "De Collegianten te Amsterdam," *Doopsgezinde Bijdragen*, n.s. 10 (1984), pp. 110–112. On the Collegiants in the eighteenth century, see also Marieke Quak, *De Collegianten te Amsterdam in de periode van 1722–1775* (doctoraalscriptie, University of Utrecht, 1985); and E. van Nimwegen, *Historie der Rijnsburgsche Vergadering* (Rotterdam, 1775).

well as by the response that he made to the criticisms of his opponents. In reply to the attacks of Kuyper and Lemmerman, Bredenburg wrote several works in which he modified his earlier views and developed his interesting "double truth" approach in defense of rationalism. In this approach Bredenburg maintained both reason and revelation as dual sources of religious truth, and even though he gave more attention to revelation as a source of truth than he had in his early works he did not correspondingly devalue the important role of human reason. This approach first became apparent in Bredenburg's *Nodige verantwoording op de ongegronde beschuldiging van Abraham Lemmerman* (Necessary answer to the baseless charge of Abraham Lemmerman [1684]). In this lengthy work Bredenburg argued that the truths presented in his *Wiskunstige demonstratie* were completely valid from the point of view of reason. He added, however, that in cases where the truths of reason conflicted with the doctrines of revelation, revelation had to be accepted above reason. This was so not because the truths of reason were false but because the authority of revelation superceded them.

Bredenburg began his reply to Lemmerman by observing that the entire controversy of which he had become the center started simply because he had undertaken to examine the principles, grounds, and nature of religion. As he contemplated the perfect essence of God, Bredenburg explained, he perceived that God had to be the necessary cause of all creation and all actions in the world. Such a consideration seemed to rule out the existence of free will, Bredenburg argued. But the miracles related in Scripture could be ascribed only to God's free will, not to the necessary laws of nature, because many such miracles openly contradicted the laws of nature. Bredenburg therefore concluded that while reason taught that the world was ruled by causal determinism, revelation taught the existence of free will and miracles. After pointing out this apparent contradiction between the conclusions of reason and the teachings of revelation, Bredenburg proclaimed that both positions could in fact be accepted as true.[30]

Reason taught that miracles could not occur because the nature of miracles was outside of reason and natural law, Bredenburg explained, but in the miracles reported by the Bible one could find no trace of untruth. Furthermore, throughout Christian history miracles had convinced people of the truth of religion. Even philosophers who once used their reason to deny God and his creation of the world had been convinced otherwise by divine miracles, Bredenburg wrote, and for this reason the apostles never needed to argue rationally against the proofs of the pagan philoso-

[30] Johannes Bredenburg, *Nodige verantwoording op de ongegronde beschuldiging van Abraham Lemmerman* (Rotterdam, 1684), pp. 26–29.

phers. God had simply used the strength of his miracles "to overcome the learning of the philosophers" and to convert them. The philosophers rejected their rational doctrines because the power of divine miracles convinced them to accept truths of revelation such as creation, resurrection, and other doctrines of the Christian faith. But the philosophers rejected their rational doctrines "not because they found their reasoning faulty," Bredenburg argued, but simply because they yielded to a superior truth. "And so it is with me," he declared, "I can be moved by miracles to put aside my rational arguments without seeing that they have been poorly or wrongly reasoned."[31] Bredenburg thus maintained that he could accept revealed truth above reason on the basis of its superior status without rejecting his rational conclusions as false. By thus separating the truths of reason from those of revelation Bredenburg allowed each to be true in its own way.

Bredenburg never doubted the veracity of biblical accounts of miracles even while he insisted on the validity of his own rational arguments against miracles, and he thus maintained that divine revelation was a valid source of religious truth despite its disagreements with reason. But even though Bredenburg elevated miracles and revelation as sources of religious truth to a higher status than he had granted them in his earlier work, he did not correspondingly devalue the importance or power of reason. His position can be compared to the ideas of Robert Boyle and other English scientists of the late seventeenth century whose Protestant beliefs allowed them to reject the validity of miracles that occurred after biblical times as part of their repudiation of Catholic doctrine, but who nevertheless accepted biblical miracles even though they contradicted scientific principles. This happy alliance between Protestantism and rationalism with regard to miracles, while it was limited by respect for the authority of Scripture, was reinforced by the belief in some Protestant quarters that the age of miracles had ended with the apostolic church. Bredenburg found himself in a similar position, caught between the Collegiants' increasing reliance on reason, which resulted in part from their belief that the gifts of the Holy Spirit had ended with the early church, and their great respect for Scripture. Concerning Boyle and his followers, Richard Westfall has written: "Without doing violence to their Protestant convictions they were able to hold a position on miracles which was not in flagrant contradiction to their scientific theories."[32] Bredenburg's doctrine of double truth was a compromise solution of this sort as well.

Elsewhere in the *Nodige verantwoording* Bredenburg dealt more specifically with several of Lemmerman's charges against him. He denied

[31] Ibid., pp. 29–30.
[32] Westfall, *Science and Religion in Seventeenth-Century England*, pp. 5–6.

Lemmerman's assertion that the *Wiskunstige demonstratie* argued that all occurrences in the world took place by natural necessity and the interaction of natural causes, remining his readers that he had stated explicitly that God was the cause of all actions in the world. He furthermore maintained that his argument that God necessarily existed and that every action in the world flowed necessarily from God was completely in accord with the orthodox Christian belief that God's eternal essence was everywhere and that the world was maintained by a constant inflowing of God's strength. To avoid giving the impression that he agreed with Spinoza's doctrine of determinism based on a God and nature that were barely distinguishable, Bredenburg again criticized Spinoza's point of view as he had done earlier in the *Enervatio*. In chapter 4 of the *Theologico-Political Treatise* Spinoza argued for a determinism consisting of the eternal linkage of natural causes, Bredenburg wrote. This argument forced Spinoza to interpret Scripture and miracles in such a way that they would not contradict his thesis of natural necessity. Bredenburg emphasized, however, that this was not his own approach. He understood Scripture, revelation, and miracles "in themselves" and did not force them to agree with nature and reason. Bredenburg was especially incensed by Kuyper's charge that he followed Spinoza in denying the existence of God with his thesis of determinism. He had not argued for a determinism of natural causes as Spinoza had done, he declared, but rather for a determinism flowing directly from the power of God. Nevertheless, his opponents had taken his proof of the necessary existence of God and turned it into a proof of atheism. In Bredenburg's view, this kind of duplicity was proof of his opponents' bad faith.[33]

Bredenburg also took issue with Lemmerman's charge that he could not believe in God because he held reason to be the chief source of metaphysical truth. While he affirmed that he did believe that reason was "the light in men's eyes and their guiding star," he insisted that he had never said that reason proved that God did not exist. But even if reason did prove that there was no God, Bredenburg continued, he could still believe in God's existence based on the evidence of revelation and miracles. Reason taught him that if he saw a miracle that appeared convincingly true he could not deny it as false, he argued. Thus, Bredenburg again claimed that he could believe something to be true on the basis of revelation even though he rationally understood it to be false, and he could do so without rejecting the conclusions of reason. For Bredenburg, reason and revelation were separate sources of truth, each existing in its own realm and each true in its own way. For this reason he again explicitly rejected Spinoza's claim that rational philosophy was the only source of metaphysical

[33] Bredenburg, *Noodige*, pp. 1–14.

truth: "Philosophy alone is not the realm of all truth; theology is also a realm of truth; one cannot call theology a realm of obedience and not truth, and thus separate it from philosophy" ("Filosofie alleen het rijk van alle waarheid niet en is, maar . . . ook de theologie een rijk van waarheid is, en (men) daarom, uyt hoofde van dat de theologie alleen een rijk van aandacht en van geen warrheid is, die zelve van de filosofie niet kan afscheyden").[34]

Leszek Kolakowski has described Bredenburg's view of reason and revelation as a new version of the medieval doctrine of double truth.[35] The term double truth has been used by some historians of philosophy to refer to the position taken by certain Averroistic arts masters at the University of Paris during the thirteenth century who read Aristotle and followed his logic to conclusions incompatible with the Christian faith. These masters attempted to resolve the apparent contradictions between faith and reason by insisting on the logical validity of the Aristotelian arguments while at the same time yielding to the superior authority of faith in the final determination of truth. People like Siger of Brabant recognized valid but conflicting truths in the realms of reason and revelation, giving greater weight to the teachings of faith. Following Aristotelian principles Siger concluded that God was ignorant of the truth value of future contingent propositions, that chance was the foundation of free will, and that personal immortality was impossible, but at the same time he maintained that the truth of these conclusions had to be subordinated to the declarations of faith. Siger thus held to Aristotelian logical rigor while insisting on the truth of the doctrines of the Christian faith. Edward Grant, the distinguished historian of medieval science, does not believe that Siger or other Paris Averroists ever explicitly endorsed a doctrine by means of which "a proposition in philosophy might be true in the natural domain and its contradictory independently true in the realm of faith."[36] Grant concedes, however, that it was the bishop of Paris's fear that certain masters did indeed hold such views that was instrumental in causing the condemnations of 1270 and 1277. Etienne Gilson has also denied that the Averroists actually maintained two equally valid but contradictory sources of truth. According to Gilson, when faced with the requirements of faith the Averroists recognized the limitations of human reason.[37] Whatever the actual beliefs of the Paris Averroists might have been, how-

---

[34] Ibid., pp. 16–23.

[35] Kolakowski, pp. 263–265. On Bredenburg's doctrine of double truth, see also Hubbeling, in Gründer and Schmidt-Biggemann, eds., p. 171.

[36] Edward Grant, *Physical Science in the Middle Ages* (Cambridge, England, 1977), pp. 26–27; *EP*, vol. 7, pp. 436–437.

[37] *EP*, vol. 1, pp. 224–225.

ever, a genuine doctrine of double truth does indeed appear to be maintained explicitly in the works of Bredenburg.

After adopting his doctrine of double truth in response to the attacks of Kuyper and Lemmerman, Bredenburg elaborated on it in a series of letters that he wrote to the Remonstrant theologian Philip van Limborch. Bredenburg's correspondence with Limborch was published in Rotterdam in 1686 under the title *Schriftelijke onderhandeling tusschen den Heer Philippus van Limborg, Professor der Remonstranten, ende Johannes Bredenburg, rakende 't gebruyk der reden in de religie* (Written discussion between Mr. Philip van Limborch, professor of the Remonstrants, and Johannes Bredenburg, dealing with the use of reason in religion). Limborch was born in Amsterdam in 1633 and educated in theology both at the University of Utrecht and at the Remonstrant Seminary in Amsterdam, where he served as professor from 1668 until his death in 1712. Moderately influenced by Cartesianism, Limborch believed in the usefulness of reason as a tool for interpreting the truths of biblical revelation. Despite his high regard for reason, however, he rejected both Socinianism and Spinoza's extreme form of rationalism. Limborch condemned all religious intolerance, and his discussions on this topic with John Locke helped to prompt Locke's famous treatise on toleration. Despite his tolerant attitude, however, Limborch found himself in serious disagreement with Bredenburg regarding the proper role of reason in religion.[38]

In his first letter to Limborch, Bredenburg revealed the main point at issue between the two men when he asked whether a rational person could sincerely believe something to be true that he knew to be contrary to the dictates of reason. Bredenburg maintained that this was possible because reason and faith were separate and autonomous sources of truth. A person could rationally understand an idea to be false while at the same time, following revelation, he believed it to be true. Limborch denied this point of view by maintaining that true rational conclusions and revealed truths could never conflict with each other, a position maintained by Descartes and common to many moderate rationalists of the time, including Boyle and the Cambridge Platonists.[39] Bredenburg saw in Limborch's po-

[38] Colie, pp. 27–29; Zilverberg, in Hoenderdaal and Luca, eds., pp. 70–71. On Limborch, see P. J. Barnouw, *Philippus van Limborch* (The Hague, 1963).

[39] Johannes Bredenburg, *Schriftelijke onderhandeling tusschen den Heer Philippus van Limborg, Professor der Remonstranten, ende Johannes Bredenburg, rakende 't gebruyk der reden in de religie* (Rotterdam, 1686), p. i. By rejecting Bredenburg's double truth separation of reason from revelation Limborch showed his own Cartesian inclinations. Descartes himself had rejected a similar idea in 1647 in a work written against Henry Regius. Descartes declared: "Since we are born men before we are made Christians, it is not credible that anyone seriously embraces opinions which he thinks contrary to right reason, which

sition the danger of branding as false any rational argument that contradicted Scripture, and it was probably at least part of Bredenburg's purpose in making reason and revelation separate realms of truth to protect reason's conclusions from falsification in this way. To buttress his claim that reason and revelation were separate sources of truth Bredenburg developed an elaborate epistemological argument.

According to Bredenburg, human understanding obtained true knowledge in two ways. The first way was through an "immediate consideration or contemplation" in which the understanding was "united with the thing itself." Here he seemed to be describing a kind of intuition or direct apprehension. The second way was through logical argument and deduction from the ideas obtained through means number 1. Bredenburg maintained that the knowledge obtained through immediate contemplation was "of worthier rank" than deductive arguments because it was "more clear and simple," and for this reason such first-rank knowledge was to be accepted above deductive arguments when the two kinds of knowledge conflicted. Revelation and miracles produced knowledge of the first rank, Bredenburg argued, and therefore this revealed truth was to be preferred to deductive rational knowledge because it was "more perfect." For example, a person might devise a rational argument based on natural principles that upheld causal determinism in nature and denied miracles. If, however, this same person was to see a miracle before his or her own eyes "clearly and distinctly, so that he [could not] doubt it," this first-rank knowledge would take precedence over rational proof.[40]

In his reply to Bredenburg, Limborch agreed that human knowledge could be divided into two parts, but he denied that these two kinds of knowledge could ever contradict each other. Limborch argued that if a person had reasoned that miracles were impossible (a reference, of course, to the *Wiskunstige demonstratie*), this person would never believe that a miracle could take place even if he or she did witness one personally. He or she would simply consider the miracle an unusual natural occurrence. By arguing in this way Limborch attempted to identify Bredenburg's conception of miracles with Spinoza's position as it appeared in chapter 6 of the *Theologico-Political Treatise*. In his next letter to Limborch, Bredenburg rejected this argument and again insisted that the truths of revelation and those of reason could disagree, and that in such cases Christians had to prefer revelation because of its "greater importance" and "in order to please God." To further emphasize the separation

---

makes us men, so that he might adhere to the faith, through which he is a Christian," see McGahagan, p. 137.

[40] Bredenburg, *Schriftelijke*, pp. 1–2. Bredenburg does not discuss the trustworthiness of sense perception nor explain how such a sense perception provides first-rank knowledge, other than by analogy.

that he believed to exist between these two realms of truth Bredenburg argued that one could never be rationally convinced of the truth of revelation because reason, which could understand only natural things, could not grasp supernatural revelation. For this reason God used miracles to convince people of the truth of revelation, and people recognized that miracles were divine because they had no basis in nature. People accepted miracles as true because of their divine origin, he argued, and thus it was not only possible but necessary for Christians to believe things that were contrary to reason. In Bredenburg's view, this kind of belief was the very foundation of religion.[41]

In Limborch's second reply to Bredenburg he again referred to Bredenburg's division of human knowledge into the knowledge gained by immediate contemplation and that gained through rational deduction. Taking as his example the geometric model of deductive method in which the valid conclusion proceeded from premises that were established as true, Limborch argued that Bredenburg's demonstration of causal necessity in the *Wiskunstige demonstratie* was a logical deduction based on first principles drawn from immediate contemplation. For this reason Limborch maintained that the conclusion of Bredenburg's rational deduction could not contradict the truths of immediate contemplation that formed its premises. But revelation and miracles came by immediate contemplation and they taught that free will existed, Limborch argued, whereas Bredenburg's rational deduction upheld the doctrine of determinism. For this reason, Limborch maintained that if Bredenburg intended to believe the truth of revelation and miracles he would have to concede that his rational deduction was false. It was simply not possible for a rational deduction to produce a valid conclusion that contradicted the premises on which it was based. "If you hold your demonstration to be true," Limborch wrote Bredenburg, "admit that there are no miracles. If you believe from the heart that miracles occur, call your demonstration false."[42]

In the face of this highly polemical line of argumentation Bredenburg's doctrine of double truth became an effort to protect the autonomous power of human reason from the control of revelation and at the same time to protect Bredenburg himself from charges of atheism. In his last letter to Limborch, Bredenburg tried to make his position clearer by further explaining some of his arguments. When he argued that a person could believe something to be true that he or she rationally understood to be false, Bredenburg explained, he did not mean that a person would rationally accept something as true while at the same time rationally understanding it to be false. When people accepted a revealed truth in prefer-

[41] Ibid., pp. 3–9.
[42] Ibid., pp. 11–17, 22.

ence to a truth of reason, they did so because they realized that revelation from God provided a "higher truth" than human reason. But even while making this choice a person had to realize that "the truths of nature and the truths of God's power can coexist." Bredenburg then concluded his argument by declaring: "Reason and belief are, then, both realms of truth, each in its own way, [but] reason must be silent where belief speaks" ("De reden en het geloof zijn dan beyde rijken der waarheid, doch ieder op zijn wijs . . . de reden zwijgen moet daar het geloof spreek").[43]

With this statement Bredenburg again distanced himself from Spinoza, who denied that revelation was a source of knowledge. But despite the pious motivation of Bredenburg's insistence on revelation as a source of metaphysical truth, his refusal to allow rational conclusions to be falsified by contradictory truths of revelation increased the epistemological power and autonomy of human reason far beyond the point reached in the thought of Balling and Jelles. According to Kolakowski, Bredenburg's thought represented the capitulation of religion to reason disguised as the capitulation of reason to religion.[44] By separating the truths of reason and those of revelation into distinct rational and nonrational realms, Bredenburg left the truths of reason as the only knowledge that could be intellectually understood by man. In this way Bredenburg closely approached Spinoza's doctrine and found himself on the verge of a purely secular philosophical rationalism.

The thought of Jan Bredenburg represented the climax of Collegiant rationalism and the culmination of a long intellectual odyssey that took the Rijnsburgers from spiritualism and millenarianism through stages of rational religion and rational spiritualism before finally arriving at a largely secular philosophical rationalism. This intellectual evolution took place within the relatively stable framework of a tolerant, individualistic, and latitudinarian religious position that defined Collegiantism as an intellectual force in Dutch life during the seventeenth century. In this process of evolution Collegiant thought mirrored the larger intellectual transformation taking place in late-seventeenth-century Europe. It would of course be misleading to portray the evolution of Collegiant thought as a monolithic movement of ideas, especially given the great toleration for many different viewpoints that made the colleges havens for a wide variety of religious and philosophical opinion. It was this very atmosphere of toleration that allowed Collegiant thought to weave together so many of the often divergent strands of seventeenth-century Dutch religious and

---

[43] Ibid., pp. 60, 63.
[44] Kolakowski, p. 273.

intellectual life. By combining elements of spiritualism, Socinianism, Cartesianism, Arminianism, millenarianism, Erasmianism, and Spinozism, Collegiant thought was able to evolve freely in its own direction. The fact that Bredenburg's rationalism could be accepted and even defended by a majority of the members of the biggest colleges in Holland during the 1680s was clear evidence of how much Collegiant thought had changed since Gijsbert van der Kodde founded the first free prophecy college in Warmond in 1620. A movement that began life as part of the Second Reformation's critique of the Protestant churches of the seventeenth century had, by the end of the century, begun to call into question the very foundations of revealed religion itself. The radical religious movement of Collegiantism had become a part of the emerging philosophical tradition of the age of reason.

Bredenburg's rationalism was influenced deeply by the philosophy of Spinoza, as to a lesser extent was the thought of Balling and Jelles. The place of Spinoza and his philosophy within the evolving tradition of Collegiant thought is highly interesting not only for the light that this relationship sheds on the intellectual background of Spinoza's own thought, but also for what this relationship reveals about the limits placed upon the role of reason in Rijnsburger religious thinking. While Spinoza never openly identified himself as a Collegiant his involvement in Rijnsburger circles was more than a marginal part of his intellectual life. Both Meinsma and Hylkema stressed Spinoza's connections to the Rijnsburger community in Amsterdam.[45] In view of his close association with the Collegiants, it is both a challenging and an interesting task to attempt to place Spinoza within the context of the developing tradition of Collegiant thought.

In many ways Spinoza was different from other Collegiants. A philosopher of genius, he far excelled the other Rijnsburgers both in the depth of his philosophical understanding and in the acuity of his intellect. There is nothing in the extensive corpus of Collegiant writings to compare with the *Ethics* in logical rigor or with the *Theologico-Political Treatise* in analytical boldness. Spinoza was a lonely figure with few close friends and even fewer intellectual companions, but he maintained closer contact with the Collegiants than with any other group after his expulsion from the Amsterdam Jewish community in 1656. Pieter Balling and Jarig Jelles were among Spinoza's closest associates in Amsterdam. He also knew Pieter Serrarius, who carried correspondence to England for him. Spinoza attended intellectual discussions that took place in the bookshop of the Collegiant publisher Jan Rieuwertsz., discussions that certainly included many Rijnsburgers. When he left Amsterdam in 1660 Spinoza chose to

---

[45] Hylkema, vol. 2, chap. 7, sec. 2; Meinsma, chaps. 4–6.

reside for a time in Rijnsburg, the cradle of Collegiantism. Perhaps he had become acquainted with the peaceful village by attending a Collegiant gathering there. While there is no direct evidence that Spinoza ever attended college meetings, given the closeness of his association with the Rijnsburgers and the openness of their meetings it would seem likely that he did so.

The Collegiant bookseller Rieuwertsz. published the *Theologico-Political Treatise* in 1670 as well as the posthumous edition of Spinoza's works in 1677—an edition prepared by Jelles and others from papers collected by Rieuwertsz. in Amsterdam.[46] Spinoza was extremely sensitive to public reaction to his ideas (his device was *"caute"* ["be cautious"] inscribed beneath a rose, the symbol of secrecy) and for this reason he published only two works during his lifetime: the *Principles of Descartes' Philosophy*, translated by Balling, and the *Theologico-Political Treatise*, which appeared anonymously. Yet Spinoza felt close enough to the Collegiants both intellectualy and spiritually to leave his most important writings in their care when he died. There is no doubt that Spinoza's ideas influenced his Collegiant friends. The works of Balling and Jelles clearly showed the influence of the frequent discussions that they had with Spinoza on Cartesian philosophy and other topics, while Bredenburg's writings were composed as a result of an active dialogue between their author and Spinoza's ideas, which Bredenburg knew in manuscript and in print in the early 1670s. But how mutual was this influence? Did Spinoza share any of the religious views of his Rijnsburger friends? Can Spinoza's rationalism be seen as an extension of the developments within Collegiant thought? Can Spinoza really be called a Rijnsburger?

While both K. O. Meinsma and C. B. Hylkema stressed Spinoza's close associations with the Amsterdam Collegiants, Madeleine Francès believed that there was little evidence to indicate a close bond between Spinoza and the Rijnsburgers. According to Francès, Spinoza never personally adhered to the Collegiant movement nor was his religious thought significantly influenced by Collegiant ideas. Spinoza apparently did not know De Breen, Boreel, or Galenus Abrahamsz., the most important leaders of the Amsterdam college, and Francès described his acquaintance with Serrarius as superficial. Francès furthermore considered Balling and Jelles to be thinkers of little breadth who had no important influence on Spinoza's thought. In her view both Balling and Jelles were basically Mennonite thinkers who managed to avoid any real Cartesian influence in their work despite their close contact with Spinoza. Savants and free spirits such as Adrian Koerbagh, Loedewijk Meyer, and Simon de Vries

[46] De Vries, pp. 200–202, 227–228; Roger Scruton, *Spinoza* (Oxford, 1985), p. 18.

played a much more important role in Spinoza's later life than did the Rijnsburgers, according to Francès.[47]

Although evidence for Spinoza's active involvement in the Collegiant movement is sparse, it would be a mistake to rule out the possibility of Rijnsburger influence on his thought. Given Spinoza's deep interest in both religious and philosophical questions it is difficult to imagine how he could not have been influenced by the Collegiant ideas of his friends Balling and Jelles, who were close associates of Galenus Abrahamsz. and who befriended Spinoza during the early and formative years of his philosophical development. Furthermore, Spinoza's own writings suggested the possibility of Rijnsburger influence. During his discussion of scriptural interpretation in chapter 7 of the *Theologico-Political Treatise* Spinoza seemed at several points to echo the Collegiant desire for a religion of individual conscience, reason, and toleration. According to Spinoza, faithfulness in religion was not produced by external constraints, such as the laws of states, but by "faithful and brotherly admonition, sound education, and, above all, free use of the individual judgement." It was precisely upon these foundations of religious education, mutual admonishment, and individual conscience that the colleges were established. Like his Rijnsburger friends Spinoza believed that each person had the right and obligation "to explain and interpret religion for himself," and he continued: "For as the highest power of Scriptural interpretation belongs to every man, the rule for such interpretation should be nothing but the natural light of reason, which is common to all—not any supernatural light nor any external authority."[48]

By indicating his desire to establish a religion of individual conscience based on the light of reason Spinoza echoed the ideas of those Collegiants who developed a rationalistic conception of the inner light of truth in part as a reaction to the extreme spiritualism of the Quakers. It was during the years 1657–1664, the years immediately following his expulsion from the Amsterdam Jewish community, that Spinoza maintained his closest contacts with Collegiant circles, and it was in these same years that Quaker missionaries first clashed with the Collegiants in Amsterdam. Spinoza's friend Pieter Balling was one of the Rijnsburgers who argued against the Quaker doctrine of the spiritual inner light, and Spinoza himself wrote in the *Theologico-Political Treatise* that no supernatural faculty or "divine gift" was necessary for the interpretation of Scripture. Spinoza argued that the Bible had been written so that it could be understood by the unconverted, who of course possessed no divine gifts, and he elaborated on

[47] Madeleine Francès, *Spinoza Dans Les Pays Neerlandais de la seconde moitie du XVIIe siècle* (Paris, 1937), pp. 138–185, 219–243.

[48] Spinoza, *A Theologico-Political Treatise*, pp. 118, 119.

this point with a remark that was perhaps directed against the Quakers: "those who demand supernatural faculties for comprehending the meaning of the prophets and apostles seem truly lacking in natural faculties, so that we should hardly suppose such persons the possessors of a divine or supernatural gift." With this sentiment Galenus, Balling, and Serrarius could readily agree. Spinoza also seemed to share Galenus's view regarding the cessation of the gifts of the Holy Spirit and the absence of divine prophets on earth when he discussed the topic of prophecy in the *Theologico-Political Treatise*: "Our conclusions on this subject must be drawn solely from Scripture, for what can we affirm about matters transcending our knowledge except what is told us by the words or writings of the prophets? And since there are, so far as I know, no prophets now alive, we have no alternative but to read the books of prophets departed."[49]

Whether such passages indicate the influence of Collegiant thought on Spinoza is diffiult to ascertain, especially given the lack of direct evidence. Spinoza could have encountered similar ideas in many other sources. The similarity between these passages and key themes of Rijnsburger religious thought, however, combined with Spinoza's close friendship with important Collegiants during a crucial period of his own intellectual and personal development, suggests a reasonable possibility of such influence. A great deal has been written concerning the various intellectual influences that shaped Spinoza's thought, including Cartesianism, Scholastic metaphysics, the Jewish tradition, and the Neoplatonism of Giordano Bruno.[50] When Spinoza is placed within the intellectual tradition of Collegiantism an interesting new perspective on his philosophy results.

Spinoza's rationalism represented a break with the past that was much more daring than that accomplished by Bredenburg, but at the same time Spinoza's position might be seen as a logical extension of the partial separation of reason from revelation present in Bredenburg's thought. Bredenburg distinguished between the rational truths of reason and the non-rational truths of revelation, but he insisted that both reason and revelation were sources of true knowledge concerning God and religion. Spinoza, on the other hand, declared rational philosophy to be the only source of true knowledge while he considered revealed religion to be a source of divine commands not understood rationally but merely obeyed. While philosophy was the realm of knowledge for Spinoza, theology was the realm of piety and obedience. According to Richard Popkin, Spinoza's

---

[49] Ibid., pp. 114, 14–15.

[50] See H. A. Wolfson; Stuart Hampshire, *Spinoza* (London, 1951; reprint 1981); Scruton; Leon Roth, *Spinoza, Descartes, and Maimonides* (Oxford, 1924); H. G. Hubbeling, *Spinoza* (Baarn, 1966); Frederick Pollock, *Spinoza: His Life and Philosophy* (London, 1880). For the relationship between Spinoza's thought and Collegiant ideas, Evenhuis, pp. 311–312; and Hubbeling in Gründer and Schmidt-Biggemann, eds., pp. 155–162.

claim that the truth of theological prescriptions could only be decided by philosophy entailed a "total scepticism about theology and religion."[51] While Bredenburg's typically Collegiant insistence on scriptural revelation as a second source of religious knowledge prevented the complete separation of faith from reason in his thought, Spinoza's demotion of revelation from a source of knowledge to a source of moral commands brought about the final division between reason and revelation. This was in fact Spinoza's purpose when he wrote the first half of the *Theologico-Political Treatise*. As he explained, he intended "to show that between faith, or theology, and philosophy, there is no connection, nor affinity."[52] In Spinoza's philosophy the separation of reason from revelation represented the final victory of reason in human thought.

Bredenburg stopped short of completely secularizing the individual conscience. In this philosophy the individual's inner ability to know truth operated primarily by reason, and reason's conclusions even took on an aspect of infallibility, but his theory of double truth preserved a place for revelation in religious thinking. Spinoza's complete separation of philosophy from theology led to the unchallenged ascendency of reason as the sole source of metaphysical truth and thus to the complete secularization of the individual conscience. As Popkin recognized, Spinoza proposed a devastating critique of revealed knowledge claims, a critique that played a significant role in the secularization of modern thought. Spinoza's rationalism could thus be seen as the final climactic step in the long Collegiant development toward a secularized conception of individual conscience. Spinoza surpassed the limited rationalism of Bredenburg by developing his uncompromisingly secular epistemology, but it was not merely the thought of Bredenburg that Spinoza surpassed. As Popkin concluded: "Spinoza's scepticism about the values of the biblical world, and his view of how it would be replaced by the rational man, was far beyond what mid-seventeenth century thinkers could accept."[53] The opposition that Spinoza's thought provoked from such thinkers as Henry More, Philip van Limborch, and even Bredenburg himself is surely proof of this contention.

The final step to a completely secular rationalism was a step that neither Bredenburg nor the other Collegiants could take. The living religious tradition of the Rijnsburgers, along with the great respect for biblical revelation that underpinned the movement, formed a limit beyond which most Collegiant thinkers could not venture. The limits to rationalism that were present within Collegiant thought reveal as much, if not perhaps

---

[51] Popkin, p. 235.
[52] Spinoza, *A Theologico-Political Treatise*, p. 189.
[53] Popkin, pp. 229, 237–238.

more, about the seventeenth-century worldview than does the secularizing tendency that so fundamentally transformed Rijnsburger thought in the years 1650–1690. Confined as they were within their own intellectual world composed of reformist ideas but ultimately conditioned by the traditions of a waning but still potent religious worldview, the Collegiants could not allow divine revelation to lose all of its truth value even as their respect for the power and importance of human reason steadily grew. Although the Collegiants were one of the most tolerant, innovative, and radical groups in seventeenth-century Dutch intellectual life, they were still very much a part of their society, a society in which the truth of revealed religion remained an important cornerstone of intellectual and spiritual life for most Europeans. Within the limitations imposed by their religious and biblical orientation, however, the Collegiants witnessed a remarkable transformation in their thought system and worldview during the second half of the seventeenth century. By 1690 Collegiant thought had become strikingly secularized and rationalistic as compared not only with its own spiritualistic beginnings but also with the intellectual outlook of most other religious groups of the day. Outside influences such as Socinianism and Cartesianism combined with the Collegiants' own deep disappointment with the outcome of the Protestant Reformation and the condition of the Christian churches of the seventeenth century to produce a profound reorientation of Rijnsburger thought. The fact that the Rijnsburgers could not take the final step into a completely secularized worldview merely emphasizes the transitional nature of Collegiant thought: It was a true intellectual bridge between Reformation spiritualism and Enlightenment rationalism. The Rijnsburgers were unable to abandon completely the old for the new. The evolution of Collegiant thought set the stage for the final breakthrough into a new worldview, but the Rijnsburgers could not make this breakthrough themselves.

It is significant that the final breakthrough was left to Spinoza. Spinoza was a thinker who was influenced by the Collegiant tradition but who was also an outsider, influenced by other sources. For this reason he was to some extent free of the limitations imposed upon other Collegiants by their own intellectual traditions, and thus he was better able to take the last critical step that caused an intellectual revolution. Perhaps it is in the nature of crucial moments of intellectual change that transitional ideas that have developed within a specific social and intellectual context need to be supplemented by new perspectives that are to an extent free of the limitations imposed by that context in order for an intellectual breakthrough to occur. It is in this sense that Spinoza's philosophy can be considered a part of the development of Collegiant thought, and Spinoza himself a Collegiant. While the evolution of Collegiant thought helped to prepare the way for Spinoza's rationalism and perhaps even contributed something to its development, Spinoza's philosophy went beyond the Collegiant tradition to attain a level of logical rigor and conceptual vision of which no other Rijnsburger thinker was capable. For this reason Spinoza made the breakthrough to a thoroughly secular philosophical rationalism that other Collegiants were unable to make. Spinoza was in part a Collegiant, but he was more. He was not without predecessors, but he was without equals.

There can be no doubt that the contributions of powerful original thinkers like Spinoza are critical to the process of intellectual change. There can likewise be no doubt, however, that the complex process of intellectual transition is not simply made up of a series of sudden, unprepared breakthroughs in which new systems or ideologies spring forth fully formed from the minds of their creators and force their way onto the historical stage by the compelling force of their own logic. Intellectual history is the story of thinkers both great and small, and like other kinds of historical change, intellectual change is a gradual, evolutionary process in which new ideas and perspectives are slowly prepared within a complex matrix of social and intellectual influences. In such a process of change, transitional systems such as Collegiant thought play a vital role in linking old to new and in providing the background against which intellectual breakthroughs can take place and be understood, accepted, and absorbed into the steady stream of intellectual tradition.

Chapter Ten

RADICAL RELIGION AND THE AGE OF REASON

> Edmund Hickhorngill, who lapsed from the
> Hexham church to become a Quaker, soon
> attained to a "better and higher dispensa-
> tion." "He propounds no other rule to himself
> but his reason, which if a man sin not
> against, he shall be happy enough." So we see
> radical religion passing into rationalism.
> —Christopher Hill

THE INTELLECTUAL origins of the secular and rationalistic worldview of the European Enlightenment lay in a world that was still deeply penetrated with religious assumptions. Collegiant thought formed an intellectual bridge linking the providential religious worldview of the Reformation era with the new worldview of science and reason that was emerging during the second half of the seventeenth century. For this reason the Dutch Collegiants provide an excellent illustration of the way in which religious ideas and attitudes provided the background against which the worldview of modern Europe evolved. By pointing out some ways in which religious ideas influenced the formation of key assumptions of the age of reason, this study of Collegiant thought has endeavored to bring to light the dynamics of intellectual transition during the late seventeenth century.

The years between 1650 and 1700 formed a crucial phase in a long and gradual process of intellectual development during which the modern secular worldview evolved organically out of the religious worldview of traditional Europe. This evolutionary process of intellectual change involved many important positive contributions made by religious ideas to the development of the modern worldview. These contributions increasingly are being recognized by recent scholarship, especially in the field of the history of science. But the positive and fruitful relationship between traditional religion and the age of reason has only begun to achieve broad recognition in the last fifty years, and even today this relationship remains controversial.

The relationship between the traditional European religious worldview and the Enlightenment worldview of reason and secularism has been discussed by modern scholarship to a large extent in terms of the relationship between religion and science in seventeenth-century England. During the nineteenth century the first histories of the relationship between religion and early-modern science emphasized the conflict and supposed incompatibility of these two systems of thought. Influenced by the progressivist ideology of scientific positivism, these works saw modern science as arising in reaction to the superstition and obscurantism of medieval religion and then moving from victory to victory against its backward foe until reason reigned supreme in the modern mind. Writers such as W.E.H. Lecky, John W. Draper, and Andrew White saw the advent of the scientific worldview as a liberating revolution directed against ignorance and superstition.[1] This interpretation was continued in the early twentieth century, although in milder form, in the work of Paul Hazard, E. A. Burtt, R. F. Jones, and Basil Wiley, all of whom stressed the essential incompatibility of science and religion.[2]

During and after World War I this view of the conflict between science and religion began to give way to an interpretation that stressed the positive influence of religious ideas on the formation of modern science. Alfred North Whitehead, R. G. Collingwood, and Charles E. Raven maintained that Christian ideas had a significant influence on the development of many of the key concepts of early-modern science despite the conflicts that existed between science and religion during the seventeenth century. In 1934 and 1935 Michael Foster published two articles in the journal *Mind* in which he argued that Christian voluntaristic theology exercised an important influence on the development of empirical science in early-modern Europe. At the same time, another group of scholars led by Irene Parker, George Rosen, and Robert K. Merton argued for the influence of English Puritanism on the development of early-modern science in Britain. In a famous book-length article in *Osiris* in 1938, Merton maintained that the psychological implications of the Puritan value system were conducive to the growth of experimental science.[3] The work of Merton was

---

[1] See W.E.H. Lecky, *History of the Rise and Influence of the Spirit of Rationalism in Europe*, 2 vols. (New York, 1865); John W. Draper, *History of the Conflict between Religion and Science* (New York, 1875); and Andrew White, *History of the Warfare of Science with Theology in Christendom*, 2 vols. (New York, 1896).

[2] E. A. Burtt, *The Metaphysical Foundations of Modern Science* (London, 1925); R. F. Jones, *Ancients and Moderns* (St. Louis, 1961); and Basil Wiley, *The Seventeenth Century Background* (London, 1934). For an interpretation of these works, see Westfall, *Science and Religion in Seventeenth-Century England*, pp. 11–12.

[3] Alfred North Whitehead, *Science and the Modern World* (New York, 1925); R. G. Collingwood, *The Idea of Nature* (Oxford, 1945); Charles E. Raven, *John Ray, Naturalist: His Life and Works* (Cambridge, 1950), and *Natural Religion and Christian Theology* (Cambridge, 1953); Michael Foster, "The Christian Doctrine of Creation and the Rise of Modern Natural Science," *Mind* 43 (1934), pp. 446–468; and "Christian Theology and the Modern

much debated in the years that followed its publication. Some critics charged that Merton's arguments were too general to establish any real link between Puritanism and science, but Merton also found many supporters who defended his methods and findings.[4]

The first investigation of the relationship between early-modern science and religion to discuss the conflicts between the two thought systems as well as the reconciliation of those conflicts achieved by seventeenth-century thinkers was Richard S. Westfall's important study *Science and Religion in Seventeenth-Century England* (1958). Westfall argued that Christian ideas played an important role in shaping the attitudes that scientists brought to the study of nature in the seventeenth century. For this reason, he maintained that religion significantly influenced the conclusions of science just as science changed the way that people thought about religion.[5] In the years after the publication of Westfall's book, a number of works appeared that stressed the important role of religious ideas in the formation of the concepts of modern science. Reijer Hooykaas's *Religion and the Rise of Modern Science* (1972) and Eugene Klaaren's *The Religious Origins of Modern Science* (1977), along with the work of J. E. McGuire, Francis Oakley, Margaret J. Osler, and Edward B. Davis have done much to deepen our appreciation for the critical role played by religious ideas and assumptions in the intellectual origins of modern science.[6]

Science of Nature," *Mind* 44 (1935), pp. 439–466; Irene Parker, *Dissenting Academies in England* (Cambridge, England, 1914); George Rosen, "Left-Wing Puritanism and Science," *Bulletin of the History of Medicine* 15 (1944), pp. 375–380; and Robert K. Merton, "Science, Technology, and Society in Seventeenth-Century England," *Osiris* 4 (1938), pp. 360–632. See also Westfall, *Science and Religion in Seventeenth-Century England*, pp. 7–11.

[4] See, for example, Eugene Klaaren, *The Religious Origins of Modern Science* (Grand Rapids, 1972), p. 9; Webster, p. 487; Westfall, *Science and Religion in Seventeenth-Century England*, p. 7; T. Aston, ed., *The Intellectual Revolution of the Seventeenth Century* (London, 1974); D. Stimson, "Puritanism and the New Philosophy in Seventeenth-Century England," *Bulletin of the Institute for the History of Medicine* 3 (1935), pp. 321–334; J. R. Jacob and M. C. Jacob, "Scientists and Society: The Saints Preserved," *Journal of European Studies* 1 (1971), pp. 87–92; Douglas Kemsley, "Religious Influences on the Rise of Modern Science," *Annals of Science* 24 (1968), pp. 199–226; Barbara Shapiro, "Debate, Science, Politics, and Religion," *Past and Present* 66 (1975), pp. 133–138; T. K. Rabb, "Puritanism and the Rise of Experimental Science in England," *Journal of World History* 7 (1962); R. L. Greaves, "Puritanism and Science: The Anatomy of a Controversy," *Journal of the History of Ideas* 30 (1969), pp. 346–360; J. R. Jacob and M. C. Jacob, "The Anglican Origins of Modern Science," *Isis* 71 (1980), pp. 251–267; John Morgan, "Puritanism and Science: A Reinterpretation," *Historical Journal* 22 (1979), pp. 535–560; P. H. Kocher, *Science and Religion in Elizabethan England* (San Marino, 1953); Barbara Shapiro, *John Wilkins, 1614–1672: An Intellectual Biography* (Berkeley, 1969), and *Probability and Certainty in Seventeenth-Century England* (Princeton, 1983).

[5] Westfall, *Science and Religion in Seventeenth-Century England*, pp. 40–69.

[6] Reijer Hooykaas, *Religion and the Rise of Modern Science* (Grand Rapids, 1972);

A number of recent works have concentrated especially on the role of radical religious groups in the development of the modern scientific worldview. In *The World Turned Upside Down: Radical Ideas during the English Revolution* (1972), Christopher Hill maintained that interest in the new mechanical philosophy was particularly prevalent among religious and political radicals during the English Revolution. He argued that there was a close connection between empirical science and radical theology, and that radical Puritans favored the teaching of science because it was of practical use to the people. In a broader sense, Hill maintained that Protestantism defeated magic and superstition and thus contributed to the process of intellectual secularization because Protestant sermons rejecting Catholic transubstantiation helped to produce a materialistic and skeptical attitude toward miracles in general.[7] In *Some Intellectual Consequences of the English Revolution* (1980), Hill maintained that after 1650 the mechanical philosophy largely replaced the supernatural worldview in part because of Puritanism's rational critique of the miracle of the mass, holy water, exorcism, and other Catholic rituals. When the mechanical philosophy put an abstract mechanism in control of the world, Hill argued, people found themselves in a universe in which God and the devil no longer took an active, day-to-day interest in humanity. The toleration and openness of the revolutionary years in England significantly contributed to the growing rationalism that led to a decline of belief in magic, and at the same time the radical millenarianism of the revolution raised hopes for a utopia on earth and linked up with Baconian scientific optimism to create a theory of progress.[8]

The influence of radical religious ideas on the developing scientific worldview was brilliantly discussed in 1975 by Charles Webster in his study *The Great Instauration: Science, Medicine, and Reform, 1626–1660.* Webster supported Merton's earlier claims by arguing for the impact of Puritan millenarian ideas on the origins of modern science. Ac-

---

Klaaren, *The Religious Origins of Modern Science*; J. E. McGuire, "Boyle's Conception of Nature," *Journal of the History of Ideas* 33 (1972), pp. 523–542; Francis Oakley, "Christian Theology and the Newtonian Science: The Rise of the Concept of Laws of Nature," in Daniel O'Connor and F. Oakley, eds., *Creation: The Impact of an Idea* (New York, 1969); Margaret J. Osler, "Descartes and Charleton on Nature and God," *Journal of the History of Ideas* 40 (1979), pp. 445–456, and "Providence and Divine Will: The Theological Background to Gassendi's Views on Scientific Knowledge," *Journal of the History of Ideas* 44 (1983), pp. 549–560. Edward B. Davis, "Creation, Contingency, and Early Modern Science: The Impact of Voluntaristic Theology on Seventeenth Century Natural Philosophy" (dissertation, Indiana University, 1984), pp. 1–14. I have relied on Davis for this bibliographical discussion.

[7] Hill, *The World Turned Upside Down*, pp. 289–292, 89.

[8] Christopher Hill, *Some Intellectual Consequences of the English Revolution* (Madison, Wis., 1980), pp. 59–66. See also Tuveson.

cording to Webster, Puritan revolutionaries employed science to add precision to the millennial outline drawn up by theologians. Following Dan. 12:4 the Puritans believed that a great revival of learning would be an integral part of the coming millennial paradise. They believed that the discoveries of science would end the intellectual decline that had begun with Adam's fall and thus help to usher in the millennium by returning humanity's original dominion over nature. They believed that this revival of learning had already started with the rejection of pagan Aristotelianism by the new experimental philosophy, and they saw Bacon's *Instauratio magna* as the blueprint for this intellectual renaissance. Bacon held that the investigation of nature would both glorify God and restore human dominion over nature, and he maintained that God had sanctioned scientific investigation by the prophecy of Daniel that foretold a millennial increase of knowledge. The *Instauratio magna* thus looked forward to a great revival of learning, and Puritan science was dominated by this millennial fervor. The Puritans pursued science for its value in confirming the power of providence as well as for its social utility. According to Webster, the growth of English science was tied closely to the growth of the Puritan party.[9]

Building upon ideas such as these, Margaret Jacob argued in *The Radical Enlightenment* (1981) that Puritanism aided the rise of modern science because the Puritans linked their desire to promote the new science with the cause of the Puritan revolution. Puritan radicals embraced the cause of science in the service of social reform, but following the failure of Puritan reform schemes during the 1640s a split occurred within the reform party. A group of moderates reacted against more radical reformers by adopting a latitudinarian religious position and a mechanical conception of the universe. This conception stressed divine providence as a source of order and harmony imposed through laws at work in nature and society. The moderates championed Newtonian science because the ordered, providentially guided, and mathematically measured universe of Newton provided a model for a stable and prosperous social order based on monarchy and supported by a rational natural religion. Opposing the moderates was a radical party that carried on the tradition of reformist Puritanism by believing the millennial paradise to be imminent. These radicals envisioned a democratic and egalitarian society without a clergy in which the spirit of God would infuse the common people and make them the inheritors of a grand new social order. Along with their social and political ideas, the radicals adopted a version of the new science that stressed materialism and pantheism. While the moderate Newtonians contributed their vision of nature and society to the mainstream of En-

---

[9] Webster, pp. xvi–30, 503.

lightenment thought represented by Voltaire and others, the radicals handed down their views to the radical wing of the Enlightenment led by people such as D'Holbach.[10]

The case of the Dutch collegiants offers a new, continental European perspective on the relationship between radical religious ideas and the coming of the age of reason. Millenarianism, toleration, anticlericalism, and universalist reform expectations were important for the Collegiants just as they were for the English Puritans, but in the colleges these ideas functioned in ways that were quite different from their role in Puritan thought. The Collegiants were seventeenth-century heirs of the religious radicalism of the continental Reformation. The three main branches of the Radical Reformation of the sixteenth century came together in the Collegiant movement after 1620 and helped to create the Rijnsburger worldview. From the Mennonites, Collegiantism took pacifist and millenarian ideas that were an important part of the Anabaptist tradition. From Socinianism, they adopted elements of rational religion, and from the radical spiritualists they took their stress on the inner light of truth. The Rijnsburgers combined these radical religious ideas with certain elements of Dutch Arminian thought to produce a scathing critique of the established churches of their own day, and in so doing they became an important part of the rising tide of religious fervor known as the Second Reformation of the seventeenth century. This attack on seventeenth-century Protestantism ultimately led the Collegiants into a skepticism about revealed religion itself and thus brought them to the threshold of a new worldview. This process of intellectual transition made Collegiant thought a bridge linking the Reformation to the Enlightenment.

From the spiritualism of the Radical Reformation the Collegiants took their conception of the essentially inner and individual nature of religious truth. For the Collegiants, the idea of inner truth became the connecting link between two otherwise quite different epistemological systems: inner-light spiritualism and natural-light rationalism. Because spiritualism and rationalism met on the common ground of the individual conscience, the Rijnsburgers were able to incorporate both into their thought and make the transition from spiritualism to rationalism. When belief in direct divine inspiration began to wane in the colleges with the spread of Galenus's ideas, belief in the spiritual inner light was replaced by belief in the natural light of reason. Like the doctrine of individual inspiration, the doctrine of inner reason was used by the Collegiants against ecclesiastical institutions because it made the intervention of external authorities such

---

[10] Jacob, *The Radical Enlightenment*, pp. 66–105, 202, and *The Newtonians and the English Revolution*.

as church and clergy irrelevant to a process in which the individual obtained religious knowledge through an inner conviction whose validity was considered self-evident and thus self-verifying.

The transition from spiritualism to rationalism in Collegiant thought took place during the 1660s and 1670s under the influence of a secularizing trend that resulted in part from a confluence of millenarian ideas with Galenus Abrahamsz.'s attack on the spiritual authority of the established churches. Millenarian thought was as important for the Collegiants as it was for the English Puritans, but while chiliasm gave the Puritans revolutionary fervor and a doctrine of progress, among the Collegiants millenarian ideas functioned in a very different way. Rijnsburger chiliastic ideas held out the promise of a divine paradise on earth for the holy people prior to the Last Judgment, but Collegiant millenarianism also stressed the corrupt and sinful nature of the secular world before the coming of this paradise. Indeed, many Collegiants saw what they considered to be the depraved state of the world in their day as evidence that the millennium was fast approaching.

In the Collegiant's pessimistic view of the premillennial world God did not actively intervene to set right the sinful affairs of humanity or stop the cruel persecution of his people. Instead, he allowed the world to rush headlong downhill into ever deepening misery, to be saved only by Christ's return and the universal reformation of the millennium. Indeed, no reform of the world could succeed before the millennium. The Collegiants thus came to see their world as a world unholy, cut off from divine intervention. During the 1660s, as the millennium repeatedly failed to arrive on the dates assigned for it, the expected universal reformation was pushed farther and farther into the indefinite future and the Collegiants learned to live with Stoic resignation in the corrupt premillennial world. Whereas the reform hopes of the English Puritans were encouraged by their belief that the English revolution marked the dawning of the millennium, Collegiant hopes for a better world were disappointed when the millennium did not arrive. This disappointment perhaps accounts for the pessimistic tone of Collegiant millenarianism as opposed to Puritan ideas of millennial progress, and it also contributed to the increasingly secular perspective of Collegiant thought.

This pessimistic view of the corrupt premillennial world fit well with Galenus's attack on the spiritual authority of the established churches. Looking back upon the religious turmoil produced by the Protestant Reformation and reflecting upon the competing claims to exclusive divine authority made by the ecclesiastical institutions of his own day, Galenus concluded that the Protestant Reformation had not been inspired by God and that the churches of the post-Reformation era were the faulty inventions of fallible humans. He saw the churches of the seventeenth century as hopelessly decayed, corrupt, and cut off from God's inspiration—totally devoid of the gifts of the Holy Spirit that had inspired the apostolic church.

Galenus concluded from what he perceived to be the failure of the Reformation that any human efforts to reform the corrupt churches would be in vain because the true reformation could only be accomplished by Christ in the millennium. As the millennium repeatedly failed to appear, however, the idea of a premillennial world unholy joined with Galenus's idea of a church unholy to produce in the colleges a growing feeling of separation from God. It seemed to many Rijnsburgers that God no longer intervened in the world to reward his friends or punish his enemies, arrange temporal affairs according to divine wishes, or inspire the church with divine truth. In the absence of a divinely inspired clergy to direct people to the truth, the Collegiants concluded that the only hope for religious knowledge was to rely on individual human reason. In the absence of any divine guidance to help people choose among the many competing religious doctrines, all doctrines had to be accepted and tolerated as equally valid. Collegiant plans for a continuation of religious life in a world unholy were thus based on a religion of reason and toleration.

Millenarianism and the ideas of Galenus Abrahamsz. inclined the Collegiants to look upon the world as primarily a realm of human activity in which the power of human reason was an increasingly valuable asset. These rational and secular ideas helped to open the colleges to the influence of Socinian rational religion during the 1660s and 1670s. The Socinians saw reason as an essential tool for understanding biblical revelation, and when the Socinians arrived in Holland after 1660 the Collegiants were prepared to adopt many of the rationalistic aspects of Socinian thought. The Rijnsburgers were also open to the influence of Cartesian rationalism, which was spreading rapidly in Dutch intellectual circles and which was introduced into the colleges by Spinoza during the years 1657–1664.

The secularizing trend in Collegiant thought gradually transformed the Rijnsburgers' conception of the individual conscience. Many Collegiants came to believe that since the world and its people were cut off from divine inspiration, the individual's inner ability to know truth could not be a product of the spiritual inner light. The first Collegiants believed that people obtained religious truth through the direct inspiration of the Holy Spirit and they founded their practice of free prophecy on this belief. After 1660, however, the Collegiants came to see the individual's inner ability to know truth as based on human reason, and their conception of free prophecy changed accordingly. The Collegiants' move away from spiritualism was given added momentum by their bitter clash with the English

Quakers from 1657 to 1670. Quaker extremism further discredited spiritualism in the colleges.

The secularization of the Collegiants' conception of the individual conscience gradually changed their idea of the spiritual inner light into an idea of the natural light of reason. This transformation can be seen clearly in the writings of Balling and Jelles, who placed reason alongside and even in the place of divine inspiration in their conception of the inner light. As the idea of the inner light came to be associated with human reason, reason assumed the spiritual inner light's function as an infallible source of true religious ideas. In this way, inner-light spiritualism of the Radical Reformation evolved into an intuitive rationalism in the colleges. This rationalism reached its fullest development in the philosophy of Jan Bredenburg. Bredenburg maintained that reason and revelation were dual sources of truth, but he clearly assigned the superior role to reason. In Bredenburg's early writings revelation was reduced to a nearly inconsequential role as a supplemental source of religious truth. Even after fierce criticism forced him to give revelation more importance as a source of religious knowledge, his theory of double truth protected reason's conclusions from falsification by revelation and left revealed truths as little more than nonrational precepts. When Bredenburg made human reason the primary source of all truth that was intelligible, the Collegiants had come to the doorstep of philosophical rationalism. It was left for Spinoza to open that door.

From a spiritualistic and millenarian worldview built on the ideas of the Radical Reformation the Collegiants developed a secular view of the world based largely on human reason. In this process of intellectual transformation the decade of the 1660s was crucial as millennial disappointments combined with the ideas of Galenus, the Socinians, Spinoza, and the Quaker controversy to create powerful forces for secularization within the colleges. Even while many Rijnsburgers debated Bredenburg's ideas on the proper role of reason in religion, other Collegiants remained attached to spiritualism. The fact that two such different worldviews could coexist within the same religious movement points out the function of Rijnsburger thought as a link between two worldviews.

All Collegiants, spiritualists and rationalists alike, were united by a common set of practices, principles, and goals that placed the Rijnsburger movement squarely in the vanguard of the Second Reformation of the seventeenth century. Their rejection of the spiritual authority of all ecclesiastical institutions and their denial of clerical authority; their call for a tolerant and morally upright, nonconfessional Christianity; their belief in the inner and individual nature of religious truth; and their devotion to free prophecy marked the Collegiants as a distinctive force in seventeenth-century Dutch religious life.[11] For the Collegiants, the intellectual consequences of the Reformation included a sense of the bankruptcy of organized religion and the separation of God from humanity. Rejection of the Reformation became a rejection of revealed religion itself and provided the foundation for the Collegiants' reliance on reason. The Collegiant movement went beyond other branches of the Second Reformation by adopting reason as the new standard for religious truth, and in this way the Rijnsburgers moved toward the natural religion of the Enlightenment.

Late in his life, Galenus Abrahamsz. looked back over the transformation in Collegiant thought that his own ideas had done so much to stimulate with a note of regret. Ever tolerant and charitable, the spiritualistic Galenus nevertheless felt left behind by the course that Collegiant thought had taken after 1660. The pious Mennonite preacher felt more at home in a world that his own ideas had helped to alter fundamentally. But while Galenus remained in his heart a spiritualist, for many other Collegiants his was a world that was passing away rapidly. It is one of the ironies of history that those who originate change are often bypassed by it as well. In 1699 Galenus wrote of his fellow Collegiants: "These men take Scripture as the one rule of their belief and life, although perhaps it can be said of them that they place a little too much value on the use of human reason in the Christian religion."[12] In these lines one can detect the anxiety and the struggle that was so much a part of the Collegiant intellectual transition from faith to reason.

[11] Kolakowski, pp. 168–176, 230–231.

[12] Galenus Abrahamsz., *Verdediging der Christenen die Doopsgezinden genaamd worden*, p. 11.

BIBLIOGRAPHY

PRIMARY SOURCES

Abrahamsz., Galenus. *Anleyding tot de kennis van de Christelyke Godsdienst.* Amsterdam, 1677.

———. *Beknopt vertoog van gelykluydende getuygenissen der H. Schrift over de voornaemste stukken der Christelyke leere.* Amsterdam, 1684.

———. *Christelyke zede-konst.* N.p., n.d.

———. *De VIII Trappen ter saligheyd.* N.p., n.d.

———. *Korte grondstellingen van de Christelyke leere.* Amsterdam, 1677.

———. *Korte verhandeling van de redelyk-bevindelyke godsdienst.* Amsterdam, 1674.

———. *Verdediging der Christenen die Doopsgezinden genaamd worden.* Amsterdam, 1699.

———. *Wederlegging van 't geschrift, genaemt: Antwoorde by forme van aenmerckingen, vragen ende redenen aen Laurens Hendricksz. . . . overghegeven.* Amsterdam, 1659.

Abrahamsz., Galenus and David Spruyt. *Bedenckingen over den Toestant der Sichtbare Kercke Christi op Aerden, Kortelijck in XIX Artikelen Voor-Ghestelt: en aen onse mede-dienaren, op den 11 Januarij 1657, Schriftelijck over-ghelevert.* Amsterdam, 1657.

———. *Nadere verklaringe van de XIX Artikelen, Voor desen Door G. Abrahamsz. ende D. Spruyt aen hare Mede-dienaren over-ghegeven: Dienende tot Wederlegging van 't Geschrift, genaemt: Antwoorde by forme van aenmerckingen, vragen, ende redenen, etc.* Amsterdam, 1659.

Alsted, J. H. *The Beloved City or The Saints Reign on Earth a Thousand Years.* London, 1643.

Ames, William. *Het Licht dat in de duisternis schijnt beweesen den weg tot God te zijn.* Amsterdam, 1660.

———. *De verborgenheden van het Rijcke Gods.* Amsterdam, 1661.

———. *Het waere Licht beschermt ende de innooselheydt van de eenvoudige bevrijt van de onwaerheden ende valsche beschuldigingen door Petrus Serrarius op haar geleyt. . . .* Amsterdam, 1661.

Anonymous. *Aenwijzing van verschiede misslagen . . . door J. D. Verburg begaan in zijn brief aan A.S.* N.p., 1687.

Anonymous. *Antwoord op Johannes Bredenburgs Korte Aanmerkingen op de Brieven van de Heer Philippus van Limborgh . . . aan Pieter Smout.* Amsterdam, n.d.

Anonymous. *Copye enes brief van sekere voor-stander der vrijheijt van spreecken in de gemeynte.* N.p., ca. 1672.

Anonymous. *Een korte bedenckinge over de stellingen van A. Lemmerman. . . .* N.p., 1685.

Anonymous. *Eenige Aanmerkingen voor den Philosopherenden Boer, met eenige vragen aan den zelven voorgestelt door die gene, diemen spots-gewijse noemt Quakers.* Rotterdam, 1676.

Anonymous. *Eenige consideratien . . . over de Schriftelichte Onderhandeling Tussen den Heer Prof. P. van Limborg en Johannes Bredenburg.* . . . N.p., 1686.

Anonymous. *Zedig tegenberigt tot verstant van Abraham Lemmerman.* N.p., n.d.

Balling, Pieter. *Het Licht op den Kandelaar.* Amsterdam, 1662.

————. *Nader verdediging van de regering der Doopsgezinde gemeente, die men de Vereenigde Hoogduytsche, Vriezen, en Vlamingen noemt, binnen Amsterdam, zijnde een wederlegging van d'Antwoort op de verdediging, etc.* Amsterdam, 1664.

————. *Verdediging van de regering der Doopsgezinde gemeente, die men de Vereenigde Vlamingen, Vriezen, en Hoogduytsche noemt, binnen Amsterdam, zijnde een wederlegging van het zoo genoemde Nootwendig Bericht, etc.* Amsterdam, 1663.

Bayle, Pierre. *Dictionnaire Historique et Critique.* Paris, 1820.

Becius, Johannes. *Apologia modesta et Christiana . . . Dat is, Sedige en Christelycke verantwoordinge van Johannes Becius Middelburger in Zeeland.* Amsterdam, 1668.

————. *Defensio apologia modestae et Christianae J. B. Dat is bescherminge van de zedige en Christelyke verantwoordinge van J. B.* Amsterdam, 1669.

————. *Dubia theologica in genere trinitatis.* N.p., 1687.

————. *Institutio Christiana, ofte Christelyk onderwys, waer in gehandelt word van veel voorname hooft-stucken, seer noodig geweten ter saligheyt.* . . . Amsterdam, 1678.

————. *Nadere beproevinge van de geest des autheurs van 't boek genaemt Arius Redivivus.* . . . N.p., 1669.

————. *Probatio Spiritus Authoris Arii Redivivi, Dat is, Beproevinge vande geest des Autheurs van Arrius Redivivus.* . . . N.p., 1669.

————. *Theologische bedenkingen den Arianen voorgestelt.* N.p., 1690.

————. *Verandwoording voor de verdrukte waerheydt welke seer onchristlijk wordt benadeelt van Jac. Oldenborge in zijn boek genaemt Nietigheyt en ongegrontheyt der Socinianensche godsdienst.* Amsterdam, 1682.

————. *Wederlegging van het tractaet welckers titul is: reden waerom de Ed. Act. magistraet den Mennisten tot Deventer niet mach toelaten conventicelen te houden.* Amsterdam, 1671.

Boreel, Adam. *Ad Legem et ad testimonium.* N.p., 1645.

Bredenburg, Johannes. *Een praetje over tafel tusschen een Remonstrant, Waterlander-Doopsgesinde ende den Waerdt.* . . . Rotterdam, 1671.

————. *Enervatio tractatus theologico-politicus.* . . . Rotterdam, 1675.

————. *Heylzame raad tot Christelijke vrede of te aanwijzing van het rechte middel tot Christelijke vereeniging.* Rotterdam, n.d.

————. *Korte Aanmerkingen op den brieven van den Hr. P. van Limborg aan Pieter Smout en N.N.* Rotterdam, 1686.

————. *Noodige verantwoording op de ongegronde beschuldiging van Abraham Lemmerman.* Rotterdam, 1684.

————. *Schriftelijke onderhandeling tusschen den Heer Philippus van Limborg,*

Professor der Remonstranten, ende Johannes Bredenburg, rakende 't gebruyk der reden in de religie. Rotterdam, 1686.

―――. *Verdediging van zijn zoo genaemde Wiskunstige Demonstratie tegen . . . F. Kuyper.* N.p., n.d.

―――. *Verhandling van de oorsprong van de kennisse Gods en van desselfs dienst, alleen uyt natuurlijke reden afgeleyd, buyten alle openbaringen of mirakelen.* Amsterdam, 1684.

―――. *Wiskunstige demonstratie dat alle verstandelijke werking noodzaakelijk is, met de weerlegging van F.K. van de wiskunstige demonstratie, uytgegeven door Abraham Lemmerman.* Amsterdam, 1684.

Bredenburg, Paulus. *Lijkreden op den earwaerdigen en Godvruchtigen Jan Dionysz. Verburg. . . .* Rotterdam, 1691.

De Breen, Daniel. *Van 't geestelyk triumpherende ryck onses heeren Jesu Christi.* Amsterdam, 1653.

―――. *Verklaring over de Openbaring van den Apostle Johannes.* N.p., n.d.

―――. *Verklaring over het boeck des H. Jobs.* Amsterdam, 1666.

―――. *Vriendelicke disputatie tegen de Joden. . . .* Rotterdam, 1664.

―――. *'t zaamen-spraak aangaande de waarheyd der Christelijke Religie.* Harlingen, 1685.

Collegianten tot Leyden. *Brief van de Collegianten tot Leyden, afgesonden na verscheyde plaatsen.* N.p., n.d.

van Dalc, Antonius. *Boer-praetjen tusschen vijf personen . . . handelende of Galenus. . . .* Amsterdam, 1664.

―――. *De Oudheid van 't Alleen spreken in de Gemeente verdedigd.* Amsterdam, 1670.

―――. *Historie van 't predikampt. . . .* N.p., n.d.

E.V.S.V.D.G.S. *Korte aanwijzinge dat de philosophie van Johannes Bredenburg zeer schadelijke is. . . .* N.p., 1688.

Fijne, Paschier de. *Kort, waerachtigh en getrouw verhael van het eerste begin en opkomen van de nieuwe seckte der propheten often Rijnsburgers in het dorp Warmont anno 1619 en 1620.* "Waertstadt," 1671.

Franck, Sebastian. *280 Paradoxes or Wondrous Sayings.* Trans. E. J. Furcha. Lewiston, N.Y., 1986.

van Geel, Joost. *Nader verklaringe eeniger zaken in zijn redenering over de algemeene kerk, tegen de overweging van J. Oudaan Fransz.* Rotterdam, 1689.

―――. *Op. F. K. en A. L. Scheurmakers deezer eeuw.* N.p., 1684.

―――. *Redenering over de algemeen kerk ofte het rijk der heiligen.* Rotterdam, 1687.

Hartigvelt, Jan. *De recht weerlooze Christen.* Rotterdam, 1678.

Higgins, John. *Eenige waerdige ende gewichtige aenmerckingen voor Galenus Abrahamsz. ende Adam Boreel ende haaere aenhangers.* Amsterdam, 1660.

Jelles, Jarig. *Belijdenisse des Algemeenen en Christelyken geloofs; vervattet in een brief aan N.N.* Amsterdam, 1684.

―――. "Voorrede." In *De Nagelate schriften van B.D.S. als Zedekunst, Staatkunde, Verbetering van 't Verstant, Brieven en Antwoorden uit Verscheide Talen in de Nederlandsche Gebragt.* Amsterdam, 1677.

Klinkhamer, Laurens. *Brief aan Pieter Smout in welke de Affschuwelijke onger-ijmdheden . . . van Jan Bredenburg ondekt worden*. . . . N.p., n.d.

——. *Losse en quaade gronden van de schuer-kerk*. Amsterdam, 1686.

——. *Verdediging van de Vryheyt van Spreken in de gemeente der gelovigen*. . . . Amsterdam, 1662.

——. *Vrijheijt van spreecken inde gemeynte der geloovigen, bewesen met ge-boden, exampelen, redenen, weerlegging van tegenwerpingen*. Leiden, 1655.

Kuyper, Frans. *Aanmerking of weerlegging van de zoo genoemd Wiskunstige de-monstratie van J.B*. Amsterdam, 1684.

——. *Aanwijzing van de groove misslagen van Daniel Zwicker*. N.p., n.d.

——. *Bewijs dat J.D. Verburg zelfs bekend, dat hij Frans Kuyper met groote onwaarheyt . . . heeft uitgemaekt*. N.p., n.d.

——. *Bewijs dat noch de schepping van natuur noch de mirakelen, die H. Schrift verhaalt, op eenigerhande wijze teegen de natuurlijke reeden strijdig zijn*. Amsterdam, 1685.

——. *De Diepten des Satans, of Geheymenissen der Atheisterij ontdekt en Ver-nielt*. . . . Rotterdam, 1677.

——. *Tweede Deel of Vervolg van de Philosopherende Boer: In Welk de geh-eyme gevoelens der Quaakers, uyt haar eygen schriften, en met haar eygen woorden, ontdekt worden*. . . . Rotterdam, 1676.

——. *Weerlegging van de verdediging van J.B. tegen de aanmerkingen van F.K*. Amsterdam, 1684.

Langedult, Pieter. *De apostolice outheyt van de vrijheijt van spreecken in de ver-gaderingen der Christenen, tegens Dr. A. van Dalens alleen-spreecken*. Haar-lem, 1672.

——. *De nietigheyt der Chiliasterye*. Haarlem, 1676.

Lemmerman, Abraham. *Eenige bewijzen dat Johannes Bredenburg staande zijn stellingen geenzins kan gelooven dat 'er zulk een God is als de H. Schrift leert. Beweezen uyt zijn eygen schriften, hier acter aangevoegt, en uyt zijn mondel-inge duydelijke bekentenis*. Amsterdam, 1684.

——. *Verdediging van de drie onfeylbaare bewijzen dat Johannes Bredenburg*. . . . Amsterdam, 1685.

Maurits, W. *Lykreden ter gedagtenis van Galenus Abrahamsz*. . . . N.p., n.d.

van Nimwegen, Elias. *Historie der Rijnsburgsche Vergadering*. Rotterdam, 1775.

Oudaan, Joachim Fransz. *Aanmerkinger over het verhaal van het eerste begin en opkomst der Rynsburgers*. . . . N.p., n.d.

——. *Bedenkelijke toepassing op eenige stukken in de Openbaringe: ten proeve voorgestelt . . . met bijvoeging der brieven van Franciscus Morstinius en Samuel Pripkovski over het onverschillig oeffenen van den godsdienst*. Rotterdam, 1689.

——. *Overwegginge eeniger grond-stellingen door J.V.G. in des zelfs redener-ing over de algemeene kerk ter neder gestelt: en der zelver onrechtmatigheid aangewezen*. Amsterdam, 1689.

Paling, Abraham. *Aanmercking en aanspraeck op Dr. Galenus geschrift aan Lau-rensz. Hendrick*. . . . Haarlem, 1665.

Park, James. *Christus Jesus verhooght/En een getuygenis gedragen tot sijn Waere*

Licht/Welck een yegelijck mensch verlicht die in de werelt komt. . . . Amsterdam, 1670.

Sartensius, Latinus Serbaltus. *Observationes quibus ostenditur J.B. esse spinosistam.* N.p., 1684.

———. *Tweede verdediging tegen de gebroaders Bredenburg.* Amsterdam, 1684.

Serrarius, Pieter. *An Awakening Warning to the Woefull World, By a Voyce in Three Nations; Uttered in a brief Dissertation Concerning that Fatal, and to be admired Conjunction of all the Planets in one and the same sign of . . . Sagitarius, the last of the Fiery Triplicity, to come to pass the 11 day of December, Anno 1662.* Amsterdam, 1662.

———. *Antwoort op 't boeck in 't jaer 1659 uytgegeven.* Amsterdam, 1661.

———. *De vertredinge des heyligen stadts, ofteen klaer bewijs van 't verval der eerste apostolische gemeente, gestelt tot antwoort op drie vragen diesaengaende aen Dr. Galenus gedaen in 't by voeghsel van seecker voor-rede op 't boecxken tegens Dr. Galenus en David Spruyt uytgegeven, ende in 't druck bevordert door Jansz. Swichtenheuvel.* Amsterdam, 1659.

Sewel, William. *The History of the Rise, Increase, and Progress of the Christian People called Quakers.* London, 1725.

Smout, Pieter. *Antwoord op het zoo genaamt waerachtig verhael van J.D. Verburg wegens de opkomst en voortgang van 't weeshuys der Collegianten tot Amsterdam.* . . . Rotterdam, 1687.

———. *Bewys dat de vier gepretendeerde regenten van het Collegianten weeshuys tot Amsterdam . . . aan veel groove stukken schuldig zijn.* Amsterdam, 1686.

———. *Copye van een brief door Pieter Smout aan Galenus Abrahamsz. geschreven in welk zijn onbehoorlijken handel tegen A.L. en F.K.* . . . N.p., 1685.

———. *Het helder licht der vryheyt, behoudster der waerheyd, vyandinne van alle meesterschap en dooling: over het godlijke vrij-propheteren in de gemeynte Jesu Christi.* Rotterdam, 1679.

———. *Vreede en vryheid onder de Rhijnsburgers.* . . . Rotterdam, 1687.

Spinoza, Benedict. *Benedict de Spinoza: On the Improvement of the Understanding, the Ethics, Correspondence.* Trans. and ed. R.H.M. Elwes. New York, 1955.

———. *A Theologico-Political Treatise and a Political Treatise.* Trans. R.H.M. Elwes. New York, 1951.

Stapel, Klaas. *Broederlijke onderhandeling van de waterdoop.* . . . Rotterdam, 1680.

Stol, Barend Joosten. *Den Philosopherenden Boer, eerste deel: Handelende van de dwalingen der hedensdaagse Christenen, Philosophen, Cartesianen en Quakers, In Verscheyden Onvermeynde Zaaken.* Rotterdam, 1676.

Swartepaert, Adrian. *Openbaringe van het ware algemeen geloof.* . . . N.p., 1678.

Toland, John. *Christianity Not Mysterious.* London, 1696.

Verburg, Jan Dionysius. *Brief aan A.S. of kort en waarachtig verhaal van de opkomst en voortgang van 't weeshuys der Collegianten.* Rotterdam, 1686.

———. *Brief aan Frans Kuyper.* Rotterdam, 1687.

———. *Brief aan J.C. behelsende een klare ontdekking van de onbedaghtheyt by de Heer P. Van Limborg.* . . . Rotterdam, 1686.

Verburg, Jan Dionysius. *Brief aan n.n. tot wederlegging van het zoo genaamde zedig berigt.* . . . Rotterdam, 1684.

──────. *Lijk-reeden over het leven en Sterven van den Godvruchtigen Jan Hartigveld.* Rotterdam, 1678.

Zwicker, Daniel. *De Nieuwe Testamentische Josias.* N.p., 1670.

──────. *De noch staende en triumpherende sichtbare kercke Christi.* . . . Amsterdam, 1660.

──────. *De verdwynende On-Apostolische vryspreecker.* N.p., 1669.

──────. *De weerloose oude kercke . . . wederom met recht bevestight.* N.p., n.d.

──────. *Het II deel van de revelatie des duyvel-dienst onder de Christenen.* . . . Amsterdam, 1675.

──────. *Openhertige vertooninge dat de Algemeene vryheyt van spreken in de Gemeynte . . . behoort Afgeschaft te worden.* N.p., 1660.

──────. *Revelatio hostium crucis Christi inter Christianos, of Acts des gesprecks tusschen D. Zwicker, aen eene, en J. Becius, D. Backer.* . . . Amsterdam, 1672.

──────. *Vredeschrift der vredeschriften of drie dubbelde regelmaet des vereenigers der hedendaghse Christenen, de gesonde reden van alle menschen, de H. Schriftuere, en de overleverlingen.* N.p., 1678.

SECONDARY SOURCES

van der Aa, A. J., ed. *Biographische woordenboek der Nederlanden.* Haarlem, 1852–1878.

Bangs, Carl. *Arminius, A Study in the Dutch Reformation.* Nashville, 1971.

Barnes, Robin B. *Prophecy and Gnosis: Apocalypticism in the Wake of the Lutheran Reformation.* Stanford, 1988.

Barnouw, P. J. *Philippus van Limborch.* The Hague, 1963.

Bergsma, Wiebe. "Aggaeus van Albada (c.1527–1587), Schwenckfeldiaan, staatsman en strijder voor verdraagzaamheid." Dissertation, University of Groningen, 1983.

de Bie, J. P., ed. *Biografisch woordenboek van Protestantsche godgelerden in Nederland.* The Hague, 1943.

de Boer, M. G. "Een unrustige geest: Johannes Rothe." *Tijdschrift voor Geschiedenis* 15 (1900), pp. 201–229.

Bonger, H. *Leven en Werken van D. V. Coornhert.* Amsterdam, 1978.

Borkowski, Stanislas von Dunin. *Der junge Spinoza.* Münster, 1910.

Bouwsma, William J. *John Calvin: A Sixteenth-Century Portrait.* Oxford, 1988.

Brienen, T., et al. *De Nadere Reformatie: Beschrijving van haar voornaamste vertegenwoordigers.* The Hague, 1986.

Bronowski, J., and Bruce Mazlish. *The Western Intellectual Tradition.* New York, 1962.

de Bruin, C. C. *Joachim Oudaan in de lijst van zijn tijd.* Groningen-Djakarta, 1955.

van Bunge, Wiep. "Johannes Bredenburg and the Korte Verhandeling." *Studia Spinoziana* 4 (1988), pp. 321–328.

──────. "A Tragic Idealist: Jacob Ostens (1630–1678)." *Studia Spinoziana* 4 (1988), pp. 263–279.

———. "Monnikhoff, Deurhoff en Spinoza." *Guest Lecturers and Seminar Papers on Spinozism* 5 (1988), pp. 1–25.

Capp, B. S. *The Fifth Monarchy Men: A Study in Seventeenth-Century English Millennarianism.* Totawa, N.J., 1972.

Cassirer, Ernst. *The Philosophy of the Enlightenment.* Princeton, 1951.

Chamberlain, E. R. *Antichrist and the Millennium.* New York, 1975.

Clark, Jon. "Immediacy and Experience: Institutional Change and Spiritual Expression in the Works of Quirinus Kuhlmann." Dissertation, University of California at Berkeley, 1986.

Cobban, Alfred. *In Search of Humanity: The Role of the Enlightenment in Modern History.* London, 1960.

Colie, Rosalie. *Light and Enlightenment: A Study of the Cambridge Platonists and Dutch Arminians.* Cambridge, England, 1957.

Cragg, Gerald R. *From Puritanism to the Age of Reason: A Study of Changes in Religious Thought within the Church of England, 1660 to 1700.* Cambridge, England, 1950.

Dijksterhuis, E. J., C. Serrurier, and P. Dibon. *Descartes et le Cartesianisme Hollandais.* Amsterdam, 1951.

van der Does, Marthe. *Antoinette Bourignon sa vie (1616–1680), son oeuvre.* Groningen, 1974.

Edwards, Paul, ed. *The Encyclopedia of Philosophy.* New York, 1972.

Eldridge, Michael. *Philosophy as Religion: A Study in Critical Devotion.* Dissertation, University of Florida, 1985.

Enno van Gelder, H. A. *Getemperde Vrijheid: Een verhandeling over de verhouding van kerk en Staat in de Republiek der Verenigde Nederlanden en de Vrijheid van meningsuiting in zake godsdienst, drukpers, en onderwijs, gedurende de 17e eeuw.* Groningen, 1972.

Erb, Peter, ed. *Schwenkfeld and Early Schwenkfeldians: Papers Presented at the Colloquium on Schwenkfeld and the Schwenkfelders, Pennsburg, Pa., September 17–22, 1984.* Pennsburg, Penn., 1984.

Evenhuis, R. B. *Ook dat was Amsterdam: de kerk der hervorming in de tweede helft van de zeventiende eeuw: nabloei en inzinking.* Vol. 3 Amsterdam, 1971.

Febvre, Lucien. *The Problem of Unbelief in the Sixteenth Century: The Religion of Rabelais.* Trans. Beatrice Gottlieb. Cambridge, Mass., 1982.

Feuer, Lewis. *Spinoza and the Rise of Liberalism.* New York, 1958.

Francès, Madeleine. *Spinoza Dans Les Pays Neerlandais de la seconde moitie du XVIIe siècle.* Paris, 1937.

Geyl, Pieter. *The Netherlands in the Seventeenth Century.* Vol. 1. New York, 1961.

Gingrich, M., C. Krahn, and O. Harms, eds. *The Mennonite Encyclopedia.* Scottsdale, Ariz., 1969–1973.

Goeters, Wilhelm. *Die Vorbereitung des Pietismus.* Leipzig, 1911.

Grant, Edward. *Physical Science in the Middle Ages.* Cambridge, England, 1977.

Groenveld, S., ed. *Daar de Orangie-appel in de gevel staat: in en om het weeshuis der Doopsgezinde Collegianten 1675–1975.* Amsterdam, 1975.

Groenveld, S., J. P. Jacobszoon, and S. L. Verheus, eds. *Wederdoopers, Menisten, Doopsgezinden in Nederland, 1530–1980*. Zutphen, 1981.

de Groot, A. "De Amsterdamse Collegiant Jan Cornelis Knol." *Doopsgezinde Bijdragen*, n.s. 10, no. 12 (1984), pp. 77–88.

Gründer, Karlfried, and Wilhelm Schmidt-Biggemann, eds. *Spinoza in der Frühzeit Seiner Religiösen Wirkung*. Heidelberg, 1984.

Haley, K.H.D. *The Dutch in the Seventeenth Century*. London, 1972.

Hampshire, Stuart. *Spinoza*. London, 1951; reprint 1981.

Hazard, Paul. *The European Mind, 1680–1715*. Cleveland, 1964.

Heering, G. J., ed. *De Remonstranten: gedenkboek bij het 300-jarig bestaan der Remonstrantsche Broederschap*. Leiden, 1919.

Herbermann, Charles, et al., eds. *Catholic Encyclopedia*. New York, 1911.

Hill, Christopher. *Some Intellectual Consequences of the English Revolution*. Madison, Wis., 1980.

———. *The World Turned Upside Down: Radical Ideas during the English Revolution*. London, 1972.

Hoenderdaal, G. J., and P. M. Luca, eds. *Staat in de vrijheid: geschiedenis van de Remonstranten*. Zutphen, 1982.

Hubbeling, H. G. *Spinoza*. Baarn, 1966.

Hull, W. I. *Benjamin Furly and Quakerism in Rotterdam*. Swarthmore, Penn., 1941.

———. *The Rise of Quakerism in Amsterdam, 1655–1665*. Swarthmore, Penn., 1938.

Hylkema, C. B. *Reformateurs: Geschiedkundige studien over de godsdienstige bewegingen uit de nadagen onzer gouden eeuw*. 2 vols. Haarlem, 1900; reprint Groningen and Amsterdam, 1978.

Jacob, Margaret. *The Newtonians and the English Revolution*. Ithaca, N.Y., 1976.

———. *The Radical Enlightenment*. London, 1981.

Jones, Rufus. *Spiritual Reformers in the Sixteenth and Seventeenth Centuries*. London, 1914.

De Jong, Otto J. *Nederlandse Kerkgeschiedenis*. Nijkerk, 1978.

Kamen, Henry. *The Rise of Toleration*. New York, 1972.

Kearns, Edward. *Ideas in Seventeenth-Century France*. Manchester, 1979.

Klassen, Peter. *Europe in the Reformation*. Englewood Cliffs, N.J., 1974.

Knox, R. Buick, ed. *Reformation, Conformity, and Dissent: Essays in Honor of Geoffrey Nuttall*. London, 1977.

Kolakowski, Leszek. *Chrétiens, sans église: la conscience religieuse et le lien confessionnel au XVIIe siècle*. Paris, 1969.

Kors, Alan C., and Paul J. Korshin, eds. *Anticipations of the Enlightenment in England, France, and Germany*. Philadelphia, 1987.

Kühler, W. J. *Het Socinianisme in Nederland*. Leiden, 1912; reprint Leeuwarden, 1980.

Lecler, Joseph. *Histoire de la tolérance au siècle de la Réforme*. 2 vols. Paris, 1955.

van der Linde, A. *Antoinette Bourignon, das Licht der Welt*. Leiden, 1895.

Lindeboom, Johannes. *Een Franc-tireur der Reformatie: Sebastiaan Franck*. Arnhem, 1952.

———. *Geschiedenis van het vrijzinnig Protestantisme*. 3 vols. Huis ter Hede, 1929–1935.

———. *Stiefkinderen van het Christendom*. The Hague, 1929; reprint Arnhem, 1973.

List, Günther. *Chiliastiche Utopie und Radicale Reformation*. Munich, 1973.

Mandrou, Robert. *From Humanism to Science, 1480–1700*. London, 1978.

Manusov, Clasina. *Pelgrims en Profeten: Bunyan's "The Pilgrim's Progress" in de Mystieke denkwereld van Jacob Böhme*. Utrecht, 1985.

Maron, Gottfried. *Individualismus und Gemeinschaft bei Caspar von Schwenkfeld*. Stuttgart, 1961.

McGahagan, Thomas A. "Cartesianism in The Netherlands, 1636–1676: The New Science and the Calvinist Counter-Reformation." Dissertation, University of Pennsylvania, 1976.

McGinn, Bernard. *Visions of the End: Apocalyptic Traditions in the Middle Ages*. New York, 1979.

McLaughlin, R. Emmet. *Caspar Schwenkfeld, Reluctant Radical*. New Haven, 1986.

Meihuizen, H. W. *Galenus Abrahamsz. 1622–1706. Strijder voor een onbeperkte verdraagzaamheid en verdediger van het Doperse Spiritualisme*. Haarlem, 1954.

Meinsma, K. O. *Spinoza en zijn kring: over Hollandse vrijgeesten*. The Hague, 1896; reprint Utrecht, 1980.

Melles, J. *Joachim Oudaan, heraut der verdaagzaamheid, 1628–1692*. Utrecht, 1958.

van Moerkerken, P. H. *Adriaan Koerbagh, een strijder voor het vrije denken*. Amsterdam, 1948.

Molhuysen, P. C., and P. J. Blok, eds., *Nieuwe Nederlandsch biografisch woordenboek*. Leiden, 1911–1937.

Moorrees, F.D.J. *D. V. Coornhert de libertijn*. Schoonhoven, 1887.

Murray, John J. *Amsterdam in the Age of Rembrandt*. Norman, Okla., 1967.

Nauta, D., et al., eds. *Biografisch Lexicon voor de geschiedenis van het Nederlandse Protestantisme*. Kampen, 1978–1988.

van Niftrik, G. C. *Spinoza en de sectariers van zijn tijd*. Leiden, 1963.

Op't Hof, W. J. *De visie op de Joden in de Nadere Reformatie tijdens het eerste kwart van de zeventiende eeuw*. Amsterdam, 1984.

Patrides, C. A., and Joseph Wittreich, eds. *The Apocalypse in English Renaissance Thought and Literature*. Ithaca, N.Y., 1984.

Pollock, Frederick. *Spinoza: His Life and Philosophy*. London, 1880.

Popkin, Richard. *The History of Scepticism from Erasmus to Spinoza*. Berkeley, 1979.

Price, J. L. *Culture and Society in the Dutch Republic during the Seventeenth Century*. London, 1974.

Quak, Marieke. "De Collegianten te Amsterdam." *Doopsgezinde Bijdragen*, n.s. 10 (1984), pp. 110–112.

Quak, Marieke. *De Collegianten te Amsterdam in de periode van 1722–1775*. Doctoraalscriptie, University of Utrecht, 1985.

―――. "De sociale status van Amsterdamse doopsgezinde Collegianten in de 18e eeuw." *Doopsgezinde Bijdragen*, n.s. 11 (1985), pp. 109–117.

Roldanus, Cornelia W. *Coenraad van Beuningen, staatsman en libertijn*. The Hague, 1931.

―――. *Zeventiende eeuwse geestesbloei*. Utrecht, 1961.

Rood, Wilhelmus. *Comenius and the Low Countries*. Amsterdam, 1970.

Roth, Leon. *Spinoza, Descartes, and Maimonides*. Oxford, 1924.

Russell, Jeffrey Burton. *Mephistopheles: The Devil in the Modern World*. Ithaca, N.Y., 1986.

Schama, Simon. *The Embarrassment of Riches: An Interpretation of Dutch Culture in the Golden Age*. New York, 1987.

Schneider, Walter. *Adam Boreel: Sein Leben und Seine Schriften*. Giessen, 1911.

Schwarz, Reinhard. *Die apokalyptische Theologie Thomas Müntzers und der Taboriten*. Tübingen, 1977.

Scruton, Roger. *Spinoza*. Oxford, 1985.

Seyppel, Joachim. *Schwenkfeld: Knight of Faith*. Pennsburg, Penn., 1961.

Shapiro, Barbara J. *Probability and Certainty in Seventeenth-Century England: A Study of the Relationships between Natural Science, Religion, History, Law, and Literature*. Princeton, 1983.

Siebrand, Heine. *Spinoza and the Netherlanders: An Inquiry into the Early Reception of His Philosophy of Religion*. Assen and Maastricht, 1988.

van Slee, J. C. *De geschiedenis van het Socinianisme in de Nederlanden*. Haarlem, 1914.

―――. *De Rijnsburger Collegianten*. Haarlem, 1895; reprint Utrecht, 1980.

Smith, Alan G. R. *Science and Society in the Sixteenth and Seventeenth Centuries*. London, 1972.

Smith, Norman Kemp, ed. *Descartes: Philosophical Writings*. New York, 1958.

Spinka, Matthew. *John Amos Comenius: That Incomparable Moravian*. New York, 1967.

Thijssen-Schoute, C. L. *Nederlands Cartesianisme*. Amsterdam, 1954.

Thomas, Keith. *Religion and the Decline of Magic*. New York, 1971.

Turnbull, G. H. *Hartlib, Dury, and Comenius*. London, 1947.

Tuveson, Ernest. *Millennium and Utopia: A Study in the Background of the Idea of Progress*. Berkeley, 1949.

Vandenbossche, Hubert. *Spinozisme en Kritiek bij Koerbagh*. Brussels, n.d.

Vekeman, Herman. *Toelichting over Galenus Korte verhandeling van de redelyk-bevindelyke godsdienst*. Veroffenlichungen des Instituts für Niederlandische Philologie der Universität Köln, 1983.

de Vries, Theun. *Spinoza: Beelden-Stormer en Wereldbouwer*. Amsterdam, 1983.

van der Wall, E.G.E. "De Hemelse tekenen en het rijk van Christus op aarde: chiliasme en astrologie bij Petrus Serrarius (1660–1669)." *Kerkhistorische Studien* (1982), pp. 45–64.

―――. "De Mystieke Chiliast Petrus Serrarius (1660–1669) en zijn Wereld." Dissertation, Leiden University, 1987.

Webster, Charles. *The Great Instauration: Science, Medicine, and Reform, 1626–1660.* New York, 1975.

Westfall, Richard S. *The Construction of Modern Science.* Cambridge, England, 1977.

———. *Science and Religion in Seventeenth-Century England.* New Haven, 1958.

Wilbur, Earl M. *A History of Unitarianism: Socinianism and its Antecedents.* Cambridge, Mass., 1946.

Williams, George Hunston. *The Radical Reformation.* Philadelphia, 1962.

Wilson, Charles. *The Dutch Republic.* London, 1968.

Wolfson, Abraham. *Spinoza: A Life of Reason.* New York, 1934.

Wolfson, Harry A. *The Philosophy of Spinoza.* Cambridge, Mass., 1934.

Wollgast, Siegfried. *Der deutsche Pantheismus im 16. Jahrhundert.* Berlin, 1972.

Young, Robert. *Comenius in England.* London, 1947.

van der Zijpp, N. *Geschiedenis der Doopsgezinden in Nederland.* Arnhem, 1952.

Zilverberg, S.B.J. *Geloof en geweten in de zeventiende eeuw.* Bussum, 1971. Reprinted as *Dissidenten in de Gouden Eeuw: Geloof en geweten in de Republiek.* Weesp, 1985.